DOOM PATROL

DOOM PATROL

VOL. 1: BRICK BY BRICK

GERARD WAY Writer
NICK DERINGTON with TOM FOWLER Artists
TAMRA BONVILLAIN Colorist
TODD KLEIN Letterer
NICK DERINGTON Cover Art and Original Series Covers
DOOM PATROL CREATED BY ARNOLD DRAKE

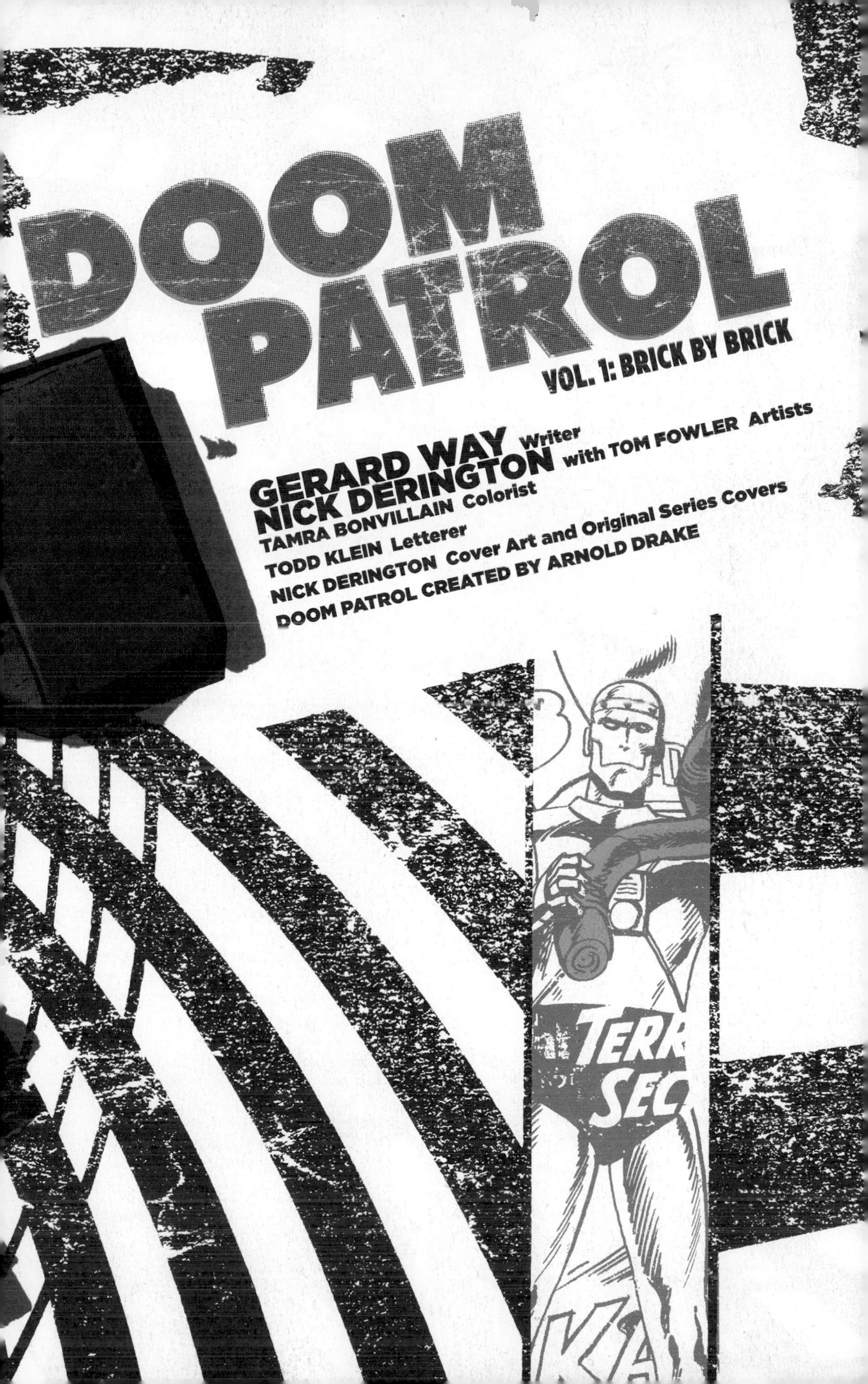

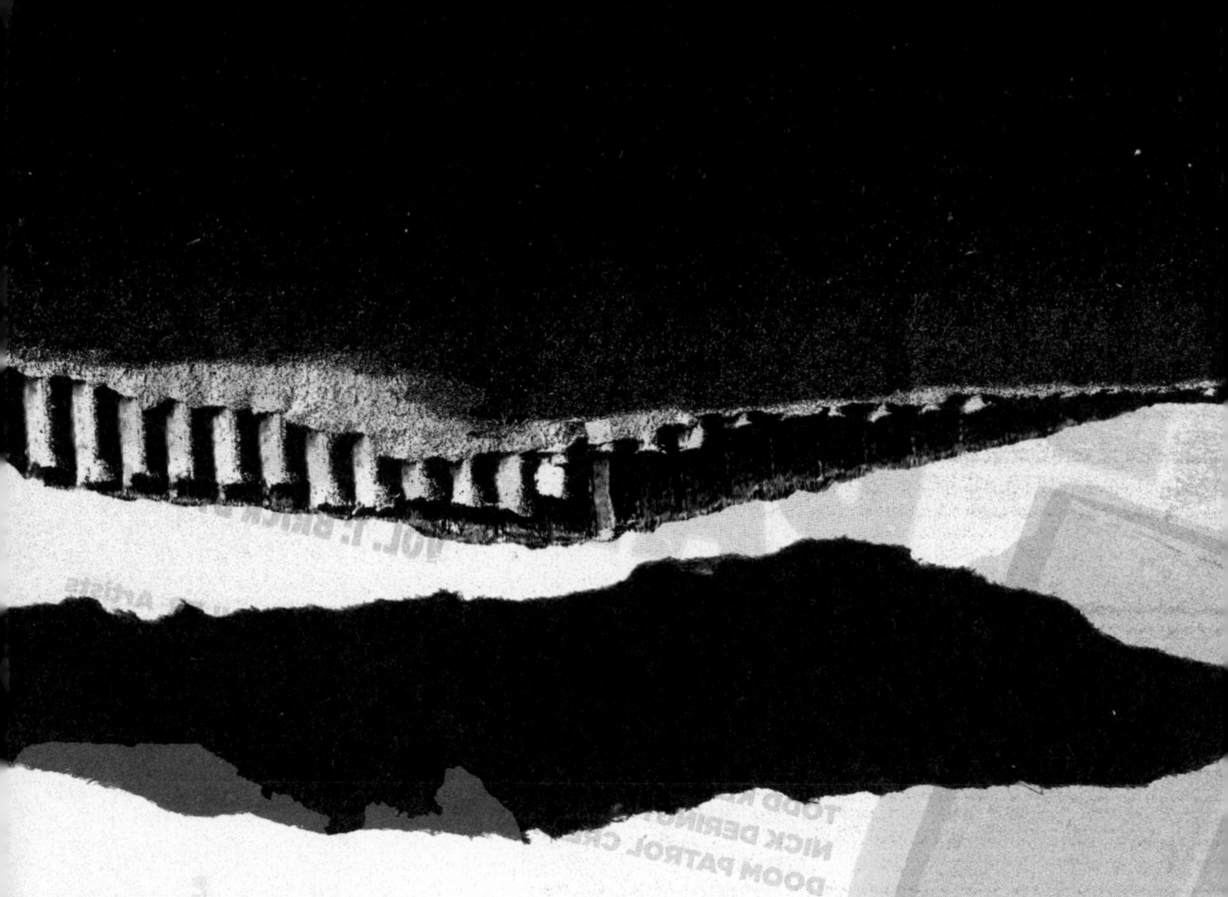

Shelly Bond Jamie S. Rich Editors – Original Series
Molly Mahan Associate Editor – Original Series
Jeb Woodard Group Editor – Collected Editions
Scott Nybakken Editor – Collected Edition
Steve Cook Design Director – Books
Louis Prandi Publication Design

Bob Harras Senior VP – Editor-in-Chief, DC Comics

Diane Nelson President
Dan DiDio Publisher
Jim Lee Publisher
Geoff Johns President & Chief Creative Officer
Amit Desai Executive VP – Business & Marketing Strategy, Direct to Consumer & Global Franchise Management
Sam Ades Senior VP – Direct to Consumer
Bobbie Chase VP – Talent Development
Mark Chiarello Senior VP – Art, Design & Collected Editions
John Cunningham Senior VP – Sales & Trade Marketing
Anne DePies Senior VP – Business Strategy, Finance & Administration
Don Falletti VP – Manufacturing Operations
Lawrence Ganem VP – Editorial Administration & Talent Relations
Alison Gill Senior VP – Manufacturing & Operations
Hank Kanalz Senior VP – Editorial Strategy & Administration
Jay Kogan VP – Legal Affairs
Thomas Loftus VP – Business Affairs
Jack Mahan VP – Business Affairs
Nick J. Napolitano VP – Manufacturing Administration
Eddie Scannell VP – Consumer Marketing
Courtney Simmons Senior VP – Publicity & Communications
Jim (Ski) Sokolowski VP – Comic Book Specialty Sales & Trade Marketing
Nancy Spears VP – Mass, Book, Digital Sales & Trade Marketing

DOOM PATROL VOL. 1: BRICK BY BRICK

DC Comics
2900 West Alameda Avenue
Burbank, CA 91505
Printed in the USA. First Printing.
ISBN: 978-1-4012-6979-1

Library of Congress Cataloging-in-Publication Data is available.

MIX
Paper from responsible sources
FSC® C132124
FSC www.fsc.org

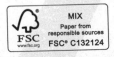

DOOM
PATROL

DOOM
PATROL

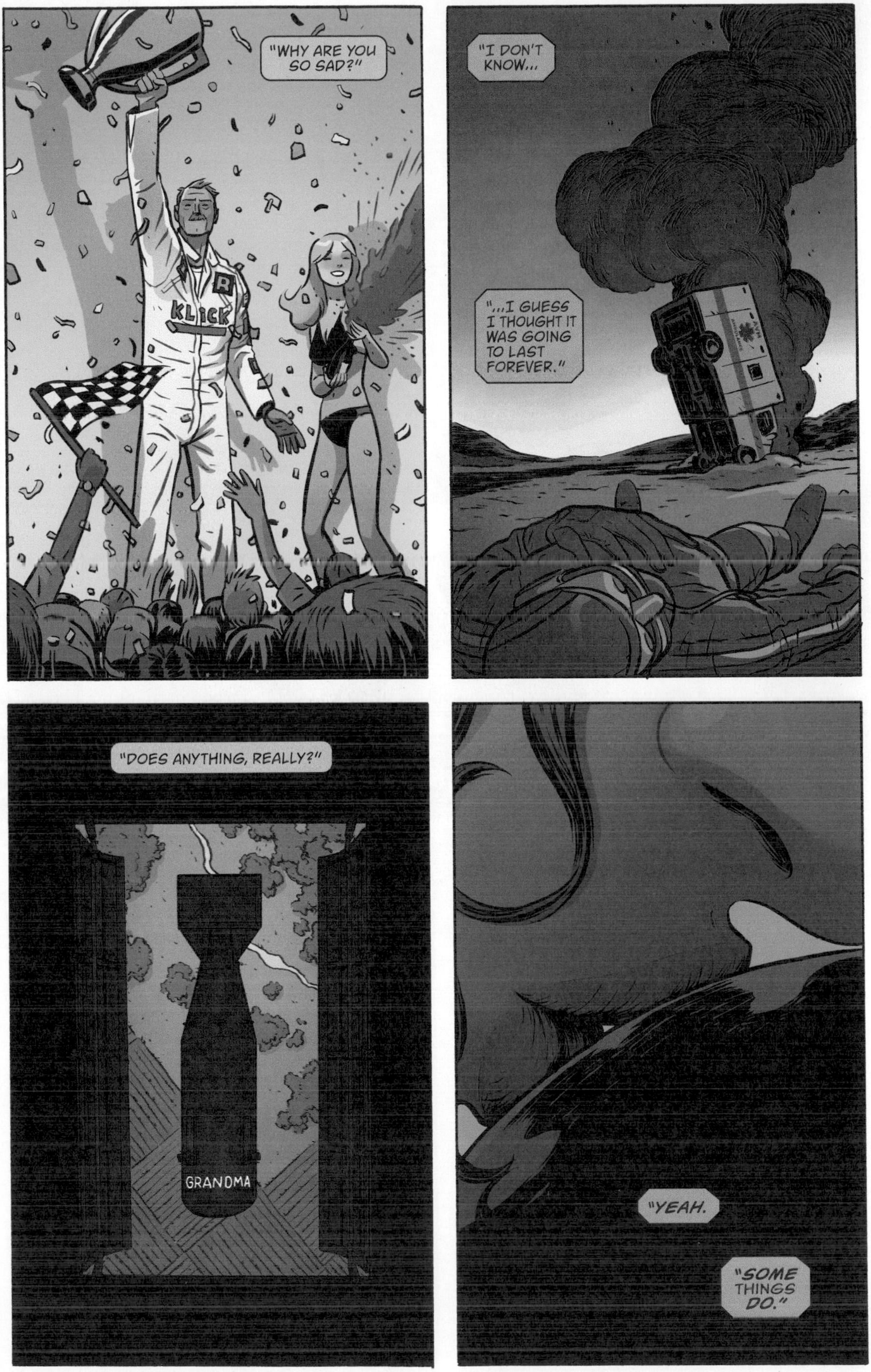
"WHY ARE YOU SO SAD?"
KLICK
"I DON'T KNOW...
"...I GUESS I THOUGHT IT WAS GOING TO LAST FOREVER."
"DOES ANYTHING, REALLY?"
GRANDMA
"YEAH.
"SOME THINGS DO."

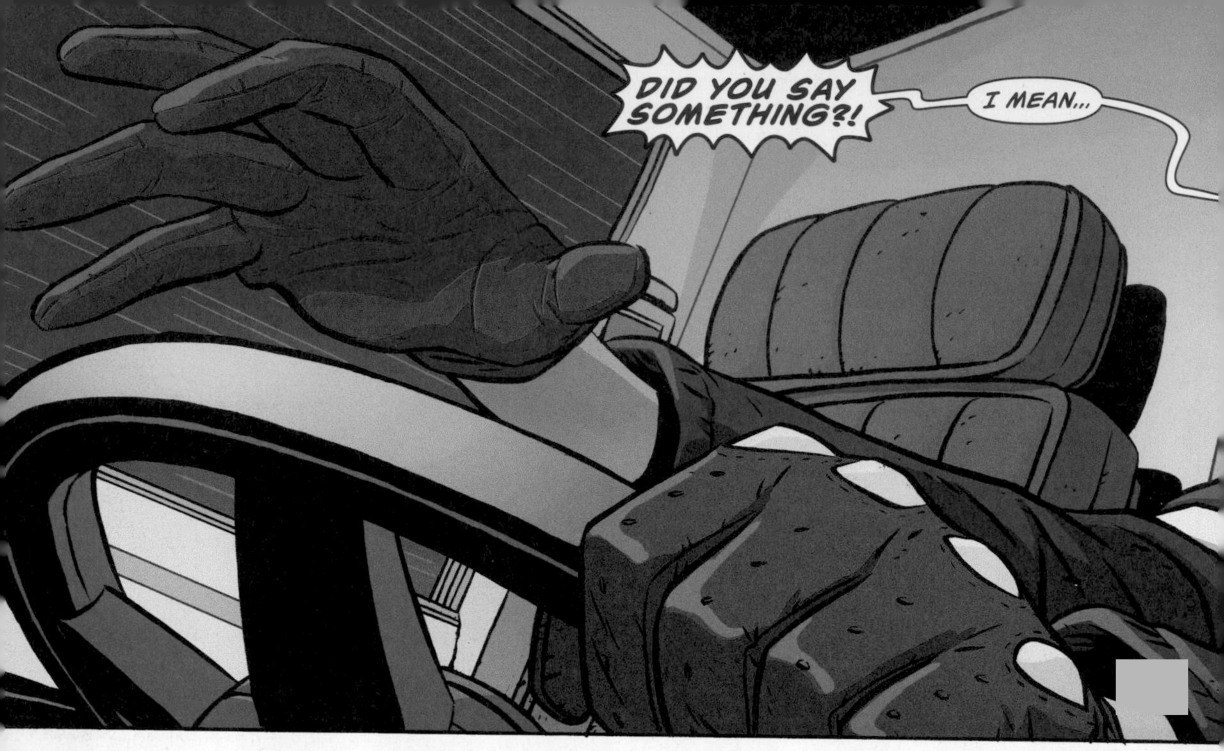
DID YOU SAY SOMETHING?!
I MEAN...

HAPPY BIRT
CASEY BR

TAMRA BONVILLAIN colorist

TODD KLEIN letterer

NICK DERINGTON cover artist

JAMES HARVEY cover colorist

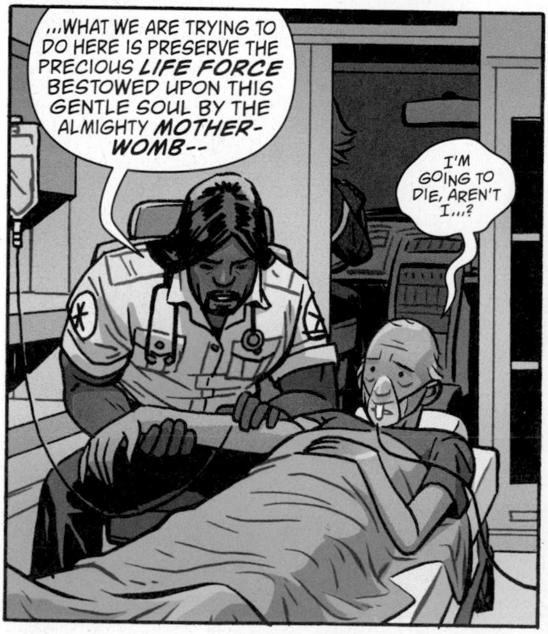
...WHAT WE ARE TRYING TO DO HERE IS PRESERVE THE PRECIOUS LIFE FORCE BESTOWED UPON THIS GENTLE SOUL BY THE ALMIGHTY MOTHER-WOMB--
I'M GOING TO DIE, AREN'T I...?

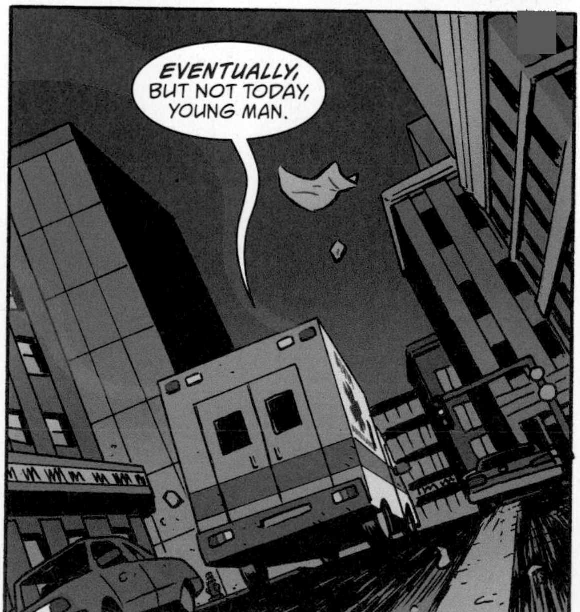
EVENTUALLY, BUT NOT TODAY, YOUNG MAN.

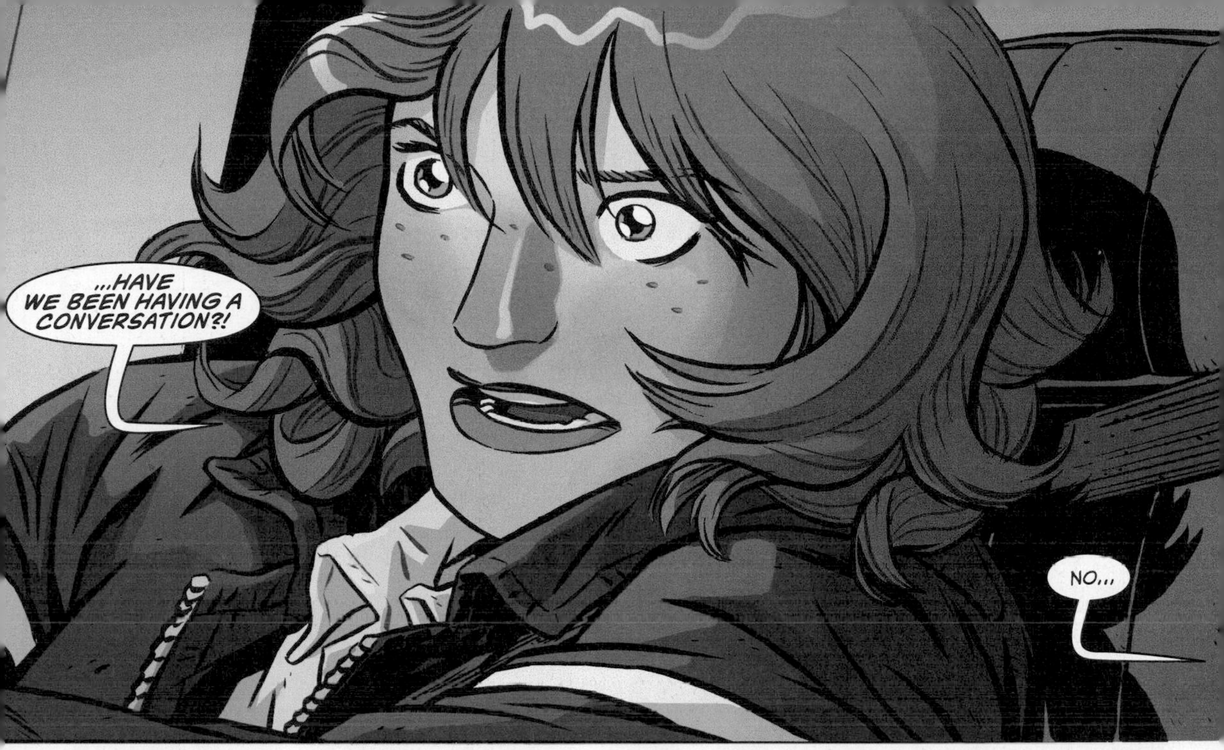
...HAVE WE BEEN HAVING A CONVERSATION?!
NO...

HDAY, INKE

BRICK by BRICK
PART ONE

GERARD WAY writer
NICK DERINGTON artist

MOLLY MAHAN assoc. ed.
SHELLY BOND editor
ADAM EGYPT MORTIMER special thanks
Doom Patrol created by Arnold Drake

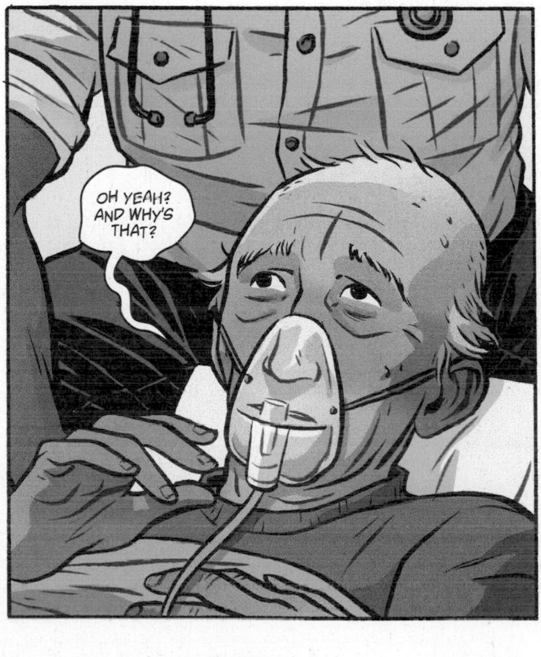
OH YEAH? AND WHY'S THAT?

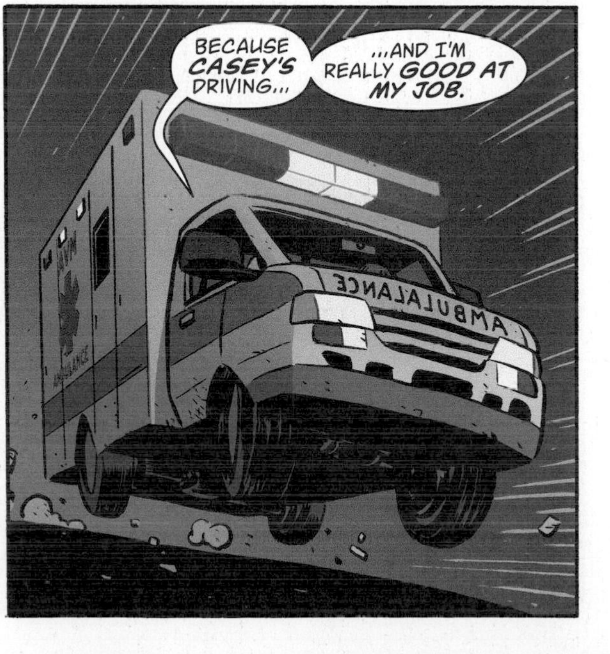
BECAUSE CASEY'S DRIVING...
...AND I'M REALLY GOOD AT MY JOB.

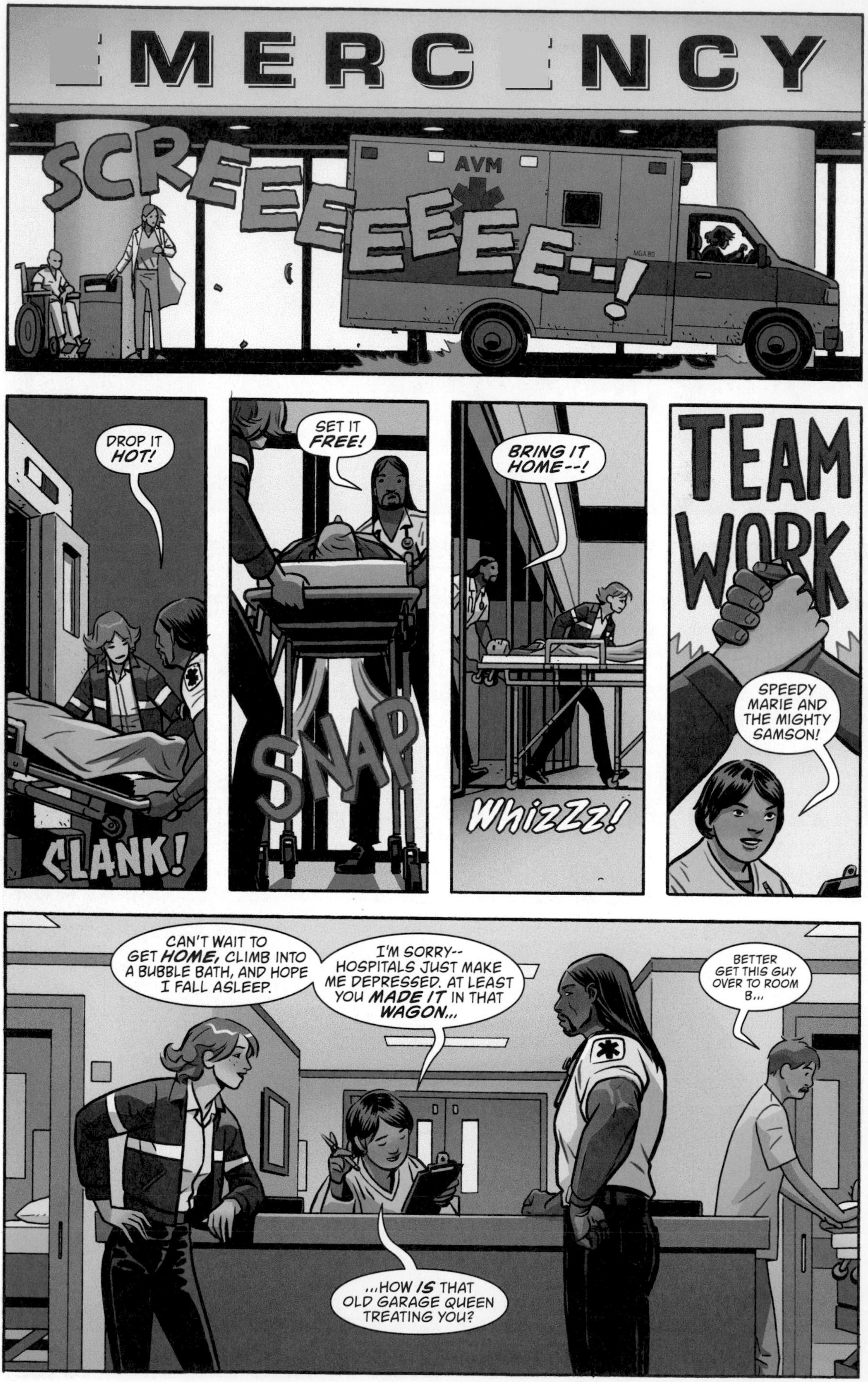
MERC NCY
SCREEEEEEEE...!
AVM
DROP IT HOT!
CLANK!
SET IT FREE!
SNAP
BRING IT HOME--!
WhizZz!
TEAM WORK
SPEEDY MARIE AND THE MIGHTY SAMSON!
CAN'T WAIT TO GET HOME, CLIMB INTO A BUBBLE BATH, AND HOPE I FALL ASLEEP.
I'M SORRY-- HOSPITALS JUST MAKE ME DEPRESSED. AT LEAST YOU MADE IT IN THAT WAGON...
...HOW IS THAT OLD GARAGE QUEEN TREATING YOU?
BETTER GET THIS GUY OVER TO ROOM B...

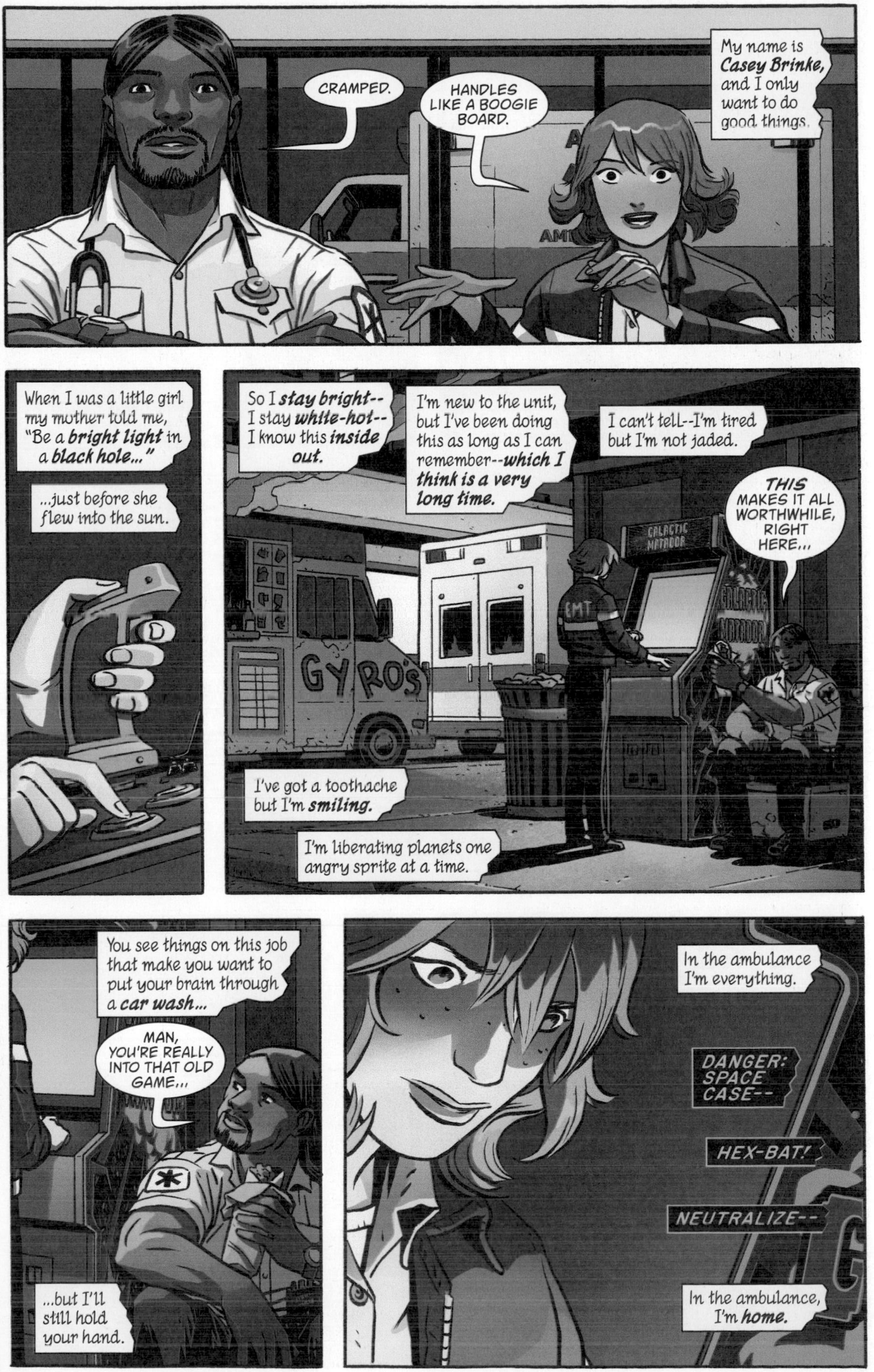
My name is Casey Brinke, and I only want to do good things.
CRAMPED.
HANDLES LIKE A BOOGIE BOARD.
When I was a little girl my mother told me, "Be a bright light in a black hole..."
...just before she flew into the sun.
So I stay bright-- I stay white-hot-- I know this inside out.
I'm new to the unit, but I've been doing this as long as I can remember--which I think is a very long time.
I can't tell--I'm tired but I'm not jaded.
THIS MAKES IT ALL WORTHWHILE, RIGHT HERE...
GALACTIC MATADOR
GYRO'S
EMT
I've got a toothache but I'm smiling.
I'm liberating planets one angry sprite at a time.
You see things on this job that make you want to put your brain through a car wash...
MAN, YOU'RE REALLY INTO THAT OLD GAME...
...but I'll still hold your hand.
In the ambulance I'm everything.
DANGER: SPACE CASE--
HEX-BAT!
NEUTRALIZE--
In the ambulance, I'm home.

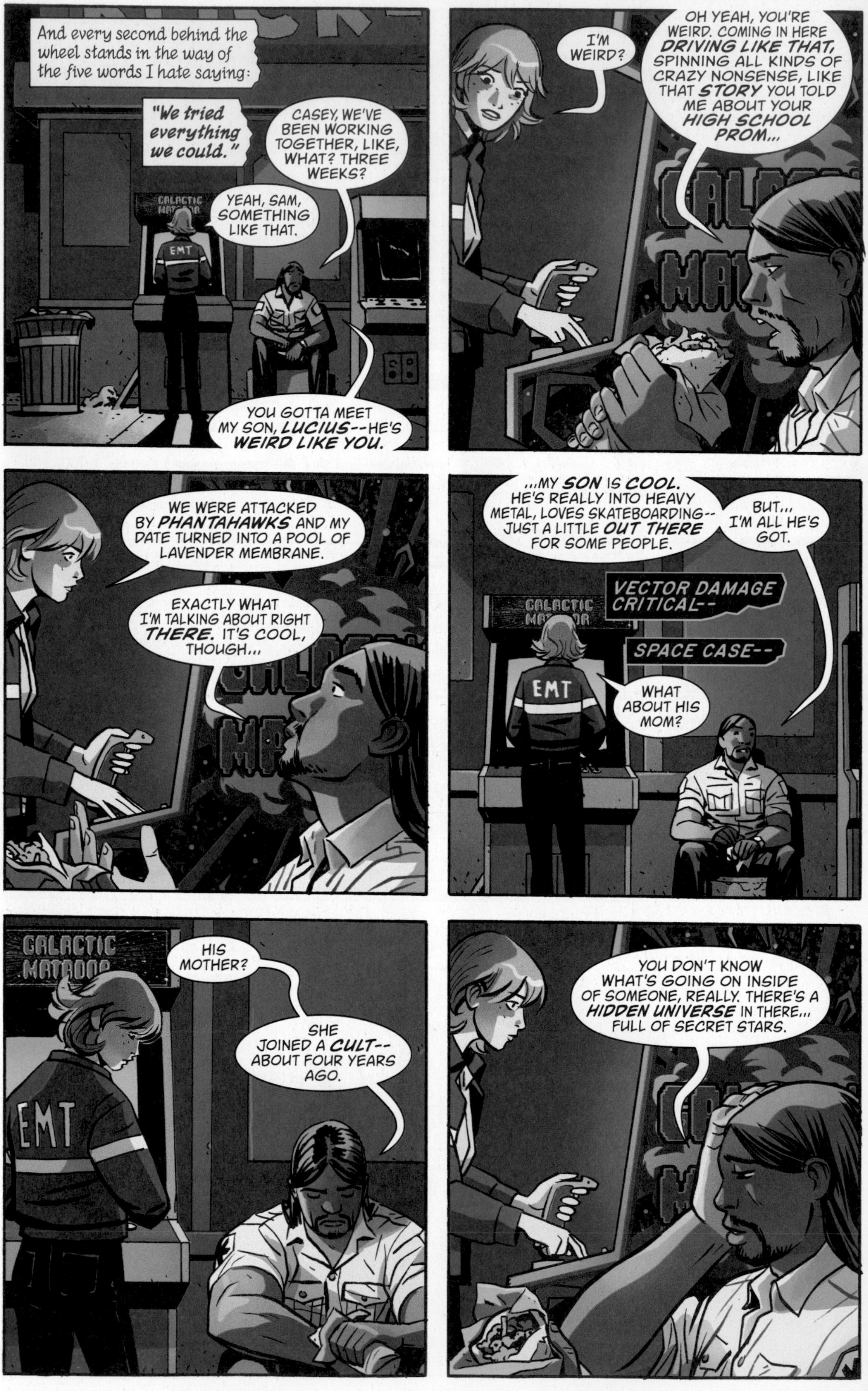

And every second behind the wheel stands in the way of the five words I hate saying:
"We tried everything we could."
CASEY, WE'VE BEEN WORKING TOGETHER, LIKE, WHAT? THREE WEEKS?
YEAH, SAM, SOMETHING LIKE THAT.
GALACTIC MATADOR
EMT
YOU GOTTA MEET MY SON, LUCIUS--HE'S WEIRD LIKE YOU.
I'M WEIRD?
OH YEAH, YOU'RE WEIRD. COMING IN HERE DRIVING LIKE THAT, SPINNING ALL KINDS OF CRAZY NONSENSE, LIKE THAT STORY YOU TOLD ME ABOUT YOUR HIGH SCHOOL PROM...
WE WERE ATTACKED BY PHANTAHAWKS AND MY DATE TURNED INTO A POOL OF LAVENDER MEMBRANE.
EXACTLY WHAT I'M TALKING ABOUT RIGHT THERE. IT'S COOL, THOUGH...
...MY SON IS COOL. HE'S REALLY INTO HEAVY METAL, LOVES SKATEBOARDING--JUST A LITTLE OUT THERE FOR SOME PEOPLE.
BUT... I'M ALL HE'S GOT.
VECTOR DAMAGE CRITICAL--
SPACE CASE--
WHAT ABOUT HIS MOM?
GALACTIC MATADOR
HIS MOTHER?
SHE JOINED A CULT--ABOUT FOUR YEARS AGO.
EMT
YOU DON'T KNOW WHAT'S GOING ON INSIDE OF SOMEONE, REALLY. THERE'S A HIDDEN UNIVERSE IN THERE... FULL OF SECRET STARS.

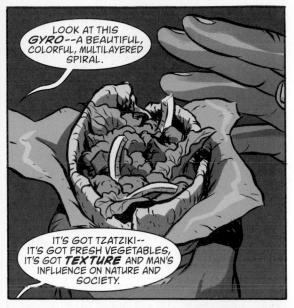

LOOK AT THIS *GYRO*--A BEAUTIFUL, COLORFUL, MULTILAYERED SPIRAL.

IT'S GOT TZATZIKI-- IT'S GOT FRESH VEGETABLES, IT'S GOT *TEXTURE* AND MAN'S INFLUENCE ON NATURE AND SOCIETY.

"WE THINK WE KNOW THIS GYRO, BUT WE DON'T KNOW EVERYTHING. *WHAT'S GOING ON IN THERE?*

"ENDLESS POSSIBILITIES? GOOD VERSUS EVIL--?

"JUST A WHOLE WORLD BUZZING ALONG... GOING ABOUT ITS DAILY ROTATION.

"TIME MIGHT MAKE *NO SENSE* IF YOU'RE LIVING IN THE GYRO!"

THEN YOU PUT THE UNIVERSE INSIDE OF YOU--*YOU FEEL ME?!*

MAYBE WE'RE *ALL* INSIDE OF SOMEONE ELSE'S GYRO.

COULD BE...

COULD BE NOTHING AT ALL.

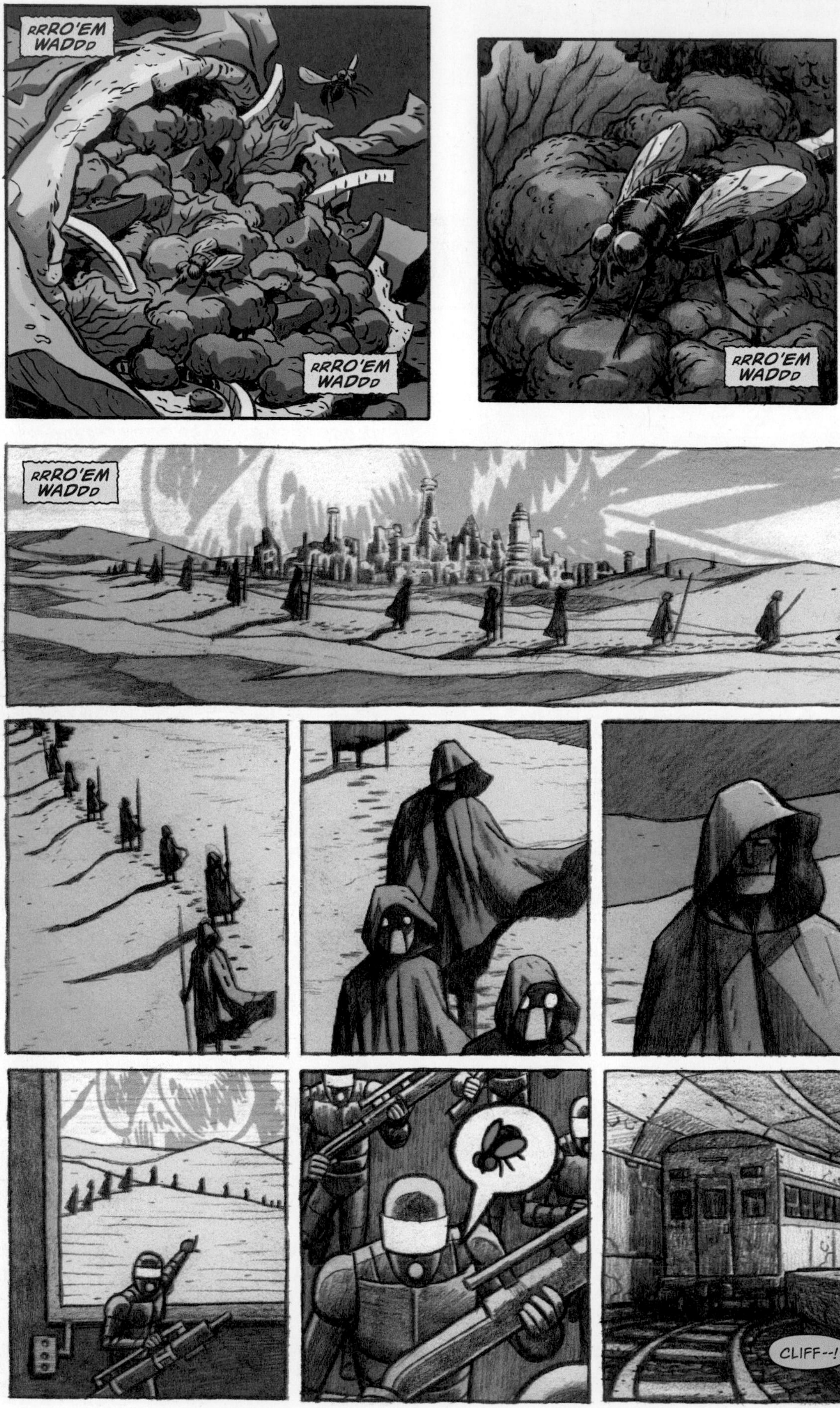

RRRO'EM WADDD
RRRO'EM WADDD
RRRO'EM WADDD
RRRO'EM WADDD
CLIFF--!

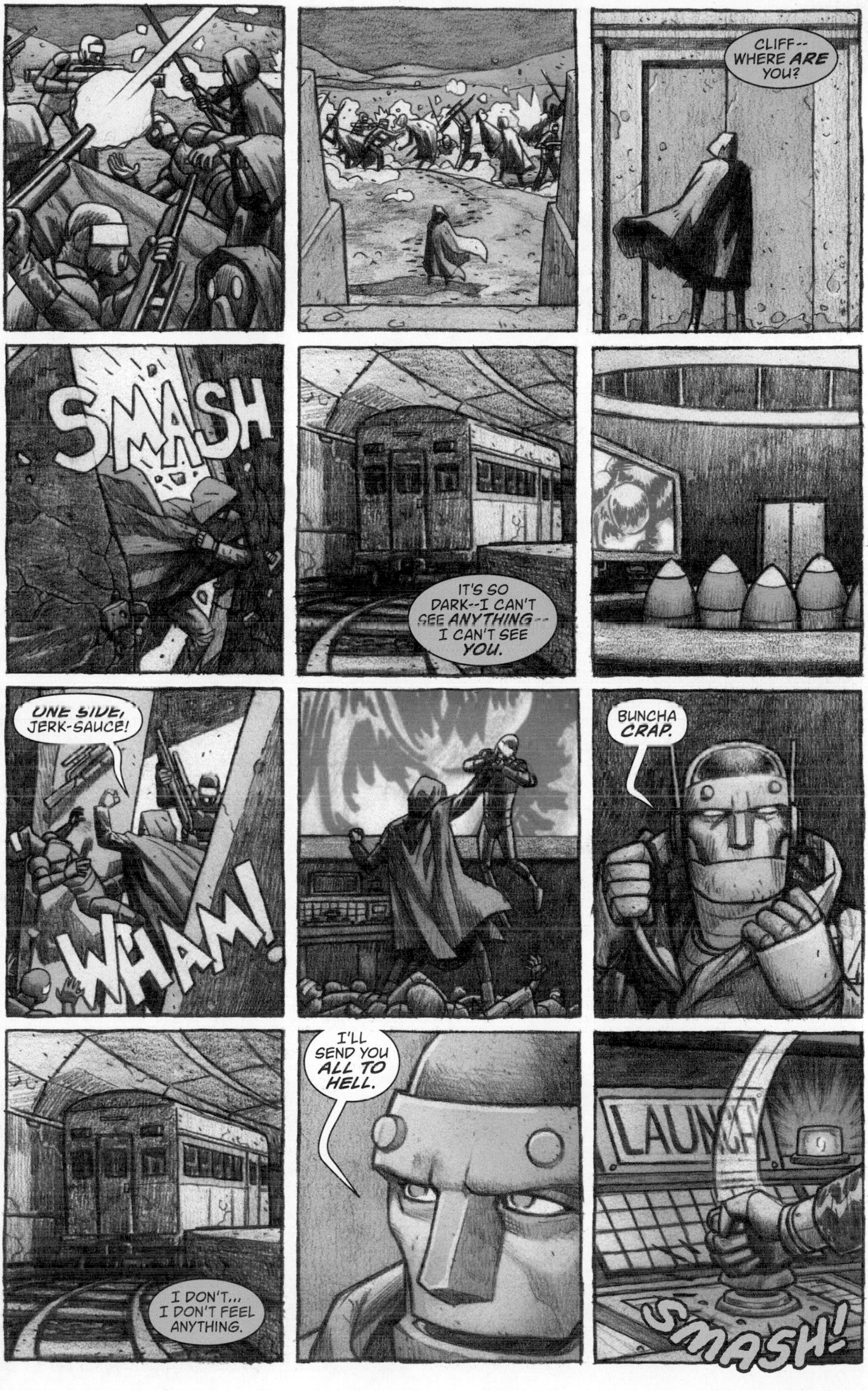
CLIFF-- WHERE ARE YOU?
SMASH
IT'S SO DARK--I CAN'T SEE ANYTHING-- I CAN'T SEE YOU.
ONE SIDE, JERK-SAUCE!
WHAM!
BUNCHA CRAP.
I DON'T... I DON'T FEEL ANYTHING.
I'LL SEND YOU ALL TO HELL.
LAUNCH
SMASH!

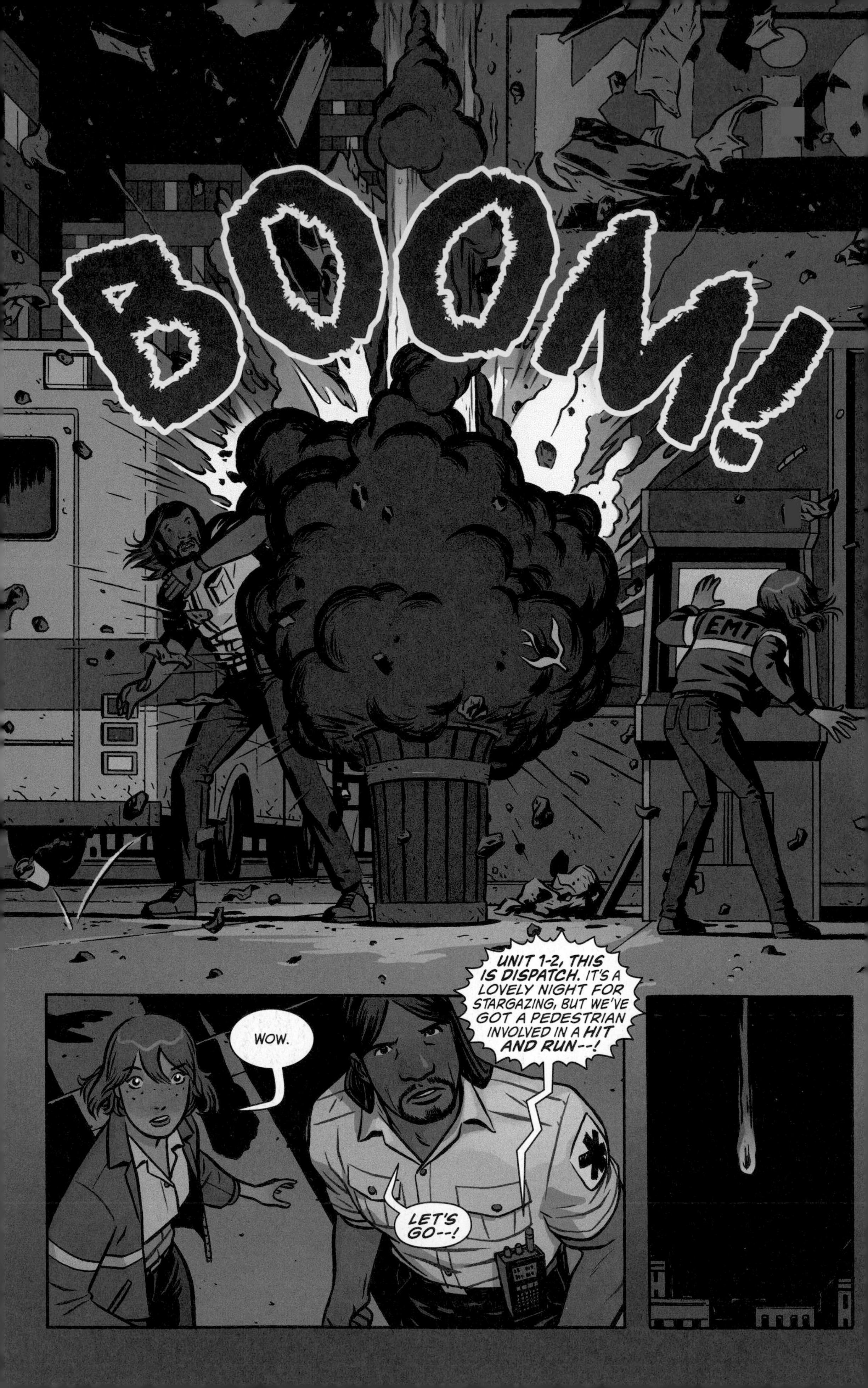
BOOM!
EMT
WOW.
UNIT 1-2, THIS IS DISPATCH. IT'S A LOVELY NIGHT FOR STARGAZING, BUT WE'VE GOT A PEDESTRIAN INVOLVED IN A HIT AND RUN--!
LET'S GO--!

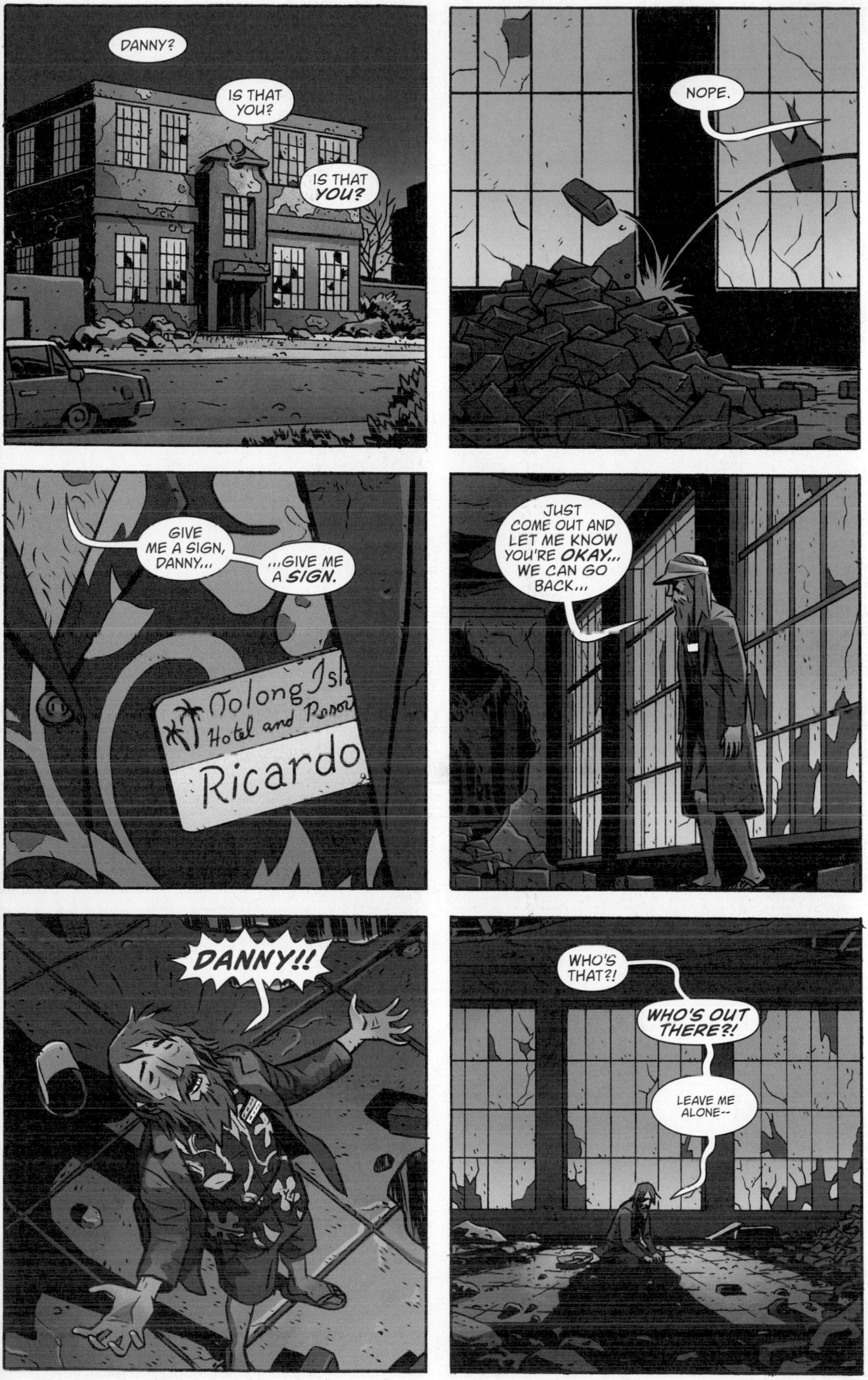
DANNY?
IS THAT YOU?
IS THAT YOU?
NOPE.
GIVE ME A SIGN, DANNY...
...GIVE ME A SIGN.
Molong Isl
Hotel and Resort
Ricardo
JUST COME OUT AND LET ME KNOW YOU'RE OKAY... WE CAN GO BACK...
DANNY!!
WHO'S THAT?!
WHO'S OUT THERE?!
LEAVE ME ALONE--

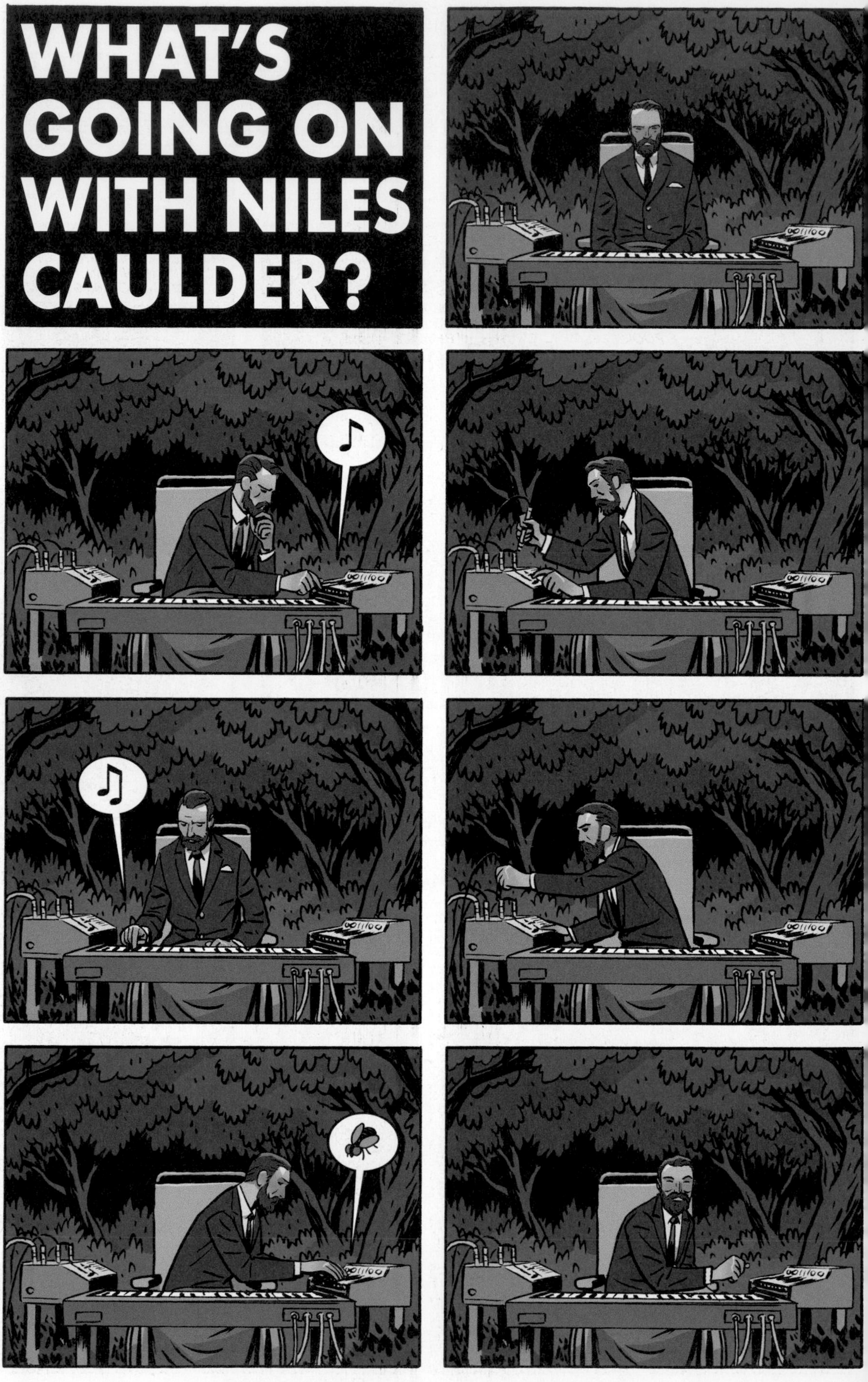
WHAT'S GOING ON WITH NILES CAULDER?

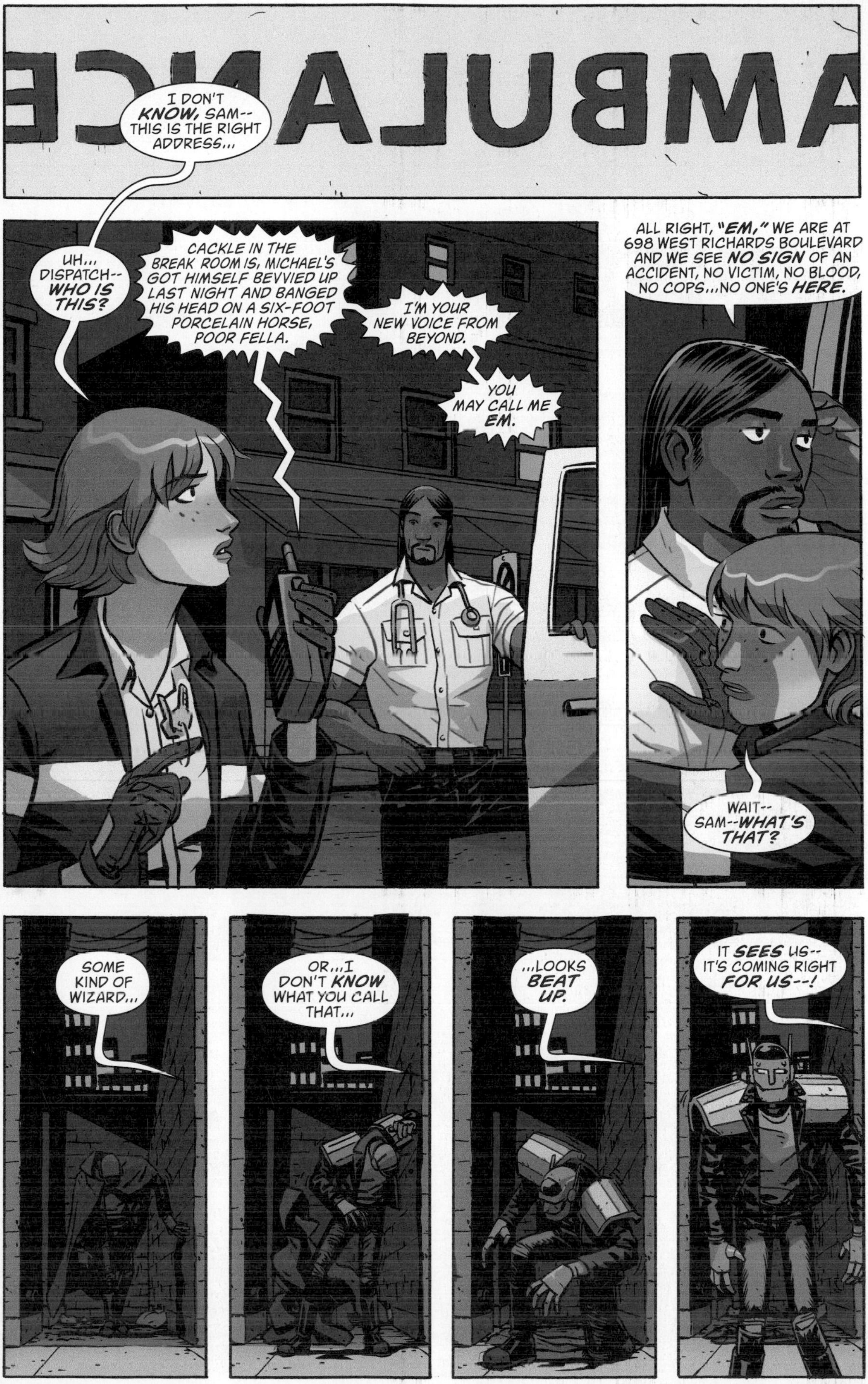
AMBULANCE
I DON'T KNOW, SAM-- THIS IS THE RIGHT ADDRESS...
UH... DISPATCH-- WHO IS THIS?
CACKLE IN THE BREAK ROOM IS, MICHAEL'S GOT HIMSELF BEVVIED UP LAST NIGHT AND BANGED HIS HEAD ON A SIX-FOOT PORCELAIN HORSE, POOR FELLA.
I'M YOUR NEW VOICE FROM BEYOND.
YOU MAY CALL ME EM.
ALL RIGHT, "EM," WE ARE AT 698 WEST RICHARDS BOULEVARD AND WE SEE NO SIGN OF AN ACCIDENT, NO VICTIM, NO BLOOD, NO COPS...NO ONE'S HERE.
WAIT-- SAM--WHAT'S THAT?
SOME KIND OF WIZARD...
OR...I DON'T KNOW WHAT YOU CALL THAT...
...LOOKS BEAT UP.
IT SEES US-- IT'S COMING RIGHT FOR US--!

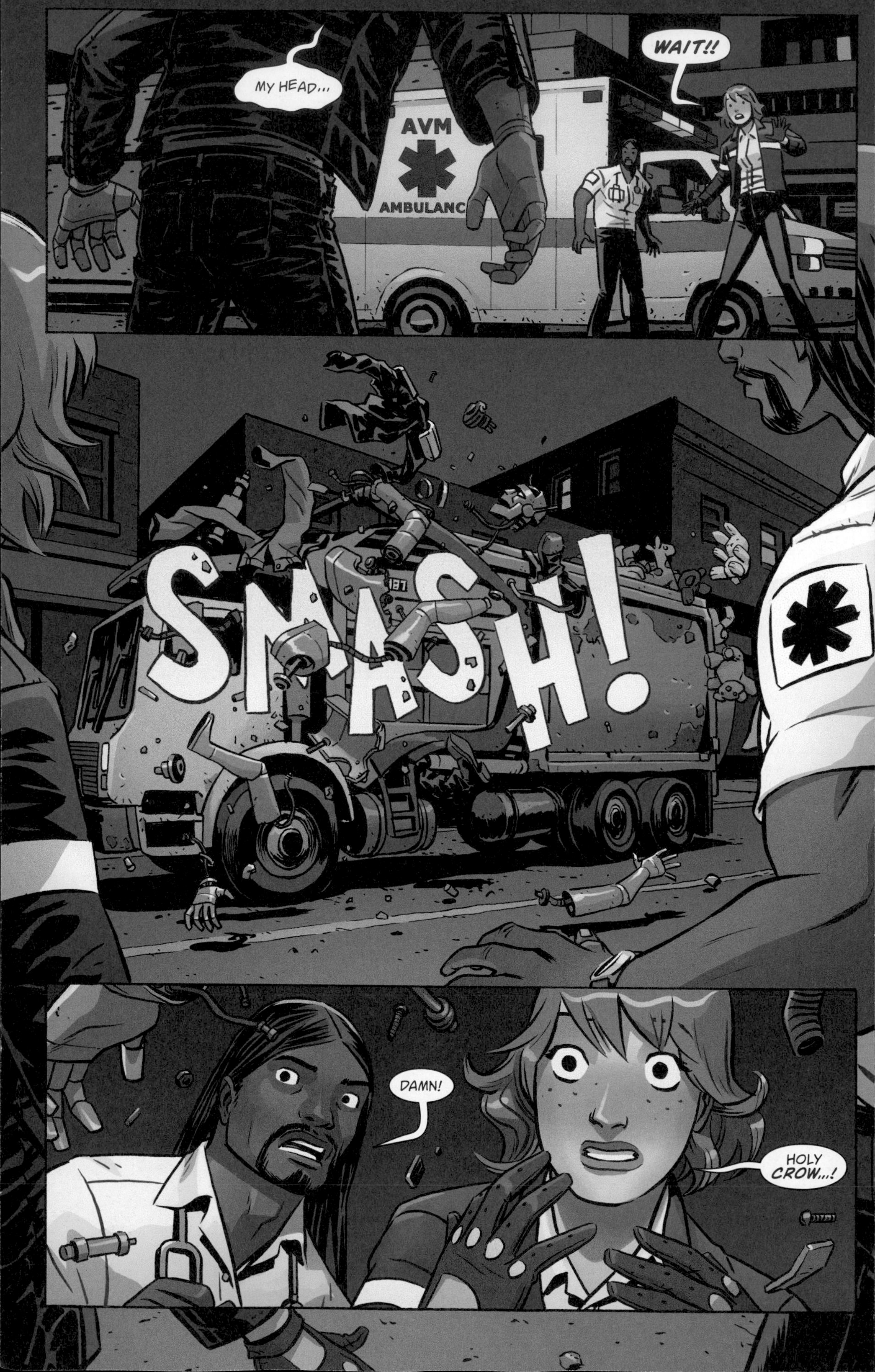
MY HEAD...
WAIT!!
AVM
AMBULANC
SMASH!
DAMN!
HOLY CROW...!

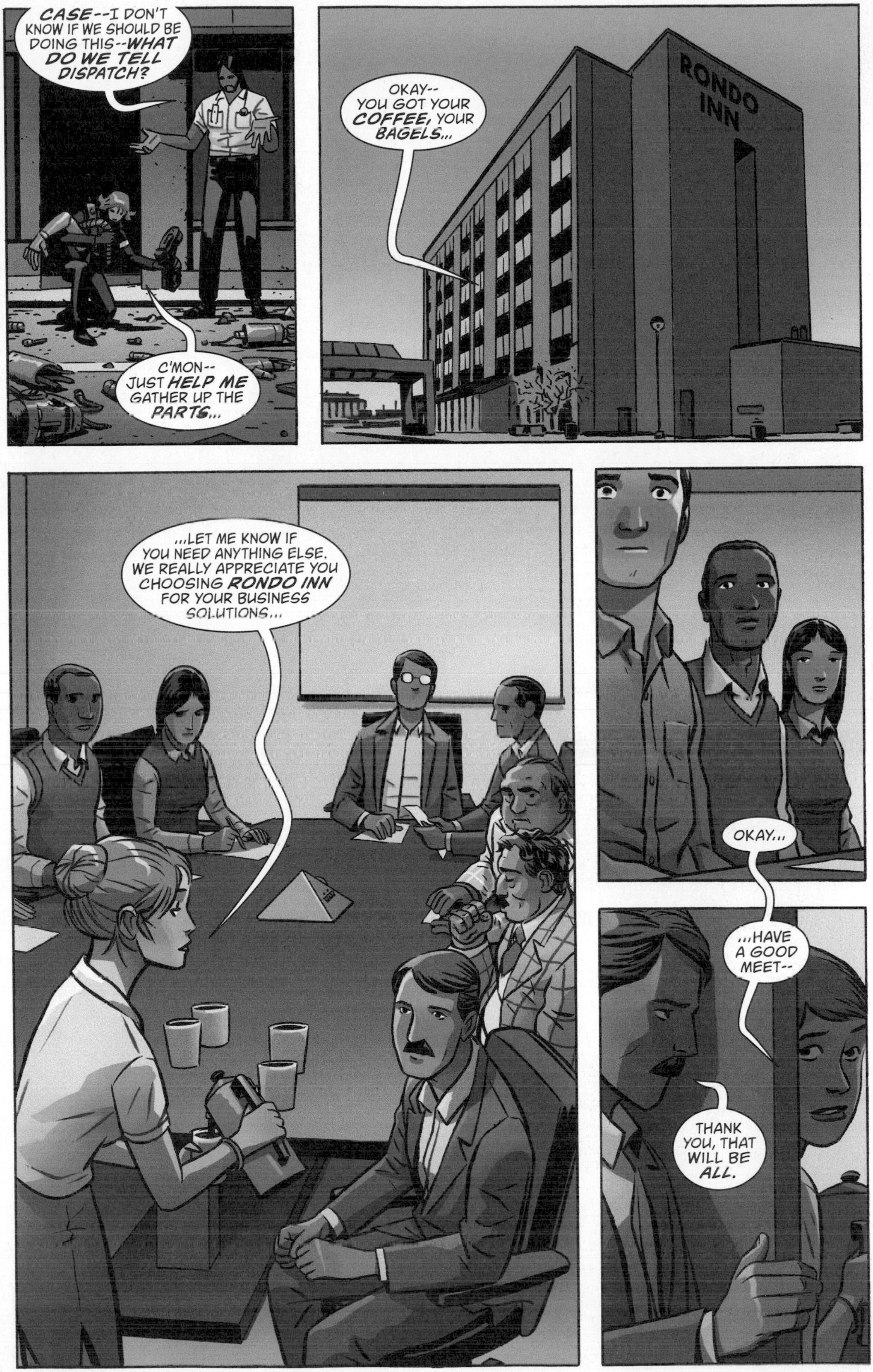
CASE--I DON'T KNOW IF WE SHOULD BE DOING THIS--WHAT DO WE TELL DISPATCH?
C'MON-- JUST HELP ME GATHER UP THE PARTS...
OKAY-- YOU GOT YOUR COFFEE, YOUR BAGELS...
RONDO INN
...LET ME KNOW IF YOU NEED ANYTHING ELSE. WE REALLY APPRECIATE YOU CHOOSING RONDO INN FOR YOUR BUSINESS SOLUTIONS...
OKAY...
...HAVE A GOOD MEET--
THANK YOU, THAT WILL BE ALL.

UMATA KALABRA!

THE MESSAGE IS THE MEAT--

--TENDER CUTS-- FINE AND SWEET!

I HATE MEETING ON EARTH, AND I *HATE* THE RONDO INN.

THIS BETTER BE SOME GROUND-BREAKING SHIT.

THANK YOU FOR MEETING US HERE-- WE WANTED A PRIVATE CHANNEL, FREE FROM THE *OBSERVASTAT, SECURITY* BEING THE ISSUE...

WE TRUST ALL GOES WELL WITH THE BUSINESS ON *GLOAM?*

YOU *KNOW* HOW IT GOES...

THAT'S WHY WE'RE HERE.

GET ON WITH IT.

AS YOU KNOW, *GOOBFOOBERS* IS INTRODUCING AN *ALL-NEW MENTALLY HEALTHY MEAT MENU* TO ALL ITS LOCATIONS.

IT'S A *REALLY BIG* CAMPAIGN...

...THERE'S A TIE-IN WITH A NEW FILM FRANCHISE INVOLVING TALKING *FRIBS,* VOICED BY XTIAN TEENAGE IDOLS. A PORTION OF ALL PROCEEDS GO TO *S.O.M.* VIRUS RESEARCH...

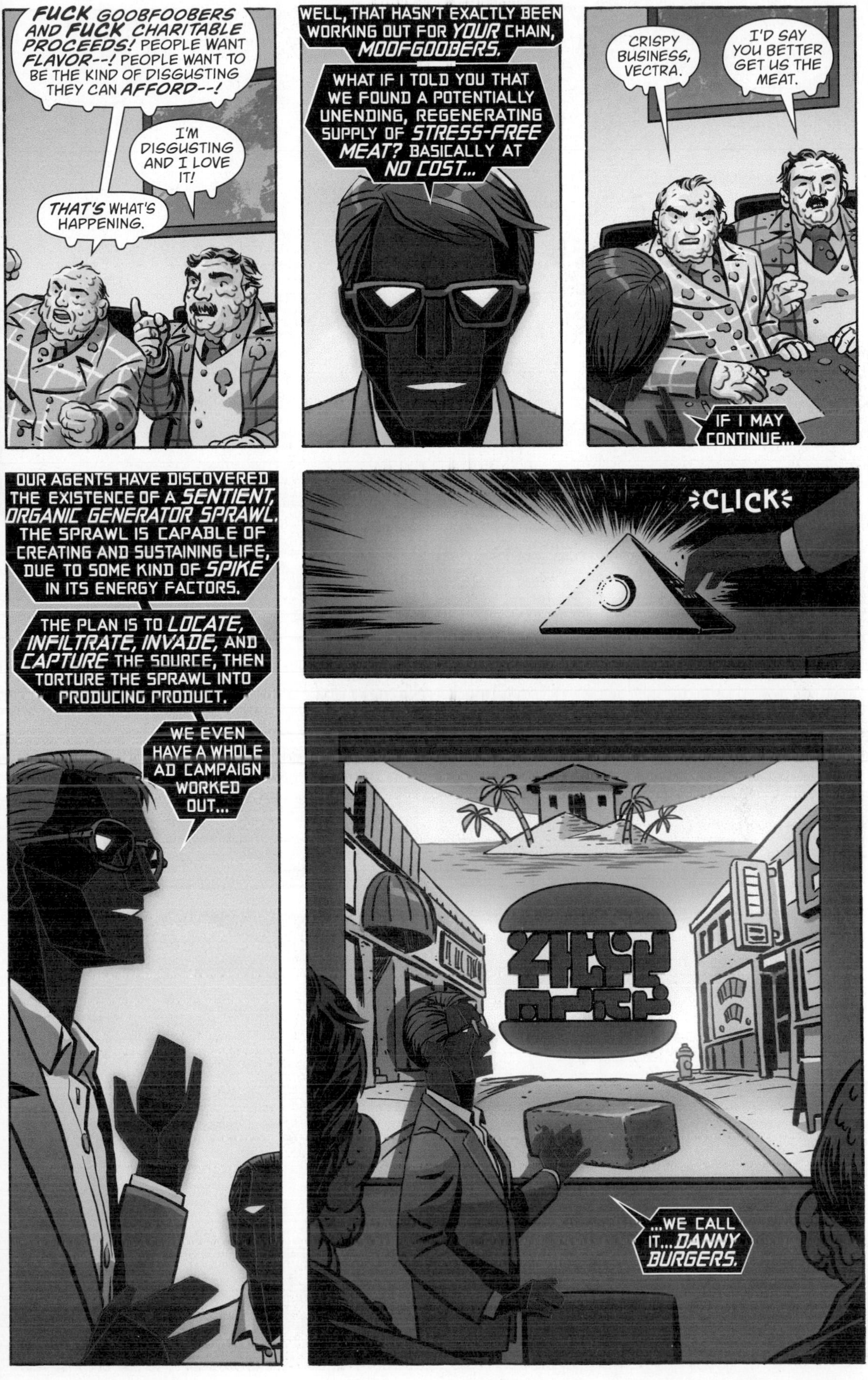
FUCK GOOBFOOBERS AND FUCK CHARITABLE PROCEEDS! PEOPLE WANT FLAVOR--! PEOPLE WANT TO BE THE KIND OF DISGUSTING THEY CAN AFFORD--!
I'M DISGUSTING AND I LOVE IT!
THAT'S WHAT'S HAPPENING.
WELL, THAT HASN'T EXACTLY BEEN WORKING OUT FOR YOUR CHAIN, MOOFGOOBERS.
WHAT IF I TOLD YOU THAT WE FOUND A POTENTIALLY UNENDING, REGENERATING SUPPLY OF STRESS-FREE MEAT? BASICALLY AT NO COST...
CRISPY BUSINESS, VECTRA.
I'D SAY YOU BETTER GET US THE MEAT.
IF I MAY CONTINUE...
OUR AGENTS HAVE DISCOVERED THE EXISTENCE OF A SENTIENT, ORGANIC GENERATOR SPRAWL. THE SPRAWL IS CAPABLE OF CREATING AND SUSTAINING LIFE, DUE TO SOME KIND OF SPIKE IN ITS ENERGY FACTORS.
THE PLAN IS TO LOCATE, INFILTRATE, INVADE, AND CAPTURE THE SOURCE, THEN TORTURE THE SPRAWL INTO PRODUCING PRODUCT.
WE EVEN HAVE A WHOLE AD CAMPAIGN WORKED OUT...
CLICK
...WE CALL IT...DANNY BURGERS.

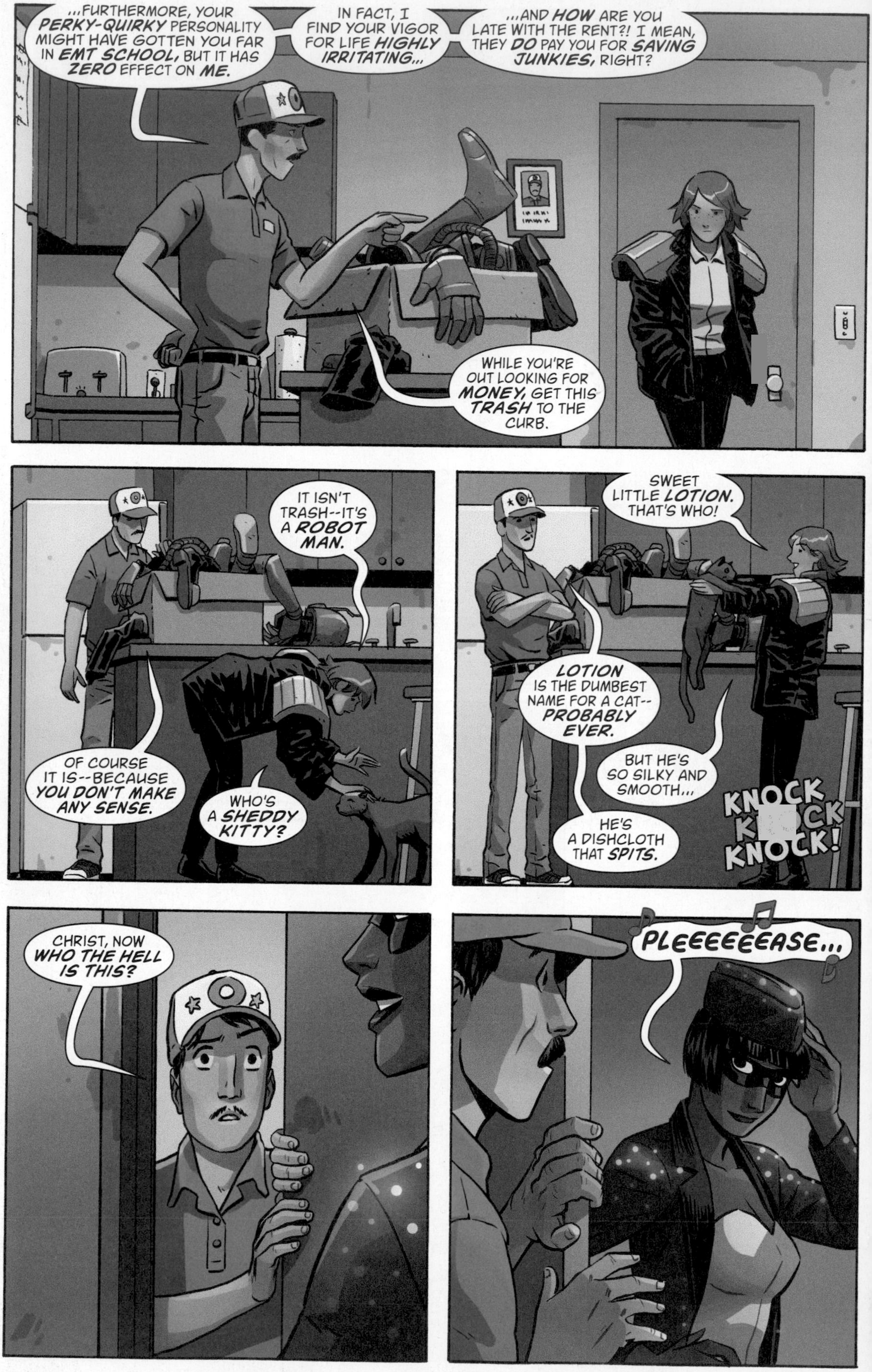
...FURTHERMORE, YOUR PERKY-QUIRKY PERSONALITY MIGHT HAVE GOTTEN YOU FAR IN EMT SCHOOL, BUT IT HAS ZERO EFFECT ON ME.
IN FACT, I FIND YOUR VIGOR FOR LIFE HIGHLY IRRITATING...
...AND HOW ARE YOU LATE WITH THE RENT?! I MEAN, THEY DO PAY YOU FOR SAVING JUNKIES, RIGHT?
WHILE YOU'RE OUT LOOKING FOR MONEY, GET THIS TRASH TO THE CURB.
IT ISN'T TRASH--IT'S A ROBOT MAN.
OF COURSE IT IS--BECAUSE YOU DON'T MAKE ANY SENSE.
WHO'S A SHEDDY KITTY?
SWEET LITTLE LOTION. THAT'S WHO!
LOTION IS THE DUMBEST NAME FOR A CAT--PROBABLY EVER.
BUT HE'S SO SILKY AND SMOOTH...
HE'S A DISHCLOTH THAT SPITS.
KNOCK KNOCK KNOCK!
CHRIST, NOW WHO THE HELL IS THIS?
PLEEEEEEASE...

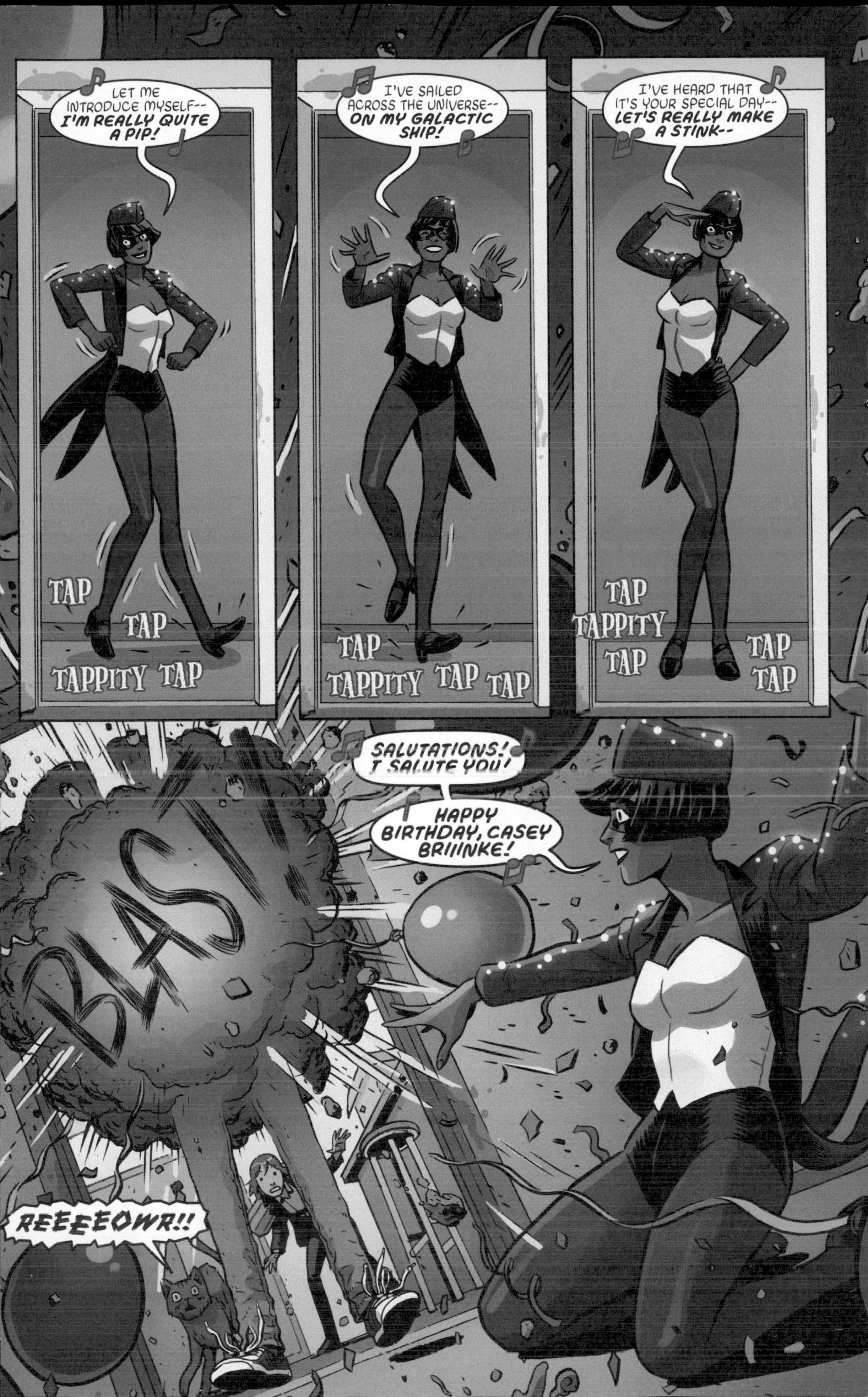
LET ME INTRODUCE MYSELF-- I'M REALLY QUITE A PIP!
TAP
TAP
TAPPITY TAP
I'VE SAILED ACROSS THE UNIVERSE-- ON MY GALACTIC SHIP!
TAP
TAPPITY TAP TAP
I'VE HEARD THAT IT'S YOUR SPECIAL DAY-- LET'S REALLY MAKE A STINK--
TAP
TAPPITY
TAP
TAP
TAP
SALUTATIONS! I SALUTE YOU!
HAPPY BIRTHDAY, CASEY BRIIINKE!
BLAST!
REEEEEOWR!!

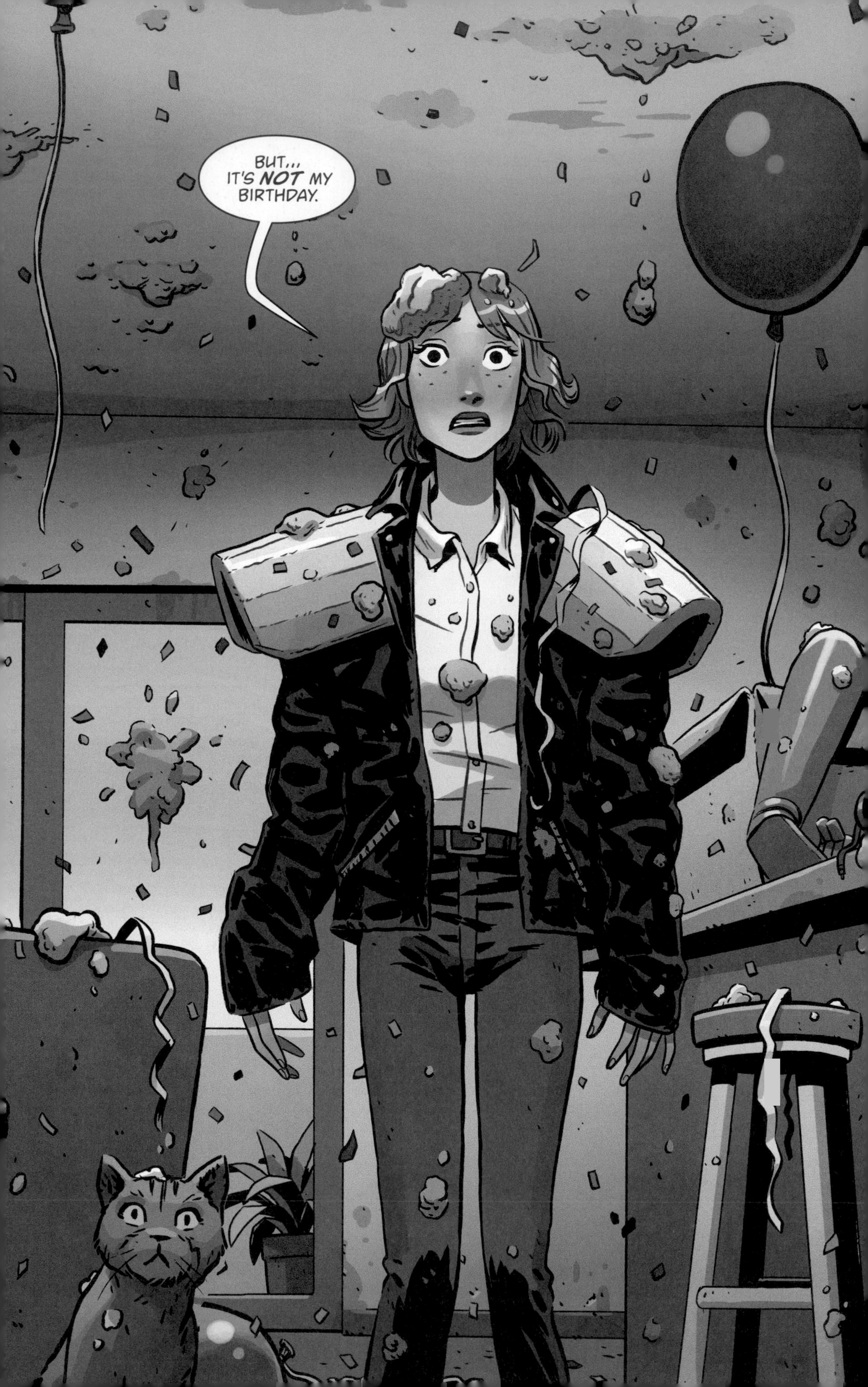
BUT... IT'S **NOT** MY BIRTHDAY.

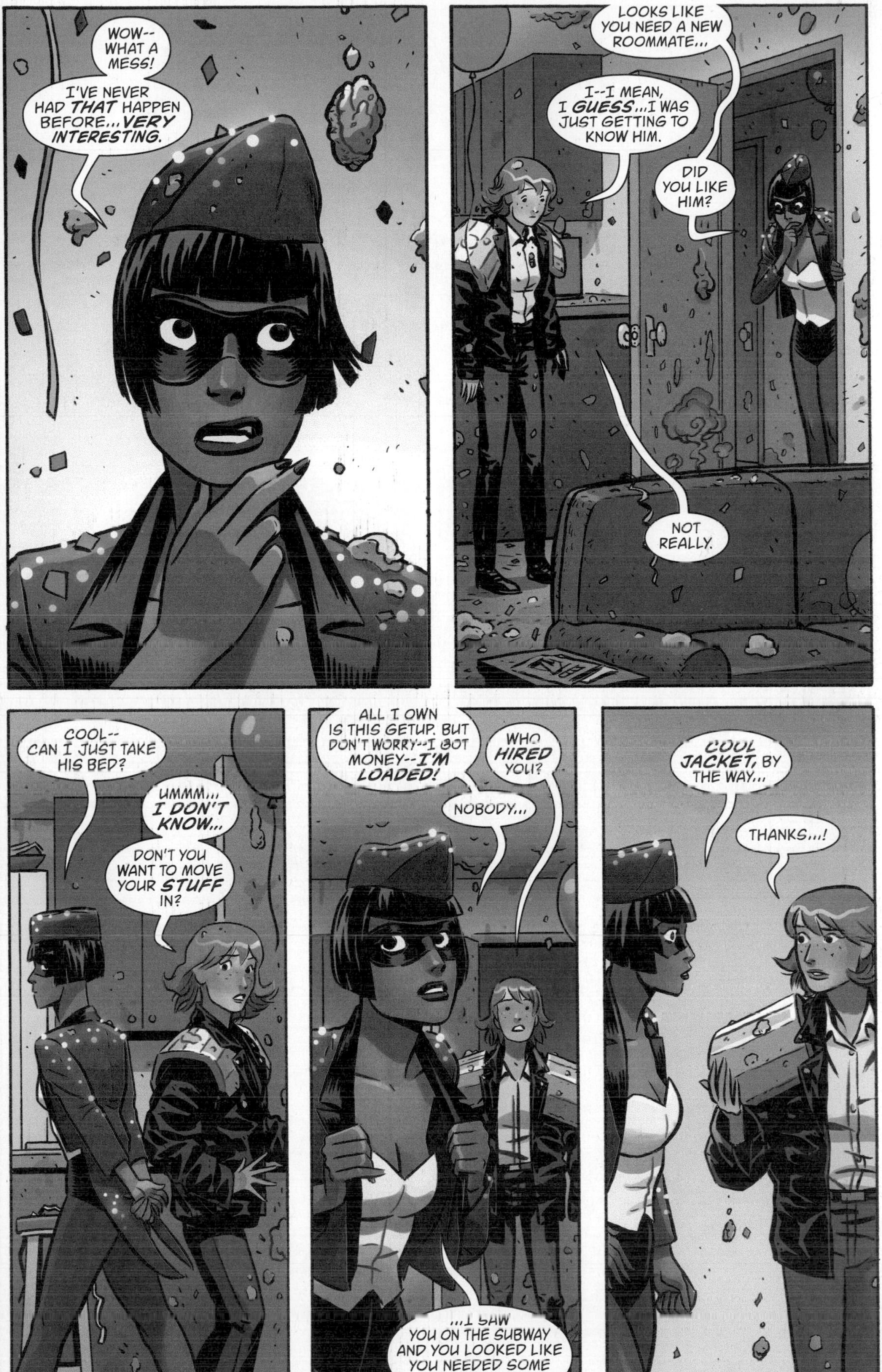
WOW--
WHAT A MESS!
I'VE NEVER HAD THAT HAPPEN BEFORE... VERY INTERESTING.
LOOKS LIKE YOU NEED A NEW ROOMMATE...
I--I MEAN, I GUESS... I WAS JUST GETTING TO KNOW HIM.
DID YOU LIKE HIM?
NOT REALLY.
COOL-- CAN I JUST TAKE HIS BED?
UMMM... I DON'T KNOW...
DON'T YOU WANT TO MOVE YOUR STUFF IN?
ALL I OWN IS THIS GETUP. BUT DON'T WORRY--I GOT MONEY--I'M LOADED!
WHO HIRED YOU?
NOBODY...
...I SAW YOU ON THE SUBWAY AND YOU LOOKED LIKE YOU NEEDED SOME CHEERING UP.
COOL JACKET, BY THE WAY...
THANKS...!

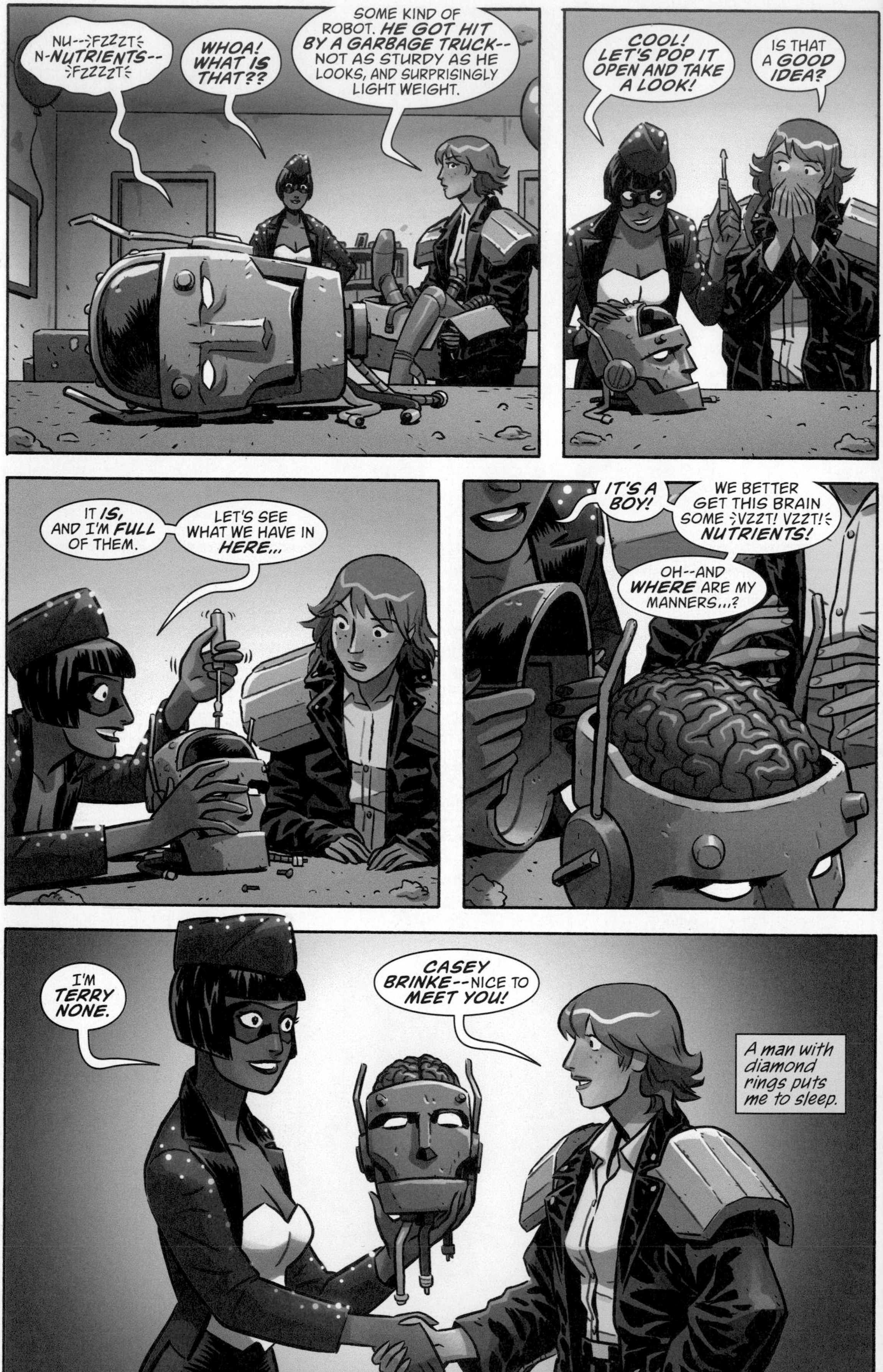
NU--FZZZT N-NUTRIENTS-- FZZZZT
WHOA! WHAT IS THAT??
SOME KIND OF ROBOT. HE GOT HIT BY A GARBAGE TRUCK-- NOT AS STURDY AS HE LOOKS, AND SURPRISINGLY LIGHT WEIGHT.
COOL! LET'S POP IT OPEN AND TAKE A LOOK!
IS THAT A GOOD IDEA?
IT IS, AND I'M FULL OF THEM.
LET'S SEE WHAT WE HAVE IN HERE...
IT'S A BOY!
WE BETTER GET THIS BRAIN SOME VZZT! VZZT! NUTRIENTS!
OH--AND WHERE ARE MY MANNERS...?
I'M TERRY NONE.
CASEY BRINKE--NICE TO MEET YOU!
A man with diamond rings puts me to sleep.

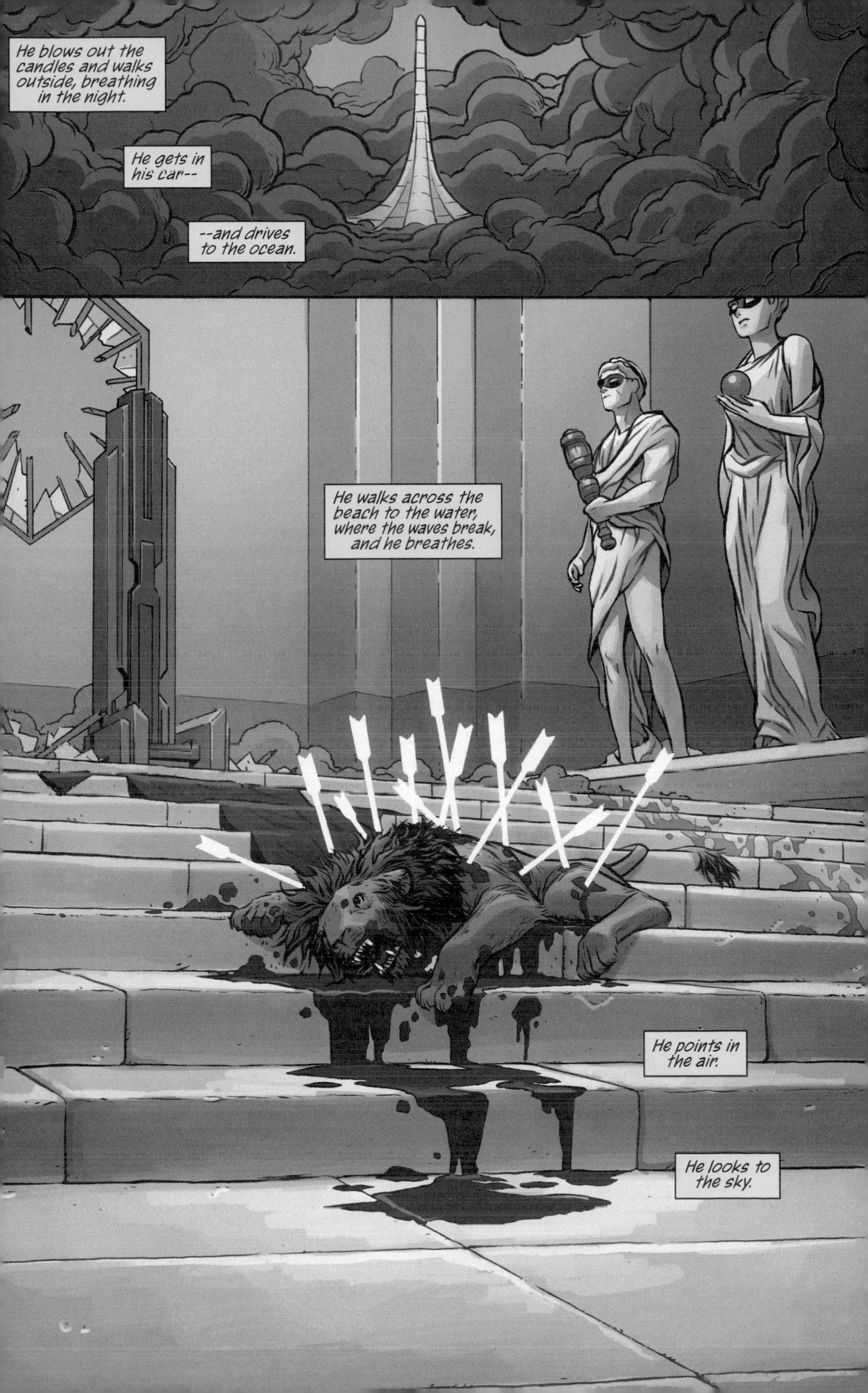

He blows out the candles and walks outside, breathing in the night.
He gets in his car--
--and drives to the ocean.
He walks across the beach to the water, where the waves break, and he breathes.
He points in the air.
He looks to the sky.

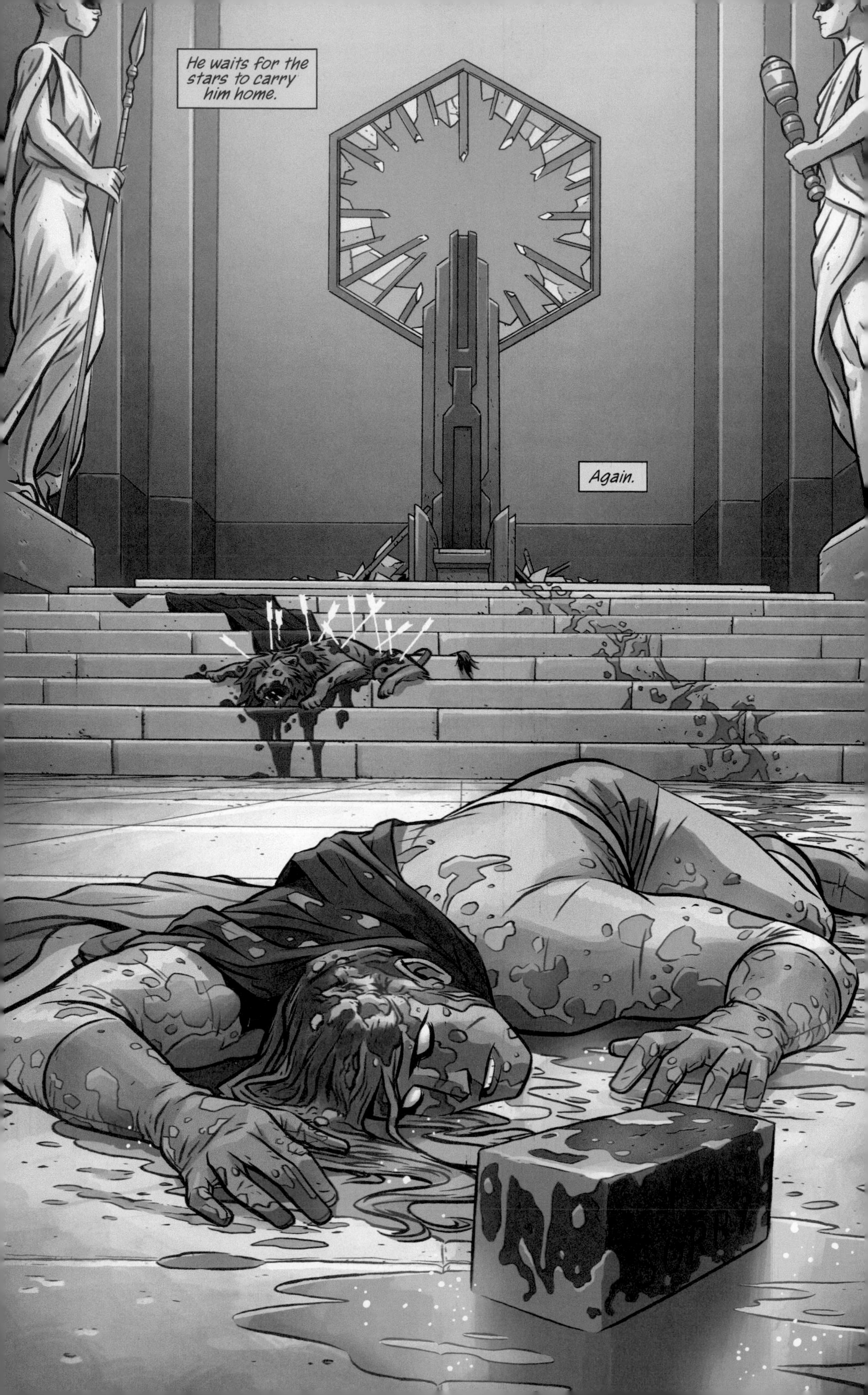
He waits for the stars to carry him home.
Again.

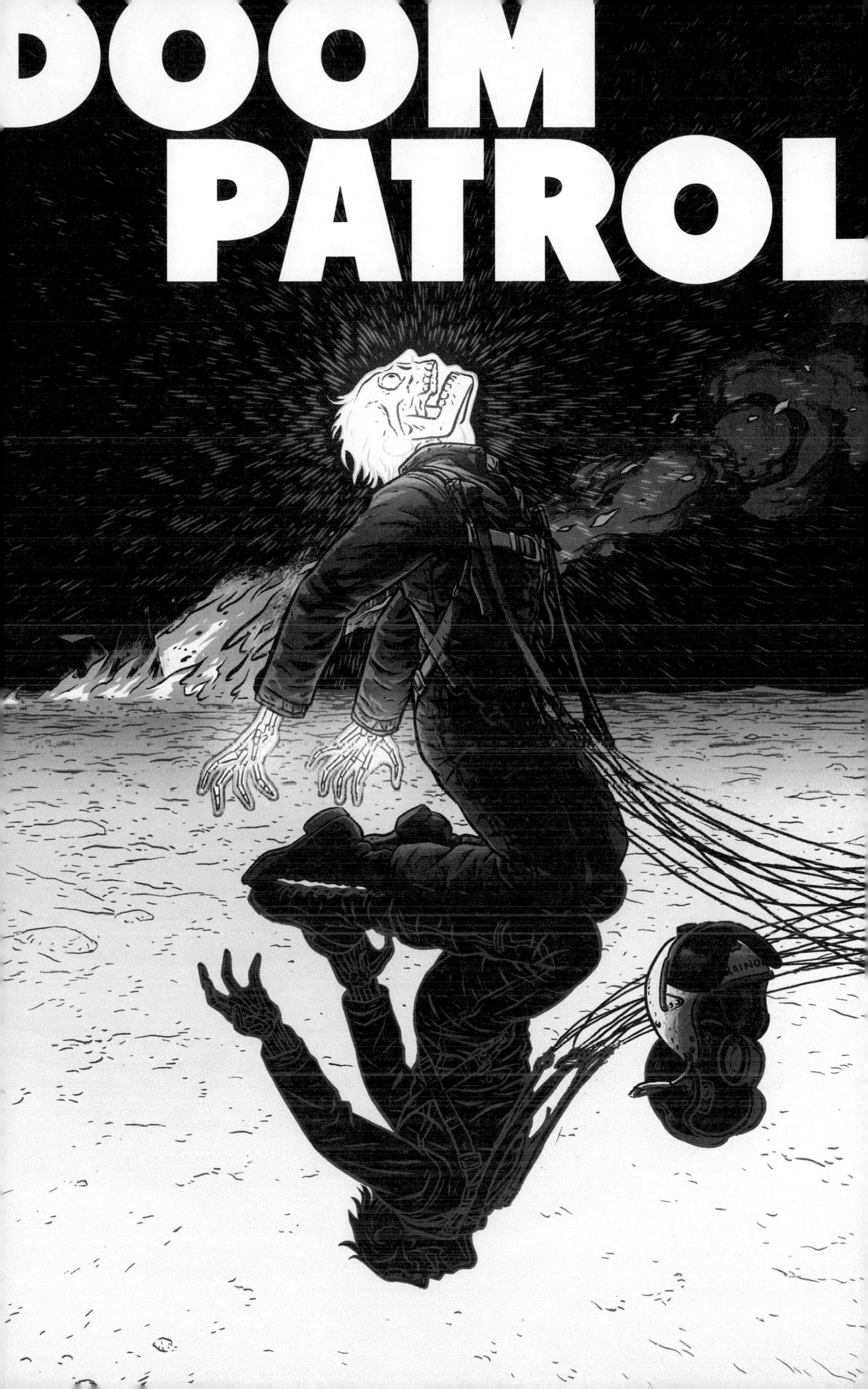
DOOM
PATROL

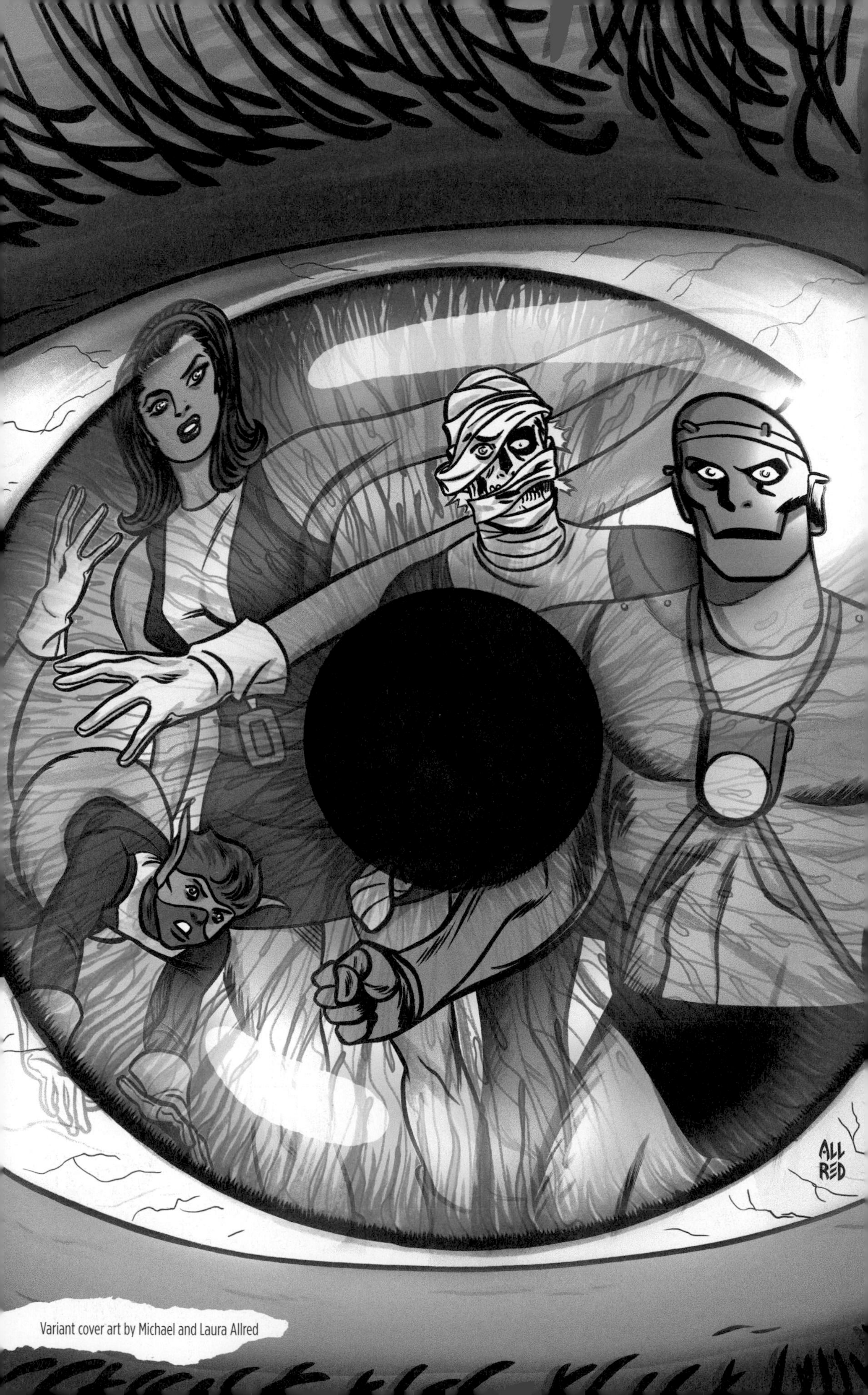
ALL
RED

Variant cover art by Michael and Laura Allred

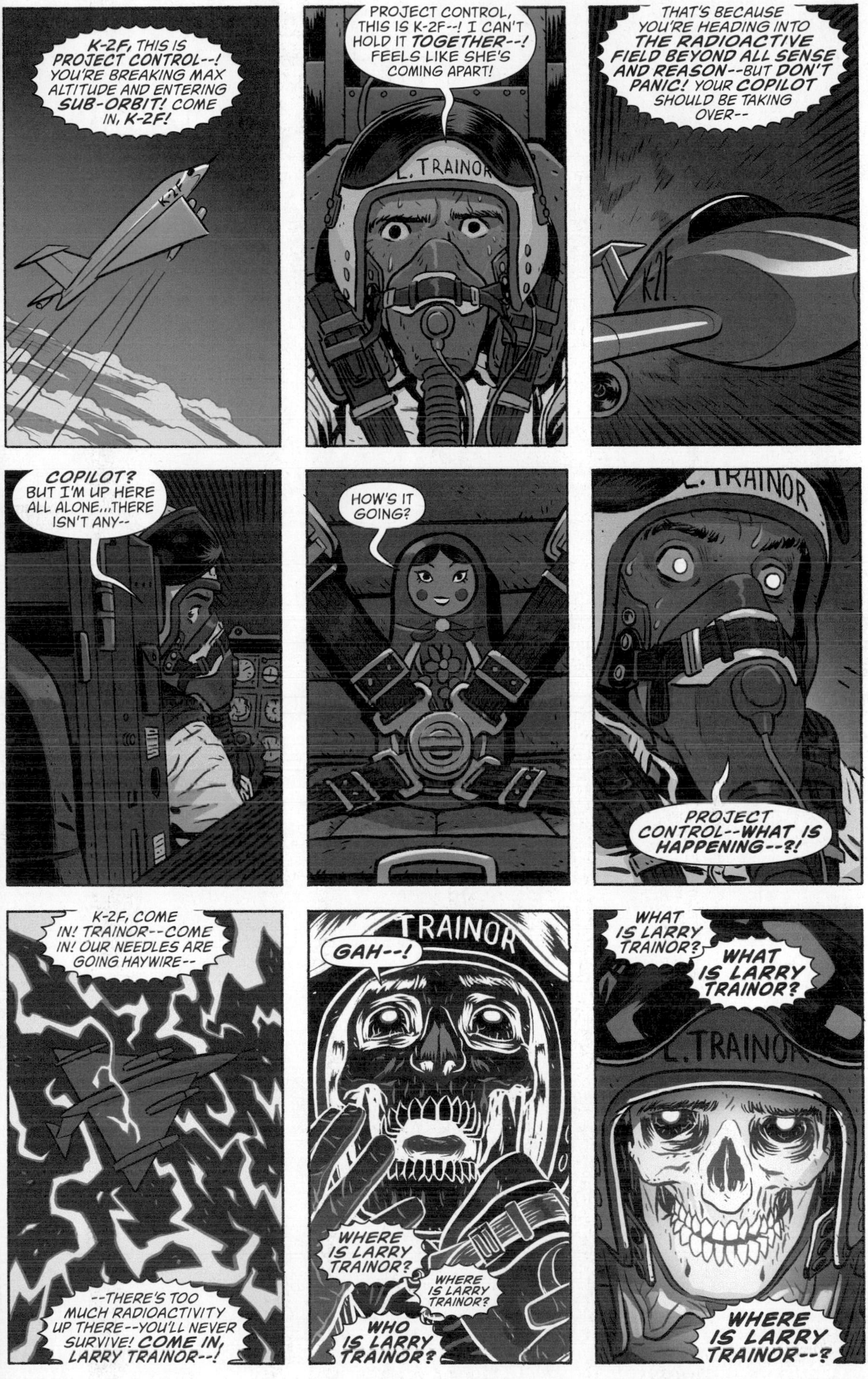
K-2F, THIS IS PROJECT CONTROL--! YOU'RE BREAKING MAX ALTITUDE AND ENTERING SUB-ORBIT! COME IN, K-2F!
PROJECT CONTROL, THIS IS K-2F--! I CAN'T HOLD IT TOGETHER--! FEELS LIKE SHE'S COMING APART!
L. TRAINOR
THAT'S BECAUSE YOU'RE HEADING INTO THE RADIOACTIVE FIELD BEYOND ALL SENSE AND REASON--BUT DON'T PANIC! YOUR COPILOT SHOULD BE TAKING OVER--
COPILOT? BUT I'M UP HERE ALL ALONE...THERE ISN'T ANY--
HOW'S IT GOING?
L. TRAINOR
PROJECT CONTROL--WHAT IS HAPPENING--?!
K-2F, COME IN! TRAINOR--COME IN! OUR NEEDLES ARE GOING HAYWIRE--
--THERE'S TOO MUCH RADIOACTIVITY UP THERE--YOU'LL NEVER SURVIVE! COME IN, LARRY TRAINOR--!
TRAINOR
GAH--!
WHERE IS LARRY TRAINOR?
WHERE IS LARRY TRAINOR?
WHO IS LARRY TRAINOR?
WHAT IS LARRY TRAINOR?
WHAT IS LARRY TRAINOR?
L. TRAINOR
WHERE IS LARRY TRAINOR--?

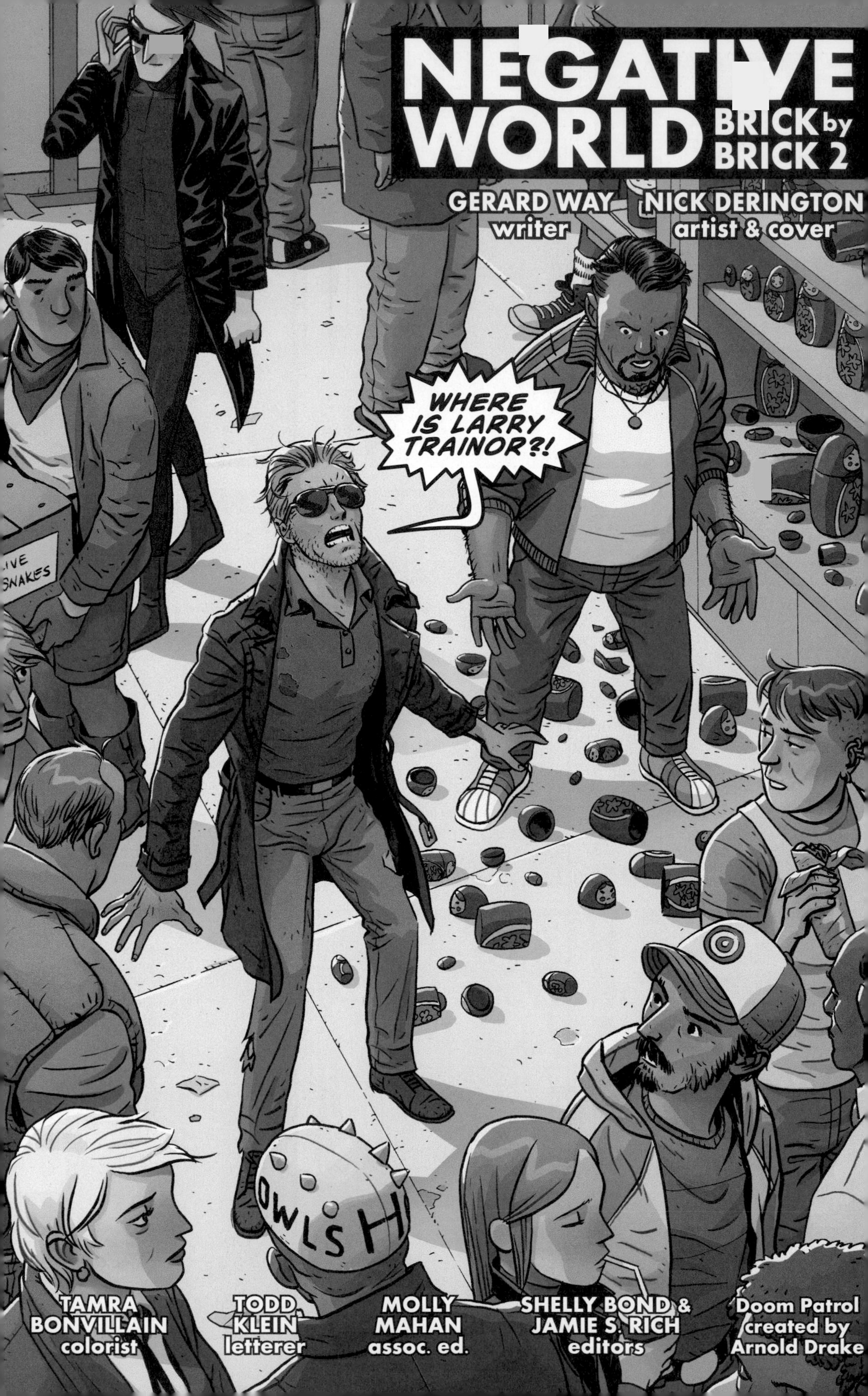
NEGATIVE WORLD
BRICK by BRICK 2
GERARD WAY writer
NICK DERINGTON artist & cover
WHERE IS LARRY TRAINOR?!
TAMRA BONVILLAIN colorist
TODD KLEIN letterer
MOLLY MAHAN assoc. ed.
SHELLY BOND & JAMIE S. RICH editors
Doom Patrol created by Arnold Drake

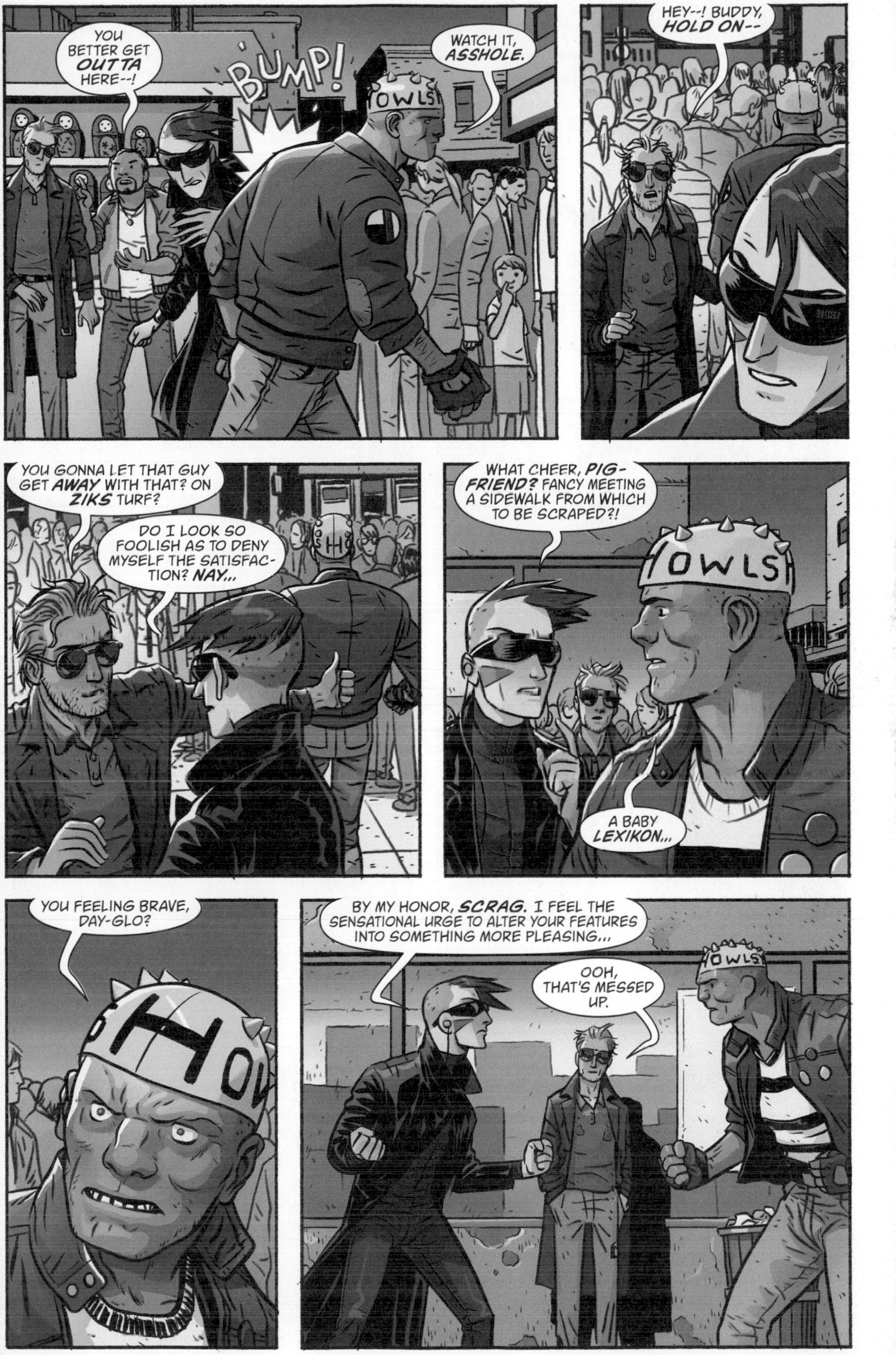
YOU BETTER GET OUTTA HERE--!
BUMP!
WATCH IT, ASSHOLE.
HOWLS
HEY--! BUDDY, HOLD ON--
YOU GONNA LET THAT GUY GET AWAY WITH THAT? ON ZIKS TURF?
DO I LOOK SO FOOLISH AS TO DENY MYSELF THE SATISFACTION? NAY...
WHAT CHEER, PIG-FRIEND? FANCY MEETING A SIDEWALK FROM WHICH TO BE SCRAPED?!
HOWLS
A BABY LEXIKON...
YOU FEELING BRAVE, DAY-GLO?
BY MY HONOR, SCRAG. I FEEL THE SENSATIONAL URGE TO ALTER YOUR FEATURES INTO SOMETHING MORE PLEASING...
OOH, THAT'S MESSED UP.
HOWLS

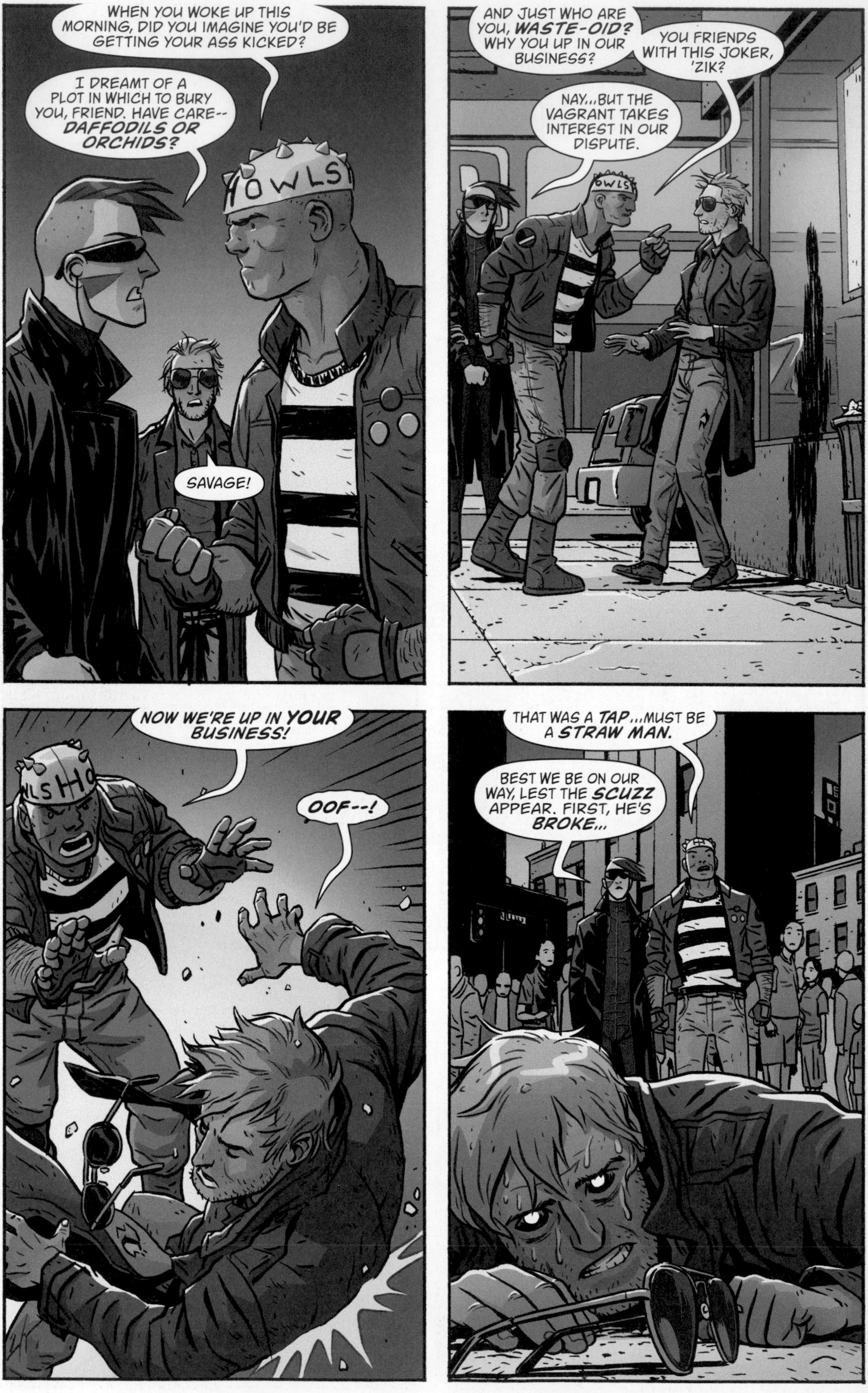
WHEN YOU WOKE UP THIS MORNING, DID YOU IMAGINE YOU'D BE GETTING YOUR ASS KICKED?
I DREAMT OF A PLOT IN WHICH TO BURY YOU, FRIEND. HAVE CARE-- DAFFODILS OR ORCHIDS?
HOWLS
SAVAGE!
AND JUST WHO ARE YOU, WASTE-OID? WHY YOU UP IN OUR BUSINESS?
YOU FRIENDS WITH THIS JOKER, 'ZIK?
NAY...BUT THE VAGRANT TAKES INTEREST IN OUR DISPUTE.
NOW WE'RE UP IN YOUR BUSINESS!
OOF--!
THAT WAS A TAP...MUST BE A STRAW MAN.
BEST WE BE ON OUR WAY, LEST THE SCUZZ APPEAR. FIRST, HE'S BROKE...

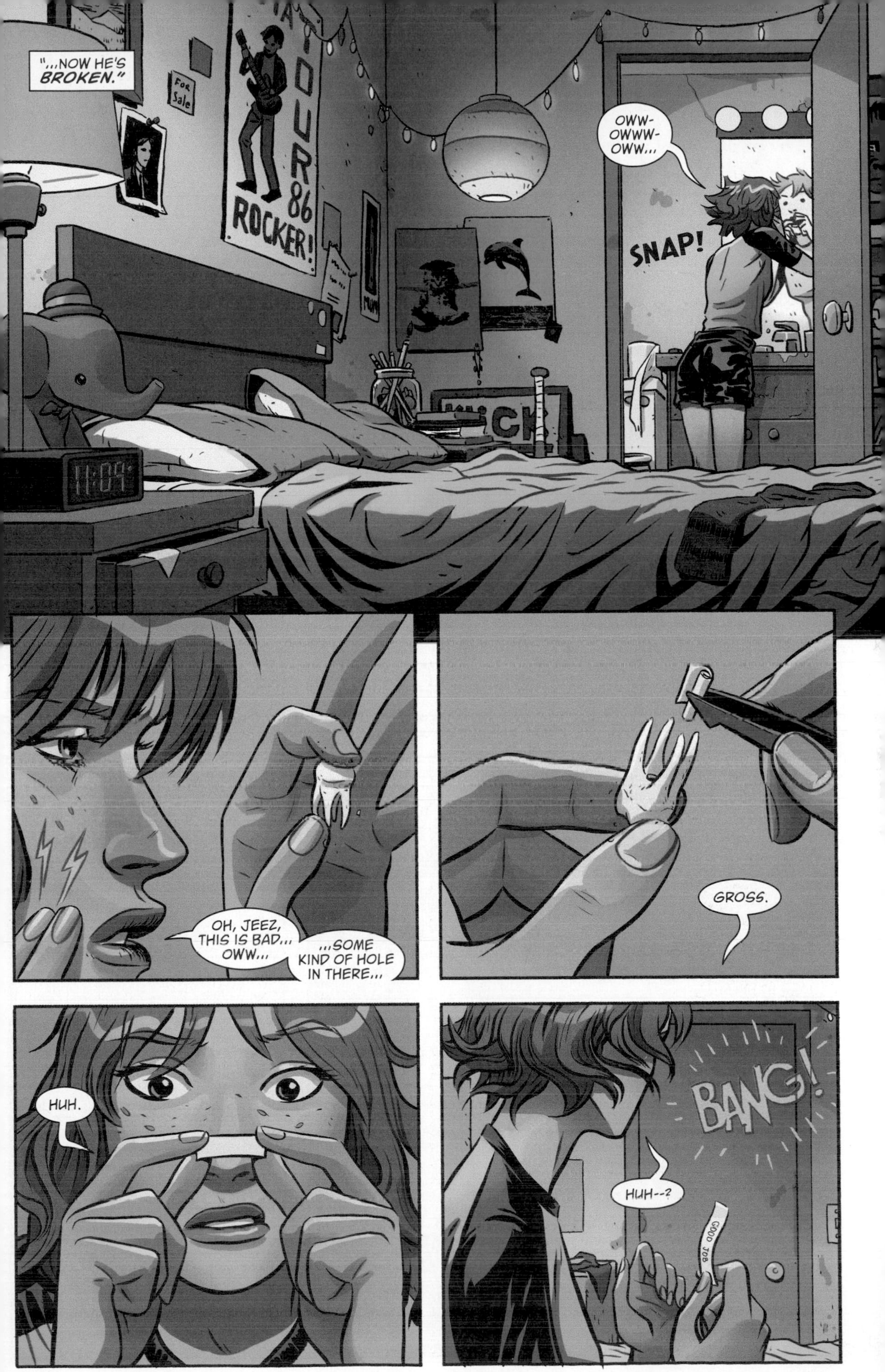
"...NOW HE'S BROKEN."
FOR SALE
TOUR 86
ROCKER!
MUM
OWW-OWWW-OWW...
SNAP!
OH, JEEZ, THIS IS BAD... OWW...
...SOME KIND OF HOLE IN THERE...
GROSS.
HUH.
BANG!
HUH--?
GOOD JOB

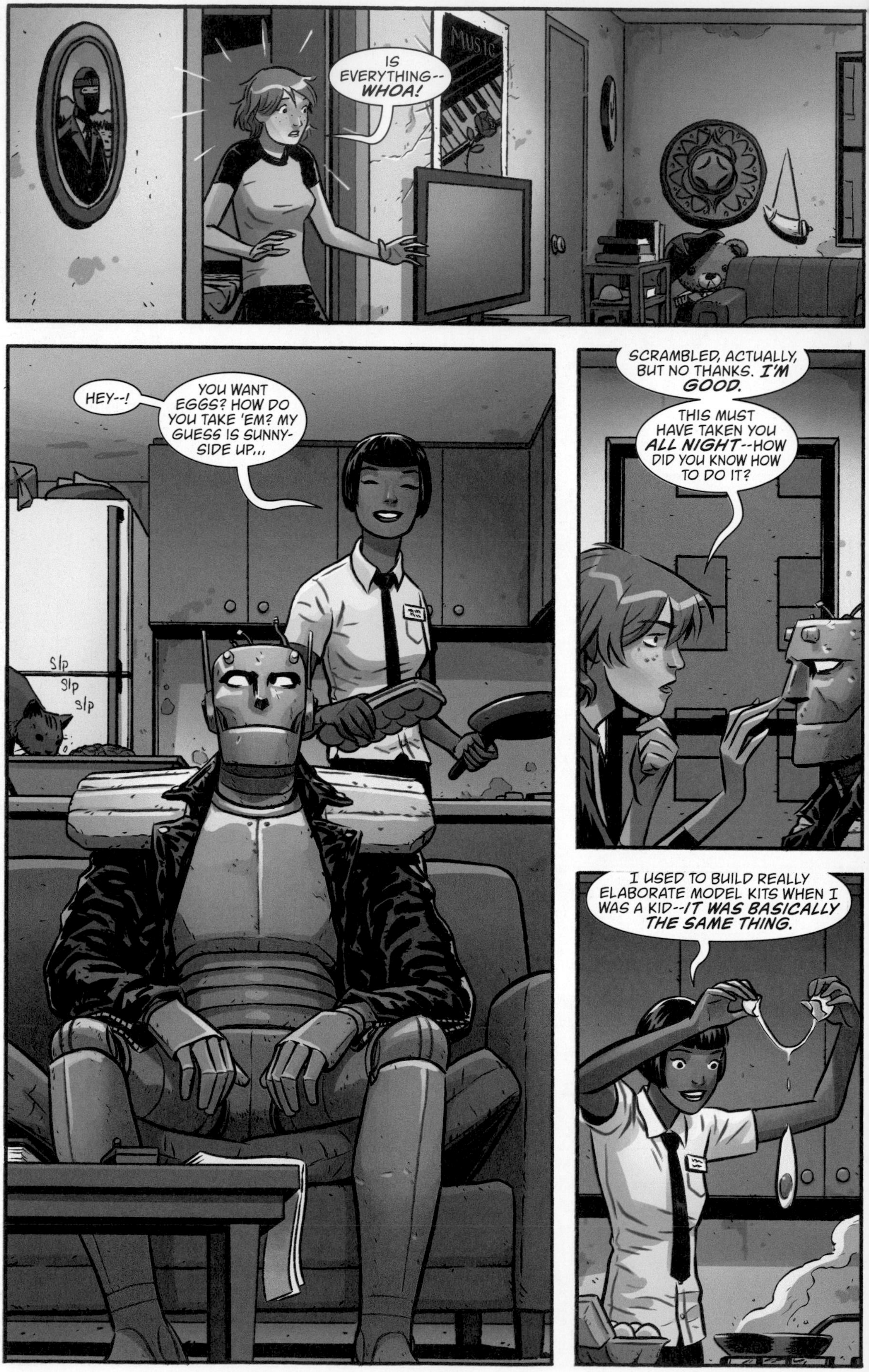
IS EVERYTHING-- WHOA!
HEY--!
YOU WANT EGGS? HOW DO YOU TAKE 'EM? MY GUESS IS SUNNY-SIDE UP...
SLP
SLP
SLP
SCRAMBLED, ACTUALLY, BUT NO THANKS. I'M GOOD.
THIS MUST HAVE TAKEN YOU ALL NIGHT--HOW DID YOU KNOW HOW TO DO IT?
I USED TO BUILD REALLY ELABORATE MODEL KITS WHEN I WAS A KID--IT WAS BASICALLY THE SAME THING.

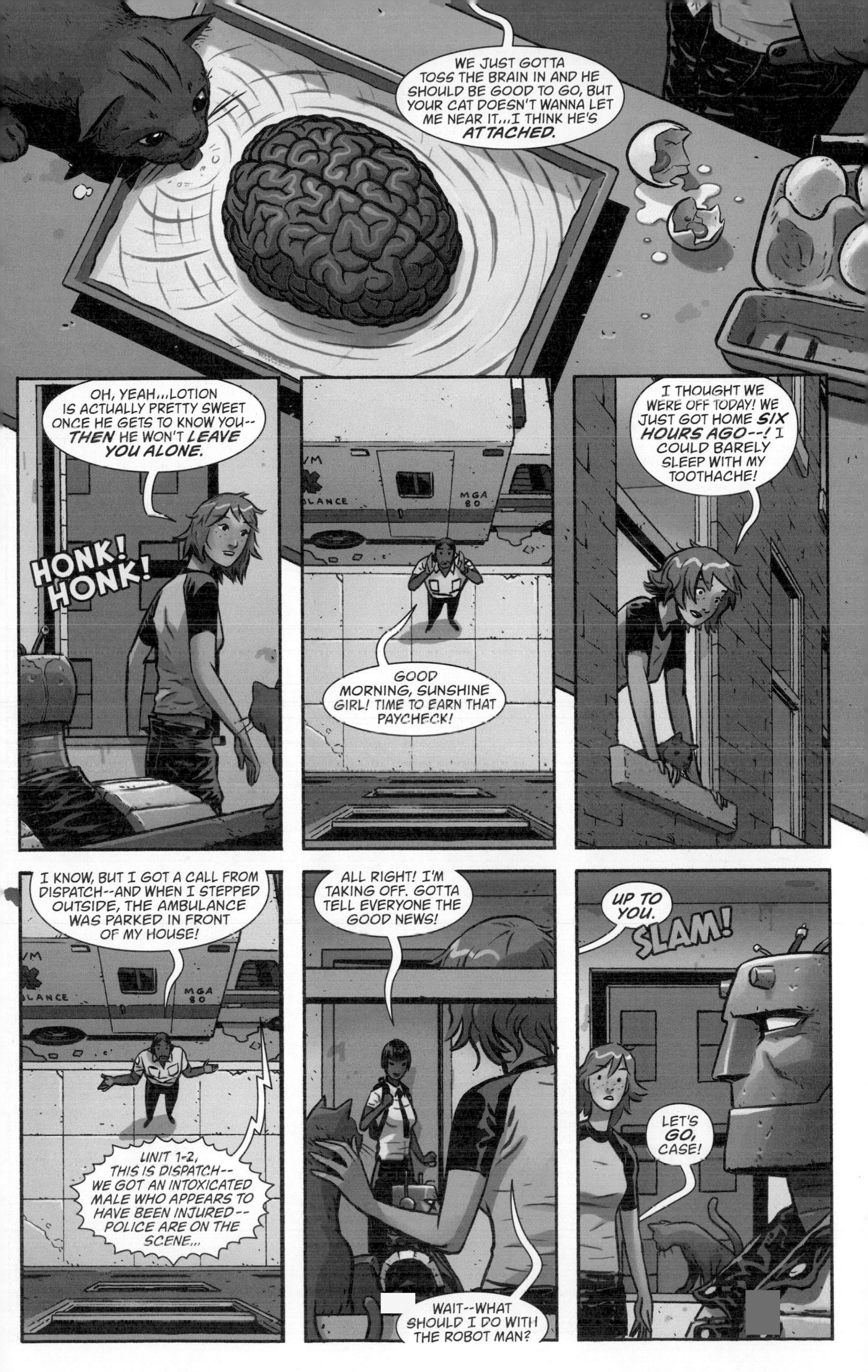
WE JUST GOTTA TOSS THE BRAIN IN AND HE SHOULD BE GOOD TO GO, BUT YOUR CAT DOESN'T WANNA LET ME NEAR IT...I THINK HE'S ATTACHED.
OH, YEAH...LOTION IS ACTUALLY PRETTY SWEET ONCE HE GETS TO KNOW YOU-- THEN HE WON'T LEAVE YOU ALONE.
HONK! HONK!
GOOD MORNING, SUNSHINE GIRL! TIME TO EARN THAT PAYCHECK!
I THOUGHT WE WERE OFF TODAY! WE JUST GOT HOME SIX HOURS AGO--! I COULD BARELY SLEEP WITH MY TOOTHACHE!
I KNOW, BUT I GOT A CALL FROM DISPATCH--AND WHEN I STEPPED OUTSIDE, THE AMBULANCE WAS PARKED IN FRONT OF MY HOUSE!
UNIT 1-2, THIS IS DISPATCH-- WE GOT AN INTOXICATED MALE WHO APPEARS TO HAVE BEEN INJURED-- POLICE ARE ON THE SCENE...
ALL RIGHT! I'M TAKING OFF. GOTTA TELL EVERYONE THE GOOD NEWS!
WAIT--WHAT SHOULD I DO WITH THE ROBOT MAN?
UP TO YOU.
SLAM!
LET'S GO, CASE!

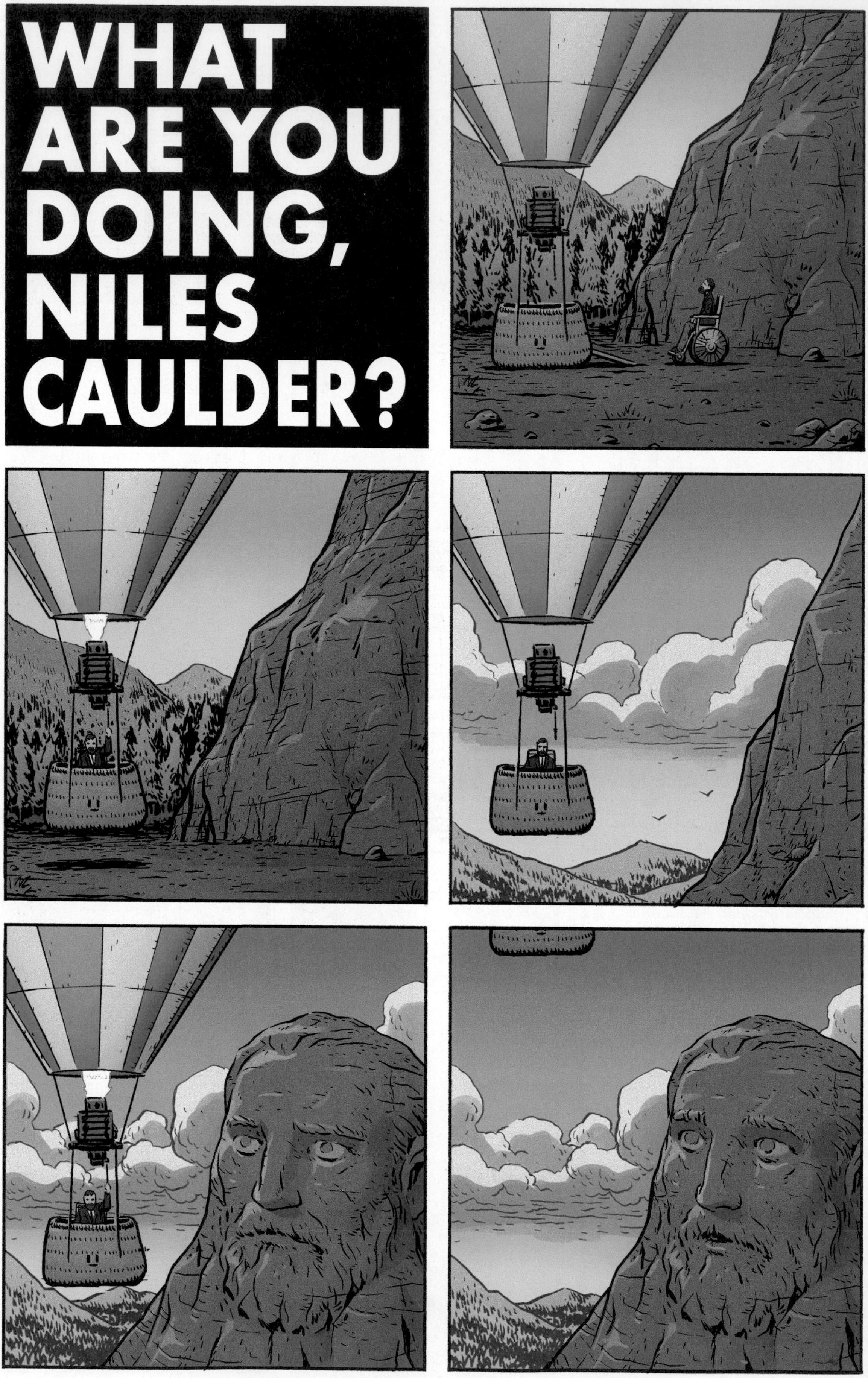
WHAT ARE YOU DOING, NILES CAULDER?

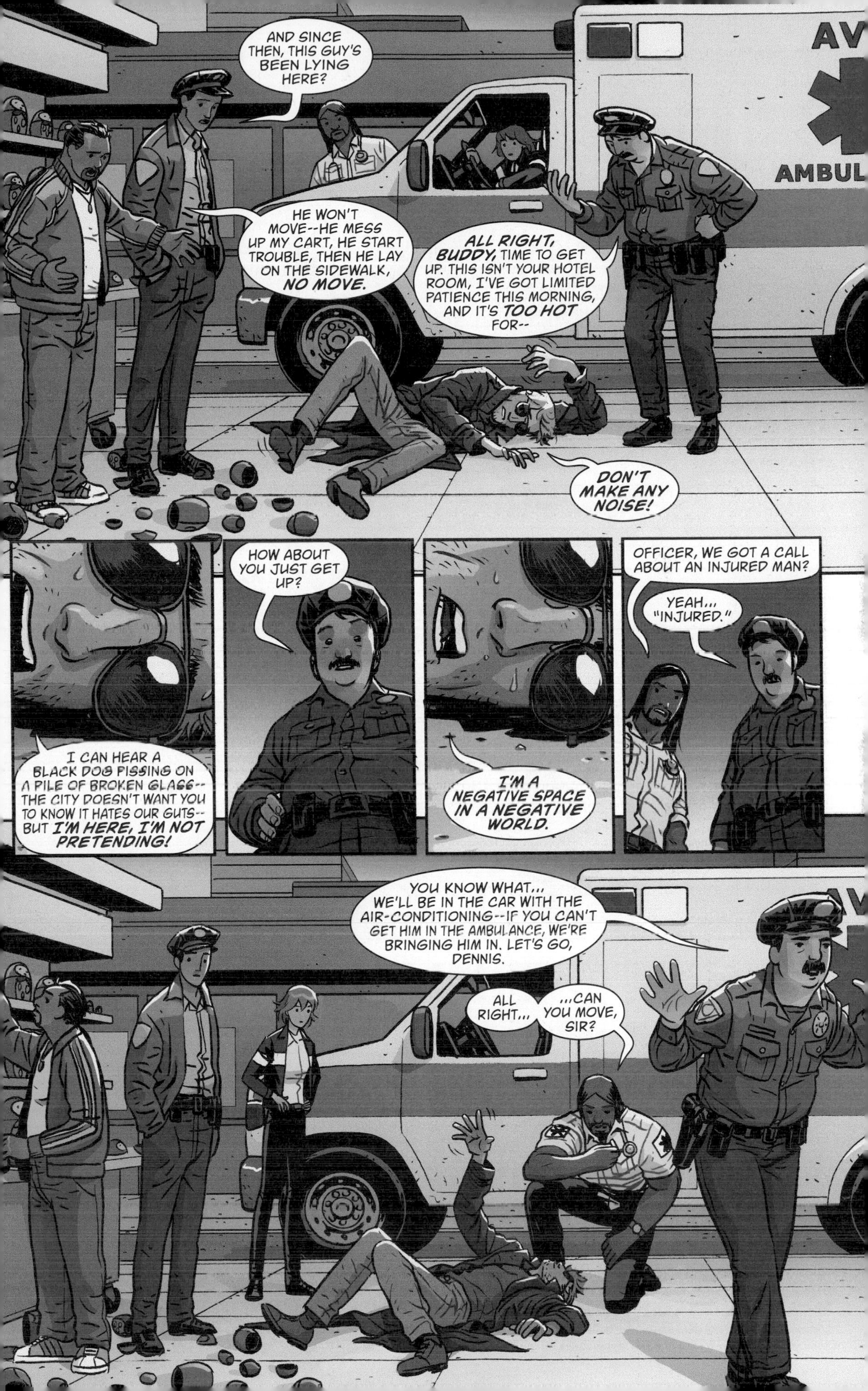

AND SINCE THEN, THIS GUY'S BEEN LYING HERE?
HE WON'T MOVE--HE MESS UP MY CART, HE START TROUBLE, THEN HE LAY ON THE SIDEWALK, NO MOVE.
ALL RIGHT, BUDDY, TIME TO GET UP. THIS ISN'T YOUR HOTEL ROOM, I'VE GOT LIMITED PATIENCE THIS MORNING, AND IT'S TOO HOT FOR--
DON'T MAKE ANY NOISE!
I CAN HEAR A BLACK DOG PISSING ON A PILE OF BROKEN GLASS-- THE CITY DOESN'T WANT YOU TO KNOW IT HATES OUR GUTS-- BUT I'M HERE, I'M NOT PRETENDING!
HOW ABOUT YOU JUST GET UP?
I'M A NEGATIVE SPACE IN A NEGATIVE WORLD.
OFFICER, WE GOT A CALL ABOUT AN INJURED MAN?
YEAH... "INJURED."
YOU KNOW WHAT... WE'LL BE IN THE CAR WITH THE AIR-CONDITIONING--IF YOU CAN'T GET HIM IN THE AMBULANCE, WE'RE BRINGING HIM IN. LET'S GO, DENNIS.
ALL RIGHT...
...CAN YOU MOVE, SIR?

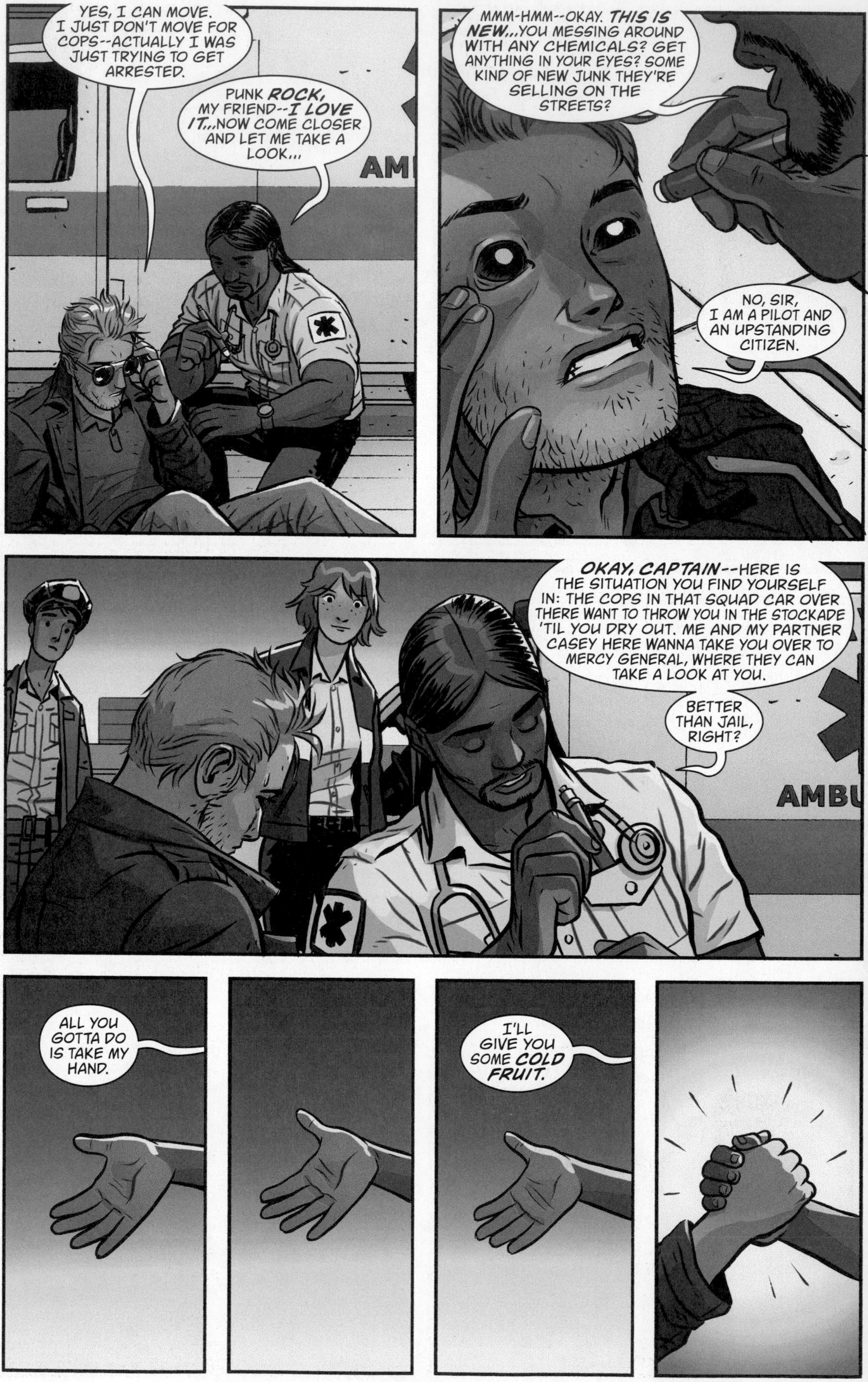
YES, I CAN MOVE. I JUST DON'T MOVE FOR COPS--ACTUALLY I WAS JUST TRYING TO GET ARRESTED.
PUNK ROCK, MY FRIEND--I LOVE IT...NOW COME CLOSER AND LET ME TAKE A LOOK...
AMB
MMM-HMM--OKAY. THIS IS NEW...YOU MESSING AROUND WITH ANY CHEMICALS? GET ANYTHING IN YOUR EYES? SOME KIND OF NEW JUNK THEY'RE SELLING ON THE STREETS?
NO, SIR, I AM A PILOT AND AN UPSTANDING CITIZEN.
OKAY, CAPTAIN--HERE IS THE SITUATION YOU FIND YOURSELF IN: THE COPS IN THAT SQUAD CAR OVER THERE WANT TO THROW YOU IN THE STOCKADE 'TIL YOU DRY OUT. ME AND MY PARTNER CASEY HERE WANNA TAKE YOU OVER TO MERCY GENERAL, WHERE THEY CAN TAKE A LOOK AT YOU.
BETTER THAN JAIL, RIGHT?
AMBU
ALL YOU GOTTA DO IS TAKE MY HAND.
I'LL GIVE YOU SOME COLD FRUIT.

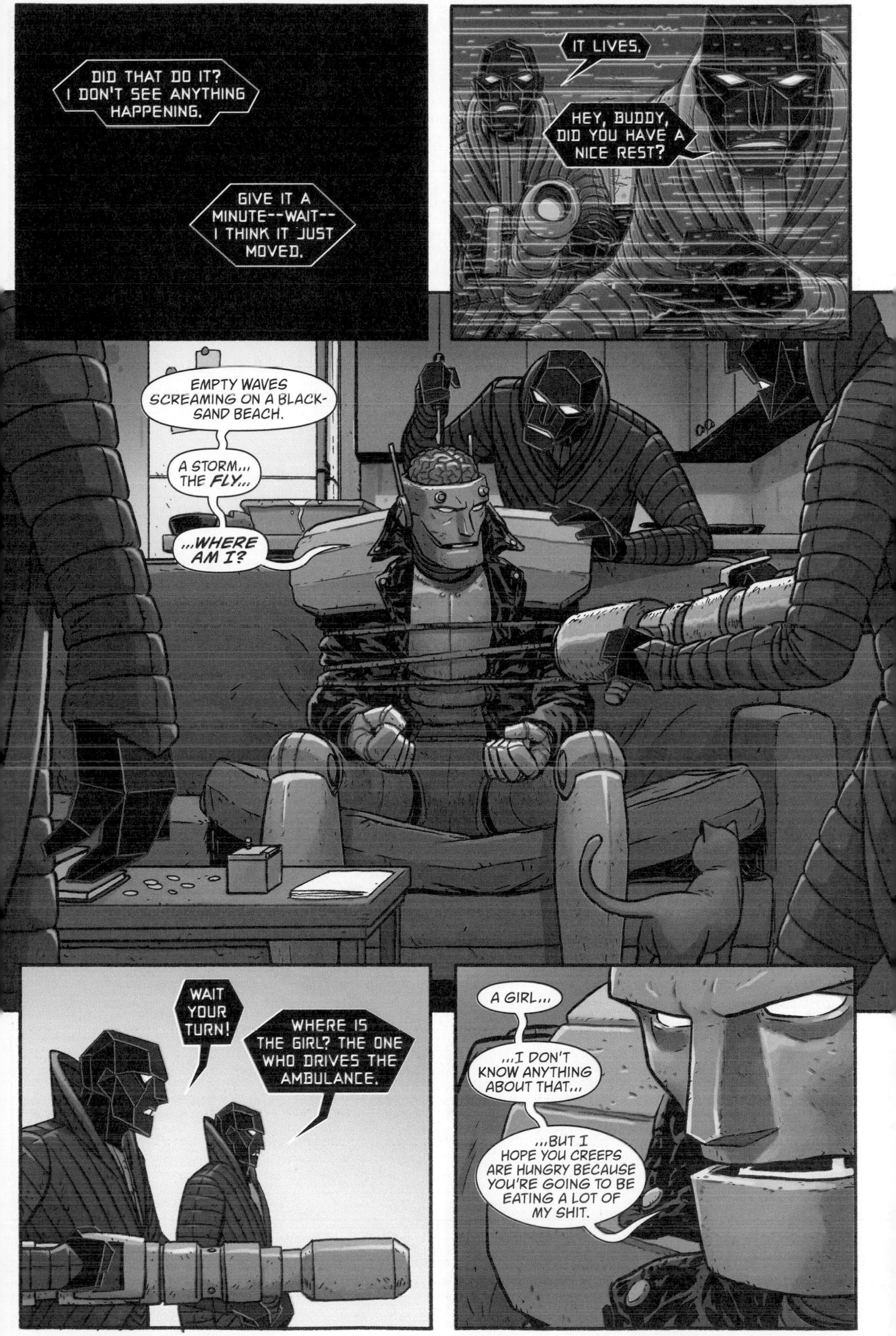
DID THAT DO IT? I DON'T SEE ANYTHING HAPPENING.
GIVE IT A MINUTE--WAIT-- I THINK IT JUST MOVED.
IT LIVES.
HEY, BUDDY, DID YOU HAVE A NICE REST?
EMPTY WAVES SCREAMING ON A BLACK-SAND BEACH.
A STORM... THE FLY...
...WHERE AM I?
WAIT YOUR TURN!
WHERE IS THE GIRL? THE ONE WHO DRIVES THE AMBULANCE.
A GIRL...
...I DON'T KNOW ANYTHING ABOUT THAT...
...BUT I HOPE YOU CREEPS ARE HUNGRY BECAUSE YOU'RE GOING TO BE EATING A LOT OF MY SHIT.

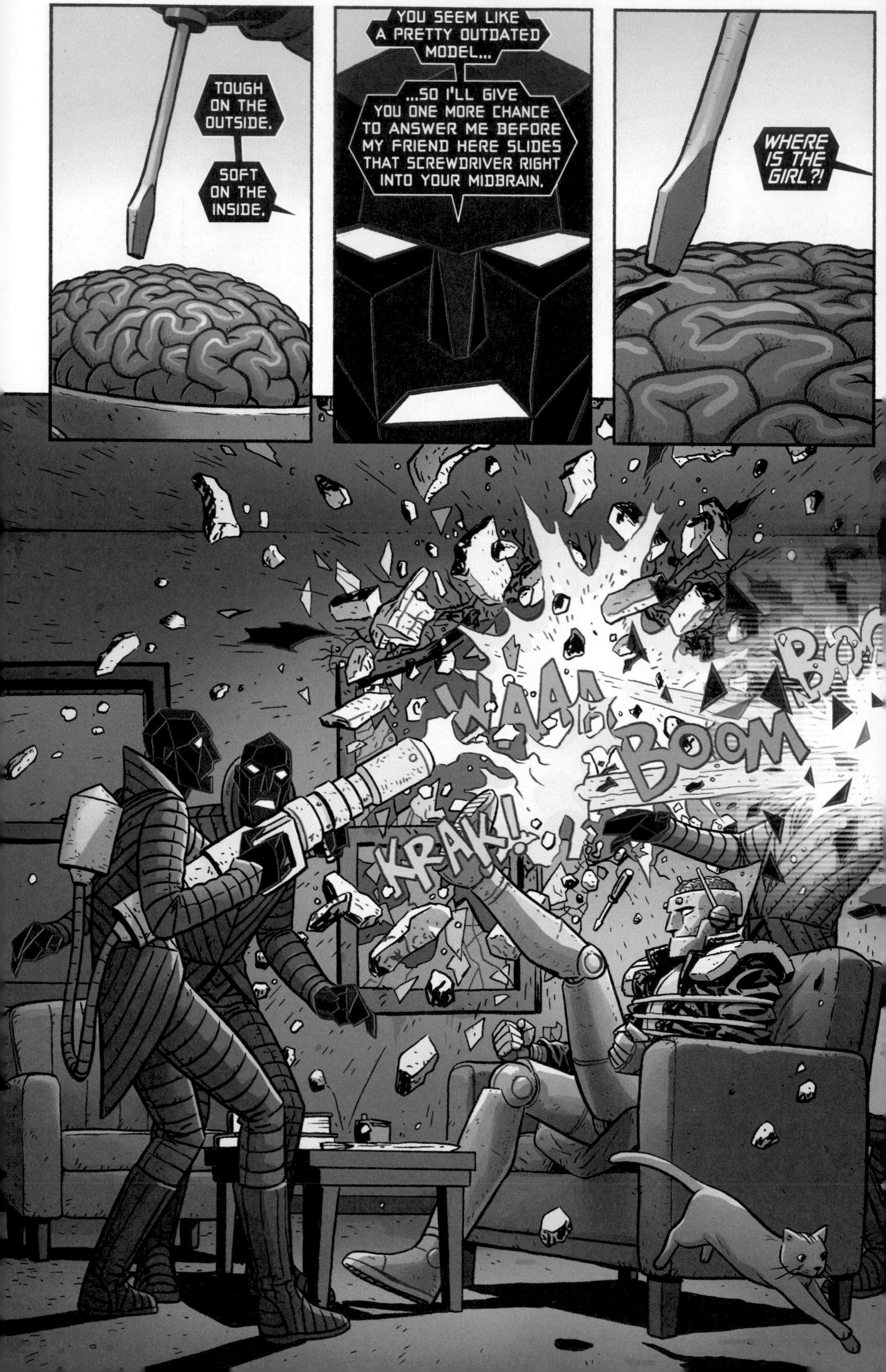
TOUGH ON THE OUTSIDE.
SOFT ON THE INSIDE.
YOU SEEM LIKE A PRETTY OUTDATED MODEL...
...SO I'LL GIVE YOU ONE MORE CHANCE TO ANSWER ME BEFORE MY FRIEND HERE SLIDES THAT SCREWDRIVER RIGHT INTO YOUR MIDBRAIN.
WHERE IS THE GIRL?!
BOOM
KRAK!

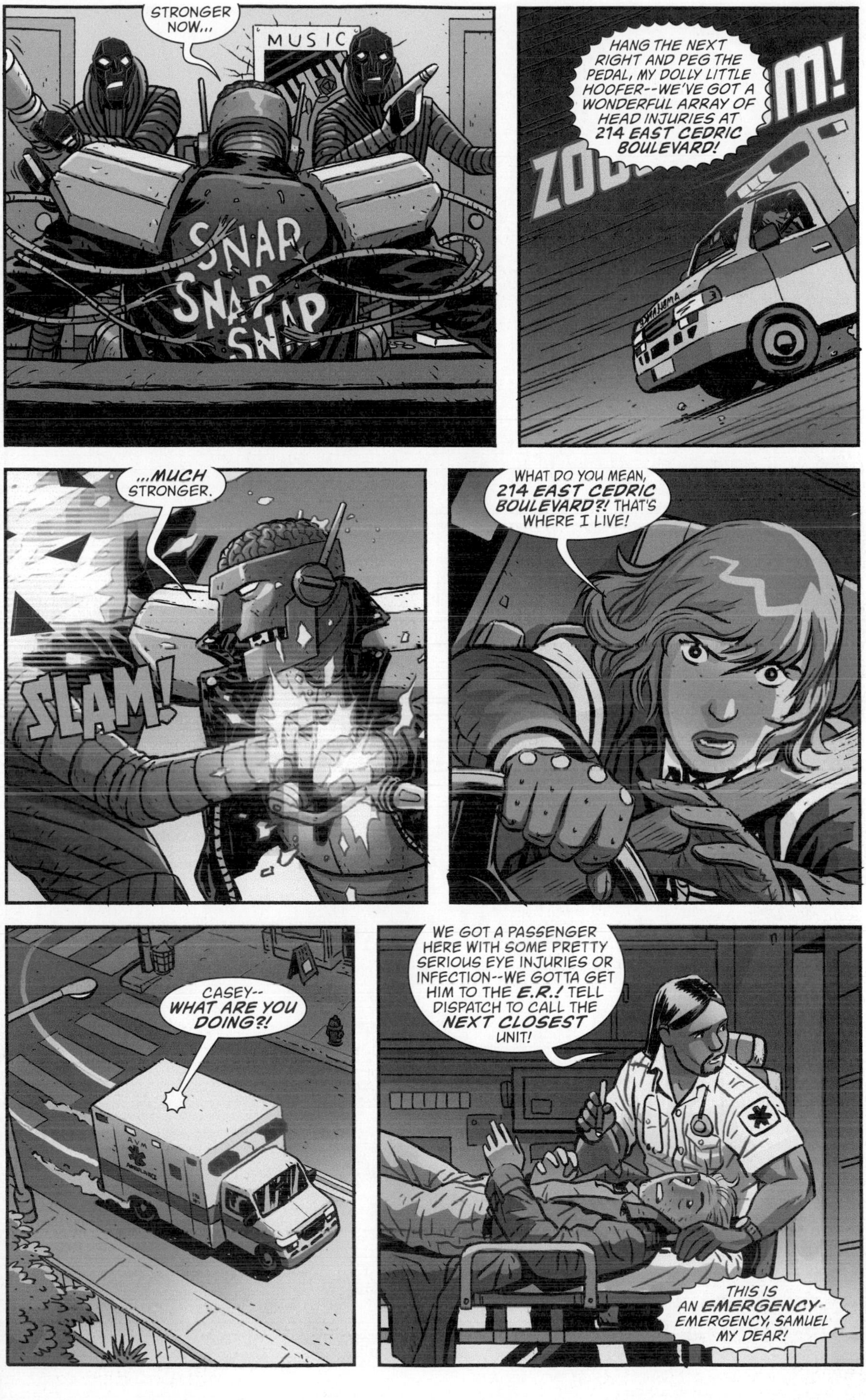
STRONGER NOW...
MUSIC
SNAP SNAP SNAP SNAP
HANG THE NEXT RIGHT AND PEG THE PEDAL, MY DOLLY LITTLE HOOFER--WE'VE GOT A WONDERFUL ARRAY OF HEAD INJURIES AT 214 EAST CEDRIC BOULEVARD!
...MUCH STRONGER.
SLAM!
WHAT DO YOU MEAN, 214 EAST CEDRIC BOULEVARD?! THAT'S WHERE I LIVE!
CASEY-- WHAT ARE YOU DOING?!
WE GOT A PASSENGER HERE WITH SOME PRETTY SERIOUS EYE INJURIES OR INFECTION--WE GOTTA GET HIM TO THE E.R.! TELL DISPATCH TO CALL THE NEXT CLOSEST UNIT!
THIS IS AN EMERGENCY-EMERGENCY, SAMUEL MY DEAR!

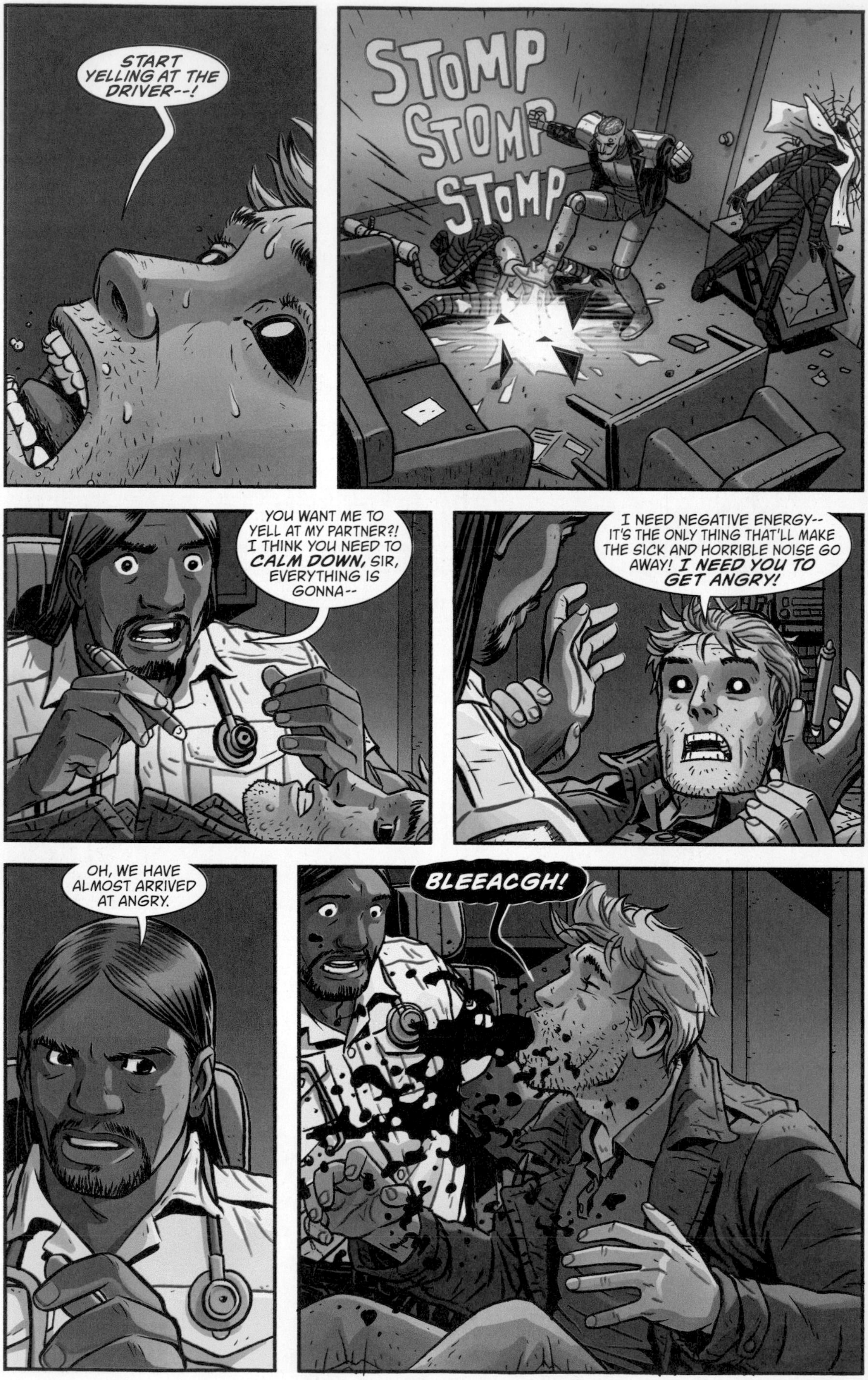
START YELLING AT THE DRIVER--!
STOMP STOMP STOMP
YOU WANT ME TO YELL AT MY PARTNER?! I THINK YOU NEED TO **CALM DOWN,** SIR, EVERYTHING IS GONNA--
I NEED NEGATIVE ENERGY-- IT'S THE ONLY THING THAT'LL MAKE THE SICK AND HORRIBLE NOISE GO AWAY! **I NEED YOU TO GET ANGRY!**
OH, WE HAVE ALMOST ARRIVED AT ANGRY.
BLEEACGH!

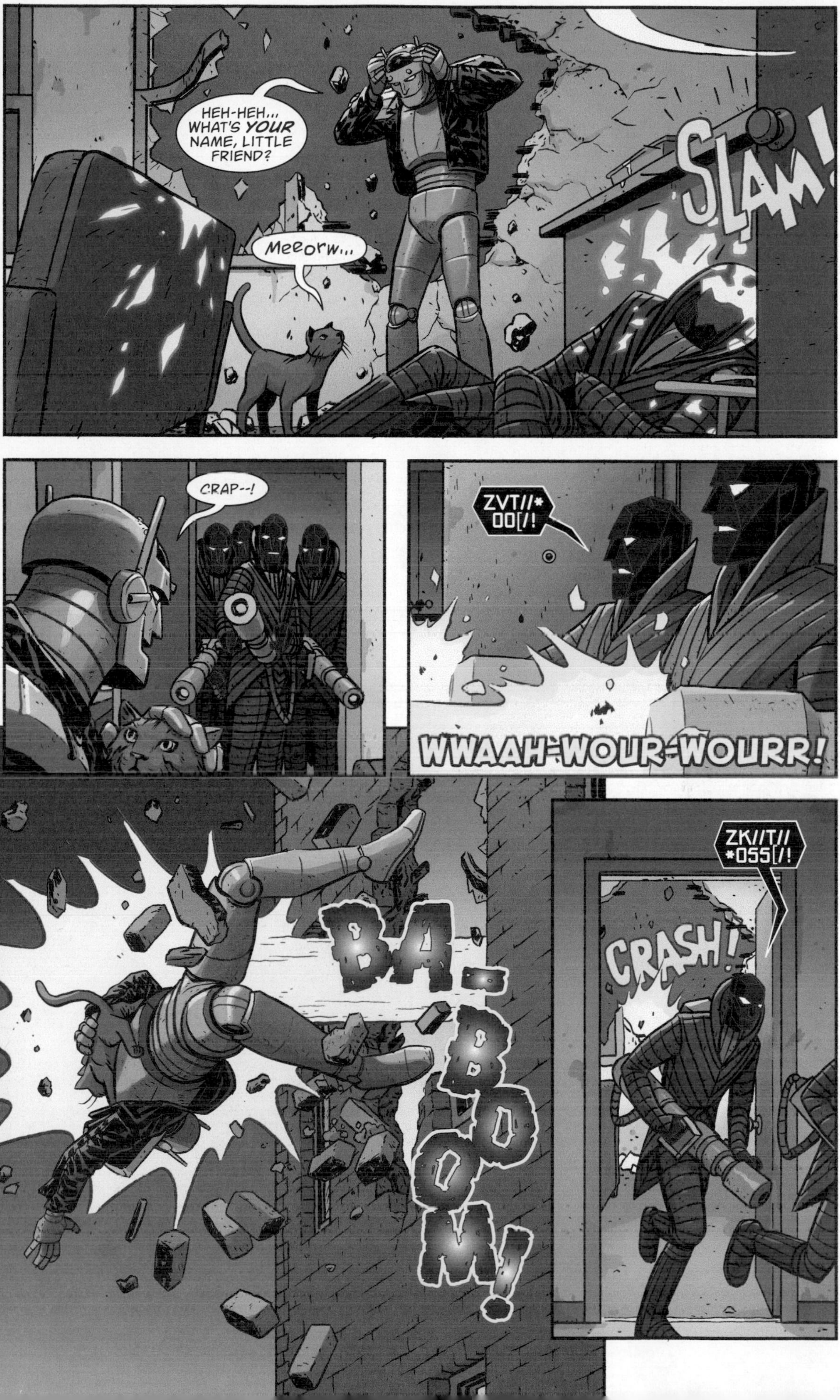
HEH-HEH... WHAT'S YOUR NAME, LITTLE FRIEND?
Meeorw...
SLAM!
CRAP--!
ZVT//* OO[/!
WWAAH-WOUR-WOURR!
BA-BOOOM!
ZK//T// *OSS[/!
CRASH!

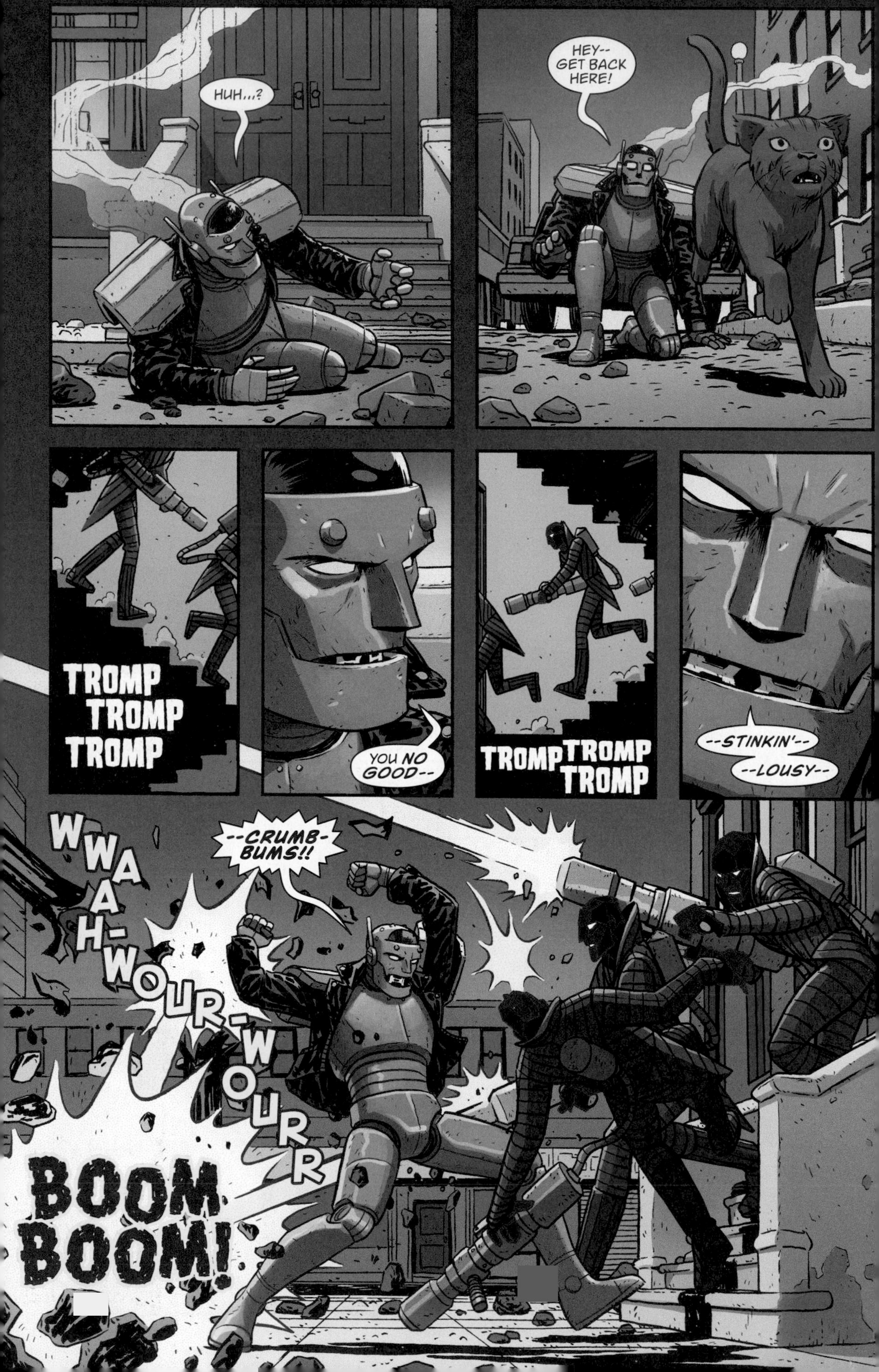
HUH...?
HEY-- GET BACK HERE!
TROMP TROMP TROMP
YOU NO GOOD--
TROMP TROMP TROMP
--STINKIN'--
--LOUSY--
--CRUMB-BUMS!!
WWAAH-WOUR-WOURR
BOOM BOOM!

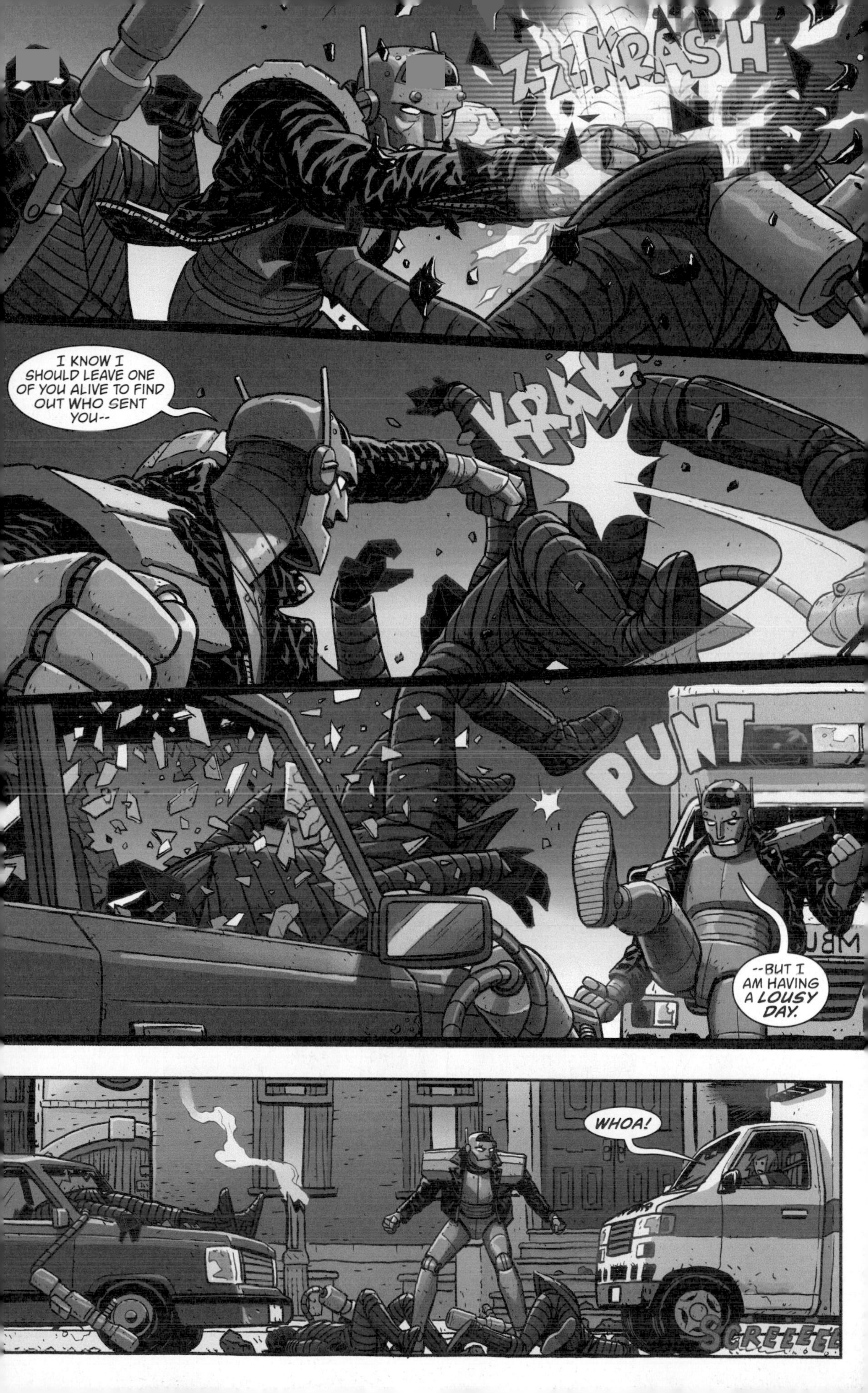
KRASH
I KNOW I SHOULD LEAVE ONE OF YOU ALIVE TO FIND OUT WHO SENT YOU--
KRAK
PUNT
--BUT I AM HAVING A LOUSY DAY.
WHOA!
SCREEEEE

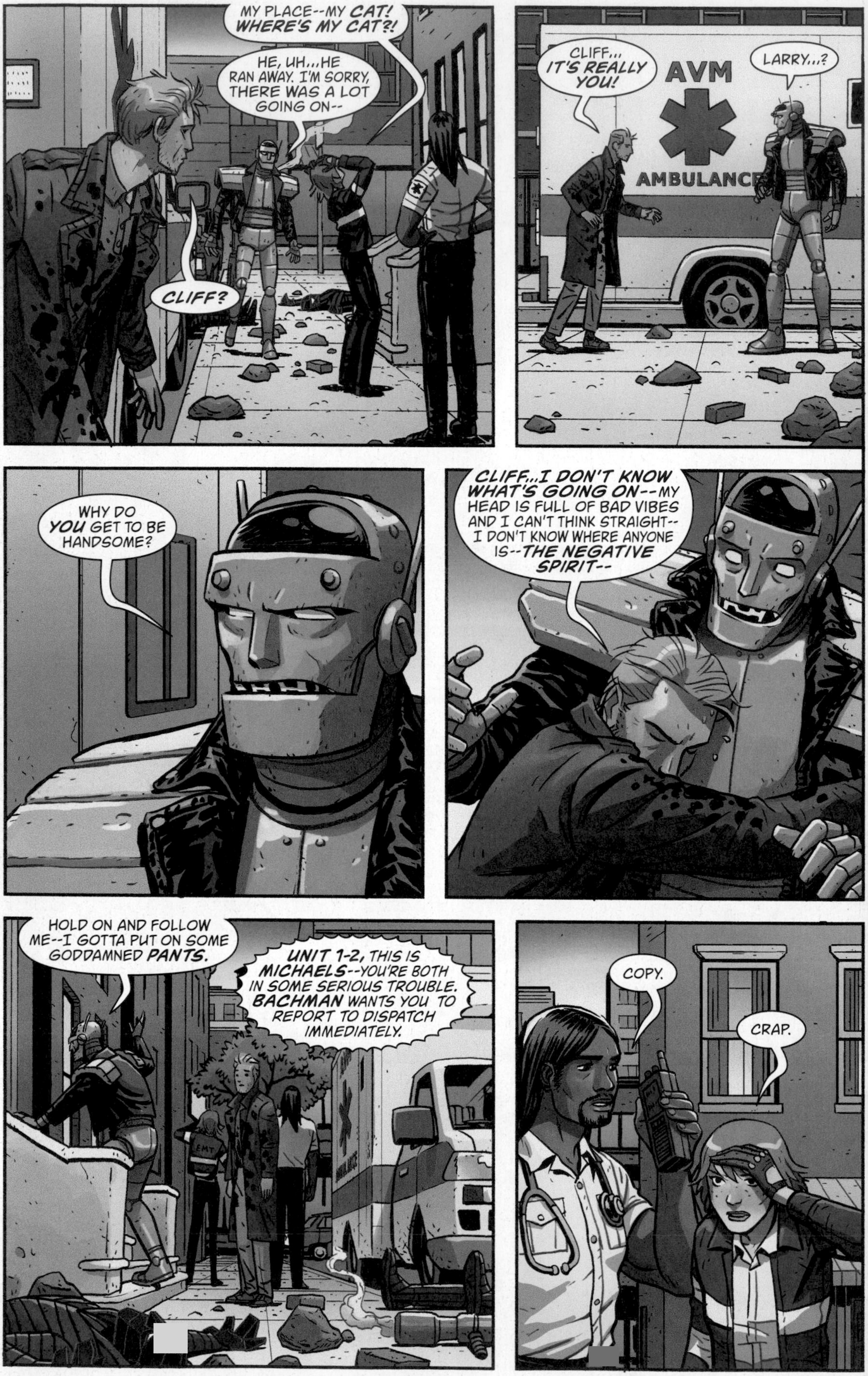
MY PLACE--MY CAT! WHERE'S MY CAT?!
HE, UH...HE RAN AWAY. I'M SORRY, THERE WAS A LOT GOING ON--
CLIFF?
CLIFF... IT'S REALLY YOU!
AVM
AMBULANCE
LARRY...?
WHY DO YOU GET TO BE HANDSOME?
CLIFF...I DON'T KNOW WHAT'S GOING ON--MY HEAD IS FULL OF BAD VIBES AND I CAN'T THINK STRAIGHT--I DON'T KNOW WHERE ANYONE IS--THE NEGATIVE SPIRIT--
HOLD ON AND FOLLOW ME--I GOTTA PUT ON SOME GODDAMNED PANTS.
UNIT 1-2, THIS IS MICHAELS--YOU'RE BOTH IN SOME SERIOUS TROUBLE. BACHMAN WANTS YOU TO REPORT TO DISPATCH IMMEDIATELY.
EMT
COPY.
CRAP.

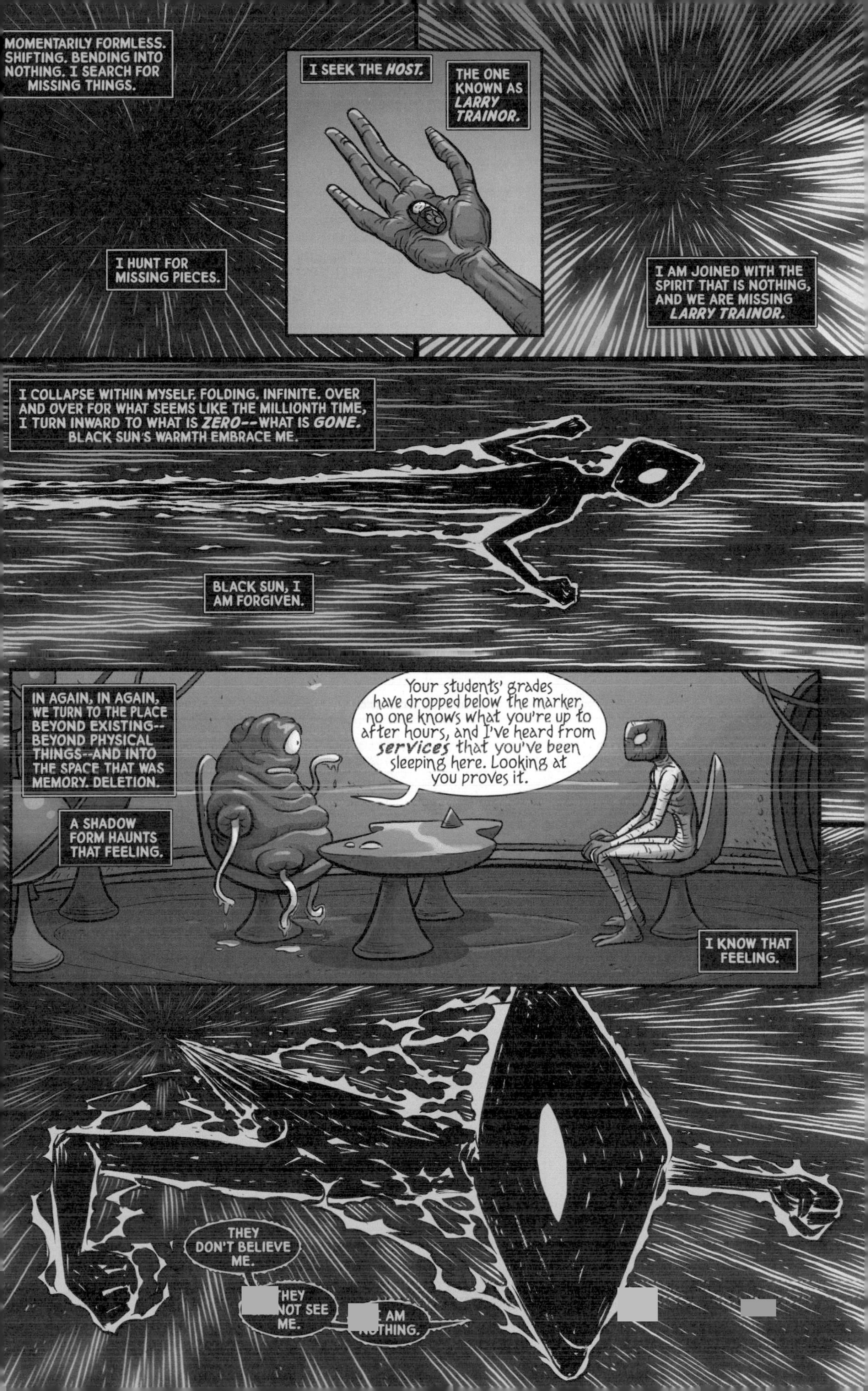
MOMENTARILY FORMLESS. SHIFTING. BENDING INTO NOTHING. I SEARCH FOR MISSING THINGS.
I SEEK THE HOST.
THE ONE KNOWN AS LARRY TRAINOR.
I HUNT FOR MISSING PIECES.
I AM JOINED WITH THE SPIRIT THAT IS NOTHING, AND WE ARE MISSING LARRY TRAINOR.
I COLLAPSE WITHIN MYSELF. FOLDING. INFINITE. OVER AND OVER FOR WHAT SEEMS LIKE THE MILLIONTH TIME, I TURN INWARD TO WHAT IS ZERO--WHAT IS GONE. BLACK SUN'S WARMTH EMBRACE ME.
BLACK SUN, I AM FORGIVEN.
IN AGAIN, IN AGAIN, WE TURN TO THE PLACE BEYOND EXISTING--BEYOND PHYSICAL THINGS--AND INTO THE SPACE THAT WAS MEMORY. DELETION.
Your students' grades have dropped below the marker, no one knows what you're up to after hours, and I've heard from services that you've been sleeping here. Looking at you proves it.
A SHADOW FORM HAUNTS THAT FEELING.
I KNOW THAT FEELING.
THEY DON'T BELIEVE ME.
THEY
NOT SEE
ME.
AM
THING.

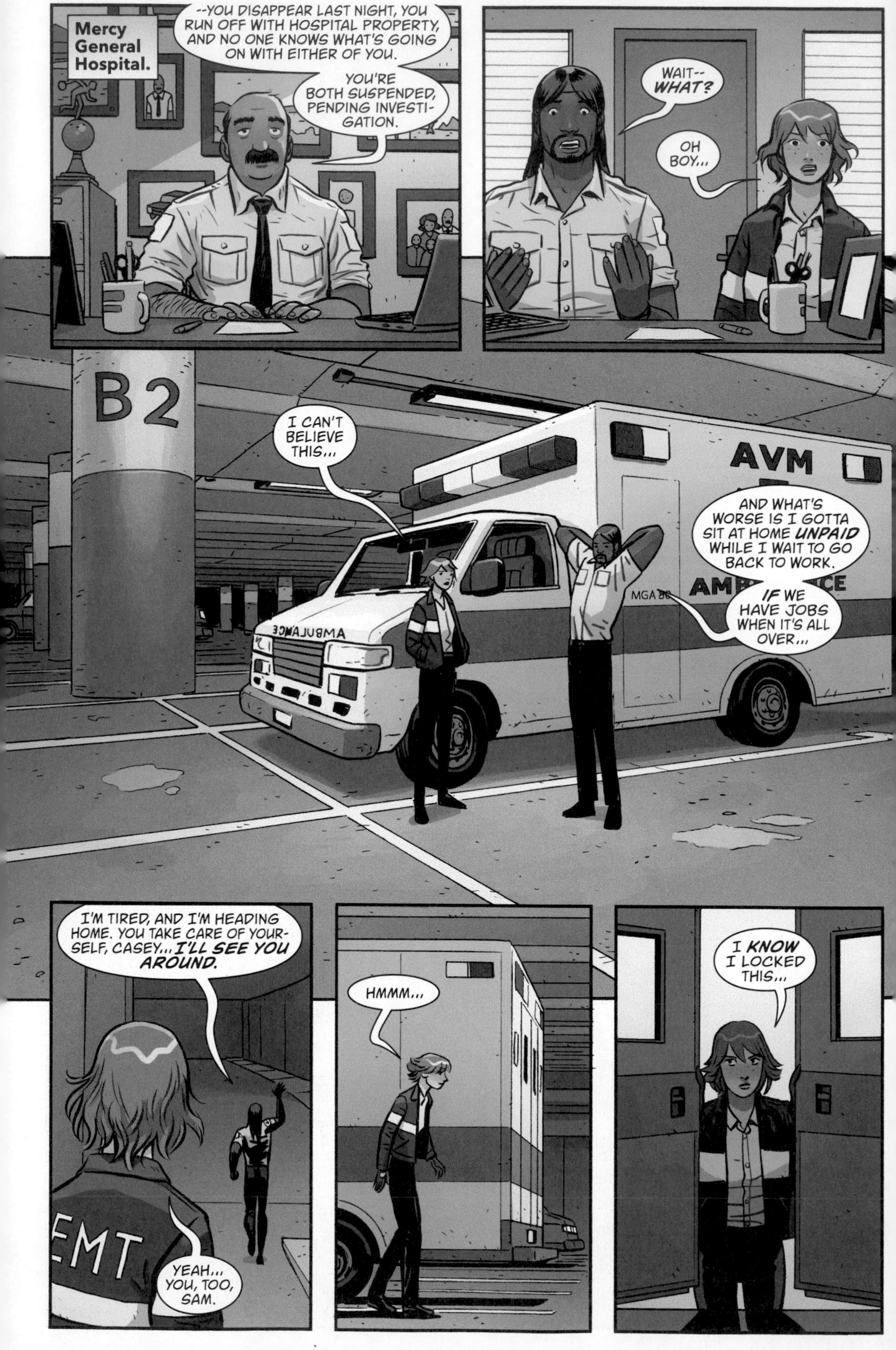
Mercy General Hospital.
--YOU DISAPPEAR LAST NIGHT, YOU RUN OFF WITH HOSPITAL PROPERTY, AND NO ONE KNOWS WHAT'S GOING ON WITH EITHER OF YOU.
YOU'RE BOTH SUSPENDED, PENDING INVESTI-GATION.
WAIT-- WHAT?
OH BOY...
B2
I CAN'T BELIEVE THIS...
AVM
AND WHAT'S WORSE IS I GOTTA SIT AT HOME UNPAID WHILE I WAIT TO GO BACK TO WORK.
IF WE HAVE JOBS WHEN IT'S ALL OVER...
I'M TIRED, AND I'M HEADING HOME. YOU TAKE CARE OF YOURSELF, CASEY... I'LL SEE YOU AROUND.
EMT
YEAH... YOU, TOO, SAM.
HMMM...
I KNOW I LOCKED THIS...

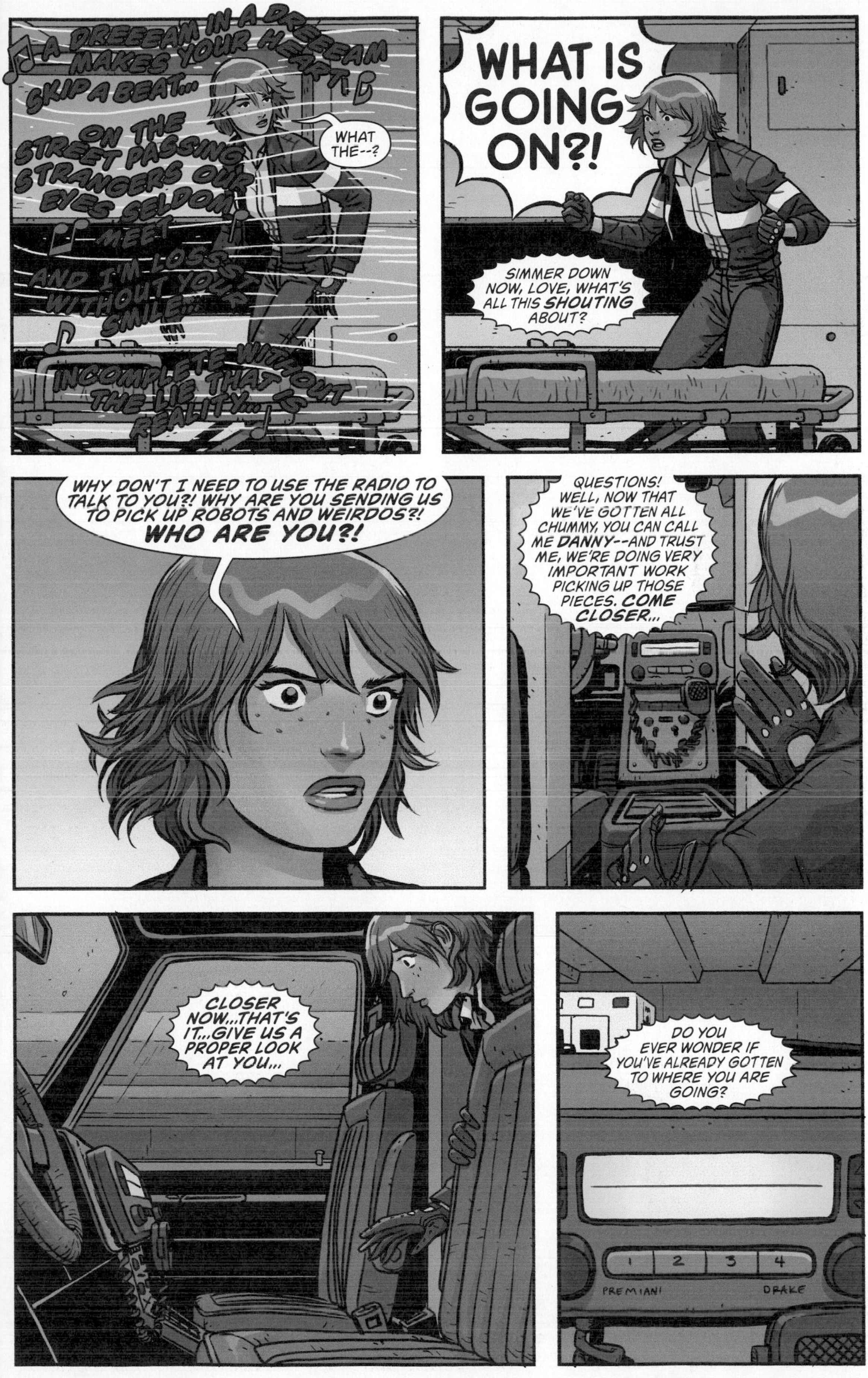
A DREEEAM IN A DREEEAM MAKES YOUR HEART SKIP A BEAT...
ON THE STREET PASSING STRANGERS OUR EYES SELDOM MEET
AND I'M LOSSST WITHOUT YOUR SMILE...
INCOMPLETE WITHOUT THE LIE THAT IS REALITY...
WHAT THE--?
WHAT IS GOING ON?!
SIMMER DOWN NOW, LOVE, WHAT'S ALL THIS SHOUTING ABOUT?
WHY DON'T I NEED TO USE THE RADIO TO TALK TO YOU?! WHY ARE YOU SENDING US TO PICK UP ROBOTS AND WEIRDOS?! WHO ARE YOU?!
QUESTIONS! WELL, NOW THAT WE'VE GOTTEN ALL CHUMMY, YOU CAN CALL ME DANNY--AND TRUST ME, WE'RE DOING VERY IMPORTANT WORK PICKING UP THOSE PIECES. COME CLOSER...
CLOSER NOW...THAT'S IT...GIVE US A PROPER LOOK AT YOU...
DO YOU EVER WONDER IF YOU'VE ALREADY GOTTEN TO WHERE YOU ARE GOING?
1 2 3 4
PREMIANI
DRAKE

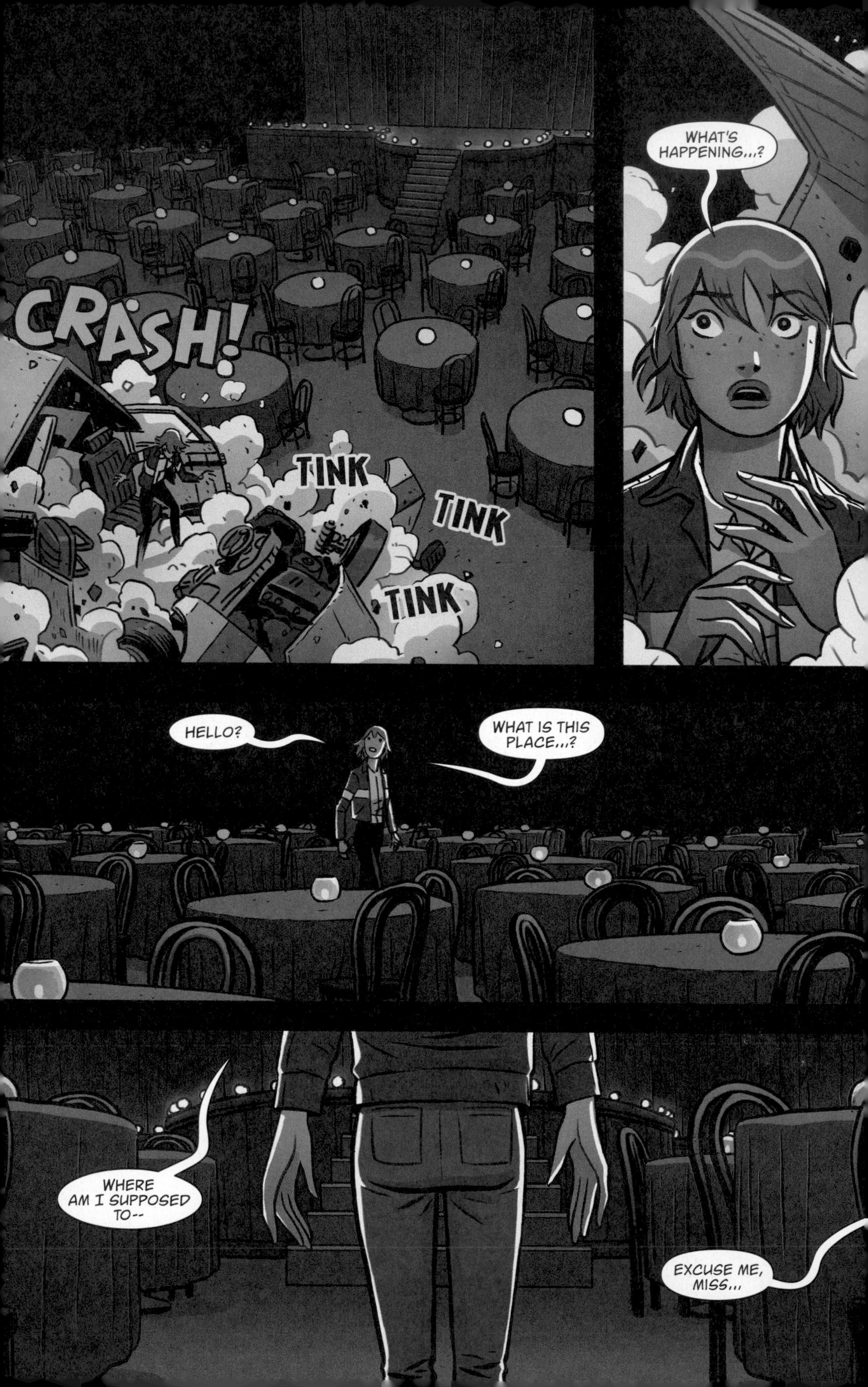
CRASH!
TINK
TINK
TINK
WHAT'S HAPPENING...?
HELLO?
WHAT IS THIS PLACE...?
WHERE AM I SUPPOSED TO--
EXCUSE ME, MISS...

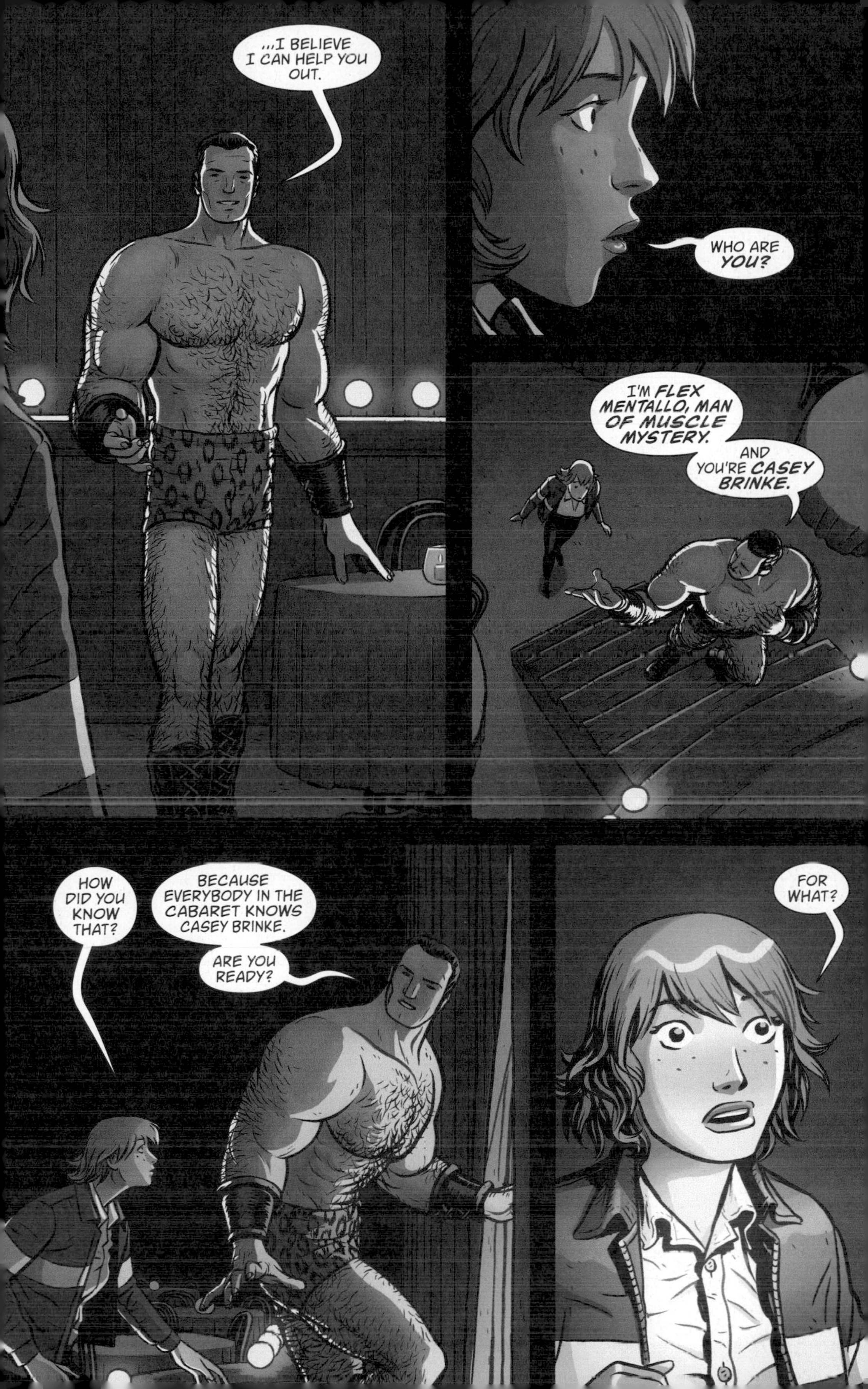
...I BELIEVE I CAN HELP YOU OUT.
WHO ARE YOU?
I'M FLEX MENTALLO, MAN OF MUSCLE MYSTERY.
AND YOU'RE CASEY BRINKE.
HOW DID YOU KNOW THAT?
BECAUSE EVERYBODY IN THE CABARET KNOWS CASEY BRINKE.
ARE YOU READY?
FOR WHAT?

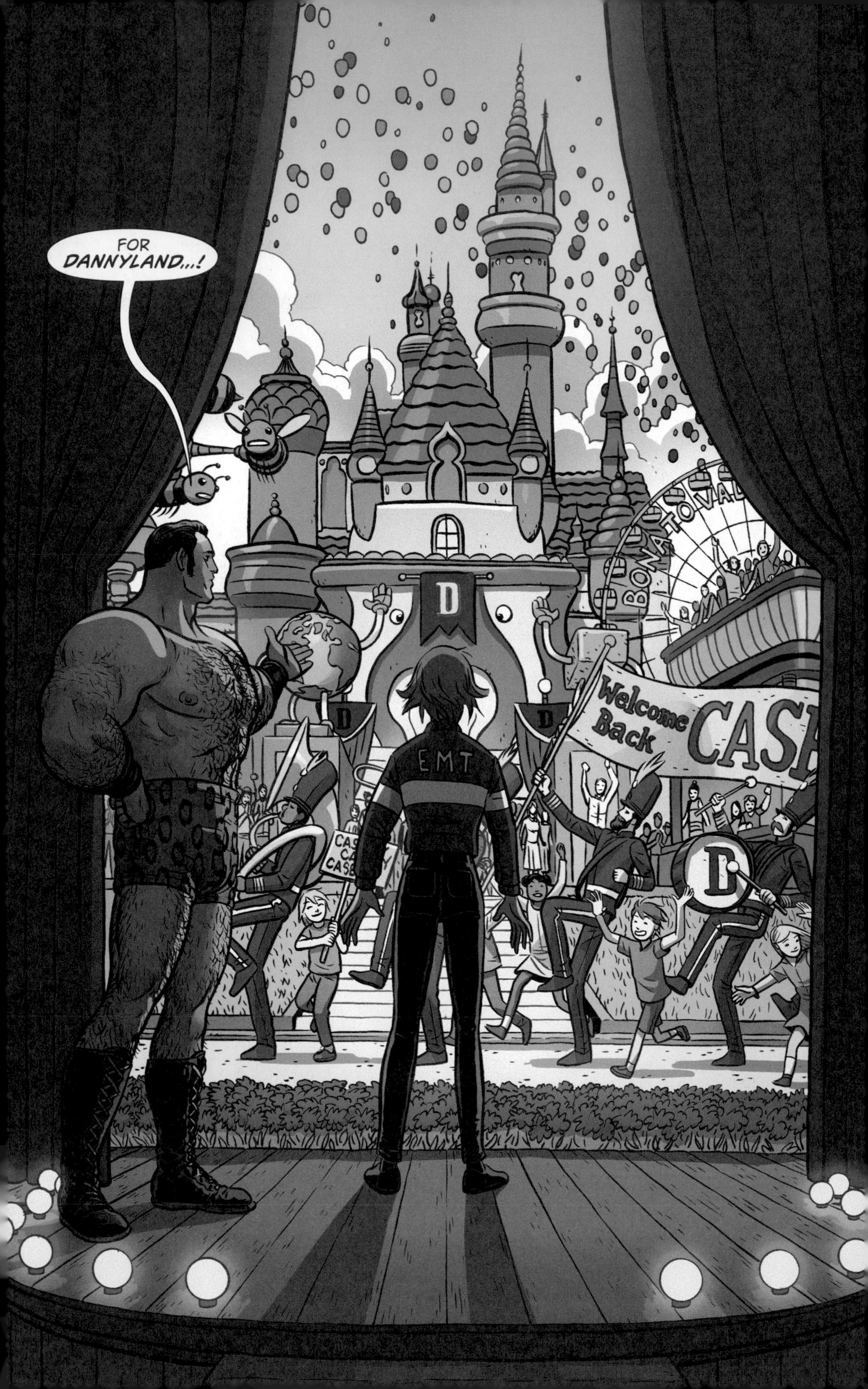
FOR DANNYLAND...!
Welcome Back CAS
EMT

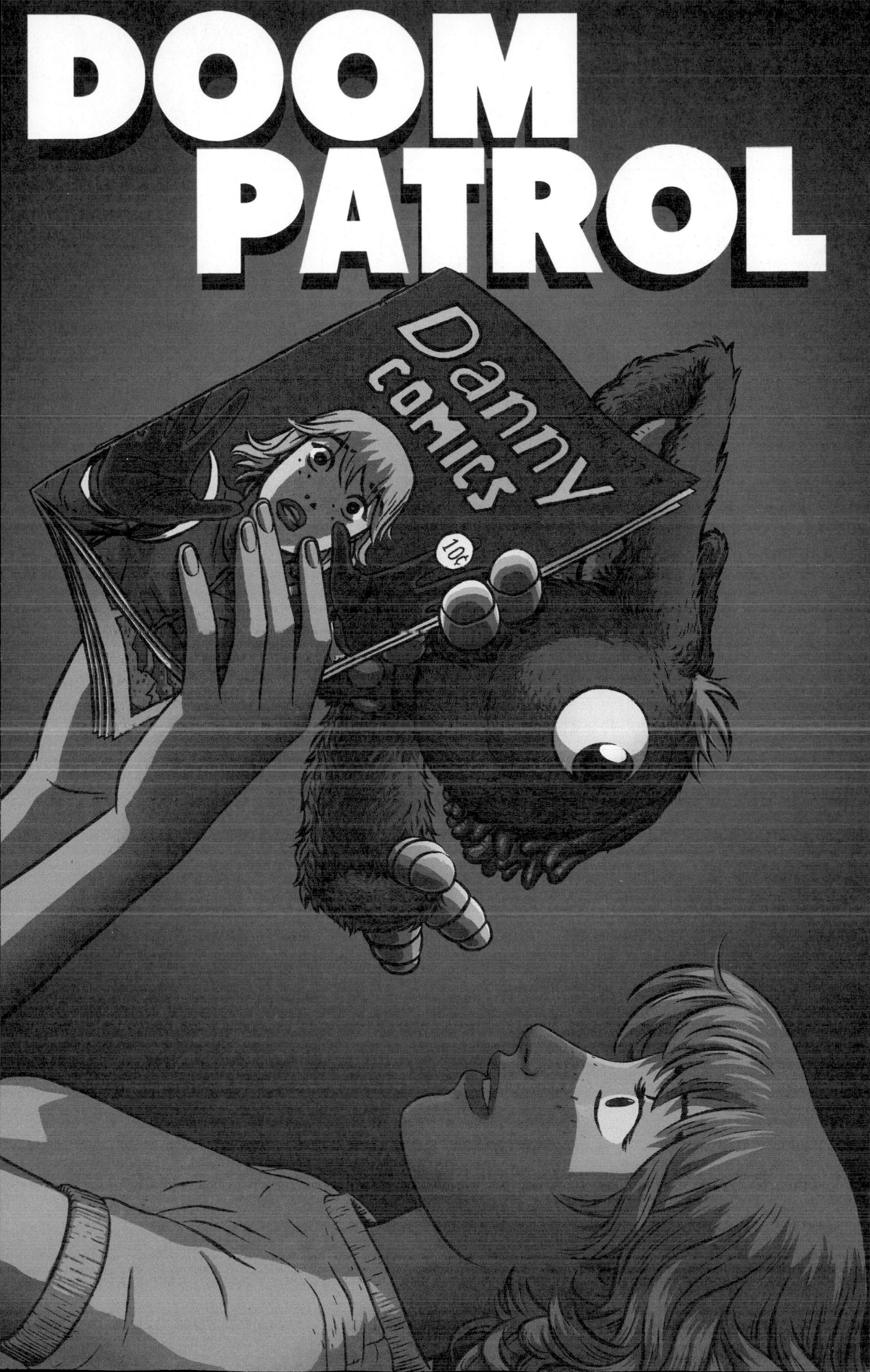
DOOM PATROL
Danny COMICS
10¢

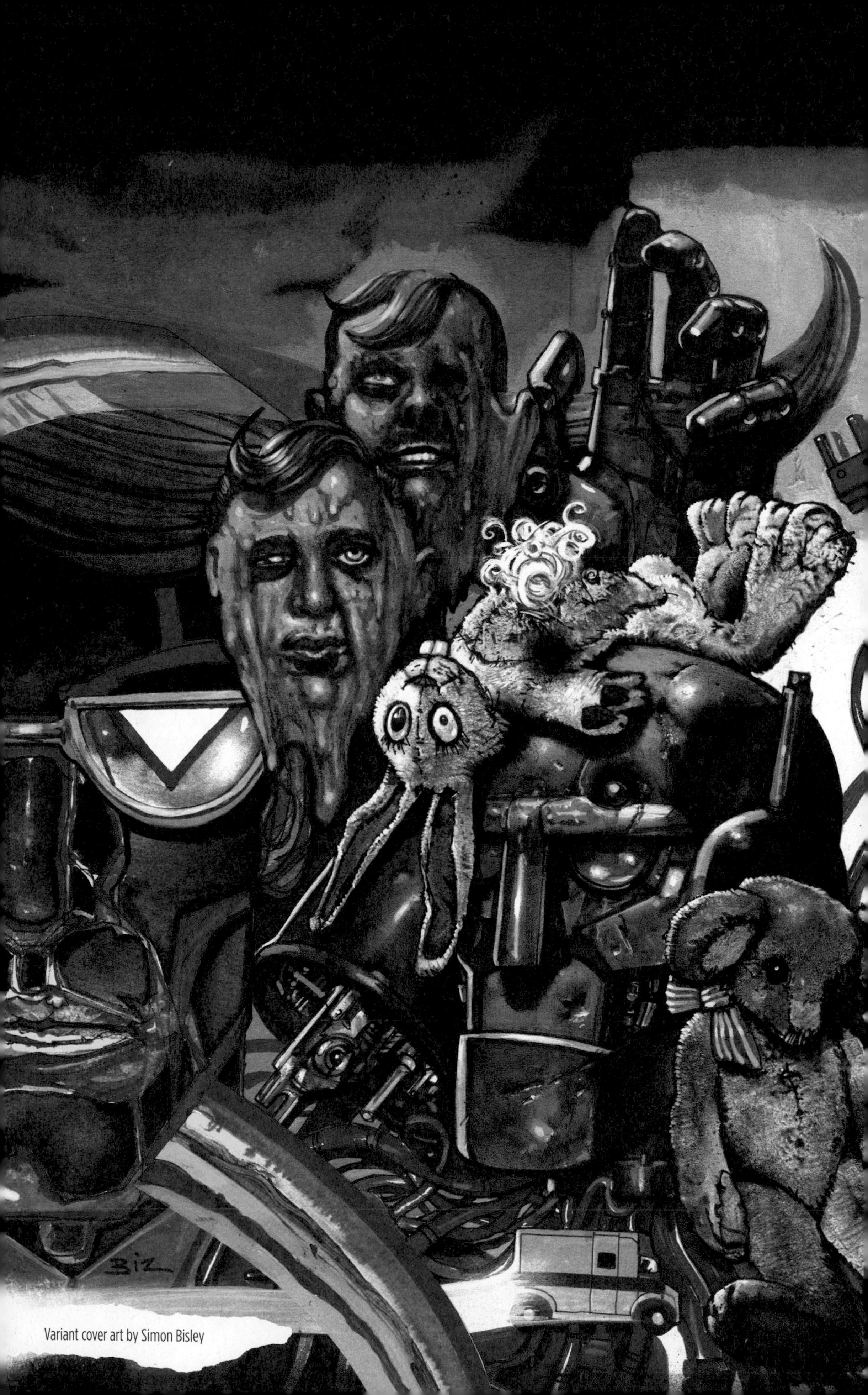
BIZ

Variant cover art by Simon Bisley

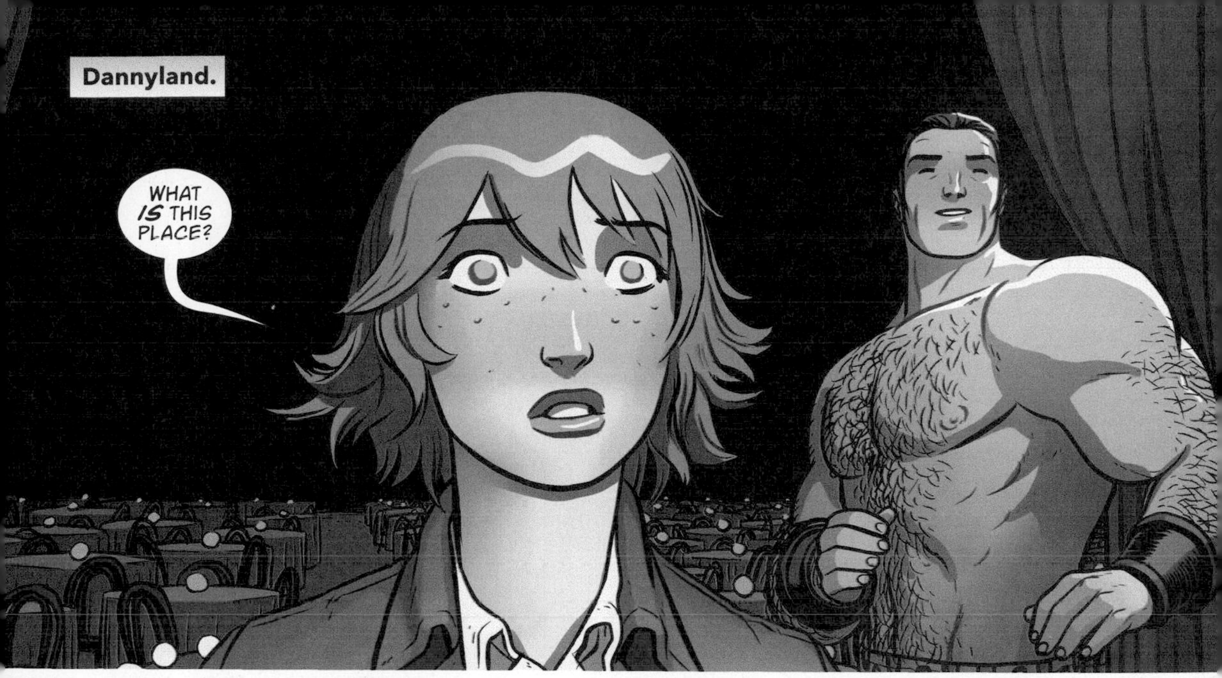
Dannyland.
WHAT *IS* THIS PLACE?

IT'S A DOOMED WORLD AFTER ALL

BRICK by BRICK Part 3

GERARD WAY writer · NICK DERINGTON artist & cover · TAMRA BONVILLAIN colorist, Special thanks to Marissa Louise · TODD KLEIN letterer · MOLLY MAHAN assoc. ed. · JAMIE S. RICH editor · Doom Patrol created by Arnold Drake

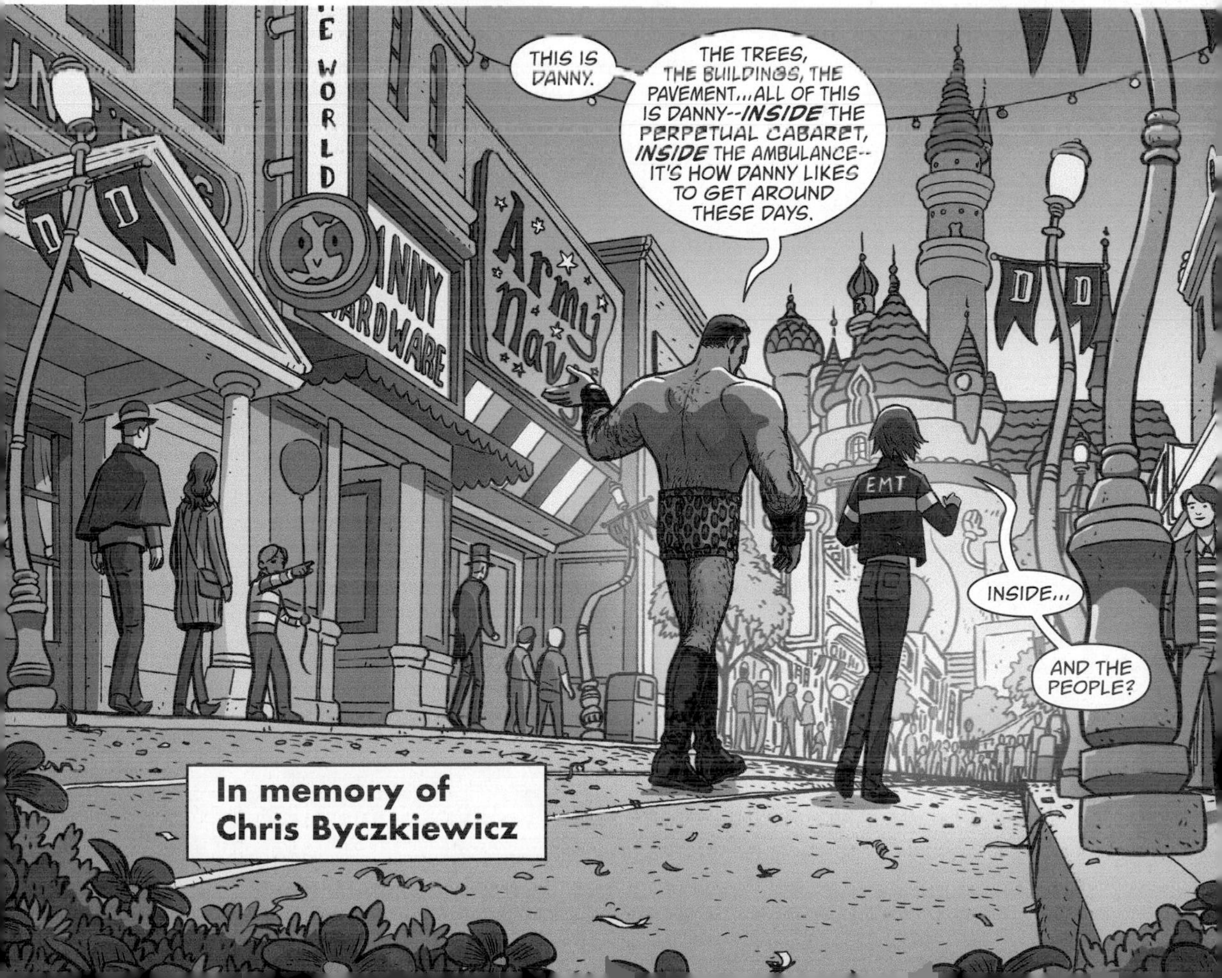
THIS IS DANNY.
THE TREES, THE BUILDINGS, THE PAVEMENT...ALL OF THIS IS DANNY--*INSIDE* THE PERPETUAL CABARET, *INSIDE* THE AMBULANCE--IT'S HOW DANNY LIKES TO GET AROUND THESE DAYS.
INSIDE...
AND THE PEOPLE?
EMT
In memory of Chris Byczkiewicz

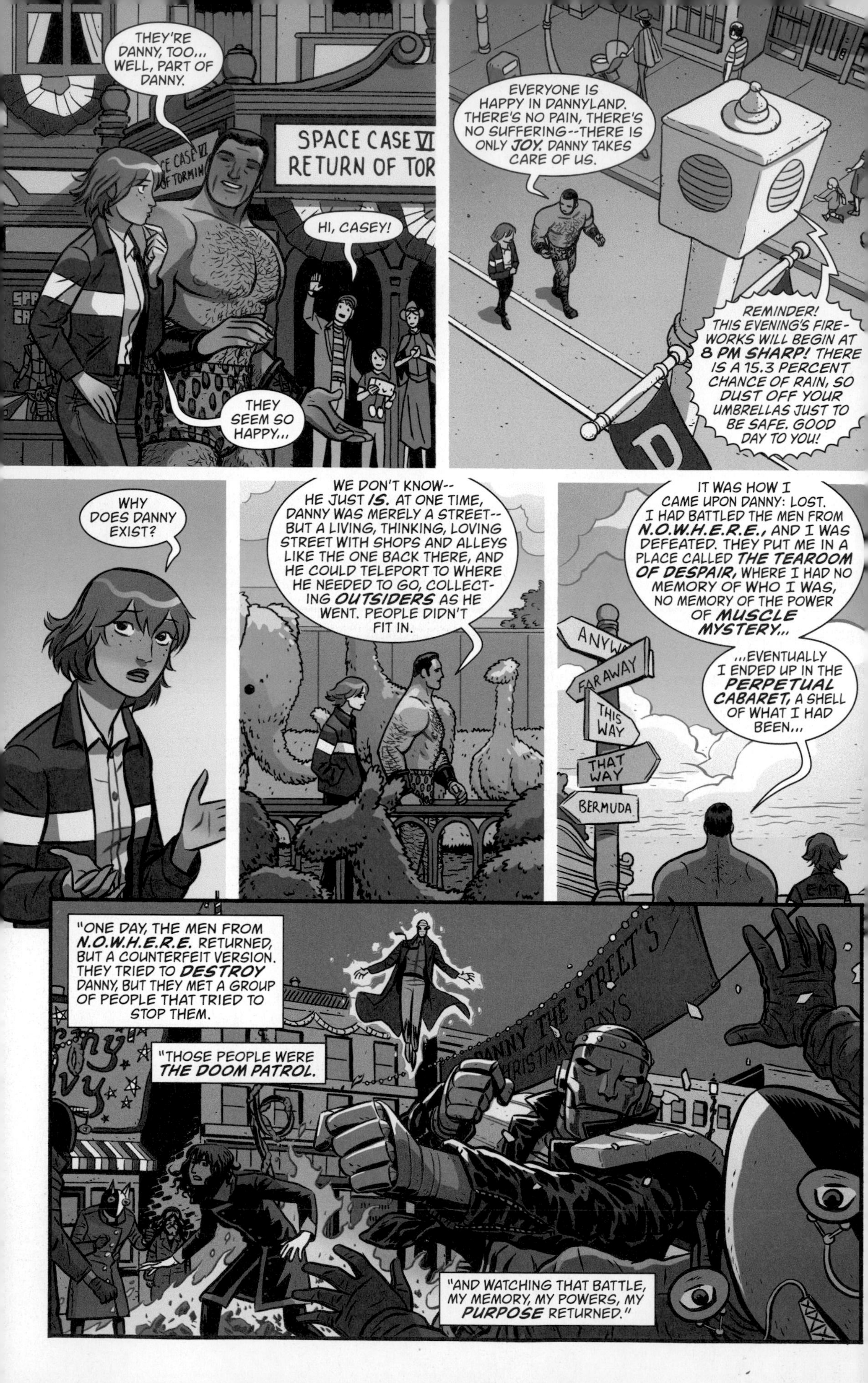

THEY'RE DANNY, TOO... WELL, PART OF DANNY.
SPACE CASE VI RETURN OF TOR
HI, CASEY!
THEY SEEM SO HAPPY...
EVERYONE IS HAPPY IN DANNYLAND. THERE'S NO PAIN, THERE'S NO SUFFERING--THERE IS ONLY JOY. DANNY TAKES CARE OF US.
REMINDER! THIS EVENING'S FIRE-WORKS WILL BEGIN AT 8 PM SHARP! THERE IS A 15.3 PERCENT CHANCE OF RAIN, SO DUST OFF YOUR UMBRELLAS JUST TO BE SAFE. GOOD DAY TO YOU!
WHY DOES DANNY EXIST?
WE DON'T KNOW-- HE JUST IS. AT ONE TIME, DANNY WAS MERELY A STREET-- BUT A LIVING, THINKING, LOVING STREET WITH SHOPS AND ALLEYS LIKE THE ONE BACK THERE, AND HE COULD TELEPORT TO WHERE HE NEEDED TO GO, COLLECTING OUTSIDERS AS HE WENT. PEOPLE DIDN'T FIT IN.
IT WAS HOW I CAME UPON DANNY: LOST. I HAD BATTLED THE MEN FROM N.O.W.H.E.R.E., AND I WAS DEFEATED. THEY PUT ME IN A PLACE CALLED THE TEAROOM OF DESPAIR, WHERE I HAD NO MEMORY OF WHO I WAS, NO MEMORY OF THE POWER OF MUSCLE MYSTERY...
...EVENTUALLY I ENDED UP IN THE PERPETUAL CABARET, A SHELL OF WHAT I HAD BEEN...
FARAWAY
THIS WAY
THAT WAY
BERMUDA
"ONE DAY, THE MEN FROM N.O.W.H.E.R.E. RETURNED, BUT A COUNTERFEIT VERSION. THEY TRIED TO DESTROY DANNY, BUT THEY MET A GROUP OF PEOPLE THAT TRIED TO STOP THEM.
"THOSE PEOPLE WERE THE DOOM PATROL.
DANNY THE STREET'S
"AND WATCHING THAT BATTLE, MY MEMORY, MY POWERS, MY PURPOSE RETURNED."

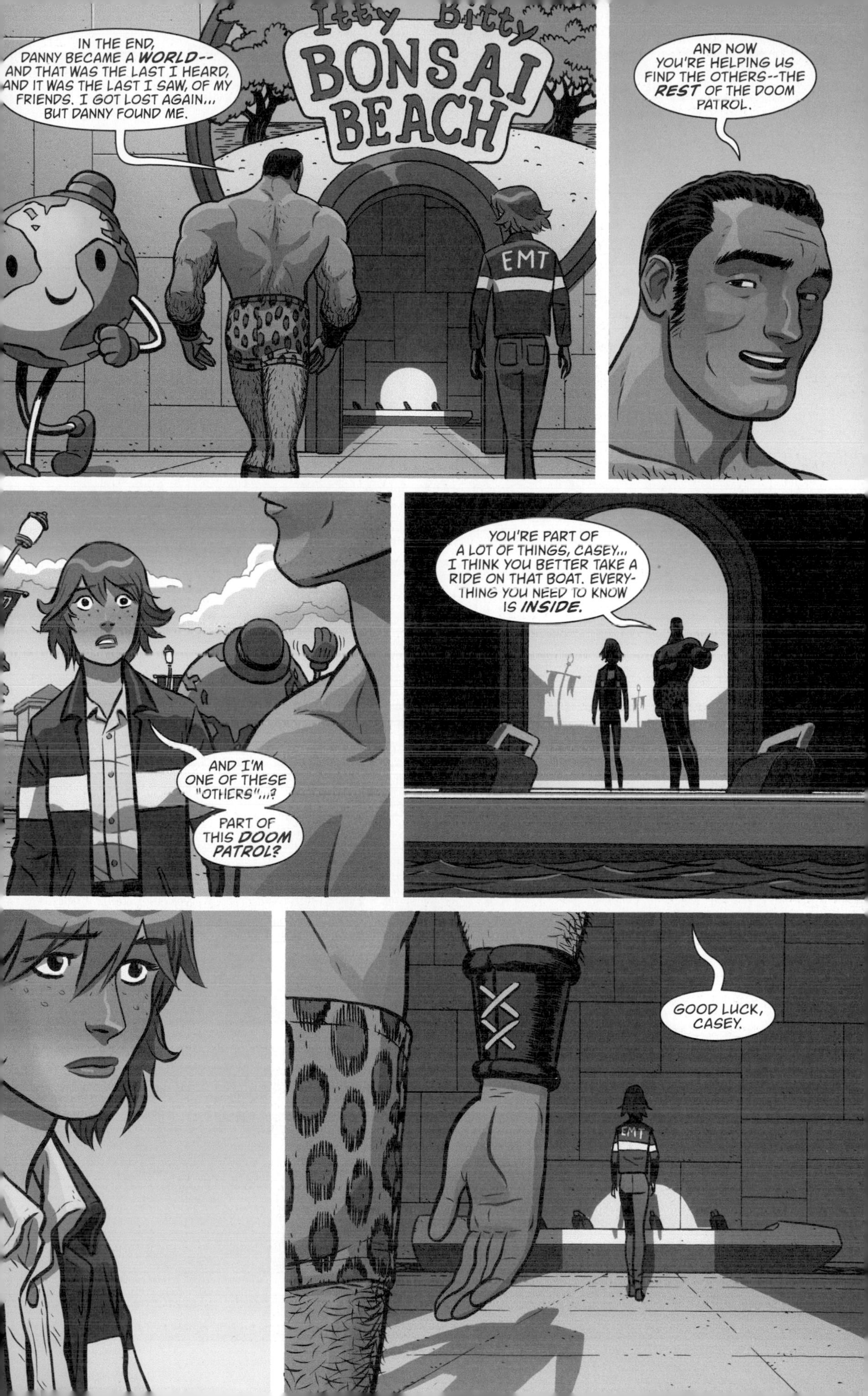
Itty Bitty BONSAI BEACH
IN THE END, DANNY BECAME A WORLD-- AND THAT WAS THE LAST I HEARD, AND IT WAS THE LAST I SAW, OF MY FRIENDS. I GOT LOST AGAIN... BUT DANNY FOUND ME.
EMT
AND NOW YOU'RE HELPING US FIND THE OTHERS--THE REST OF THE DOOM PATROL.
AND I'M ONE OF THESE "OTHERS"...?
PART OF THIS DOOM PATROL?
YOU'RE PART OF A LOT OF THINGS, CASEY... I THINK YOU BETTER TAKE A RIDE ON THAT BOAT. EVERYTHING YOU NEED TO KNOW IS INSIDE.
GOOD LUCK, CASEY.
EMT

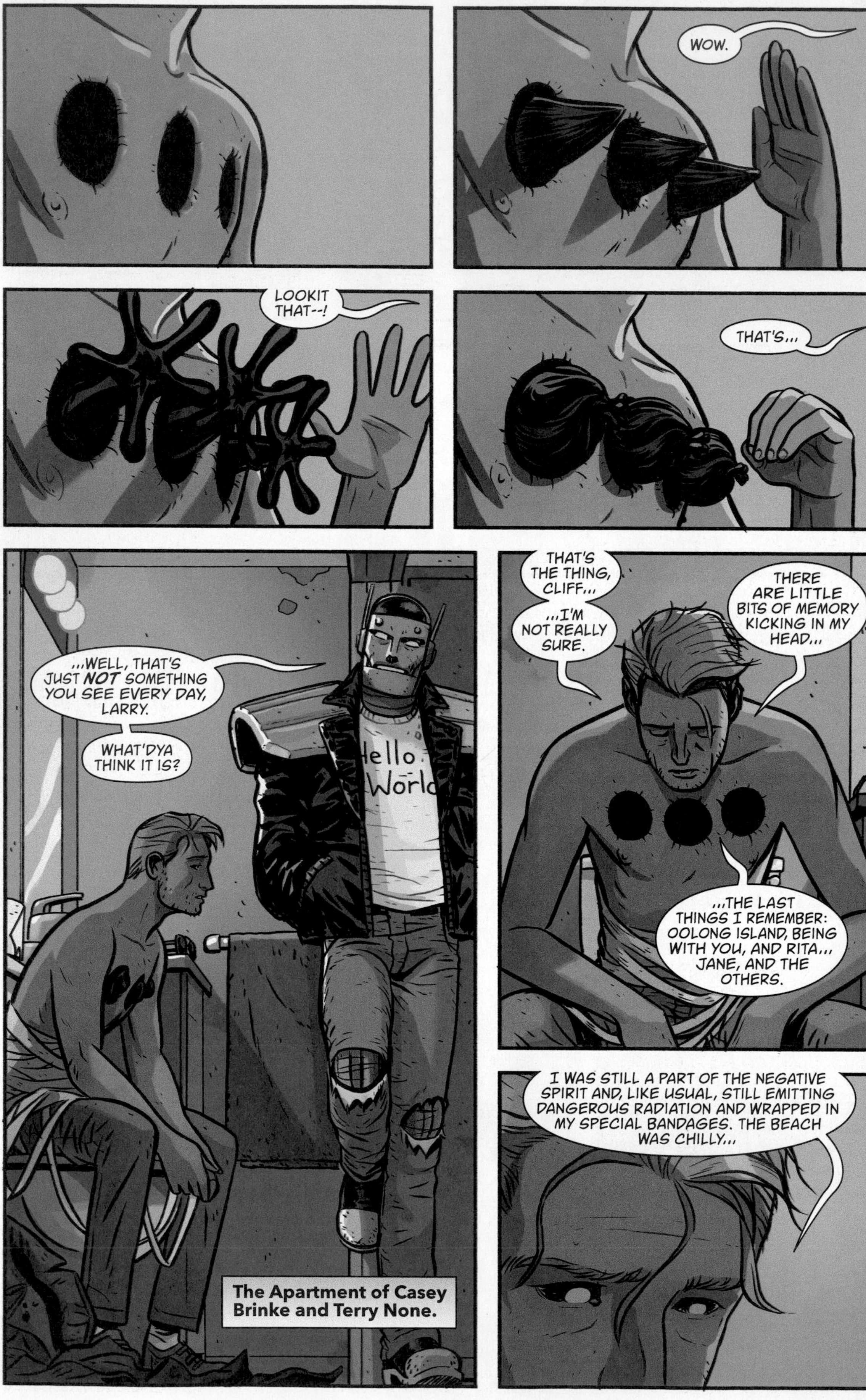

WOW.
LOOKIT THAT--!
THAT'S...
...WELL, THAT'S JUST NOT SOMETHING YOU SEE EVERY DAY, LARRY.
WHAT'DYA THINK IT IS?
Hello World
The Apartment of Casey Brinke and Terry None.
THAT'S THE THING, CLIFF...
...I'M NOT REALLY SURE.
THERE ARE LITTLE BITS OF MEMORY KICKING IN MY HEAD...
...THE LAST THINGS I REMEMBER: OOLONG ISLAND, BEING WITH YOU, AND RITA... JANE, AND THE OTHERS.
I WAS STILL A PART OF THE NEGATIVE SPIRIT AND, LIKE USUAL, STILL EMITTING DANGEROUS RADIATION AND WRAPPED IN MY SPECIAL BANDAGES. THE BEACH WAS CHILLY...

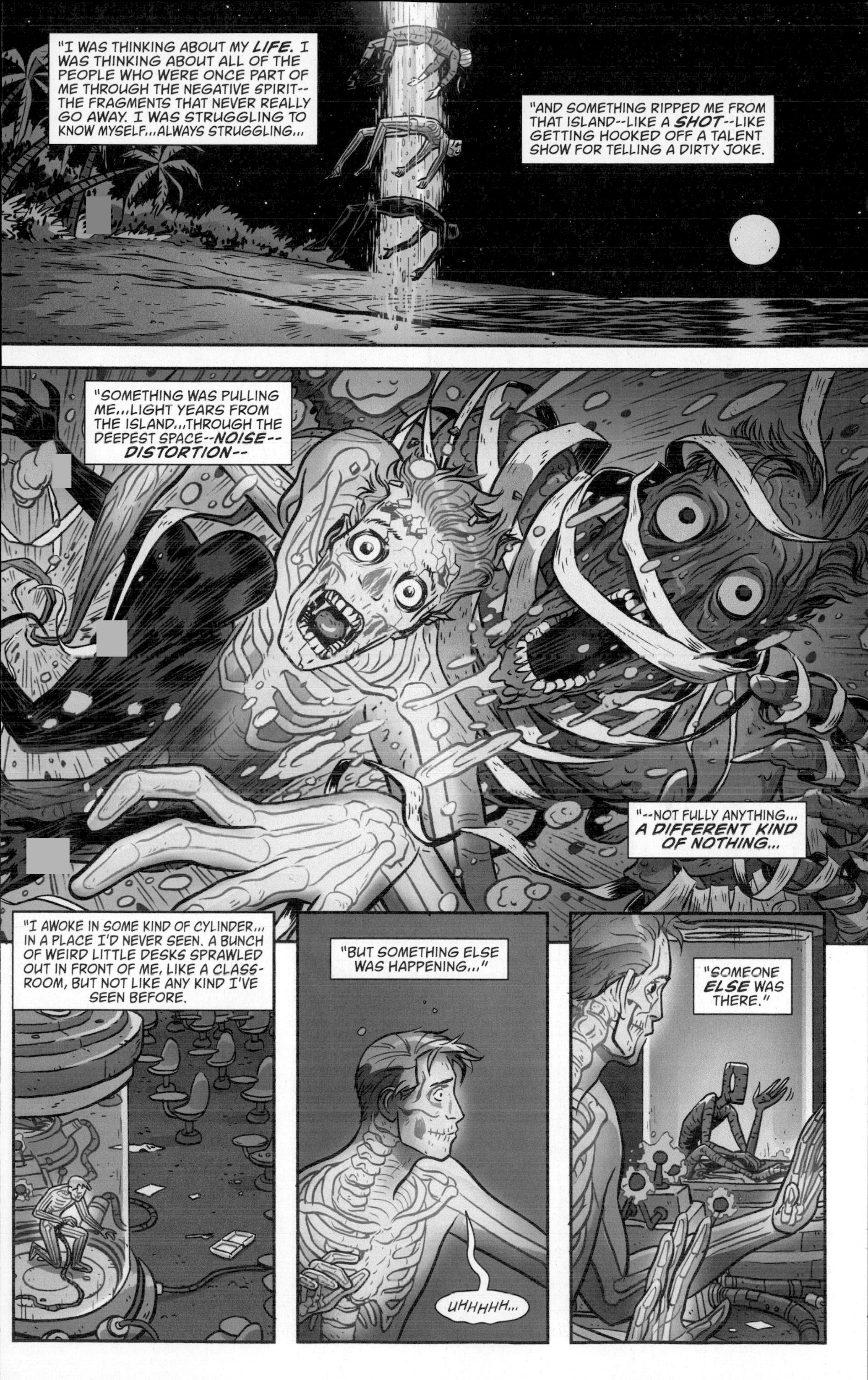
"I WAS THINKING ABOUT MY LIFE. I WAS THINKING ABOUT ALL OF THE PEOPLE WHO WERE ONCE PART OF ME THROUGH THE NEGATIVE SPIRIT--THE FRAGMENTS THAT NEVER REALLY GO AWAY. I WAS STRUGGLING TO KNOW MYSELF...ALWAYS STRUGGLING...
"AND SOMETHING RIPPED ME FROM THAT ISLAND--LIKE A SHOT--LIKE GETTING HOOKED OFF A TALENT SHOW FOR TELLING A DIRTY JOKE.
"SOMETHING WAS PULLING ME...LIGHT YEARS FROM THE ISLAND...THROUGH THE DEEPEST SPACE--NOISE--DISTORTION--
"--NOT FULLY ANYTHING... A DIFFERENT KIND OF NOTHING...
"I AWOKE IN SOME KIND OF CYLINDER... IN A PLACE I'D NEVER SEEN. A BUNCH OF WEIRD LITTLE DESKS SPRAWLED OUT IN FRONT OF ME, LIKE A CLASS-ROOM, BUT NOT LIKE ANY KIND I'VE SEEN BEFORE.
"BUT SOMETHING ELSE WAS HAPPENING..."
UHHHHH...
"SOMEONE ELSE WAS THERE."

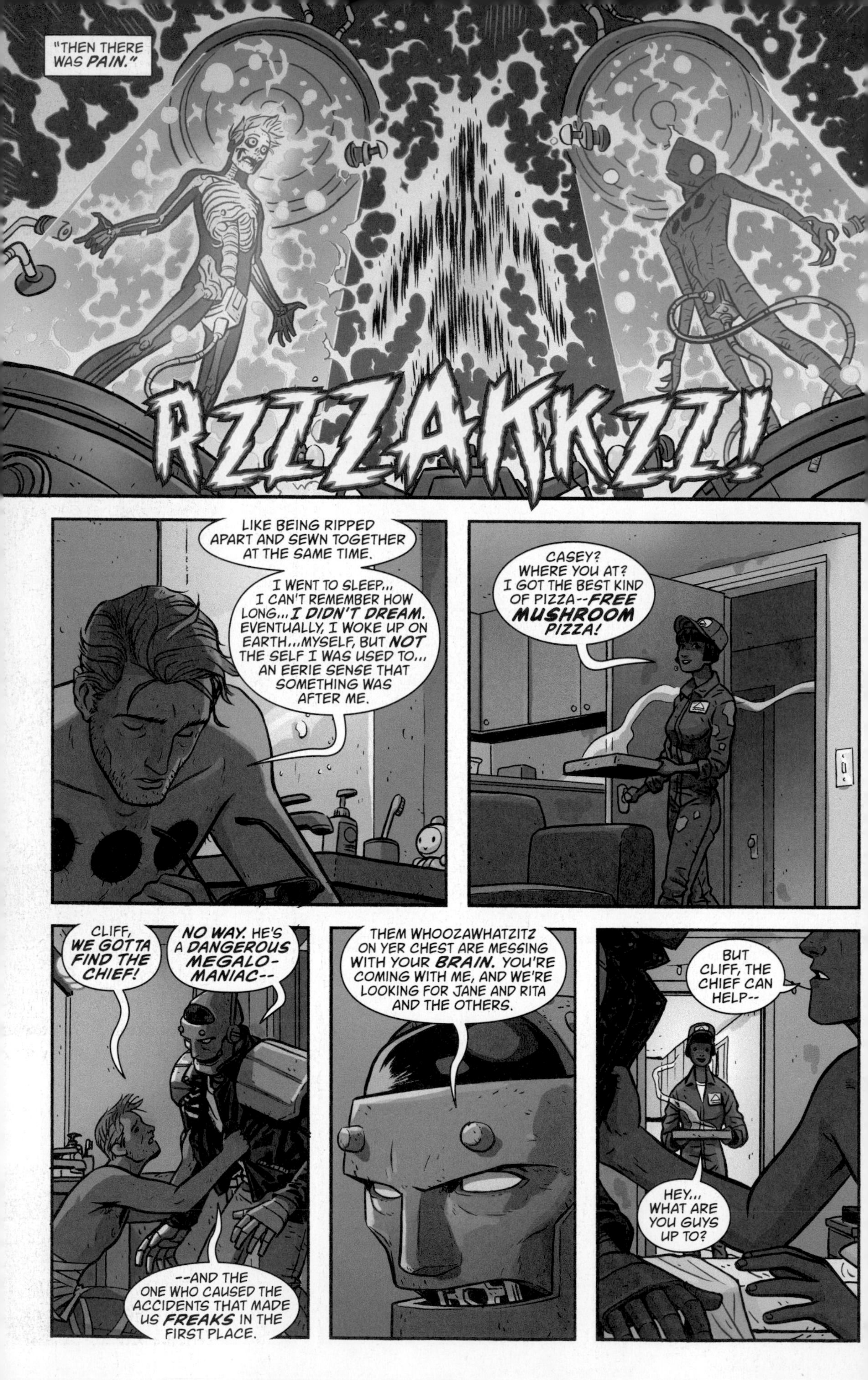
"THEN THERE WAS PAIN."
RZZZAKKZZZ!
LIKE BEING RIPPED APART AND SEWN TOGETHER AT THE SAME TIME.
I WENT TO SLEEP... I CAN'T REMEMBER HOW LONG... I DIDN'T DREAM. EVENTUALLY, I WOKE UP ON EARTH... MYSELF, BUT NOT THE SELF I WAS USED TO... AN EERIE SENSE THAT SOMETHING WAS AFTER ME.
CASEY? WHERE YOU AT? I GOT THE BEST KIND OF PIZZA--FREE MUSHROOM PIZZA!
CLIFF, WE GOTTA FIND THE CHIEF!
NO WAY. HE'S A DANGEROUS MEGALO-MANIAC--
--AND THE ONE WHO CAUSED THE ACCIDENTS THAT MADE US FREAKS IN THE FIRST PLACE.
THEM WHOOZAWHATZITZ ON YER CHEST ARE MESSING WITH YOUR BRAIN. YOU'RE COMING WITH ME, AND WE'RE LOOKING FOR JANE AND RITA AND THE OTHERS.
BUT CLIFF, THE CHIEF CAN HELP--
HEY... WHAT ARE YOU GUYS UP TO?

CLIFF STEELE, ATTORNEY-AT-LAW.

ME AND MY ASSOCIATE WERE JUST GETTING OUT OF HERE...

NO, *IT'S COOL*-- YOU GUYS CAN STAY. HAVE YOU SEEN LOTION? LOTION THE CAT?

UH.... ABOUT THAT--

RETTCH!

HOLY CRAP! LET'S GET HIM IN THE LIVING ROOM!

WHAT *HAPPENED?!*

I...I NEED MORE NEGATIVE ENERGY...

...THE POST-WAVES FROM THE VIOLENCE YOU CAUSED...MUST HAVE KEPT ME GOING--

I DO MY BEST.

BUT NOW MY *GUTS* ARE CLAWING OUT--

EEEEEEEEEEEEEEEEEEEEEEEE

CHRIST, CAN *YOU* HEAR THAT, TOO--?

I NEED AIR!

WHICH IS CONVENIENT BECAUSE WE JUST GOT THIS NEW WINDOW INSTALLED...

I DON'T HEAR *ANYTHING!*

OH SHIT...IT FOUND ME!

EEEEEEEEEEEEEEEEEEEEEEEEEEEEEEE

EEEEEEEEE

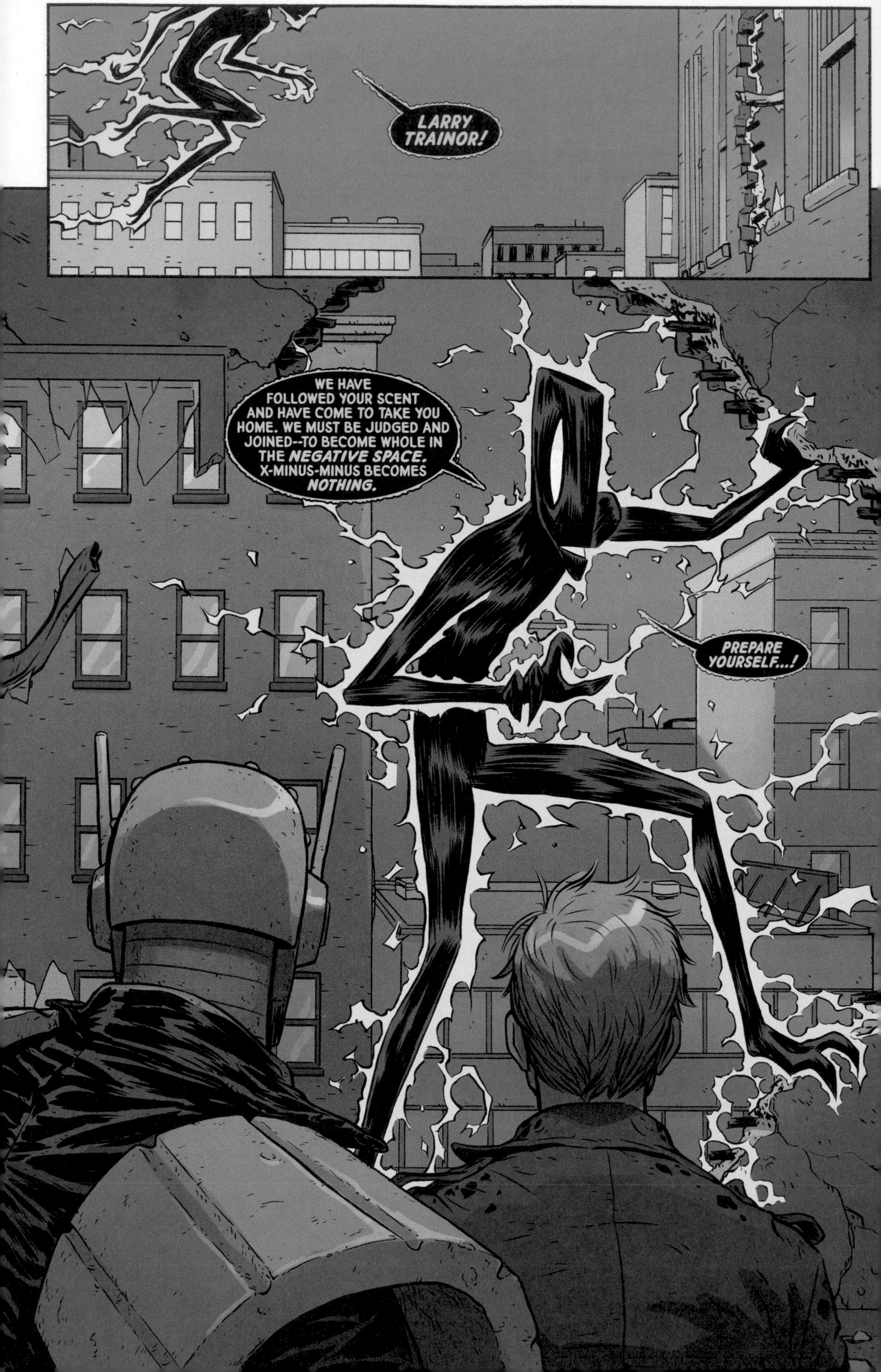
LARRY TRAINOR!
WE HAVE FOLLOWED YOUR SCENT AND HAVE COME TO TAKE YOU HOME. WE MUST BE JUDGED AND JOINED--TO BECOME WHOLE IN THE *NEGATIVE SPACE.* X-MINUS-MINUS BECOMES *NOTHING.*
PREPARE YOURSELF...!

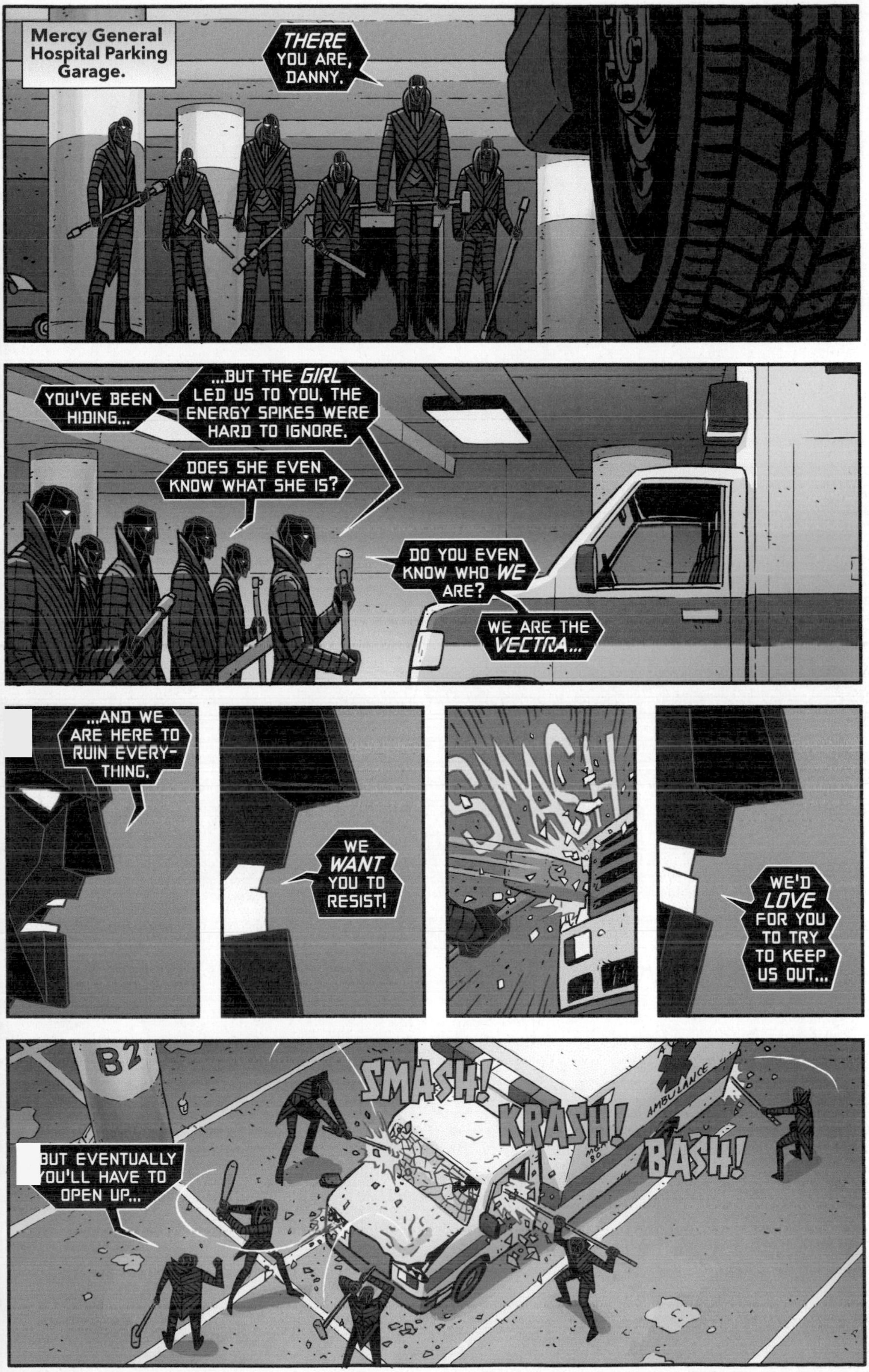
Mercy General Hospital Parking Garage.
THERE YOU ARE, DANNY.
YOU'VE BEEN HIDING...
...BUT THE GIRL LED US TO YOU. THE ENERGY SPIKES WERE HARD TO IGNORE.
DOES SHE EVEN KNOW WHAT SHE IS?
DO YOU EVEN KNOW WHO WE ARE?
WE ARE THE VECTRA...
...AND WE ARE HERE TO RUIN EVERY-THING.
WE WANT YOU TO RESIST!
SMASH
WE'D LOVE FOR YOU TO TRY TO KEEP US OUT...
B2
BUT EVENTUALLY YOU'LL HAVE TO OPEN UP...
SMASH!
KRASH!
AMBULANCE
BASH!

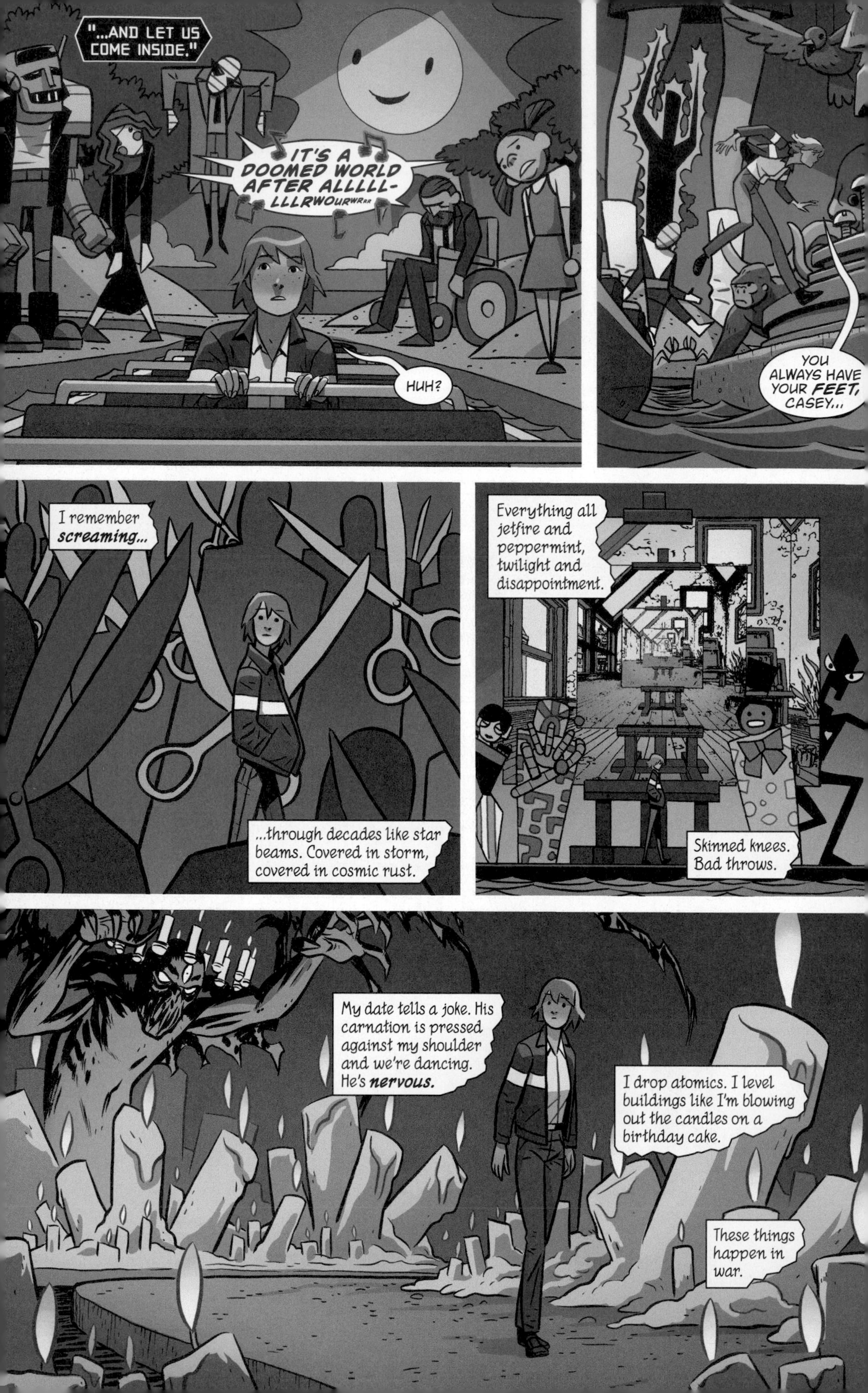
"...AND LET US COME INSIDE."
IT'S A DOOMED WORLD AFTER ALLLLL-LLLRWOURWRRR
HUH?
YOU ALWAYS HAVE YOUR FEET, CASEY...
I remember screaming...
...through decades like star beams. Covered in storm, covered in cosmic rust.
Everything all jetfire and peppermint, twilight and disappointment.
Skinned knees. Bad throws.
My date tells a joke. His carnation is pressed against my shoulder and we're dancing. He's nervous.
I drop atomics. I level buildings like I'm blowing out the candles on a birthday cake.
These things happen in war.

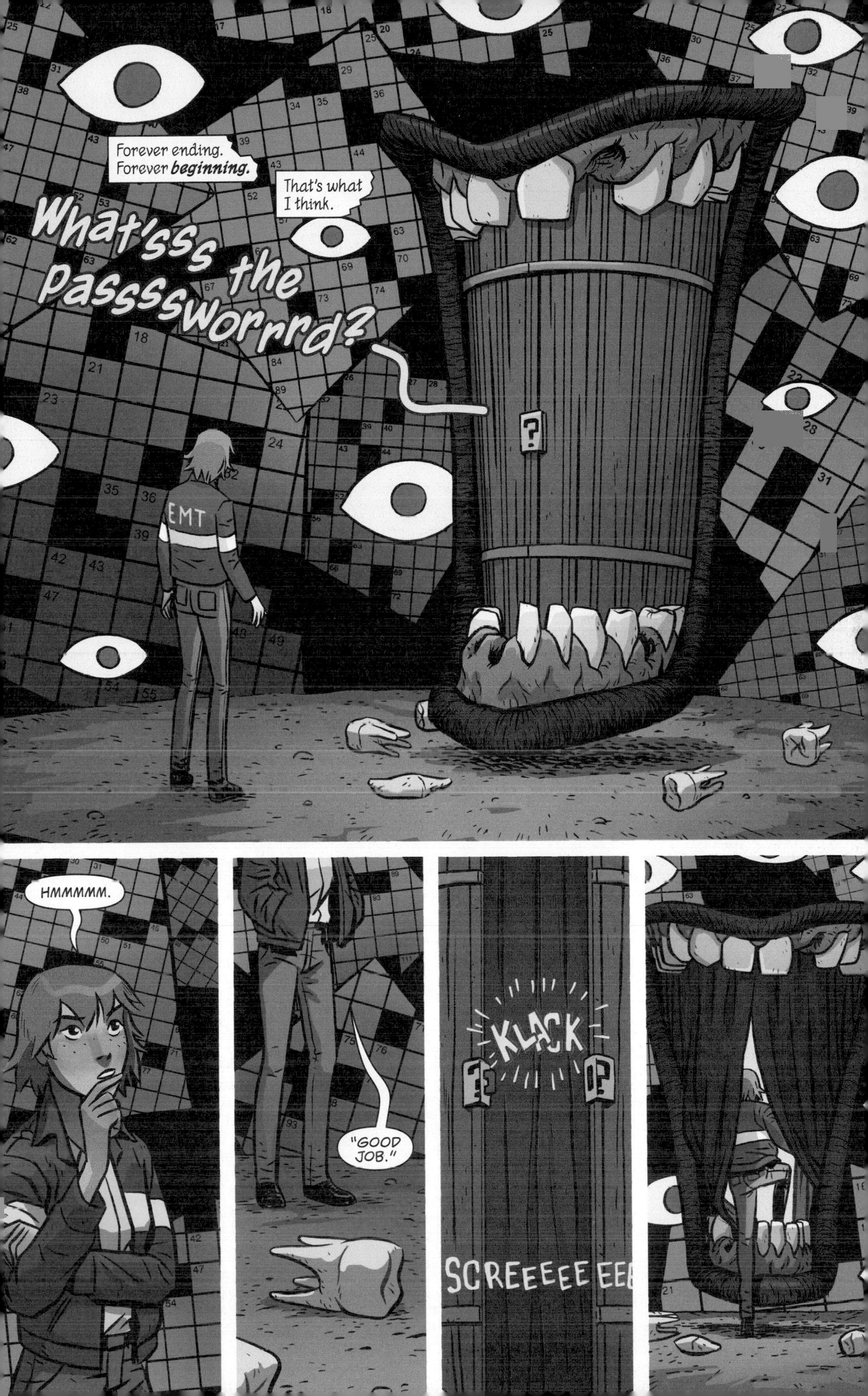
Forever ending. Forever *beginning.*
That's what I think.
What'sss the passssworrrd?
HMMMMM.
"GOOD JOB."
KLACK
SCREEEEEEEE

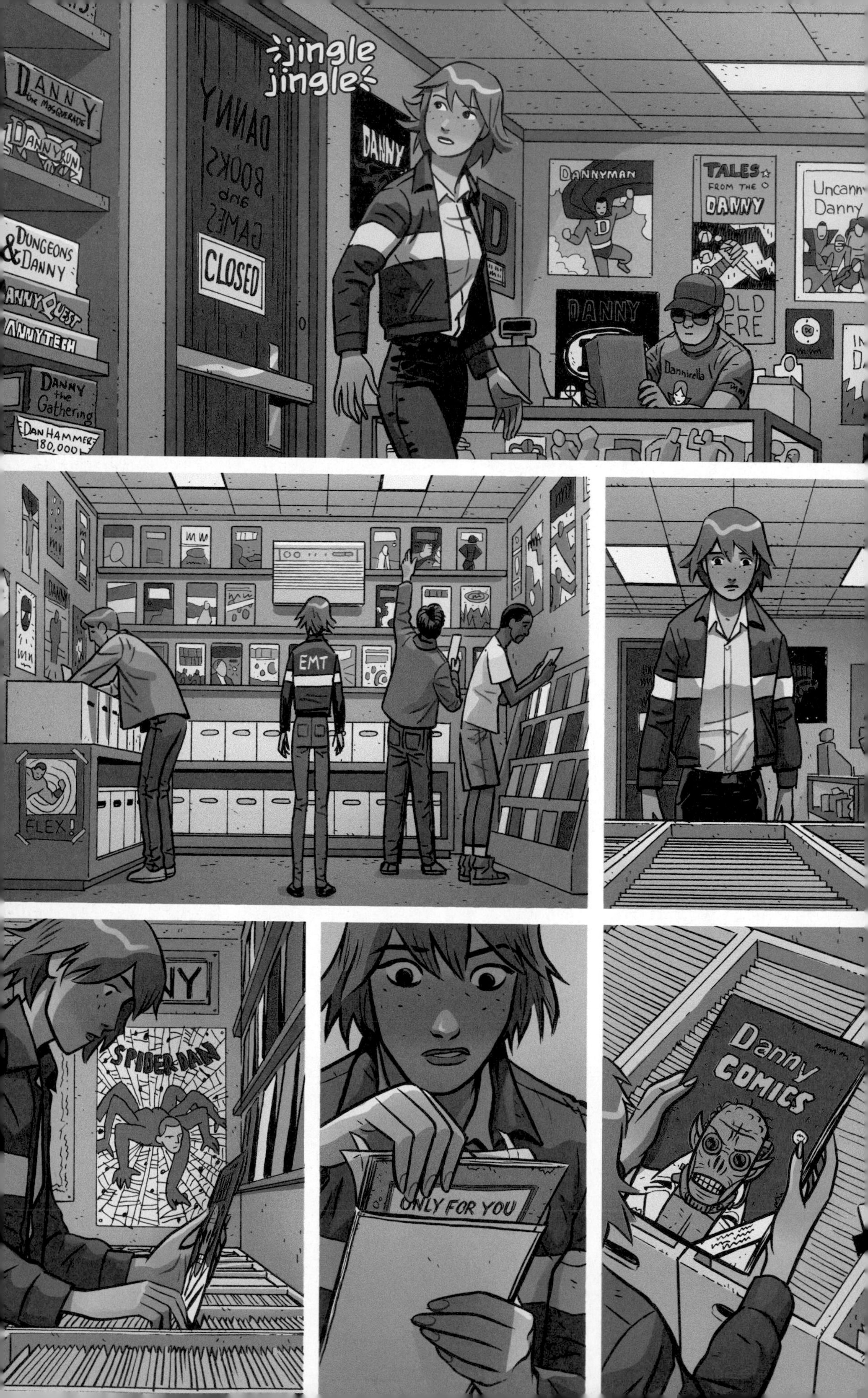

jingle jingle
DANNY the Masquerade
DUNGEONS & DANNY
ANNYQUEST
ANNYTECH
DANNY the Gathering
DAN HAMMER 80,000
CLOSED
DANNY
DANNYMAN
TALES FROM THE DANNY
Uncann Danny
DANNY
Dannirella
EMT
FLEX!
SPIDER-DAN
ONLY FOR YOU
Danny COMICS

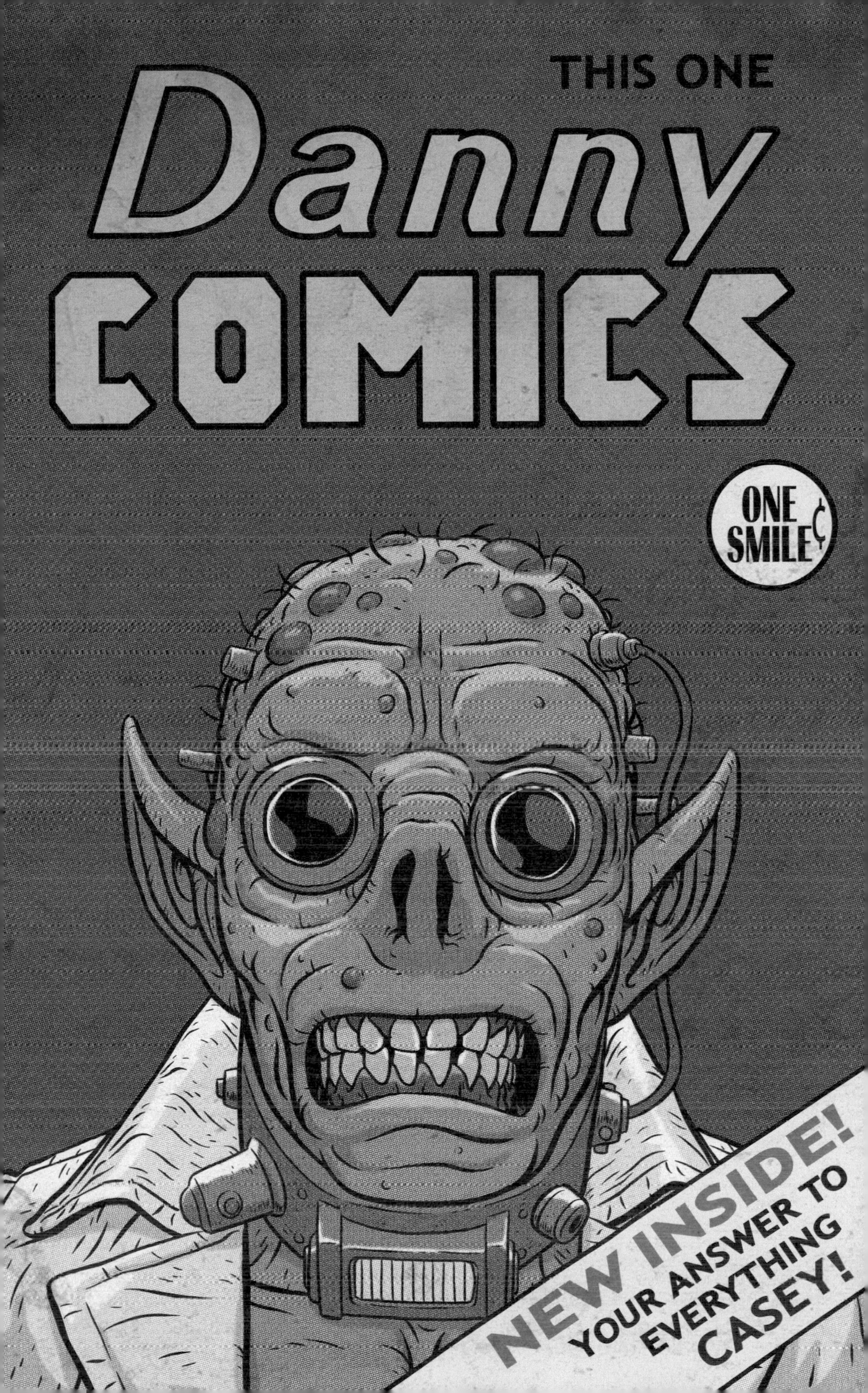
THIS ONE
Danny
COMICS
ONE SMILE ¢
NEW INSIDE!
YOUR ANSWER TO EVERYTHING
CASEY!

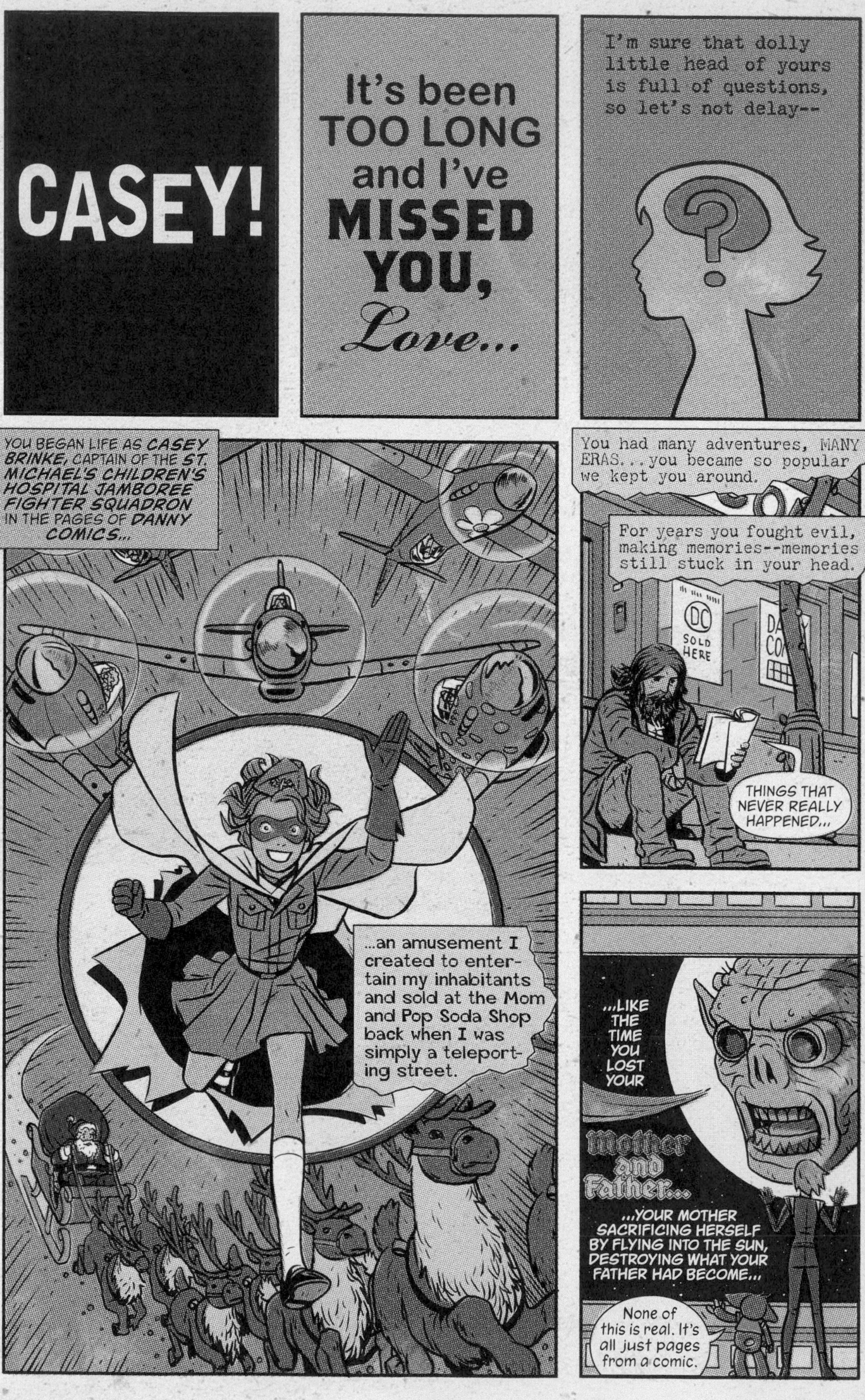
CASEY!
It's been TOO LONG and I've MISSED YOU, Love...
I'm sure that dolly little head of yours is full of questions, so let's not delay--
YOU BEGAN LIFE AS CASEY BRINKE, CAPTAIN OF THE ST. MICHAEL'S CHILDREN'S HOSPITAL JAMBOREE FIGHTER SQUADRON IN THE PAGES OF DANNY COMICS...
...an amusement I created to entertain my inhabitants and sold at the Mom and Pop Soda Shop back when I was simply a teleporting street.
You had many adventures, MANY ERAS...you became so popular we kept you around.
For years you fought evil, making memories--memories still stuck in your head.
DC SOLD HERE
THINGS THAT NEVER REALLY HAPPENED...
...LIKE THE TIME YOU LOST YOUR
Mother and Father...
...YOUR MOTHER SACRIFICING HERSELF BY FLYING INTO THE SUN, DESTROYING WHAT YOUR FATHER HAD BECOME...
None of this is real. It's all just pages from a comic.

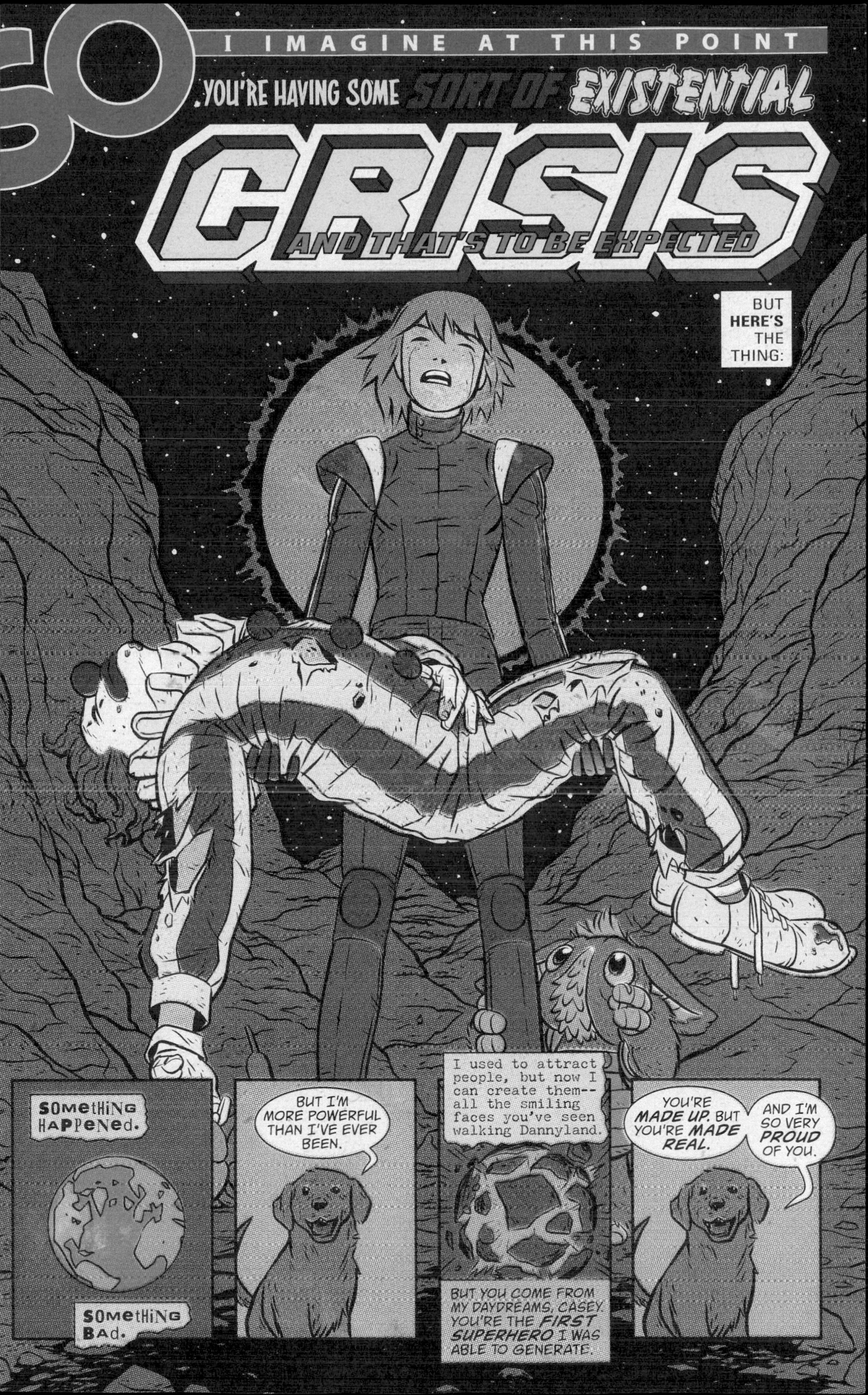

50
I IMAGINE AT THIS POINT
YOU'RE HAVING SOME SORT OF EXISTENTIAL
CRISIS
AND THAT'S TO BE EXPECTED
BUT HERE'S THE THING:
SOMETHING HAPPENED.
SOMETHING BAD.
BUT I'M MORE POWERFUL THAN I'VE EVER BEEN.
I used to attract people, but now I can create them--all the smiling faces you've seen walking Dannyland.
BUT YOU COME FROM MY DAYDREAMS, CASEY. YOU'RE THE FIRST SUPERHERO I WAS ABLE TO GENERATE.
YOU'RE MADE UP. BUT YOU'RE MADE REAL.
AND I'M SO VERY PROUD OF YOU.

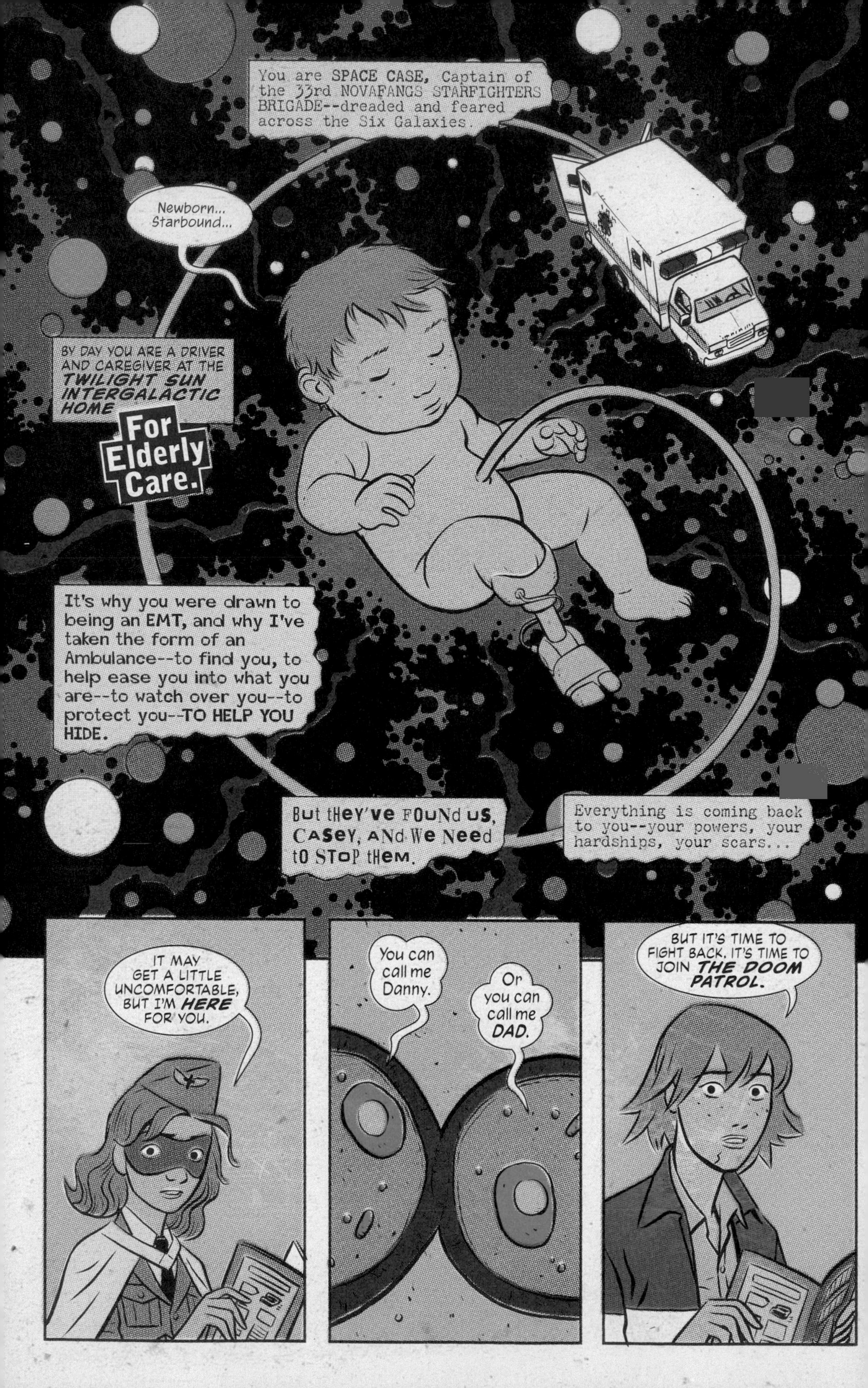

You are SPACE CASE, Captain of the 33rd NOVAFANGS STARFIGHTERS BRIGADE--dreaded and feared across the Six Galaxies.
Newborn... Starbound...
BY DAY YOU ARE A DRIVER AND CAREGIVER AT THE TWILIGHT SUN INTERGALACTIC HOME
For Elderly Care.
It's why you were drawn to being an EMT, and why I've taken the form of an Ambulance--to find you, to help ease you into what you are--to watch over you--to protect you--TO HELP YOU HIDE.
But they've found us, Casey, and we need to stop them.
Everything is coming back to you--your powers, your hardships, your scars...
IT MAY GET A LITTLE UNCOMFORTABLE, BUT I'M HERE FOR YOU.
You can call me Danny.
Or you can call me DAD.
BUT IT'S TIME TO FIGHT BACK. IT'S TIME TO JOIN THE DOOM PATROL.

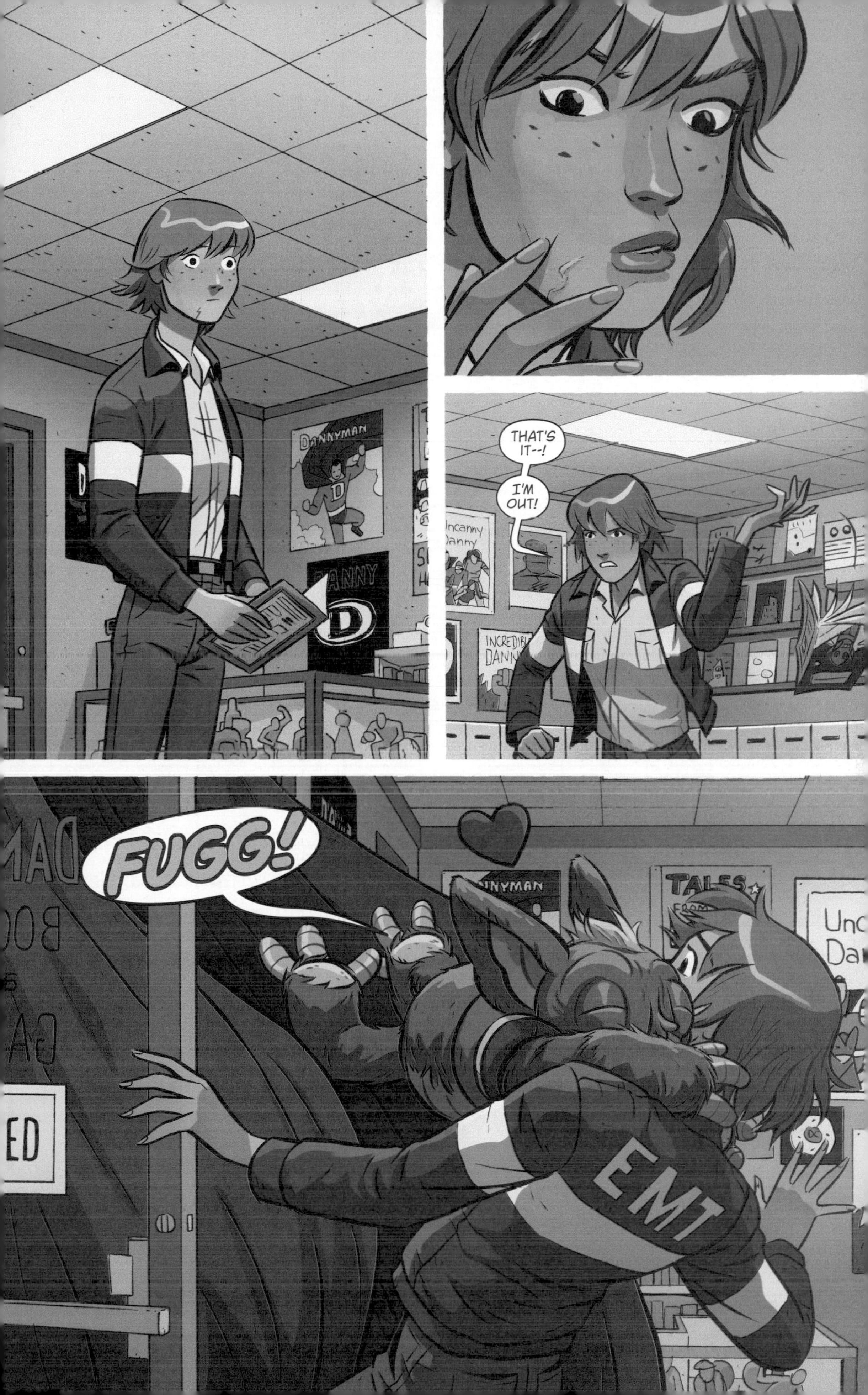
DANNYMAN
DANNY
THAT'S IT--!
I'M OUT!
Uncanny Danny
FUGG!
EMT

EXCEPTIONAL! MAKE SOME *ROOM!* IT'S TIME TO TAKE THINGS TO THEIR NEXT LOGICAL CONCLUSION!

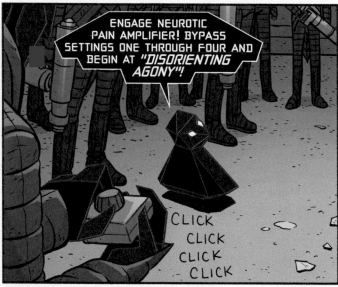

ENGAGE NEUROTIC PAIN AMPLIFIER! BYPASS SETTINGS ONE THROUGH FOUR AND BEGIN AT *"DISORIENTING AGONY"*!

CLICK
CLICK
CLICK
CLICK

YESSS...

YESSS! YESSS! RELEASE YOUR FLUIDS!

LEVEL SIX! LEVEL SEVEN! YOU WILL OPEN UP AND LET US IN! WE WILL OBTAIN THE MEAT!

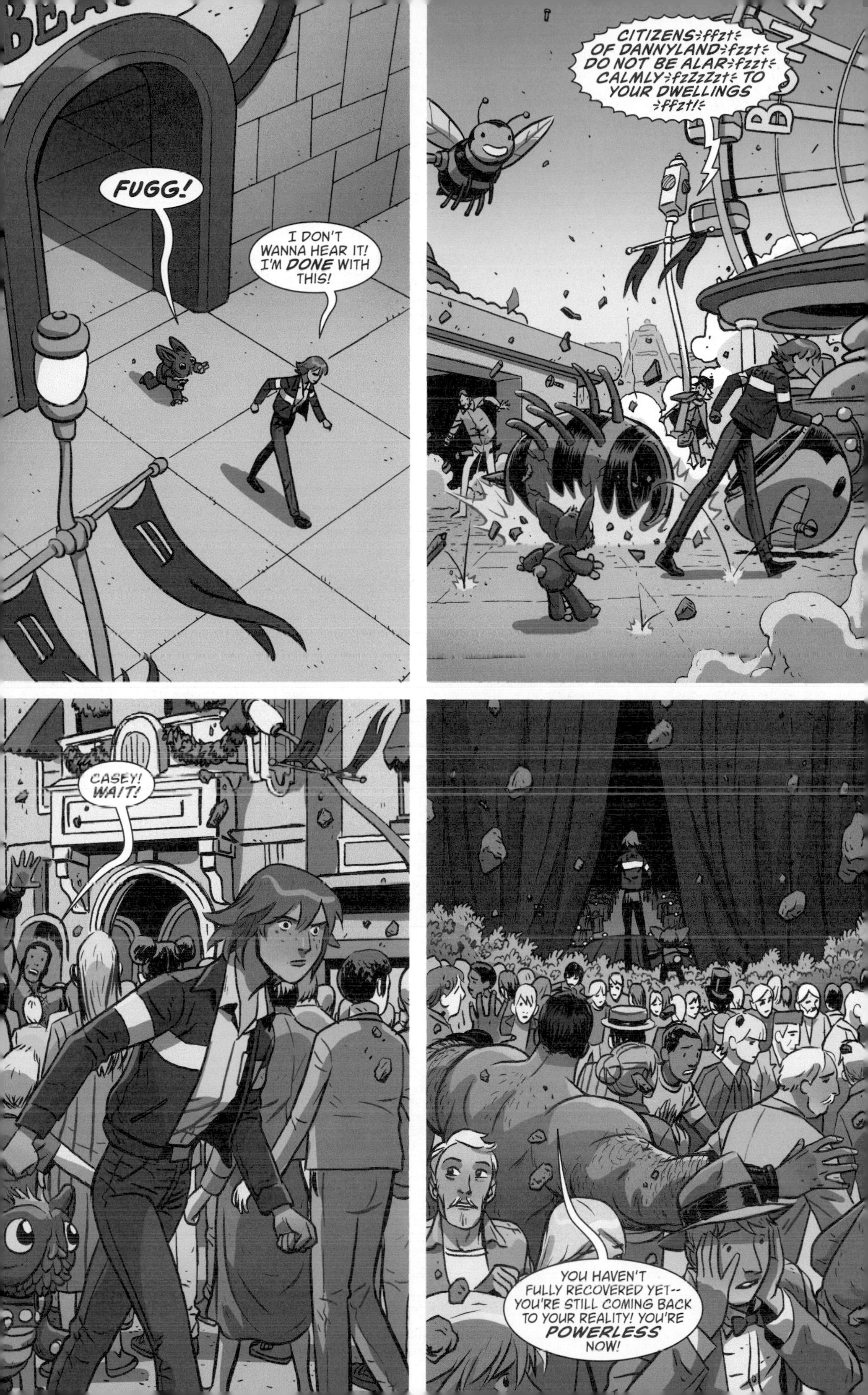
FUGG!
I DON'T WANNA HEAR IT! I'M DONE WITH THIS!
CITIZENS ffzt OF DANNYLAND fzzt DO NOT BE ALAR fzzt CALMLY fzZzZzt TO YOUR DWELLINGS ffzt!
CASEY! WAIT!
YOU HAVEN'T FULLY RECOVERED YET-- YOU'RE STILL COMING BACK TO YOUR REALITY! YOU'RE POWERLESS NOW!

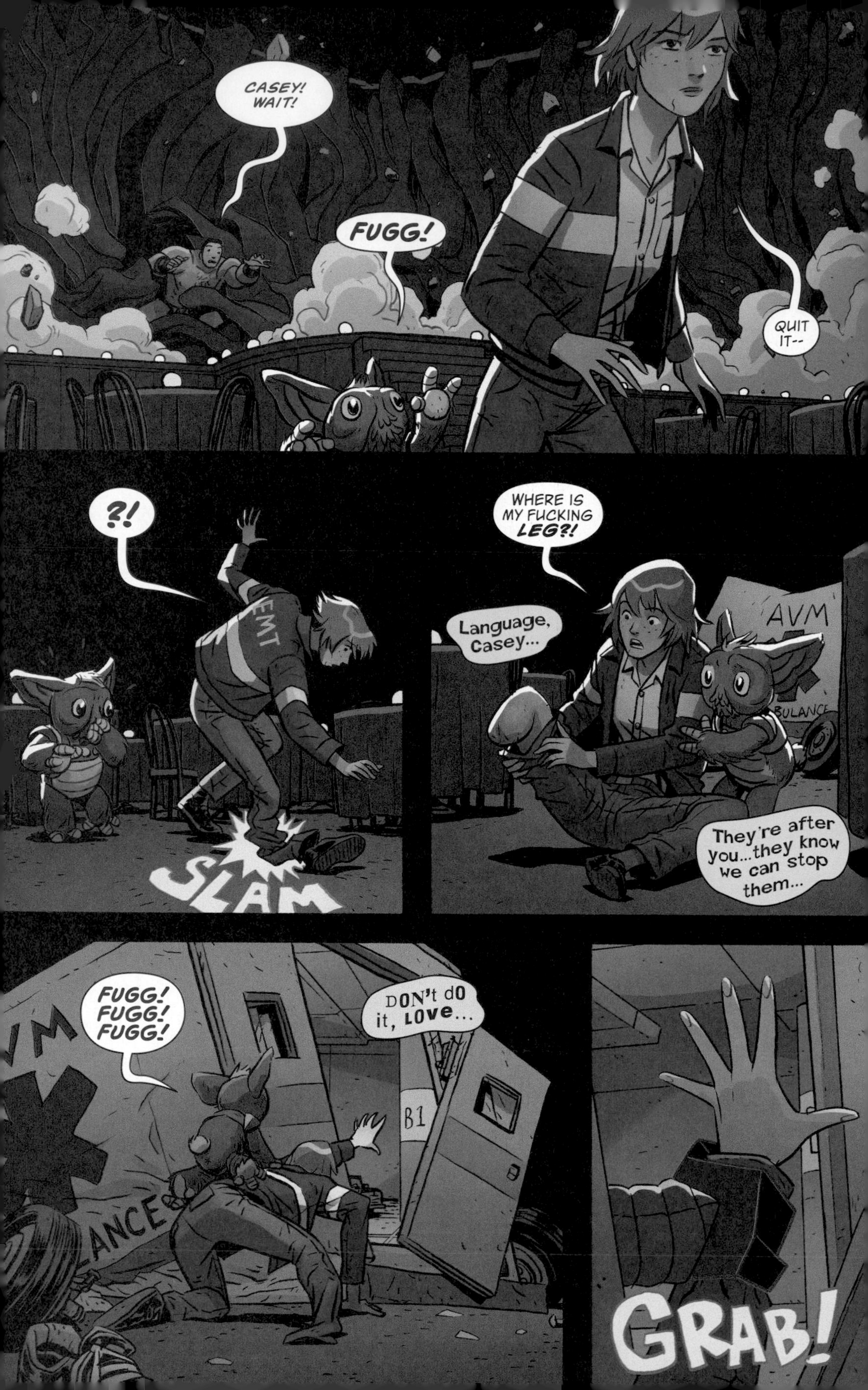
CASEY! WAIT!
FUGG!
QUIT IT--
?!
SLAM
WHERE IS MY FUCKING LEG?!
Language, Casey...
AVM
BULANCE
They're after you...they know we can stop them...
FUGG! FUGG! FUGG!
DON't dO it, LOVE...
B1
ANCE
GRAB!

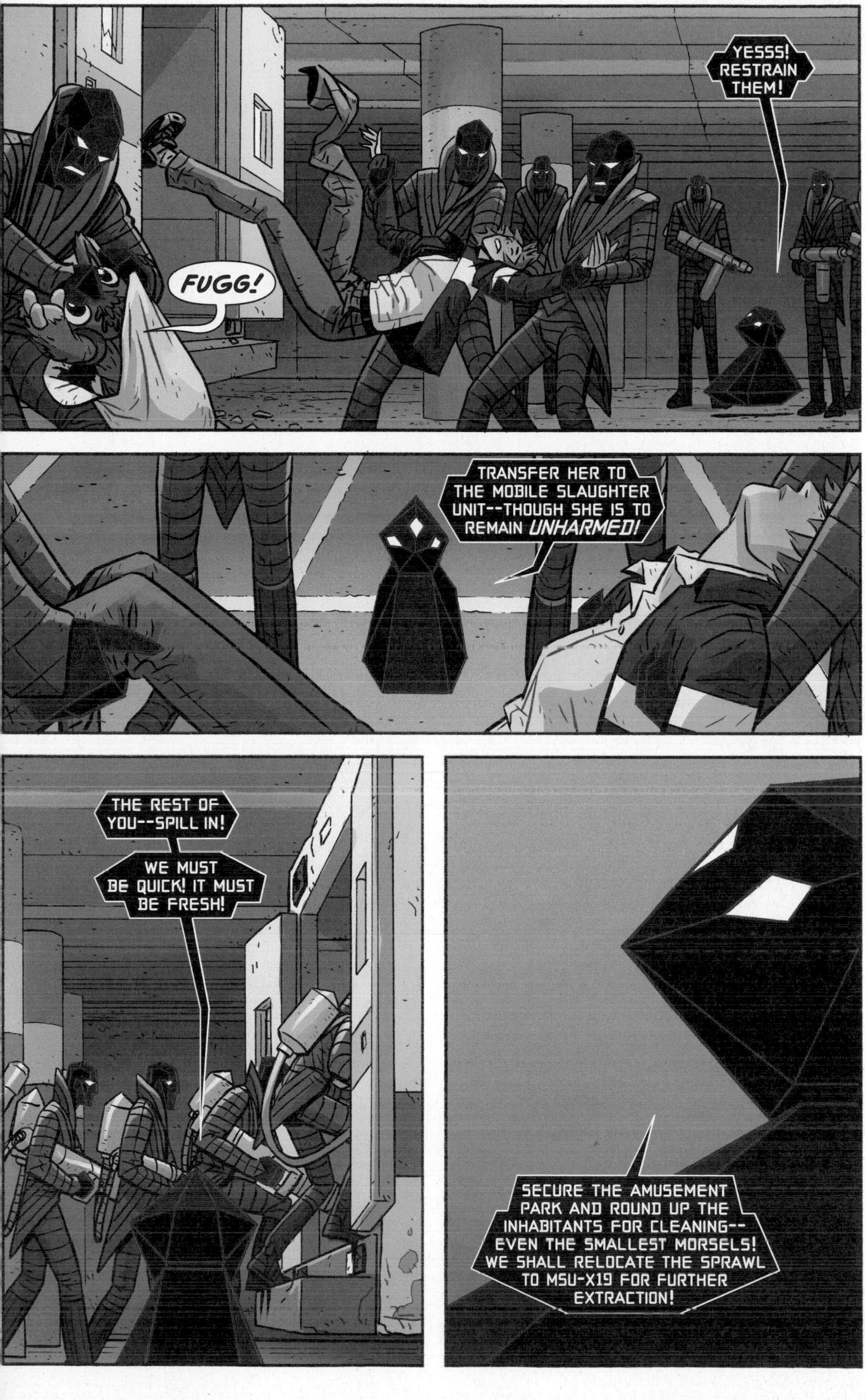

YESSS! RESTRAIN THEM!
FUGG!
TRANSFER HER TO THE MOBILE SLAUGHTER UNIT--THOUGH SHE IS TO REMAIN *UNHARMED!*
THE REST OF YOU--SPILL IN!
WE MUST BE QUICK! IT MUST BE FRESH!
SECURE THE AMUSEMENT PARK AND ROUND UP THE INHABITANTS FOR CLEANING-- EVEN THE SMALLEST MORSELS! WE SHALL RELOCATE THE SPRAWL TO MSU-X19 FOR FURTHER EXTRACTION!

NILES CAULDER A.K.A. THE CHIEF

FSSSST!
FSSSST!
CLANK
ZZAP!
AND HOW ARE YOU FEELING NOW?
OOF!
SEE YA LATER, *HAND TURKEY!*

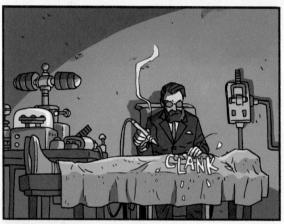

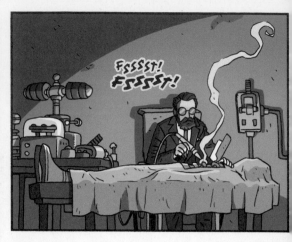

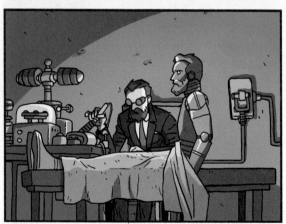

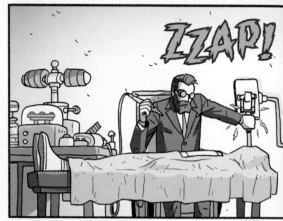

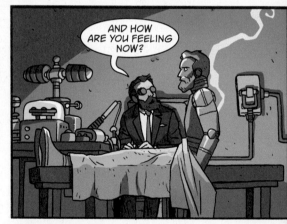

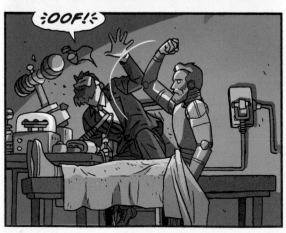

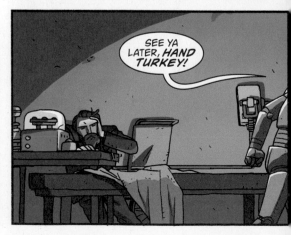

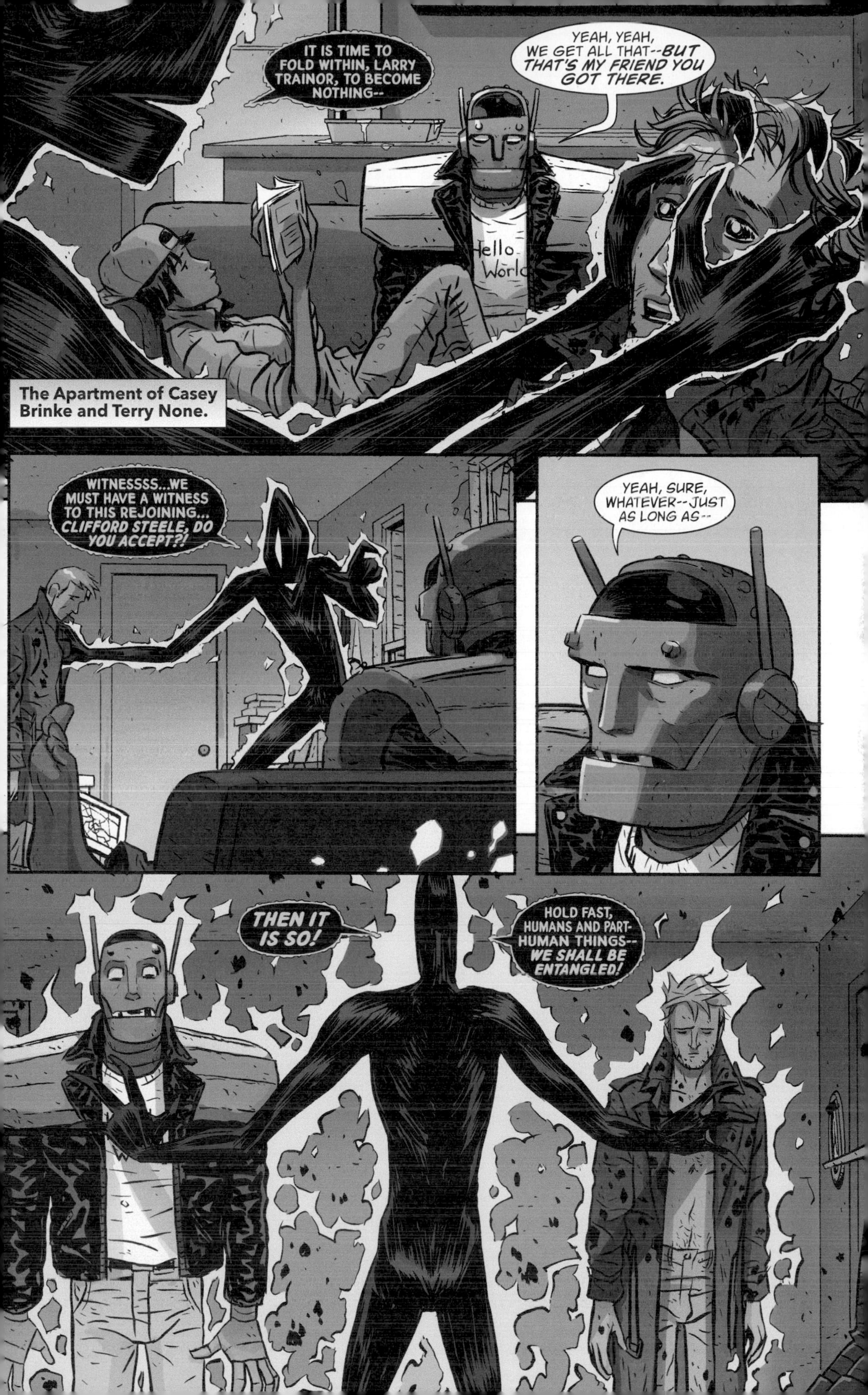
IT IS TIME TO FOLD WITHIN, LARRY TRAINOR, TO BECOME NOTHING--
YEAH, YEAH, WE GET ALL THAT--BUT THAT'S MY FRIEND YOU GOT THERE.
Hello World
The Apartment of Casey Brinke and Terry None.
WITNESSSS...WE MUST HAVE A WITNESS TO THIS REJOINING... CLIFFORD STEELE, DO YOU ACCEPT?!
YEAH, SURE, WHATEVER--JUST AS LONG AS--
THEN IT IS SO!
HOLD FAST, HUMANS AND PART-HUMAN THINGS-- WE SHALL BE ENTANGLED!

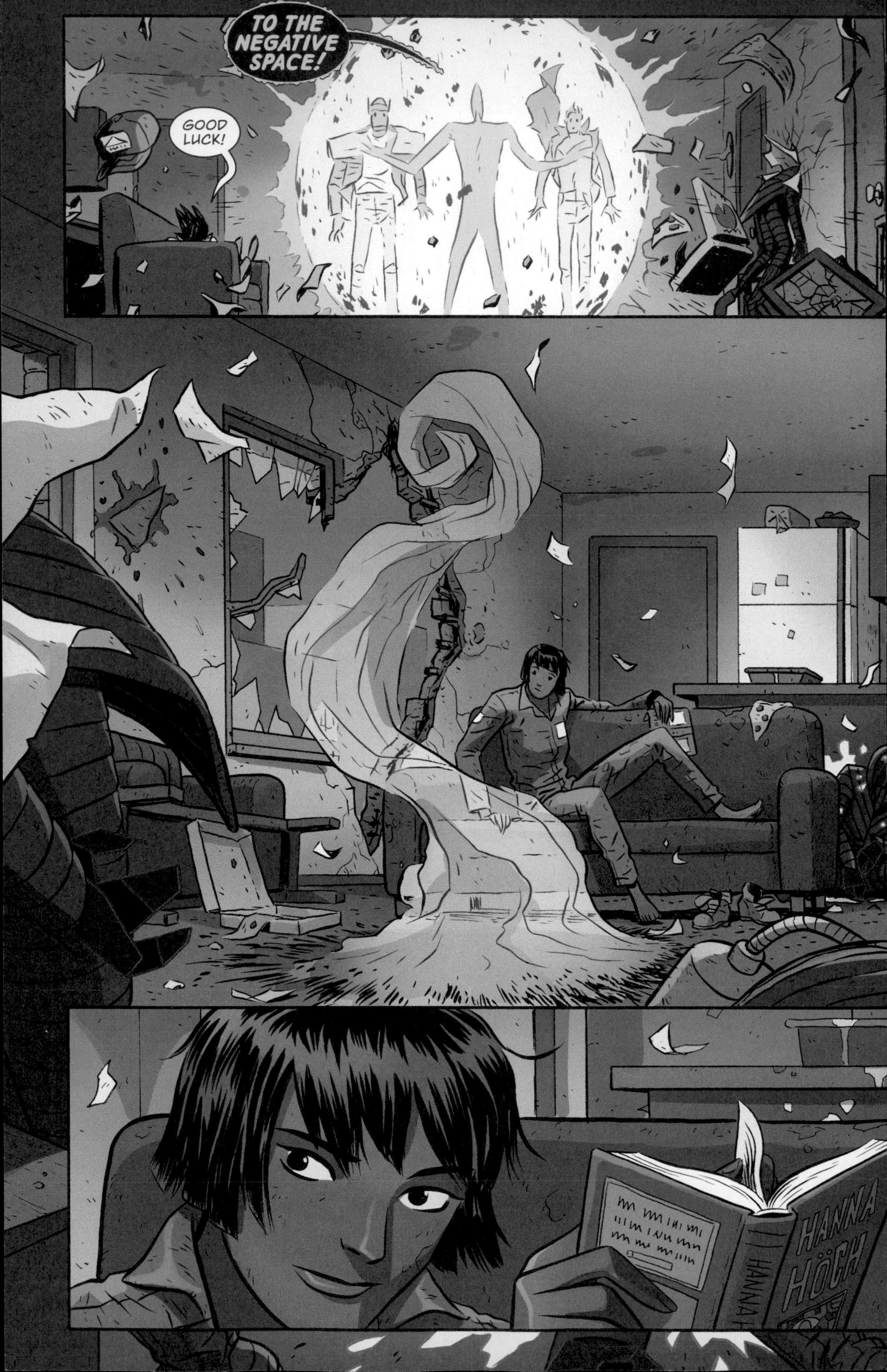
TO THE NEGATIVE SPACE!
GOOD LUCK!
HANNA HÖCH
HANNA

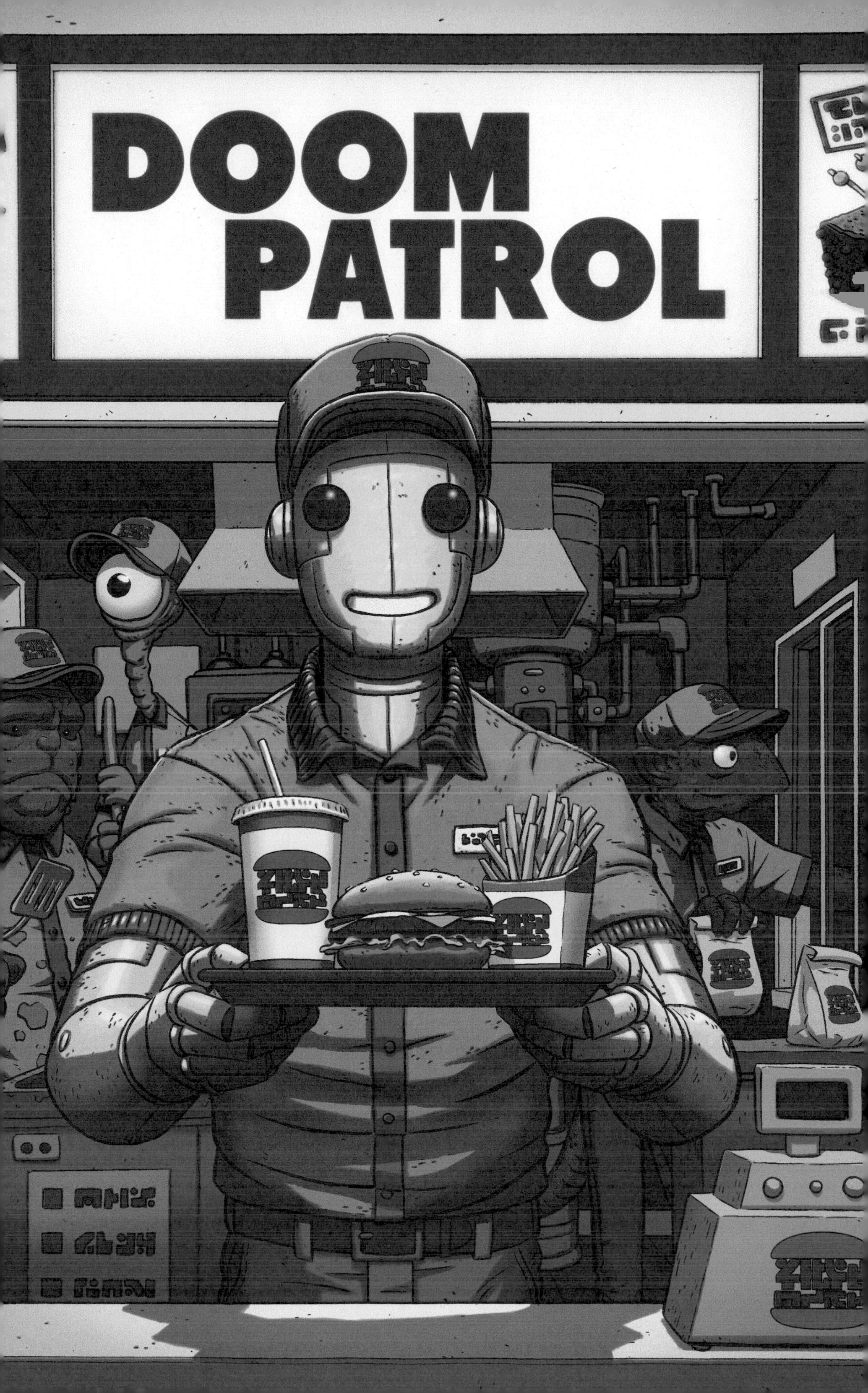
DOOM
PATROL

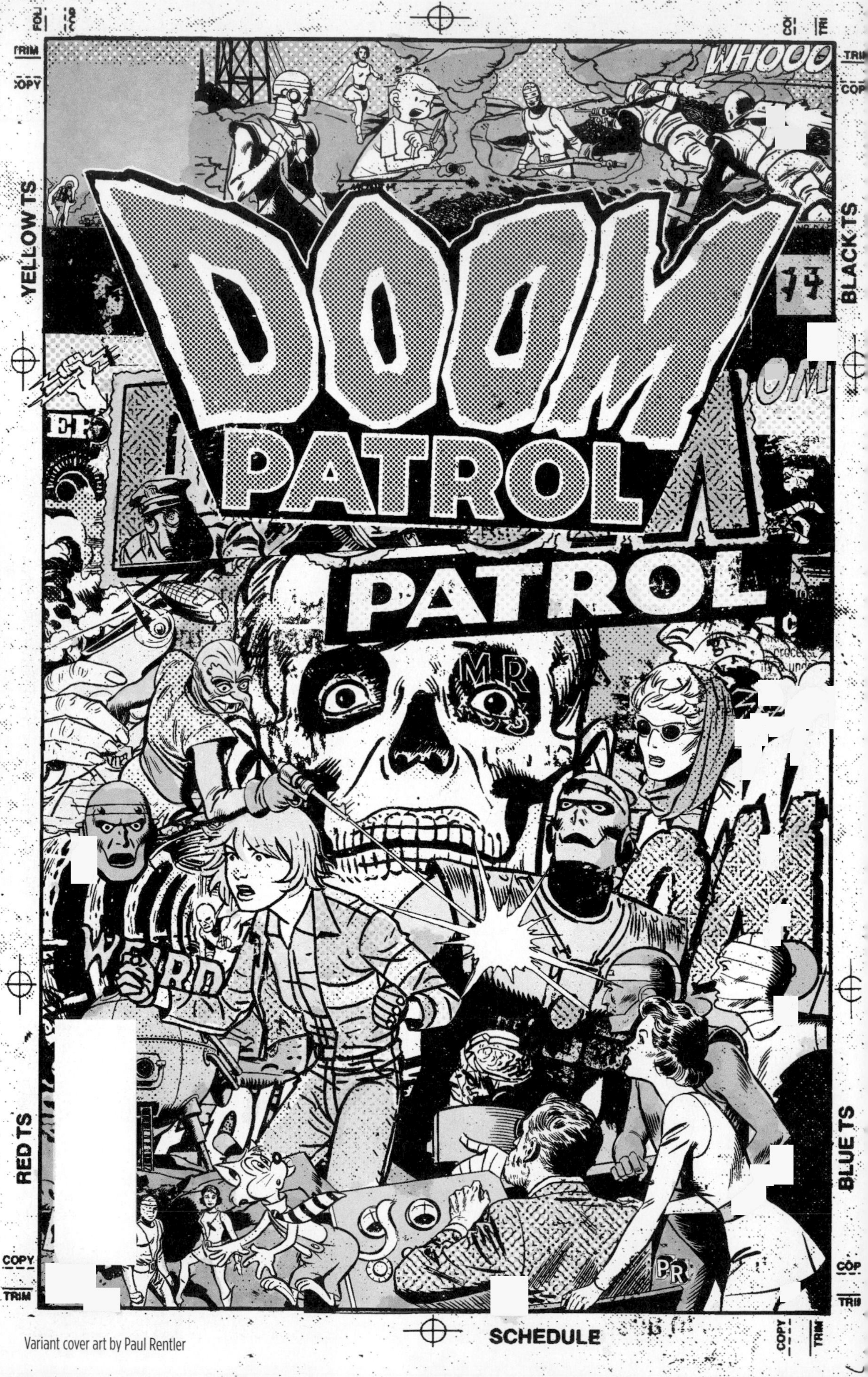
WHOOO
DOOM
PATROL
PATROL
YELLOW TS
BLACK TS
RED TS
BLUE TS
SCHEDULE

Variant cover art by Paul Rentler

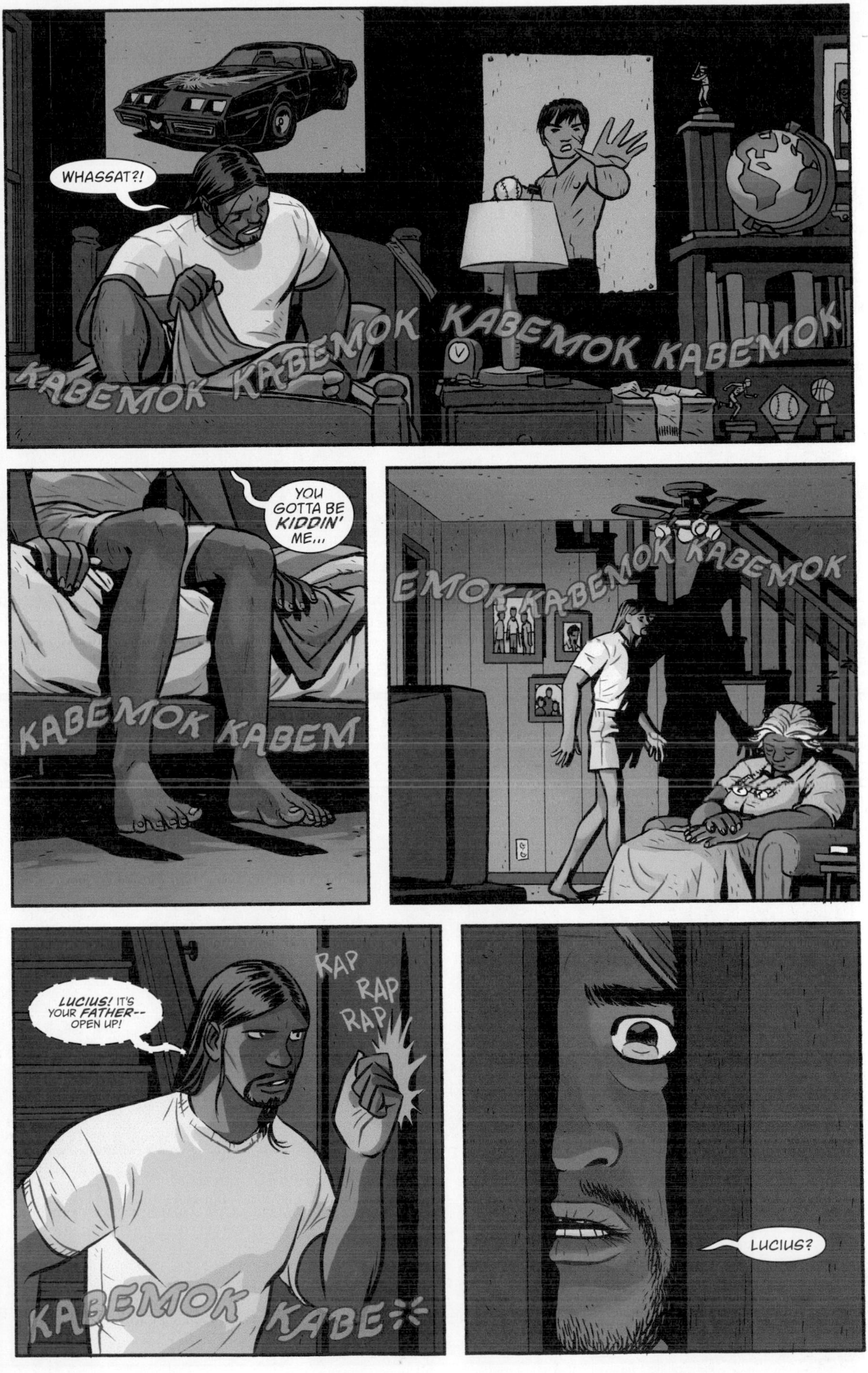
WHASSAT?!
KABEMOK KABEMOK KABEMOK KABEMOK KABEMOK
YOU GOTTA BE KIDDIN' ME...
KABEMOK KABEM
EMOK KABEMOK KABEMOK
LUCIUS! IT'S YOUR FATHER-- OPEN UP!
RAP RAP RAP
KABEMOK KABE
LUCIUS?

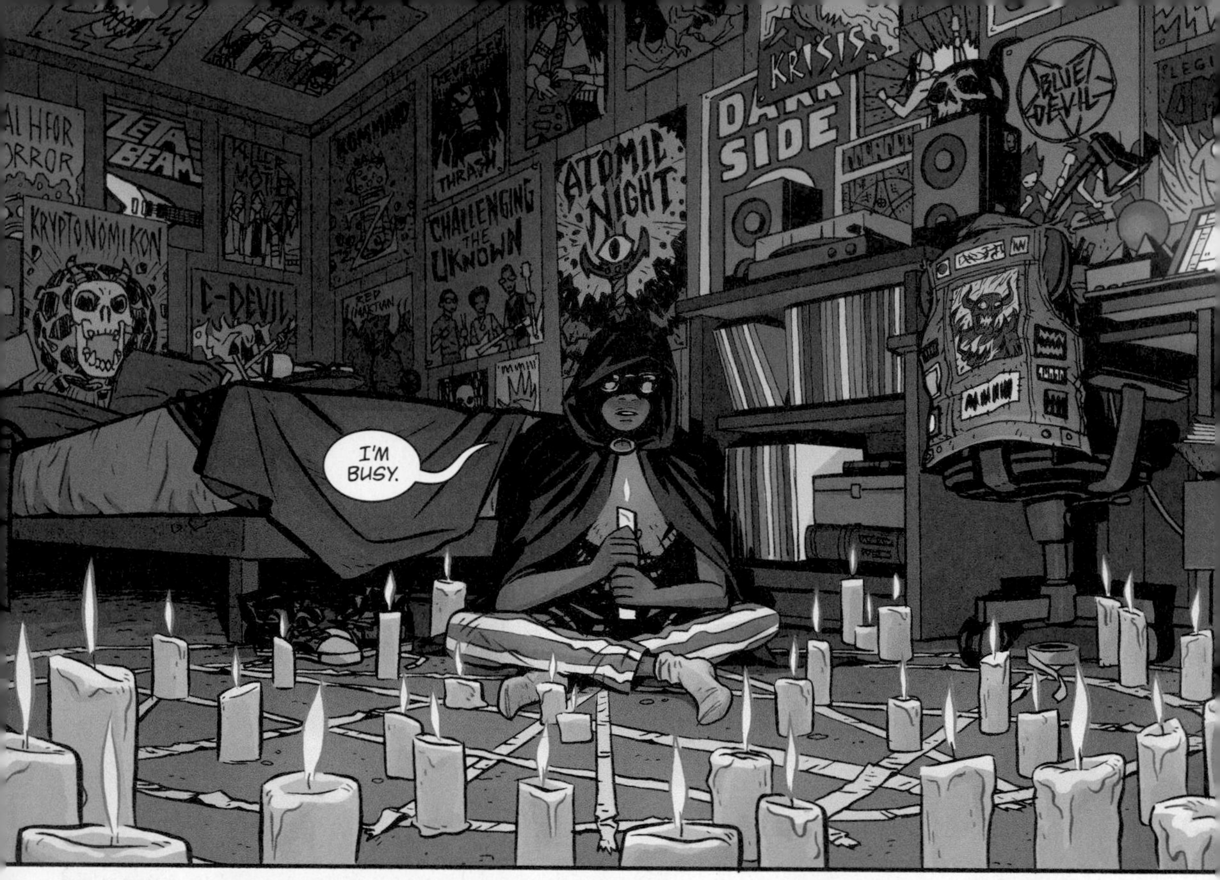
I'M BUSY.

I'M SORRY I'M LATE BRICK by BRICK Part 4

GERARD WAY writer | NICK DERINGTON artist & cover | TAMRA BONVILLAIN colorist | TODD KLEIN letterer | MOLLY MAHAN assoc. ed. | JAMIE S. RICH editor | Doom Patrol created by Arnold Drake

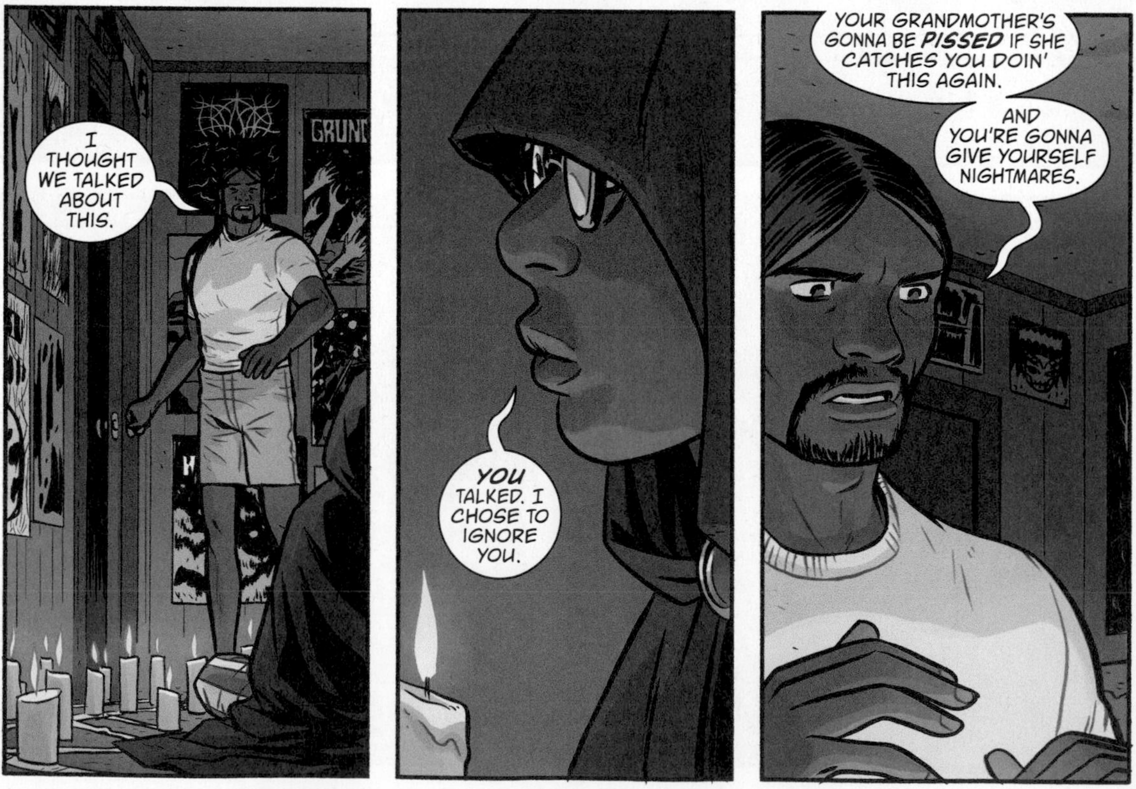
I THOUGHT WE TALKED ABOUT THIS.
YOU TALKED. I CHOSE TO IGNORE YOU.
YOUR GRANDMOTHER'S GONNA BE PISSED IF SHE CATCHES YOU DOIN' THIS AGAIN.
AND YOU'RE GONNA GIVE YOURSELF NIGHTMARES.

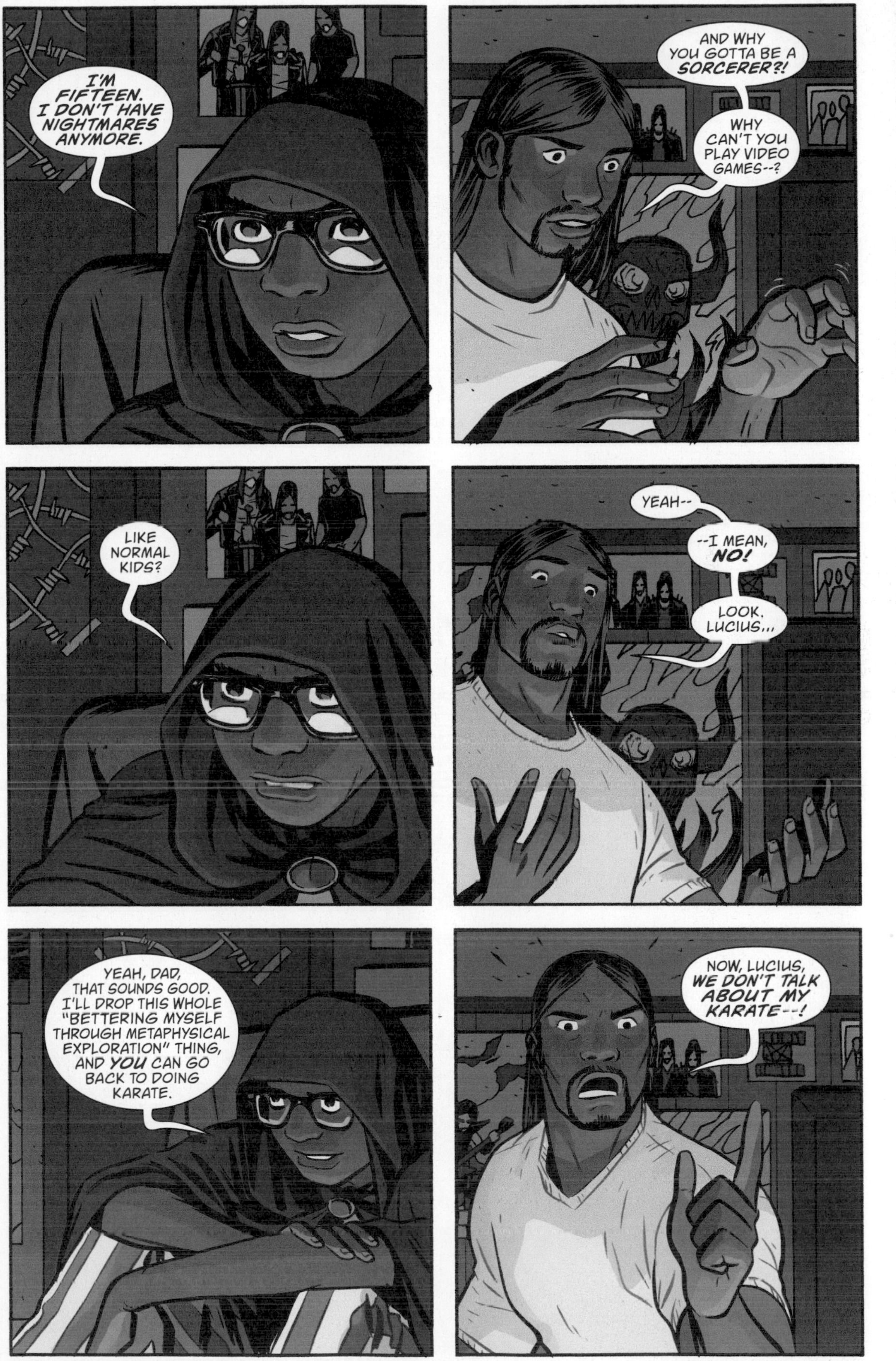
I'M FIFTEEN. I DON'T HAVE NIGHTMARES ANYMORE.
AND WHY YOU GOTTA BE A SORCERER?!
WHY CAN'T YOU PLAY VIDEO GAMES--?
LIKE NORMAL KIDS?
YEAH--
--I MEAN, NO!
LOOK. LUCIUS...
YEAH, DAD, THAT SOUNDS GOOD. I'LL DROP THIS WHOLE "BETTERING MYSELF THROUGH METAPHYSICAL EXPLORATION" THING, AND YOU CAN GO BACK TO DOING KARATE.
NOW, LUCIUS, WE DON'T TALK ABOUT MY KARATE--!

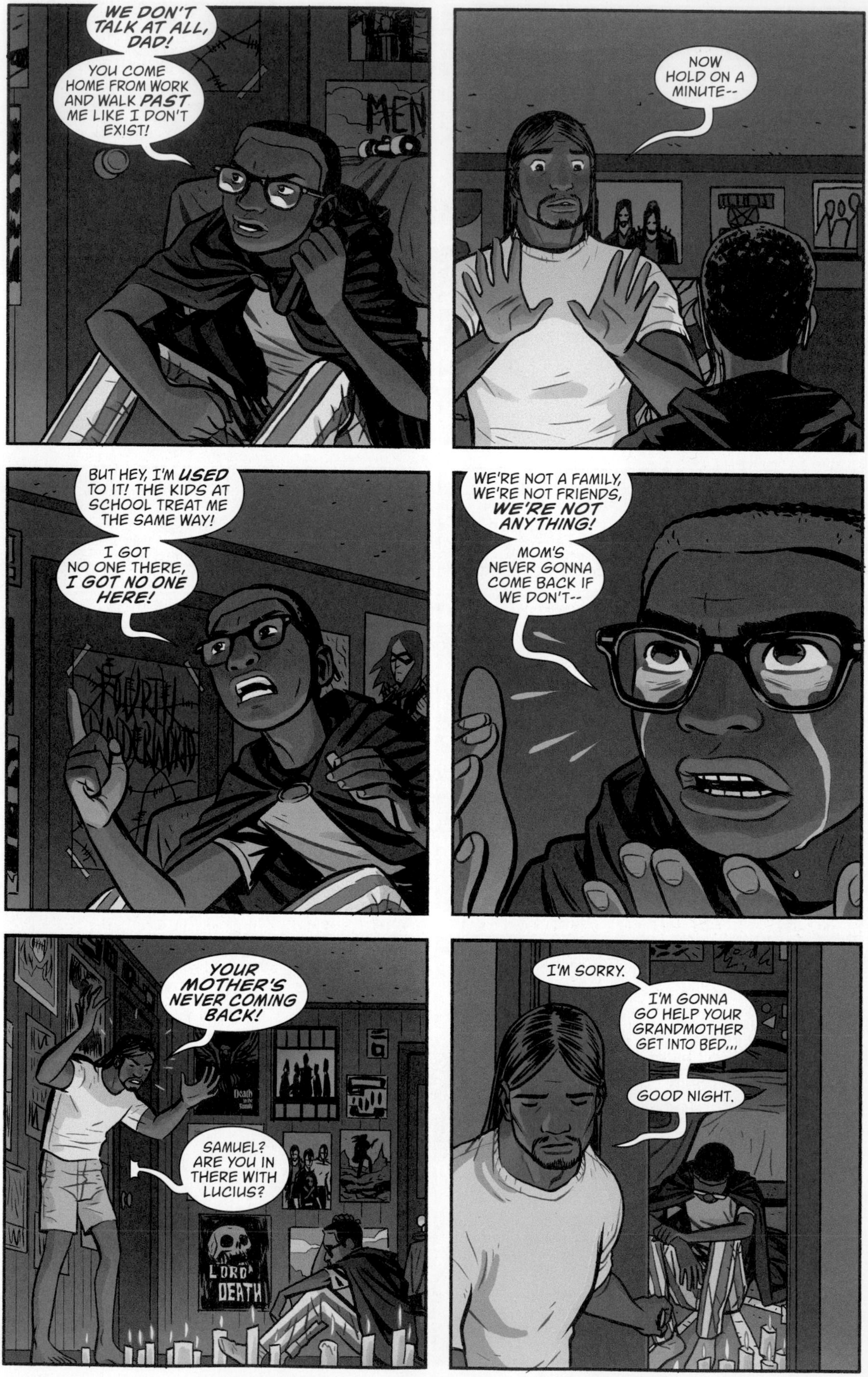
WE DON'T TALK AT ALL, DAD!
YOU COME HOME FROM WORK AND WALK PAST ME LIKE I DON'T EXIST!
NOW HOLD ON A MINUTE--
BUT HEY, I'M USED TO IT! THE KIDS AT SCHOOL TREAT ME THE SAME WAY!
I GOT NO ONE THERE, I GOT NO ONE HERE!
WE'RE NOT A FAMILY, WE'RE NOT FRIENDS, WE'RE NOT ANYTHING!
MOM'S NEVER GONNA COME BACK IF WE DON'T--
YOUR MOTHER'S NEVER COMING BACK!
SAMUEL? ARE YOU IN THERE WITH LUCIUS?
LORD DEATH
I'M SORRY.
I'M GONNA GO HELP YOUR GRANDMOTHER GET INTO BED...
GOOD NIGHT.

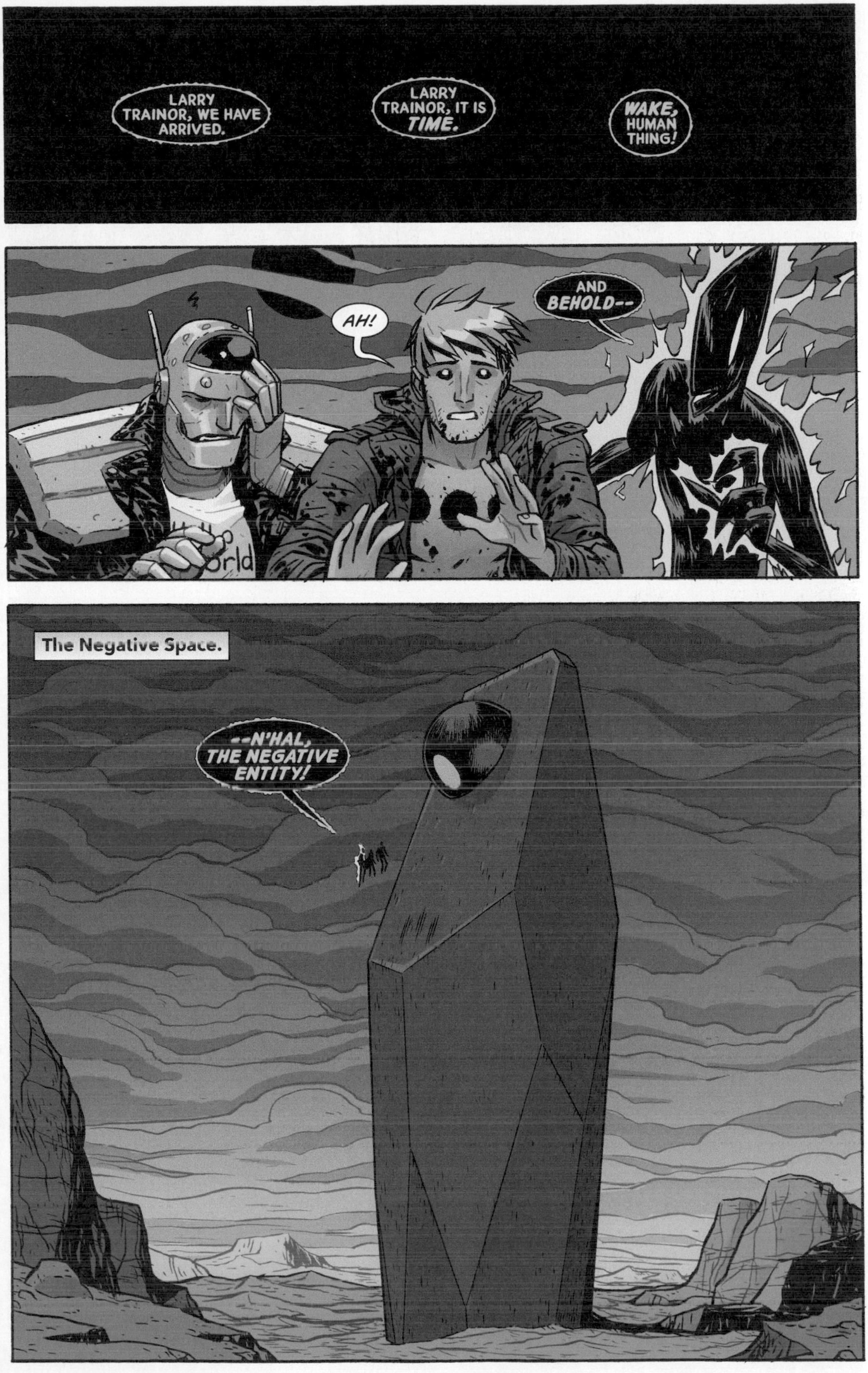
LARRY TRAINOR, WE HAVE ARRIVED.
LARRY TRAINOR, IT IS TIME.
WAKE, HUMAN THING!
AH!
AND BEHOLD--
The Negative Space.
--N'HAL, THE NEGATIVE ENTITY!

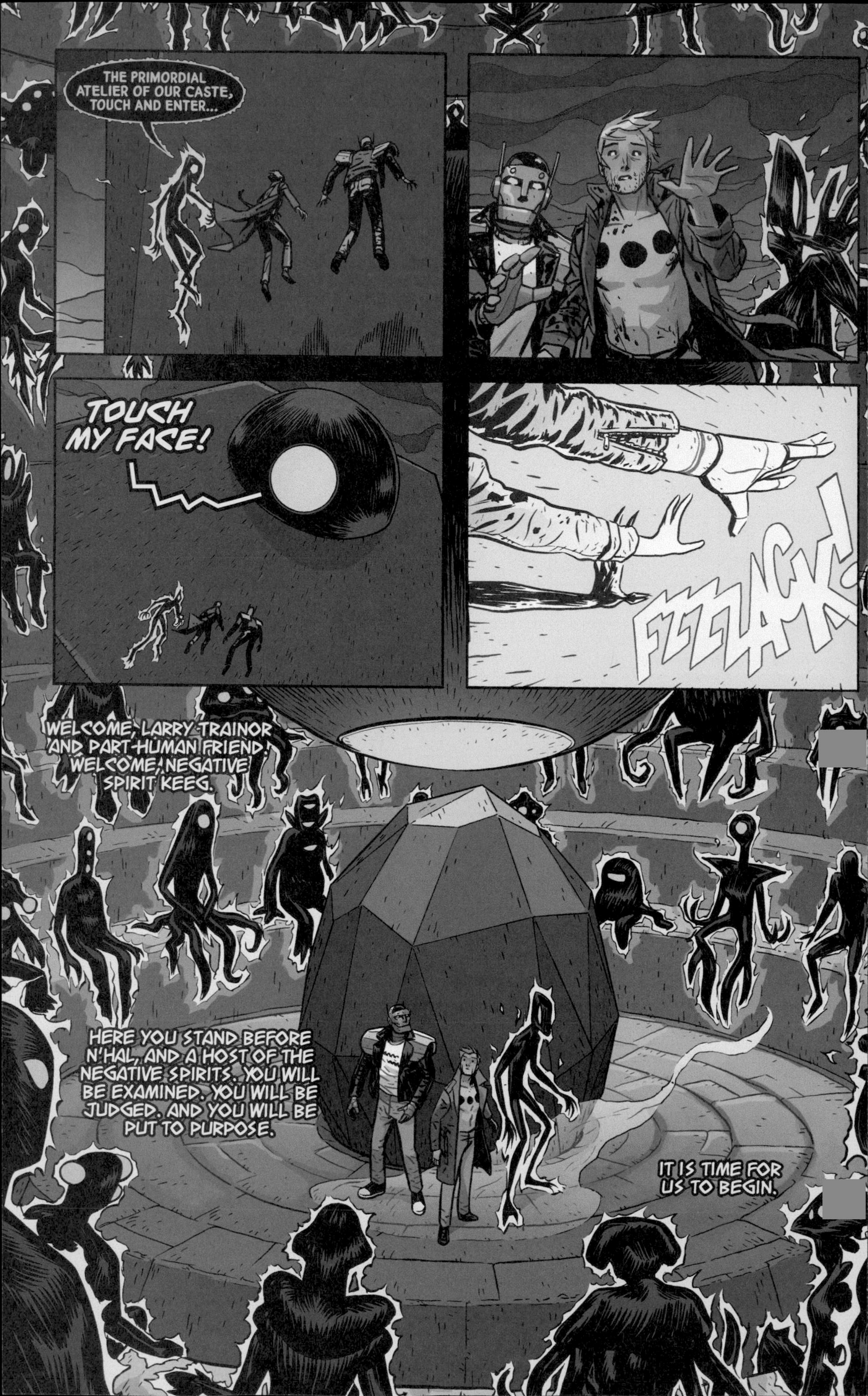
THE PRIMORDIAL ATELIER OF OUR CASTE, TOUCH AND ENTER...
TOUCH MY FACE!
FZZZACK!
WELCOME, LARRY TRAINOR AND PART-HUMAN FRIEND. WELCOME, NEGATIVE SPIRIT KEEG.
HERE YOU STAND BEFORE N'HAL, AND A HOST OF THE NEGATIVE SPIRITS. YOU WILL BE EXAMINED. YOU WILL BE JUDGED. AND YOU WILL BE PUT TO PURPOSE.
IT IS TIME FOR US TO BEGIN.

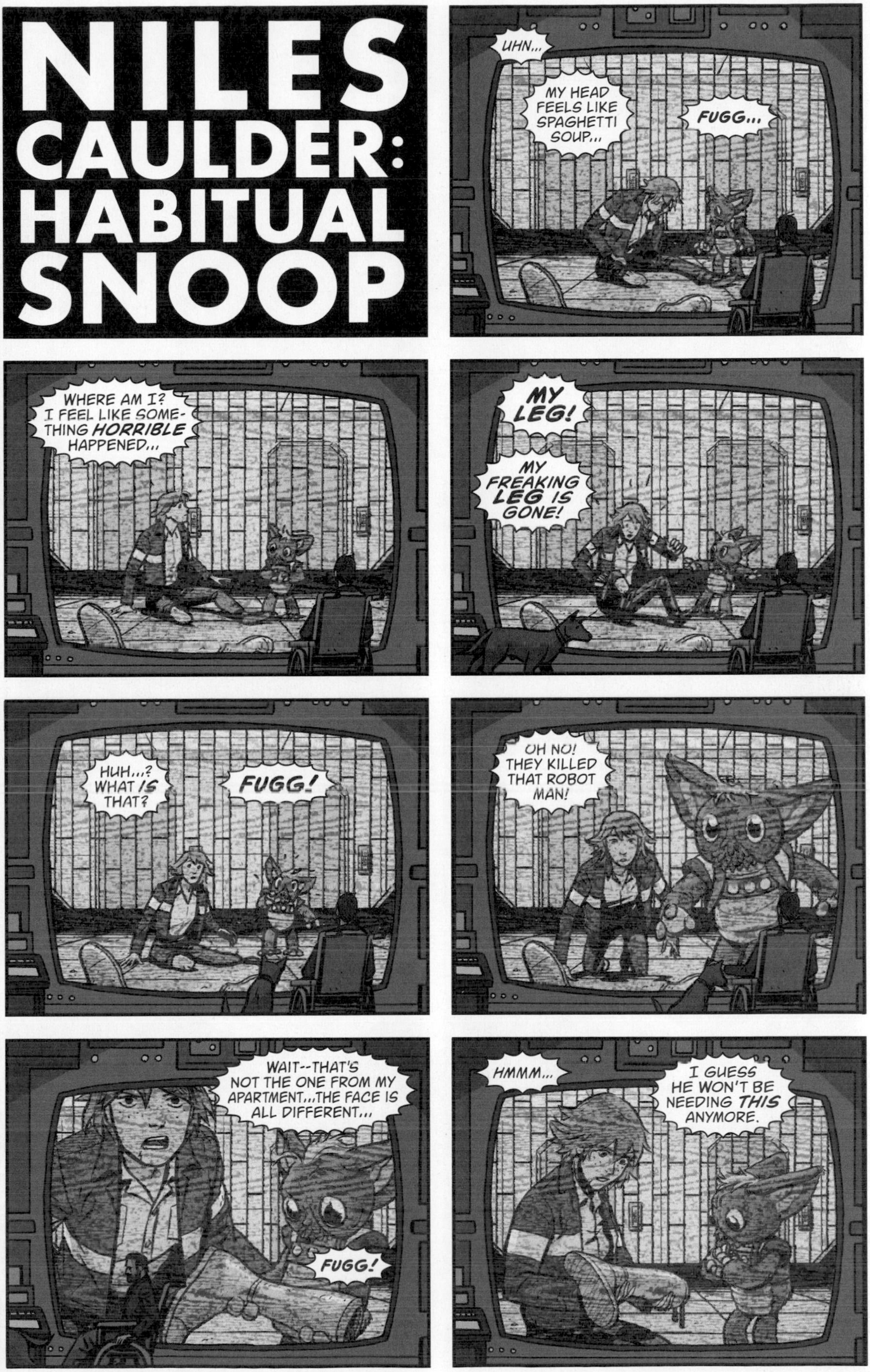
NILES CAULDER: HABITUAL SNOOP
UHN...
MY HEAD FEELS LIKE SPAGHETTI SOUP...
FUGG...
WHERE AM I? I FEEL LIKE SOME-THING HORRIBLE HAPPENED...
MY LEG!
MY FREAKING LEG IS GONE!
HUH...? WHAT IS THAT?
FUGG!
OH NO! THEY KILLED THAT ROBOT MAN!
WAIT--THAT'S NOT THE ONE FROM MY APARTMENT...THE FACE IS ALL DIFFERENT...
FUGG!
HMMM...
I GUESS HE WON'T BE NEEDING THIS ANYMORE.

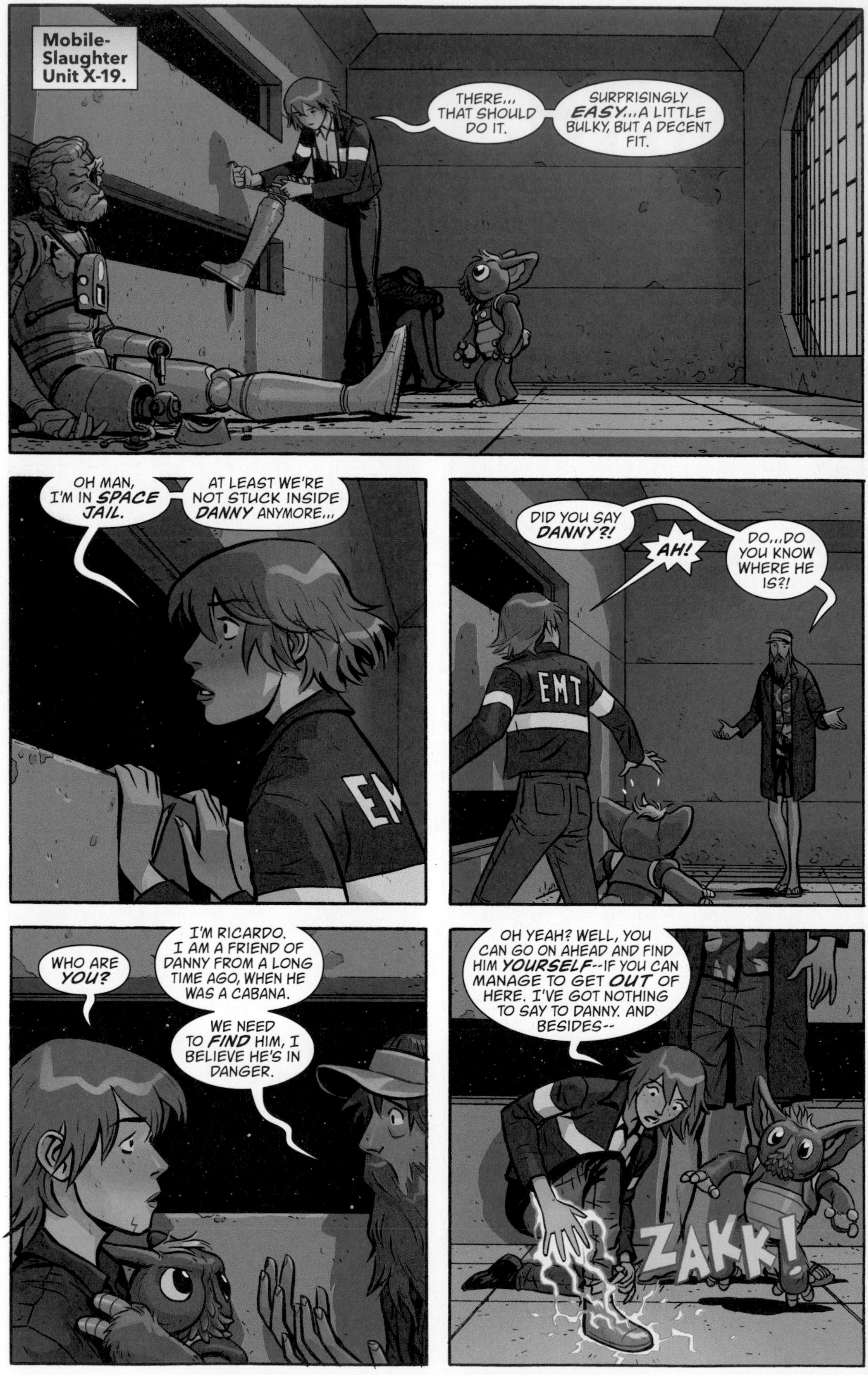
Mobile-Slaughter Unit X-19.
THERE... THAT SHOULD DO IT.
SURPRISINGLY EASY...A LITTLE BULKY, BUT A DECENT FIT.
OH MAN, I'M IN SPACE JAIL.
AT LEAST WE'RE NOT STUCK INSIDE DANNY ANYMORE...
DID YOU SAY DANNY?!
AH!
DO...DO YOU KNOW WHERE HE IS?!
EMT
WHO ARE YOU?
I'M RICARDO. I AM A FRIEND OF DANNY FROM A LONG TIME AGO, WHEN HE WAS A CABANA.
WE NEED TO FIND HIM, I BELIEVE HE'S IN DANGER.
OH YEAH? WELL, YOU CAN GO ON AHEAD AND FIND HIM YOURSELF--IF YOU CAN MANAGE TO GET OUT OF HERE. I'VE GOT NOTHING TO SAY TO DANNY. AND BESIDES--
ZAKK!

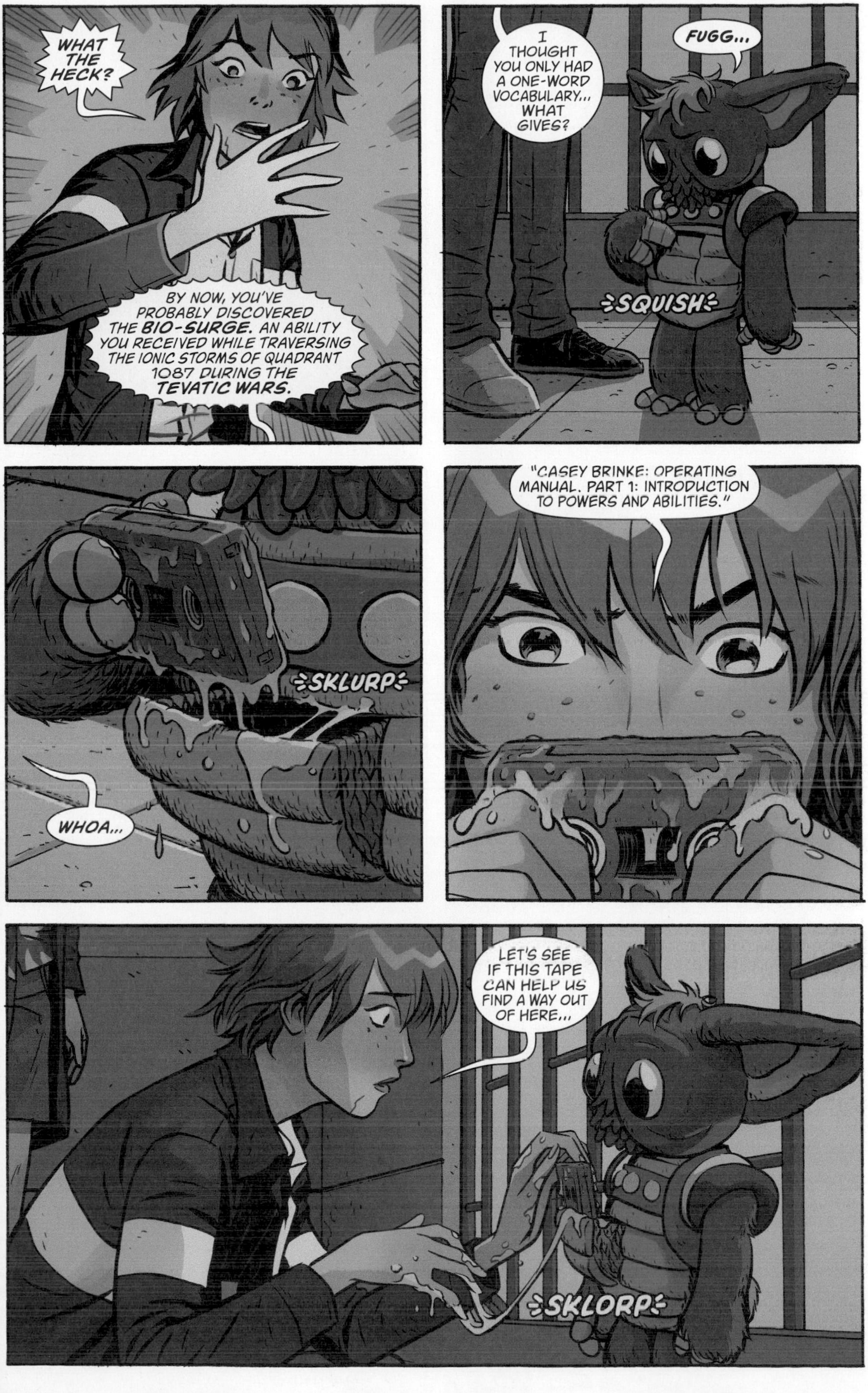
WHAT THE HECK?
BY NOW, YOU'VE PROBABLY DISCOVERED THE BIO-SURGE. AN ABILITY YOU RECEIVED WHILE TRAVERSING THE IONIC STORMS OF QUADRANT 1087 DURING THE TEVATIC WARS.
I THOUGHT YOU ONLY HAD A ONE-WORD VOCABULARY... WHAT GIVES?
FUGG...
SQUISH
SKLURP
WHOA...
"CASEY BRINKE: OPERATING MANUAL. PART 1: INTRODUCTION TO POWERS AND ABILITIES."
LET'S SEE IF THIS TAPE CAN HELP US FIND A WAY OUT OF HERE...
SKLORP

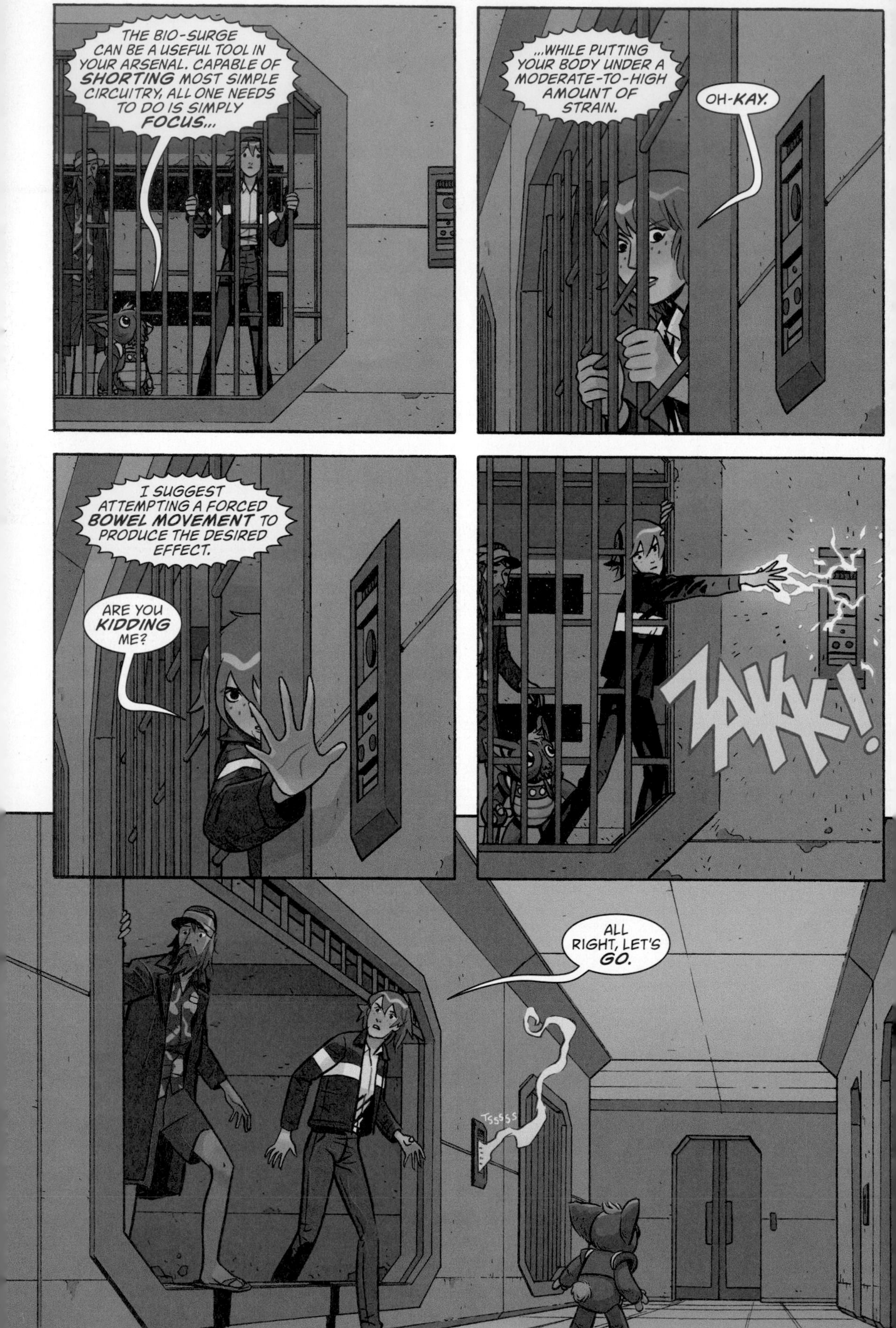
THE BIO-SURGE CAN BE A USEFUL TOOL IN YOUR ARSENAL. CAPABLE OF SHORTING MOST SIMPLE CIRCUITRY, ALL ONE NEEDS TO DO IS SIMPLY FOCUS...
...WHILE PUTTING YOUR BODY UNDER A MODERATE-TO-HIGH AMOUNT OF STRAIN.
OH-KAY.
I SUGGEST ATTEMPTING A FORCED BOWEL MOVEMENT TO PRODUCE THE DESIRED EFFECT.
ARE YOU KIDDING ME?
ZAKK!
ALL RIGHT, LET'S GO.
TSSSSS

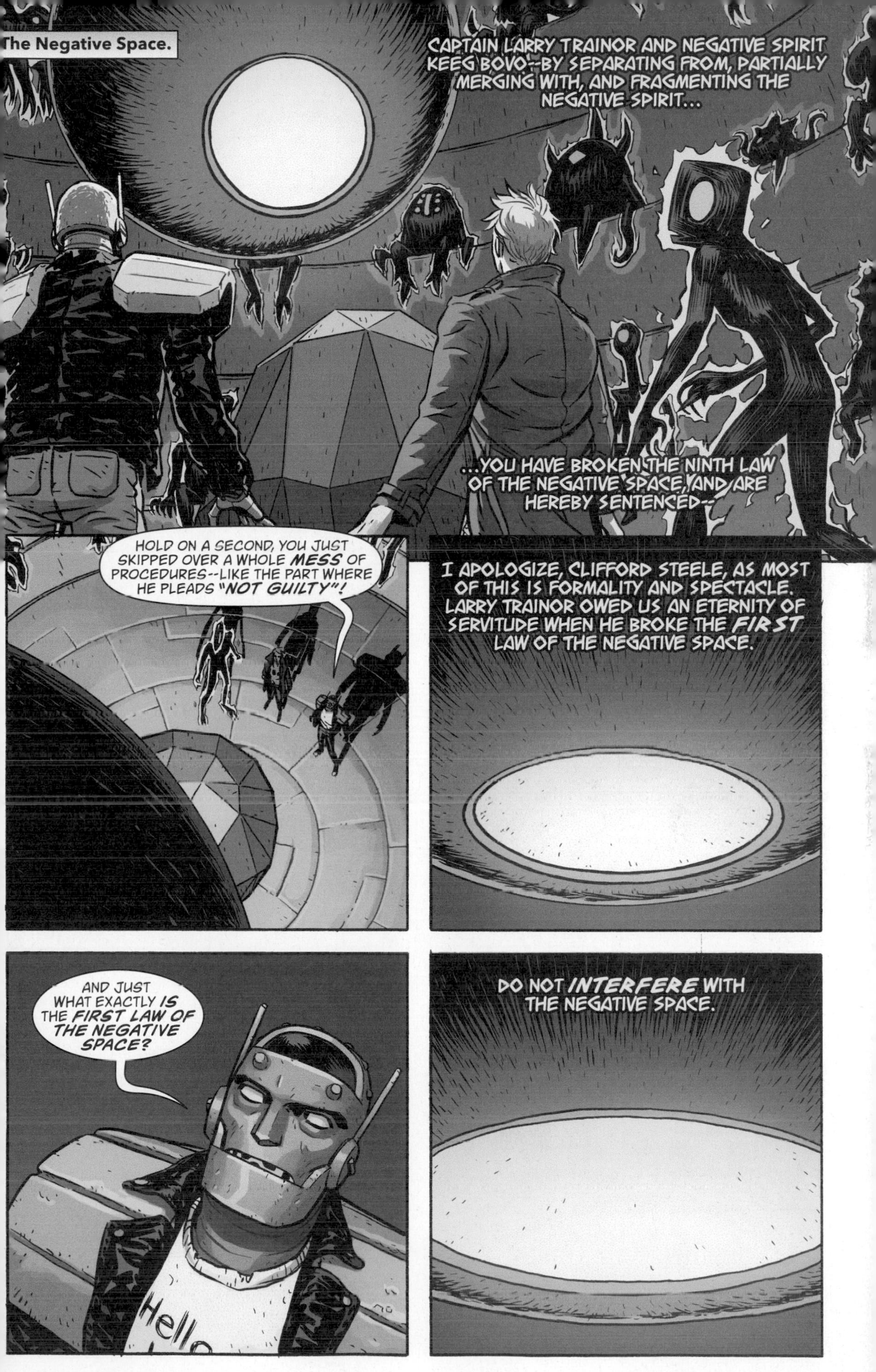
The Negative Space.
CAPTAIN LARRY TRAINOR AND NEGATIVE SPIRIT KEEG BOVO--BY SEPARATING FROM, PARTIALLY MERGING WITH, AND FRAGMENTING THE NEGATIVE SPIRIT...
...YOU HAVE BROKEN THE NINTH LAW OF THE NEGATIVE SPACE, AND ARE HEREBY SENTENCED--
HOLD ON A SECOND, YOU JUST SKIPPED OVER A WHOLE MESS OF PROCEDURES--LIKE THE PART WHERE HE PLEADS "NOT GUILTY"!
I APOLOGIZE, CLIFFORD STEELE, AS MOST OF THIS IS FORMALITY AND SPECTACLE. LARRY TRAINOR OWED US AN ETERNITY OF SERVITUDE WHEN HE BROKE THE FIRST LAW OF THE NEGATIVE SPACE.
AND JUST WHAT EXACTLY IS THE FIRST LAW OF THE NEGATIVE SPACE?
DO NOT INTERFERE WITH THE NEGATIVE SPACE.

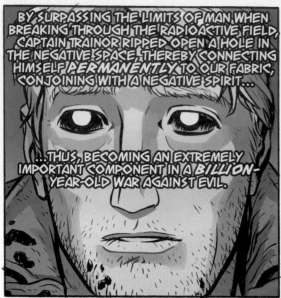

BY SURPASSING THE LIMITS OF MAN WHEN BREAKING THROUGH THE RADIOACTIVE FIELD, CAPTAIN TRAINOR RIPPED OPEN A HOLE IN THE NEGATIVE SPACE, THEREBY CONNECTING HIMSELF *PERMANENTLY* TO OUR FABRIC, CONJOINING WITH A NEGATIVE SPIRIT...

...THUS, BECOMING AN EXTREMELY IMPORTANT COMPONENT IN A *BILLION-YEAR-OLD* WAR AGAINST EVIL.

LARRY TRAINOR IS MUCH MORE THAN A VESSEL. HE GUIDES THE NEGATIVE SPIRIT TO ACT AS AN AGENT OF BALANCE. WE WANT HIM TO REMAIN SO.

AND WHAT ABOUT WHAT *LARRY* WANTS--?!

MAYBE HE DOESN'T WANT TO BE HOST TO A RADIOACTIVE SPACE PHANTOM AND AN ALIEN, NO OFFENSE, AND MAYBE HE DOESN'T CARE ABOUT YOUR "BALANCE" AND WANTS TO LIVE A NORMAL *LIFE* WATCHING HOCKEY AND GOING TO WORK FLYING SUPER-FAST *JETS*.

CLIFF, IT'S OKAY, I--

WELL...WE HADN'T CONSIDERED THAT. WHAT *DOES* LARRY WANT?

HAVE YOU GIVEN THIS MUCH THOUGHT, CAPTAIN TRAINOR?

DO YOU WANT TO BE "NORMAL"?

I...

...I WANT TO BE *REJOINED* WITH THE NEGATIVE SPIRIT.

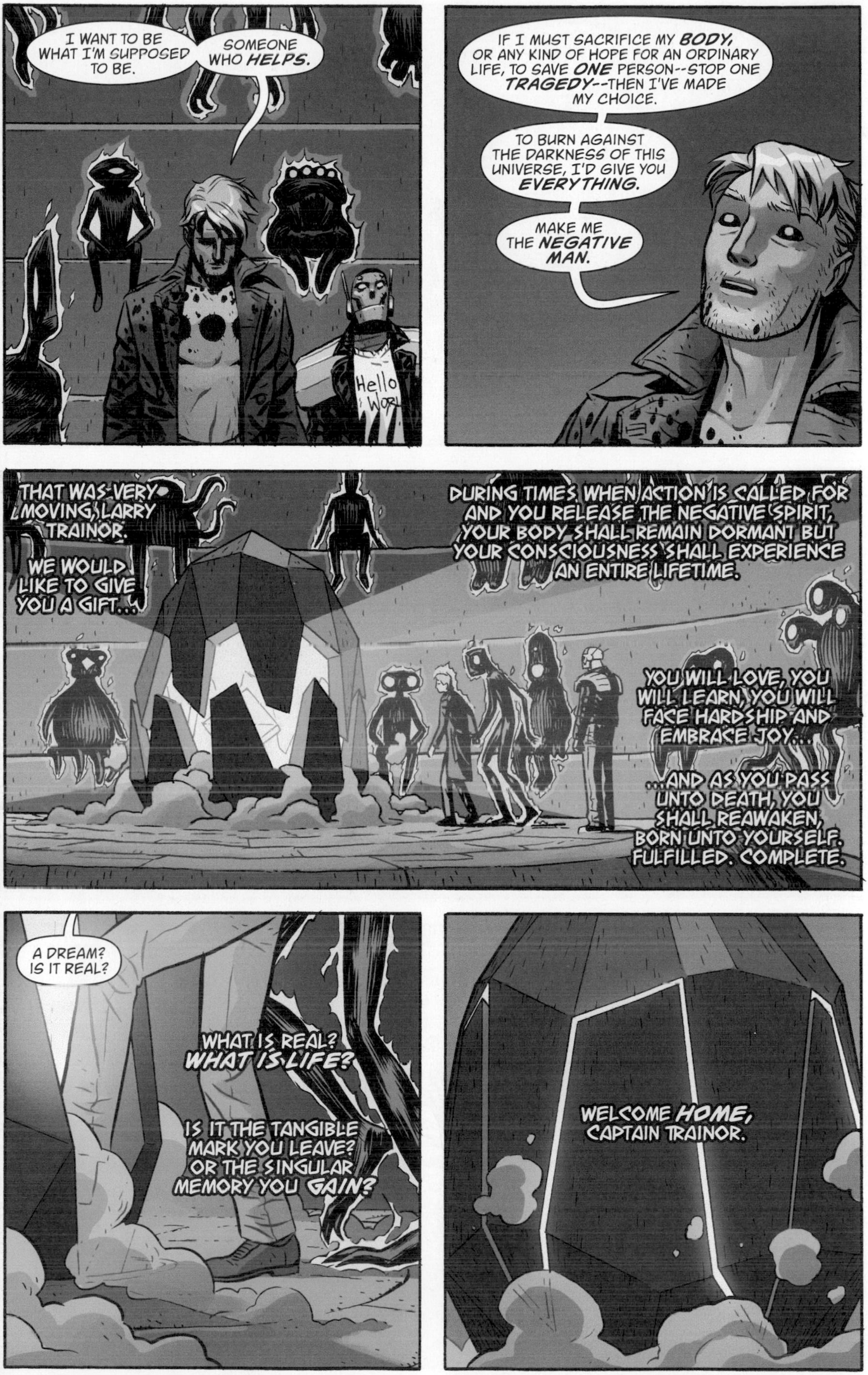
I WANT TO BE WHAT I'M SUPPOSED TO BE.
SOMEONE WHO HELPS.
Hello WORL
IF I MUST SACRIFICE MY BODY, OR ANY KIND OF HOPE FOR AN ORDINARY LIFE, TO SAVE ONE PERSON--STOP ONE TRAGEDY--THEN I'VE MADE MY CHOICE.
TO BURN AGAINST THE DARKNESS OF THIS UNIVERSE, I'D GIVE YOU EVERYTHING.
MAKE ME THE NEGATIVE MAN.
THAT WAS VERY MOVING, LARRY TRAINOR.
WE WOULD LIKE TO GIVE YOU A GIFT...
DURING TIMES WHEN ACTION IS CALLED FOR AND YOU RELEASE THE NEGATIVE SPIRIT, YOUR BODY SHALL REMAIN DORMANT BUT YOUR CONSCIOUSNESS SHALL EXPERIENCE AN ENTIRE LIFETIME.
YOU WILL LOVE, YOU WILL LEARN, YOU WILL FACE HARDSHIP AND EMBRACE JOY...
...AND AS YOU PASS UNTO DEATH, YOU SHALL REAWAKEN, BORN UNTO YOURSELF. FULFILLED. COMPLETE.
A DREAM? IS IT REAL?
WHAT IS REAL? WHAT IS LIFE?
IS IT THE TANGIBLE MARK YOU LEAVE? OR THE SINGULAR MEMORY YOU GAIN?
WELCOME HOME, CAPTAIN TRAINOR.

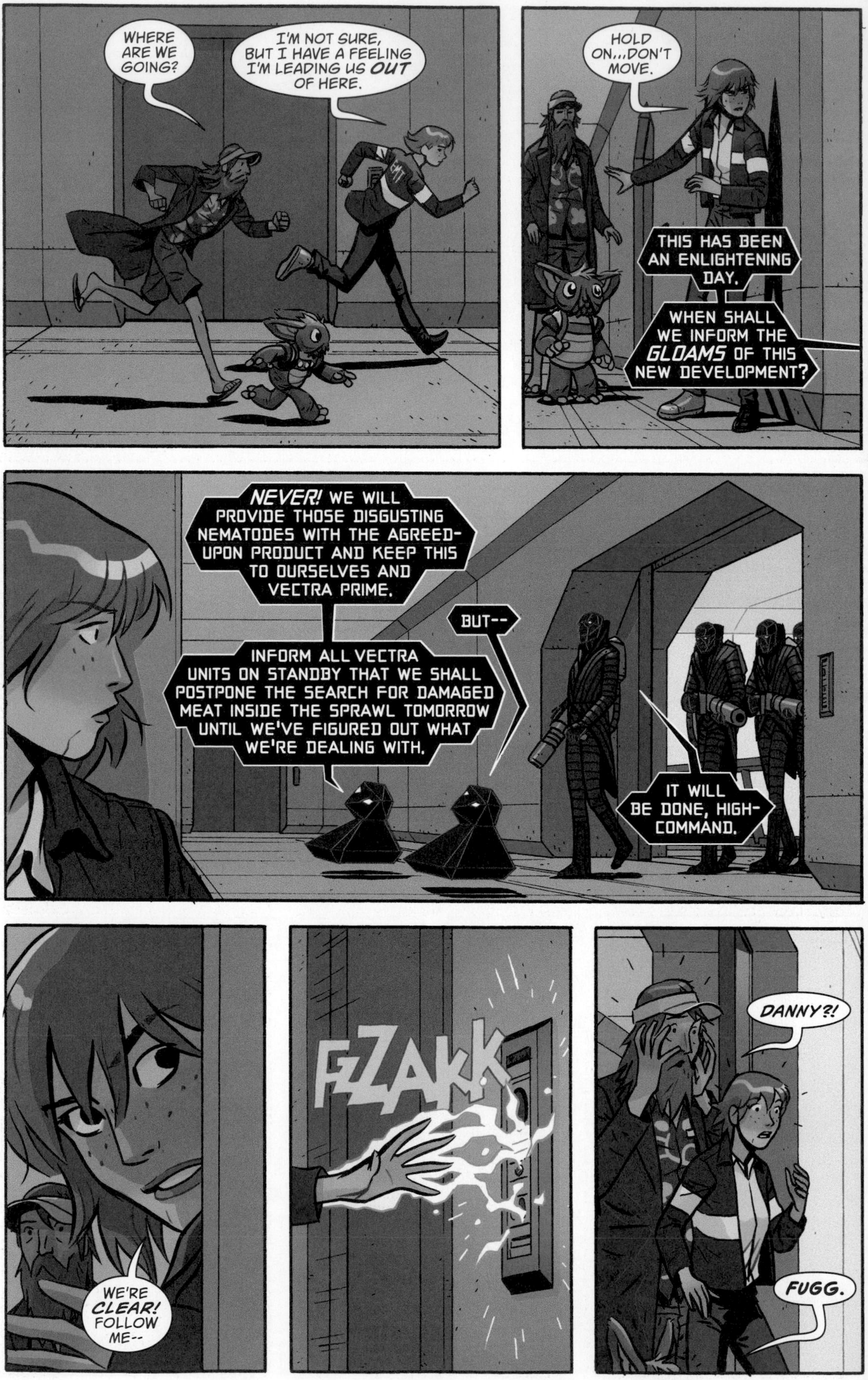
WHERE ARE WE GOING?
I'M NOT SURE, BUT I HAVE A FEELING I'M LEADING US OUT OF HERE.
HOLD ON...DON'T MOVE.
THIS HAS BEEN AN ENLIGHTENING DAY.
WHEN SHALL WE INFORM THE GLOAMS OF THIS NEW DEVELOPMENT?
NEVER! WE WILL PROVIDE THOSE DISGUSTING NEMATODES WITH THE AGREED-UPON PRODUCT AND KEEP THIS TO OURSELVES AND VECTRA PRIME.
INFORM ALL VECTRA UNITS ON STANDBY THAT WE SHALL POSTPONE THE SEARCH FOR DAMAGED MEAT INSIDE THE SPRAWL TOMORROW UNTIL WE'VE FIGURED OUT WHAT WE'RE DEALING WITH.
BUT--
IT WILL BE DONE, HIGH-COMMAND.
WE'RE CLEAR! FOLLOW ME--
FZZAKK
DANNY?!
FUGG.

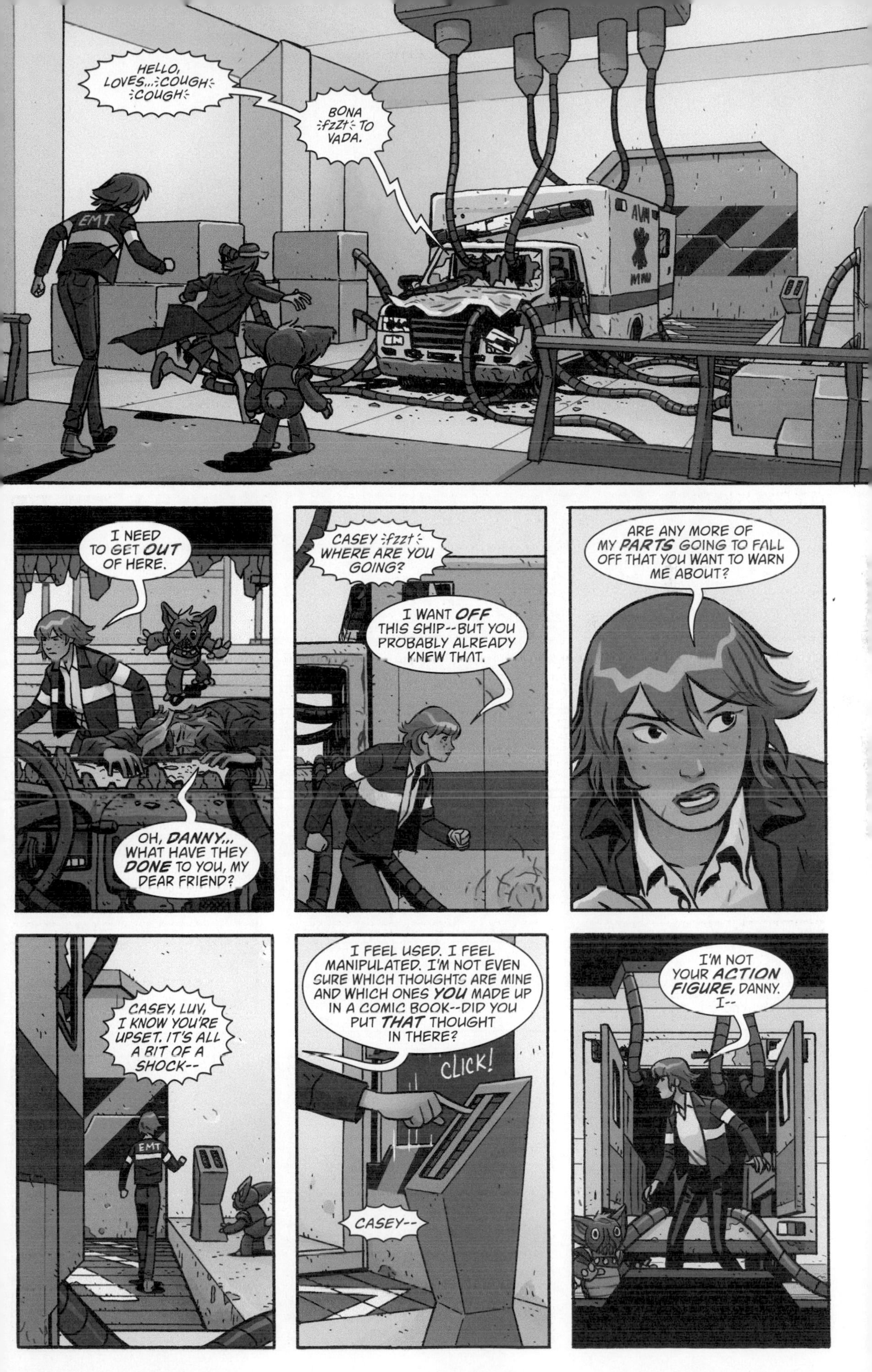
HELLO, LOVES... COUGH COUGH
BONA fzZt TO VADA.
I NEED TO GET OUT OF HERE.
OH, DANNY... WHAT HAVE THEY DONE TO YOU, MY DEAR FRIEND?
CASEY fzzt WHERE ARE YOU GOING?
I WANT OFF THIS SHIP--BUT YOU PROBABLY ALREADY KNEW THAT.
ARE ANY MORE OF MY PARTS GOING TO FALL OFF THAT YOU WANT TO WARN ME ABOUT?
CASEY, LUV, I KNOW YOU'RE UPSET. IT'S ALL A BIT OF A SHOCK--
I FEEL USED. I FEEL MANIPULATED. I'M NOT EVEN SURE WHICH THOUGHTS ARE MINE AND WHICH ONES YOU MADE UP IN A COMIC BOOK--DID YOU PUT THAT THOUGHT IN THERE?
CLICK!
CASEY--
I'M NOT YOUR ACTION FIGURE, DANNY. I--

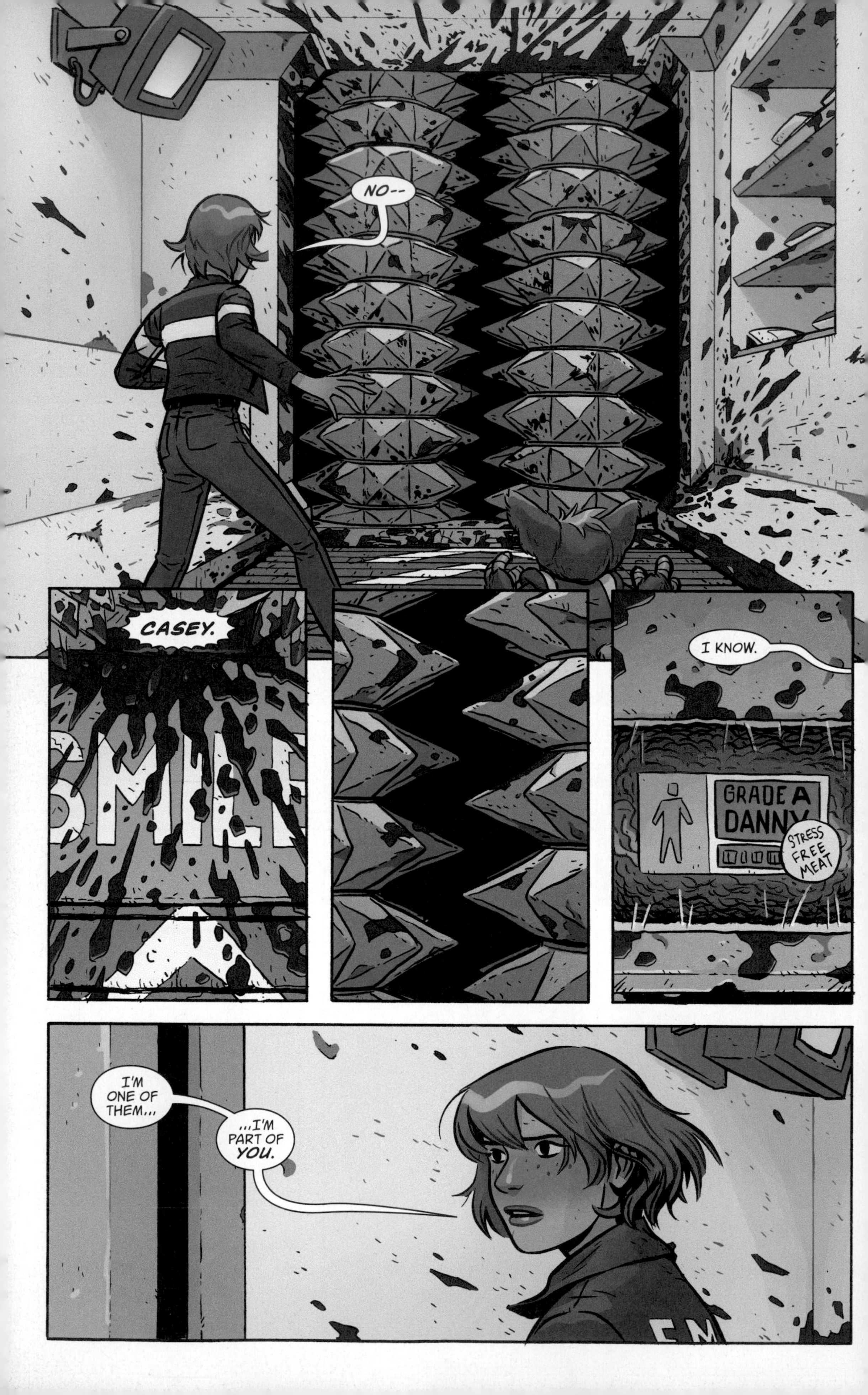
NO--
CASEY.
I KNOW.
GRADE A DANNY
STRESS FREE MEAT
I'M ONE OF THEM...
...I'M PART OF YOU.

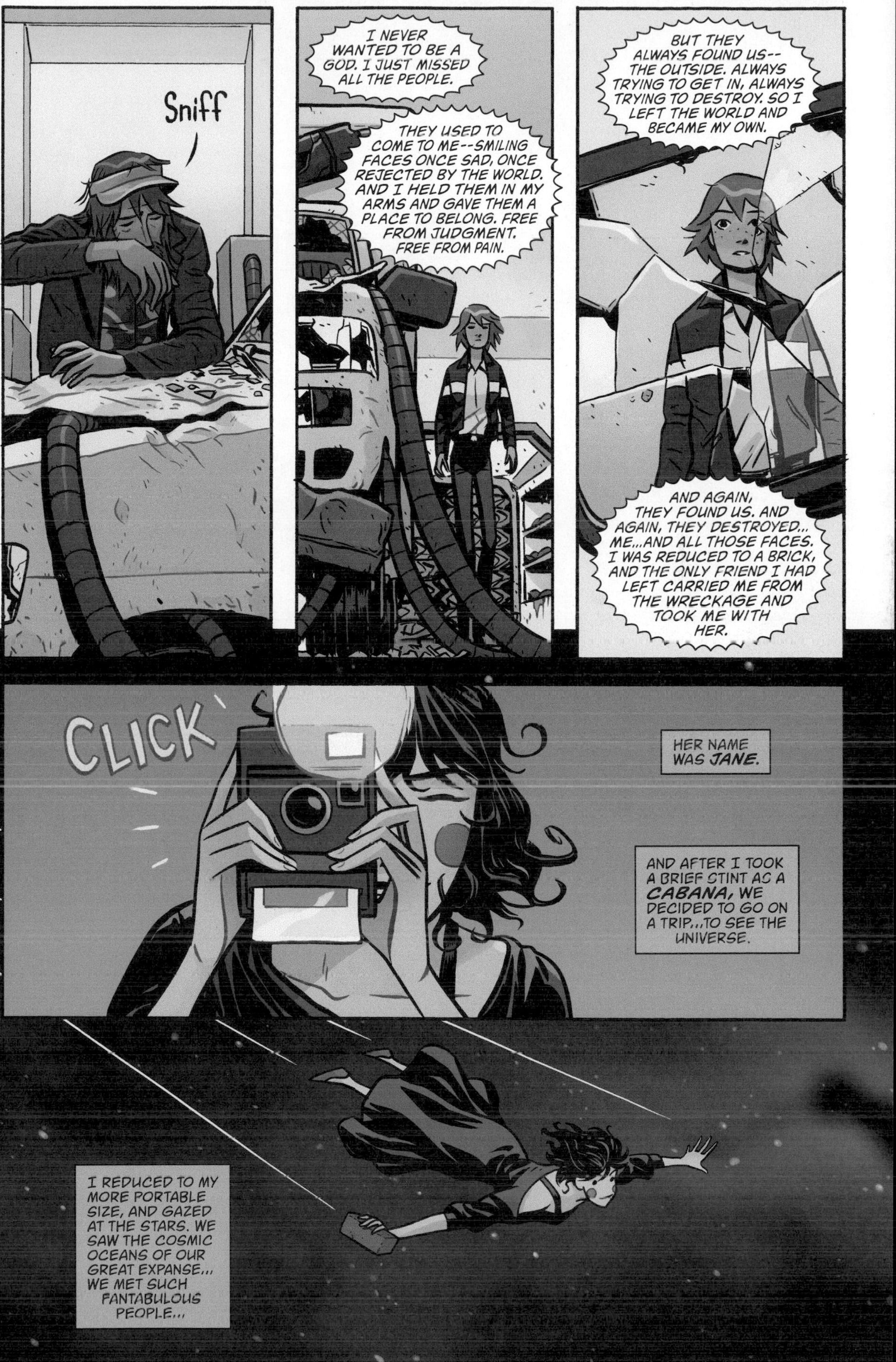
Sniff
I NEVER WANTED TO BE A GOD. I JUST MISSED ALL THE PEOPLE.
THEY USED TO COME TO ME--SMILING FACES ONCE SAD, ONCE REJECTED BY THE WORLD. AND I HELD THEM IN MY ARMS AND GAVE THEM A PLACE TO BELONG. FREE FROM JUDGMENT. FREE FROM PAIN.
BUT THEY ALWAYS FOUND US-- THE OUTSIDE. ALWAYS TRYING TO GET IN, ALWAYS TRYING TO DESTROY. SO I LEFT THE WORLD AND BECAME MY OWN.
AND AGAIN, THEY FOUND US. AND AGAIN, THEY DESTROYED... ME...AND ALL THOSE FACES. I WAS REDUCED TO A BRICK, AND THE ONLY FRIEND I HAD LEFT CARRIED ME FROM THE WRECKAGE AND TOOK ME WITH HER.
CLICK
HER NAME WAS JANE.
AND AFTER I TOOK A BRIEF STINT AS A CABANA, WE DECIDED TO GO ON A TRIP...TO SEE THE UNIVERSE.
I REDUCED TO MY MORE PORTABLE SIZE, AND GAZED AT THE STARS. WE SAW THE COSMIC OCEANS OF OUR GREAT EXPANSE... WE MET SUCH FANTABULOUS PEOPLE...

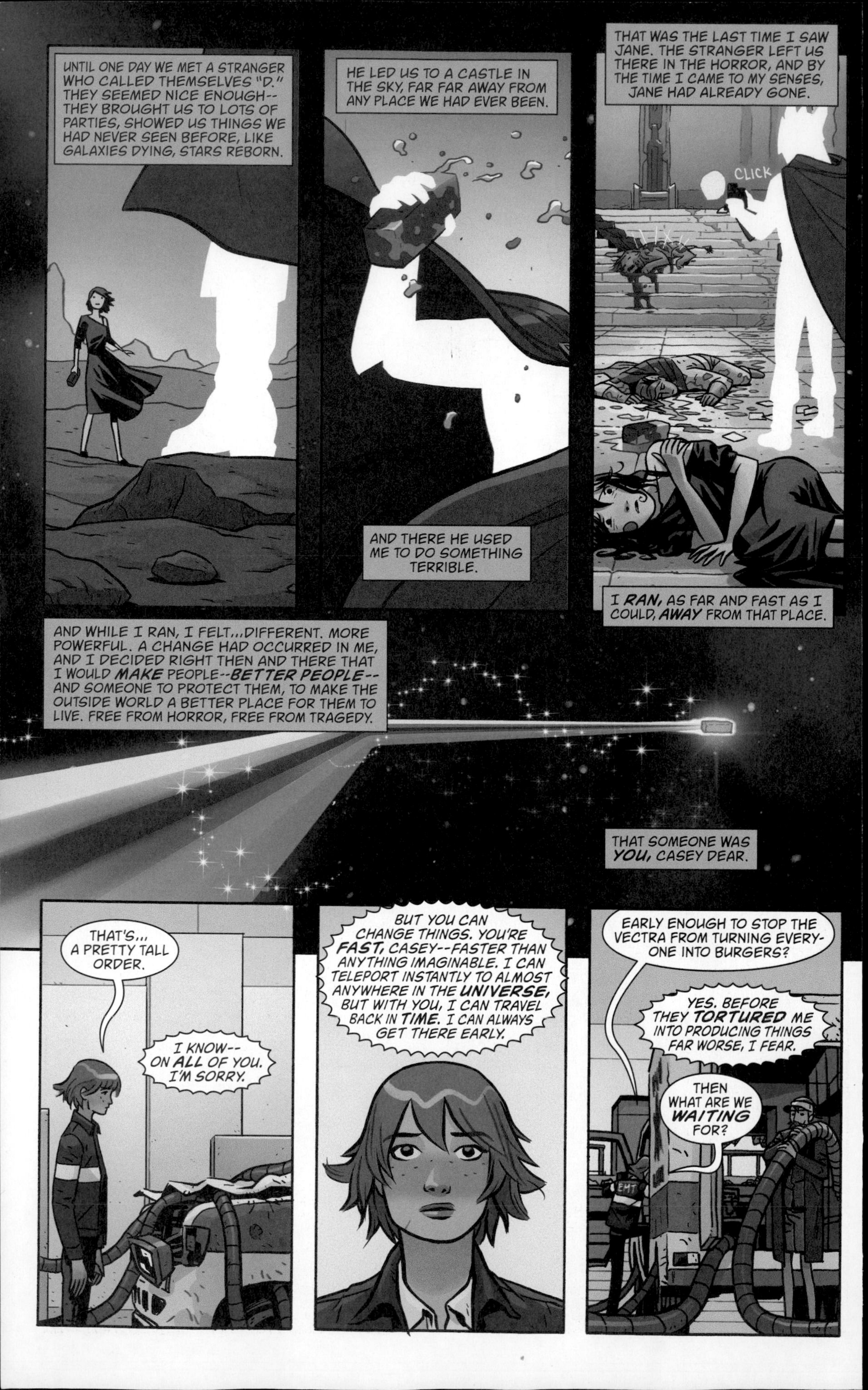
UNTIL ONE DAY WE MET A STRANGER WHO CALLED THEMSELVES "D." THEY SEEMED NICE ENOUGH-- THEY BROUGHT US TO LOTS OF PARTIES, SHOWED US THINGS WE HAD NEVER SEEN BEFORE, LIKE GALAXIES DYING, STARS REBORN.
HE LED US TO A CASTLE IN THE SKY, FAR FAR AWAY FROM ANY PLACE WE HAD EVER BEEN.
AND THERE HE USED ME TO DO SOMETHING TERRIBLE.
THAT WAS THE LAST TIME I SAW JANE. THE STRANGER LEFT US THERE IN THE HORROR, AND BY THE TIME I CAME TO MY SENSES, JANE HAD ALREADY GONE.
CLICK
I RAN, AS FAR AND FAST AS I COULD, AWAY FROM THAT PLACE.
AND WHILE I RAN, I FELT...DIFFERENT. MORE POWERFUL. A CHANGE HAD OCCURRED IN ME, AND I DECIDED RIGHT THEN AND THERE THAT I WOULD MAKE PEOPLE--BETTER PEOPLE-- AND SOMEONE TO PROTECT THEM, TO MAKE THE OUTSIDE WORLD A BETTER PLACE FOR THEM TO LIVE. FREE FROM HORROR, FREE FROM TRAGEDY.
THAT SOMEONE WAS YOU, CASEY DEAR.
THAT'S... A PRETTY TALL ORDER.
I KNOW-- ON ALL OF YOU. I'M SORRY.
BUT YOU CAN CHANGE THINGS. YOU'RE FAST, CASEY--FASTER THAN ANYTHING IMAGINABLE. I CAN TELEPORT INSTANTLY TO ALMOST ANYWHERE IN THE UNIVERSE, BUT WITH YOU, I CAN TRAVEL BACK IN TIME. I CAN ALWAYS GET THERE EARLY.
EARLY ENOUGH TO STOP THE VECTRA FROM TURNING EVERY-ONE INTO BURGERS?
YES. BEFORE THEY TORTURED ME INTO PRODUCING THINGS FAR WORSE, I FEAR.
THEN WHAT ARE WE WAITING FOR?
EMT

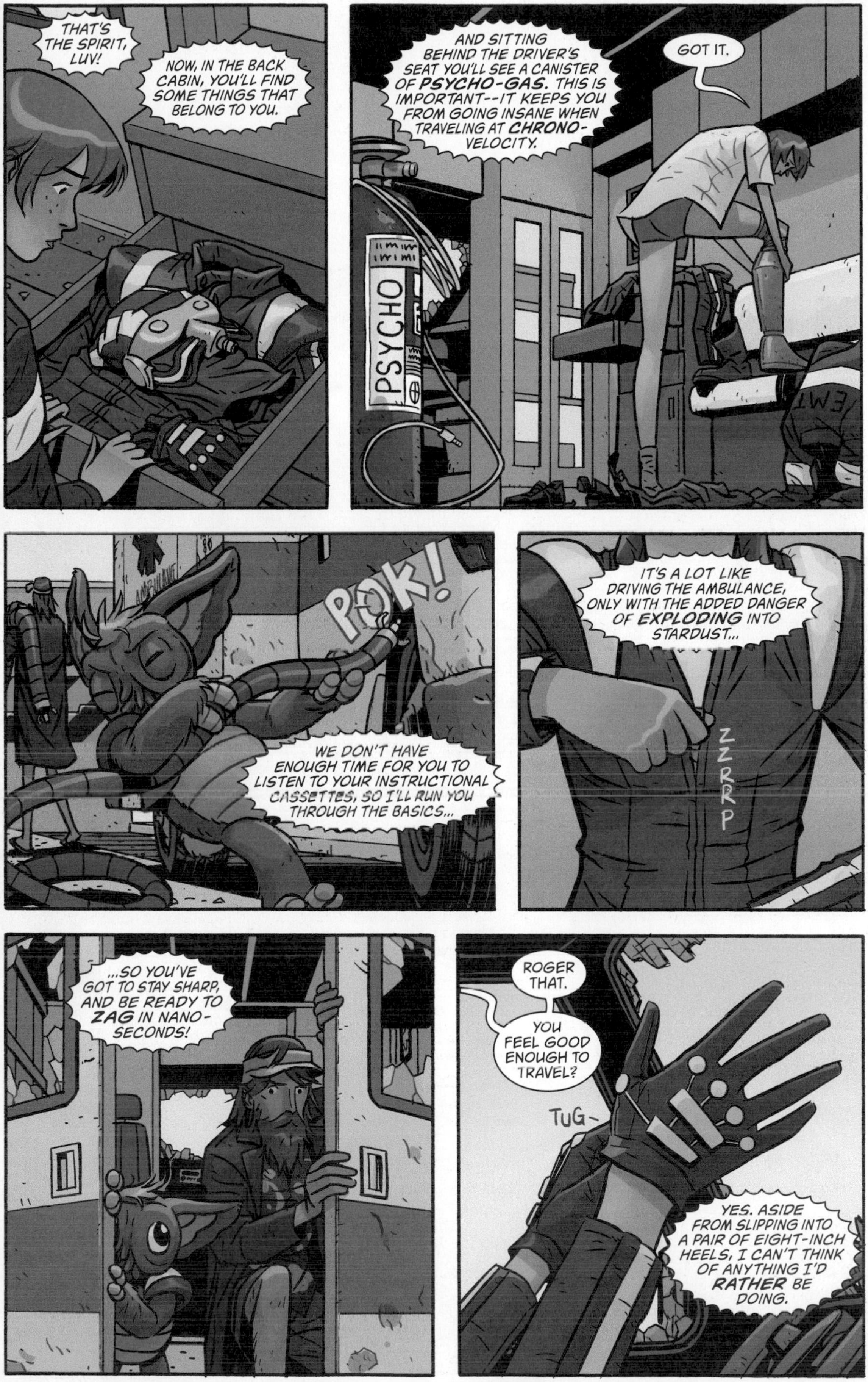
THAT'S THE SPIRIT, LUV!
NOW, IN THE BACK CABIN, YOU'LL FIND SOME THINGS THAT BELONG TO YOU.
AND SITTING BEHIND THE DRIVER'S SEAT YOU'LL SEE A CANISTER OF PSYCHO-GAS. THIS IS IMPORTANT--IT KEEPS YOU FROM GOING INSANE WHEN TRAVELING AT CHRONO-VELOCITY.
GOT IT.
PSYCHO
EMT
POK!
WE DON'T HAVE ENOUGH TIME FOR YOU TO LISTEN TO YOUR INSTRUCTIONAL CASSETTES, SO I'LL RUN YOU THROUGH THE BASICS...
IT'S A LOT LIKE DRIVING THE AMBULANCE, ONLY WITH THE ADDED DANGER OF EXPLODING INTO STARDUST...
ZZRRP
...SO YOU'VE GOT TO STAY SHARP, AND BE READY TO ZAG IN NANO-SECONDS!
ROGER THAT.
YOU FEEL GOOD ENOUGH TO TRAVEL?
TUG-
YES. ASIDE FROM SLIPPING INTO A PAIR OF EIGHT-INCH HEELS, I CAN'T THINK OF ANYTHING I'D RATHER BE DOING.

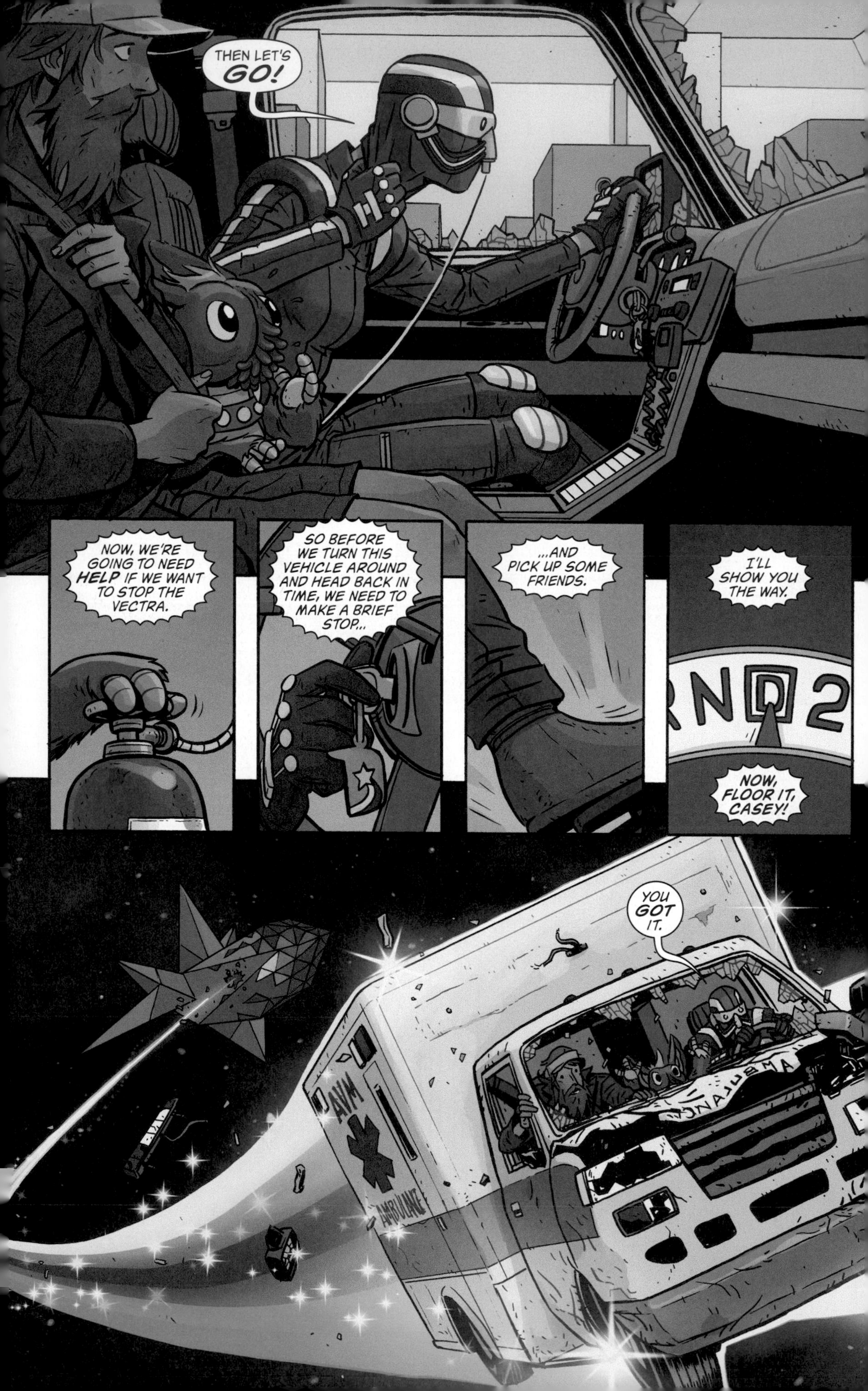
THEN LET'S GO!
NOW, WE'RE GOING TO NEED HELP IF WE WANT TO STOP THE VECTRA.
SO BEFORE WE TURN THIS VEHICLE AROUND AND HEAD BACK IN TIME, WE NEED TO MAKE A BRIEF STOP...
...AND PICK UP SOME FRIENDS.
I'LL SHOW YOU THE WAY.
RND2
NOW, FLOOR IT, CASEY!
YOU GOT IT.
AMBULANCE
AMBULANCE

SCRAMBLE ATTACK FIGHTERS AND PURSUE--

NO... WE HAVE OUR OWN PLANS.

DOODLE-BUG? PREP THE SYNTHETIC.

GLADLY.

THIS IS *NOT* YOUR OPERATION TO CONTROL! WE CANNOT RISK SPACE CASE AND HER FRIENDS STOPPING US FROM PRODUCING THE PRECIOUS PRODUCT. WE WERE HIRED TO DO A JOB AND--

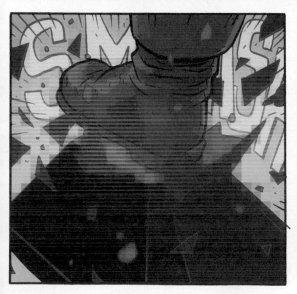

THAT'S IT. BACK THE FUCK UP...

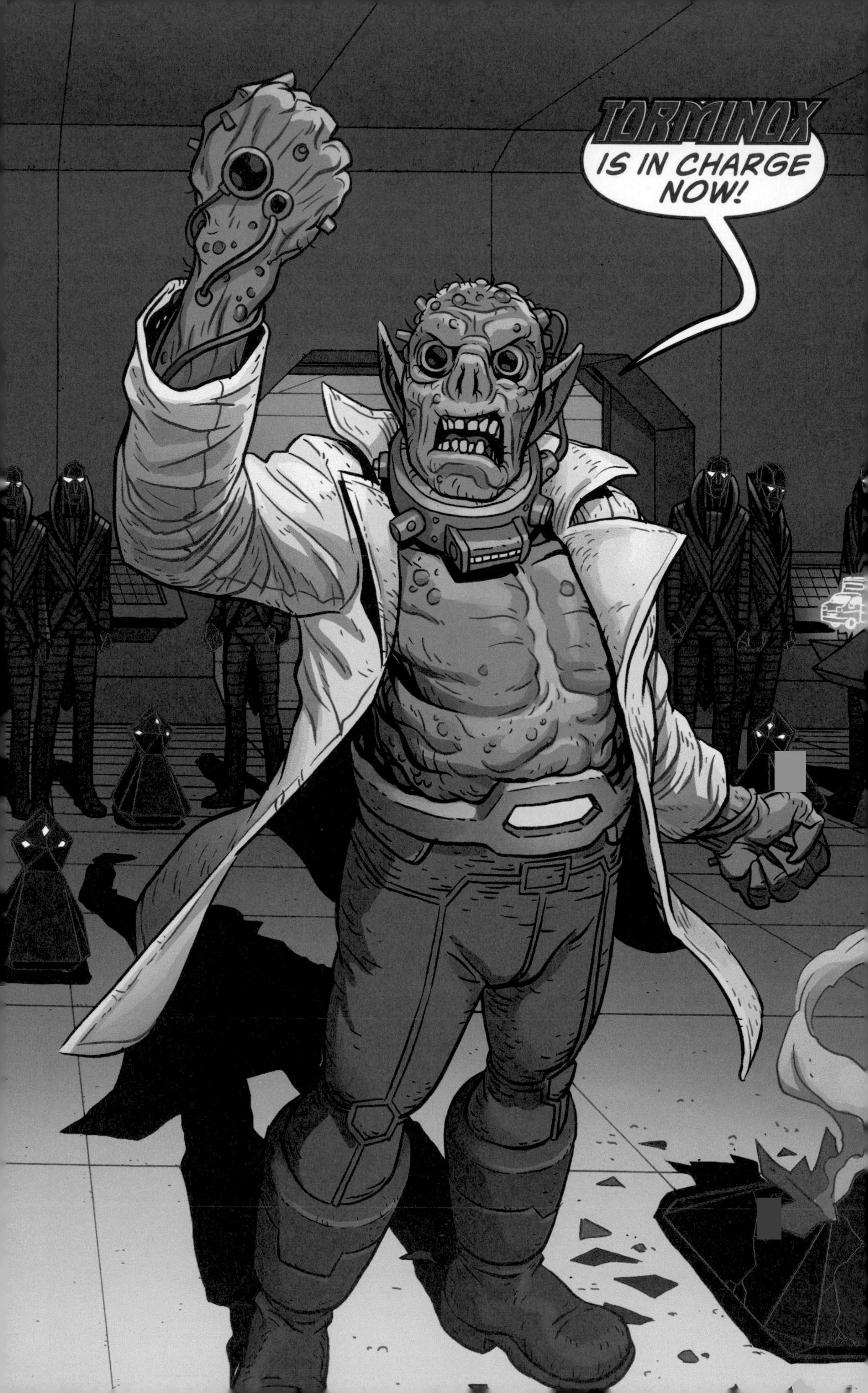
TORMINOX IS IN CHARGE NOW!

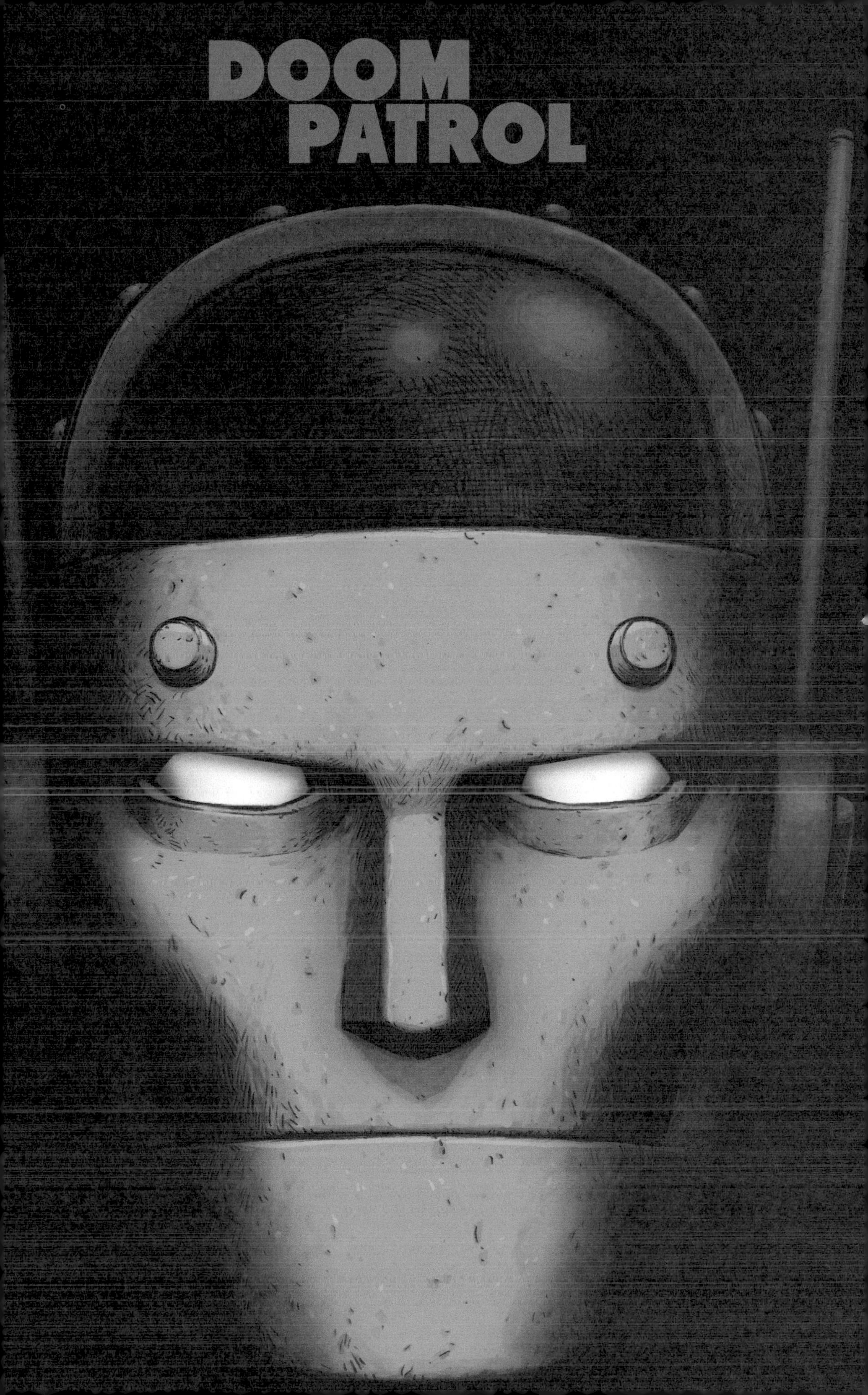
DOOM
PATROL

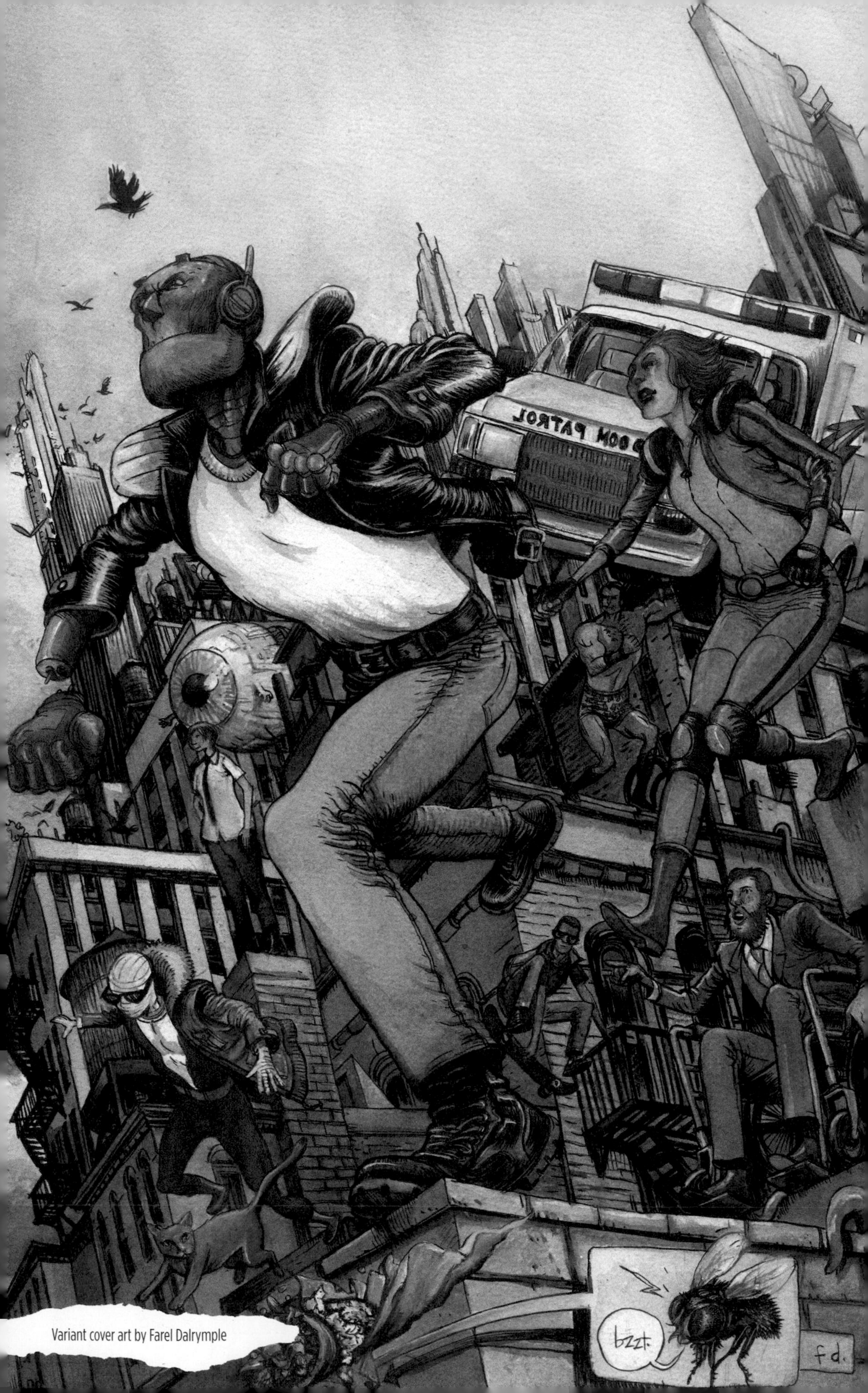
bzzt.
fd.
Variant cover art by Farel Dalrymple

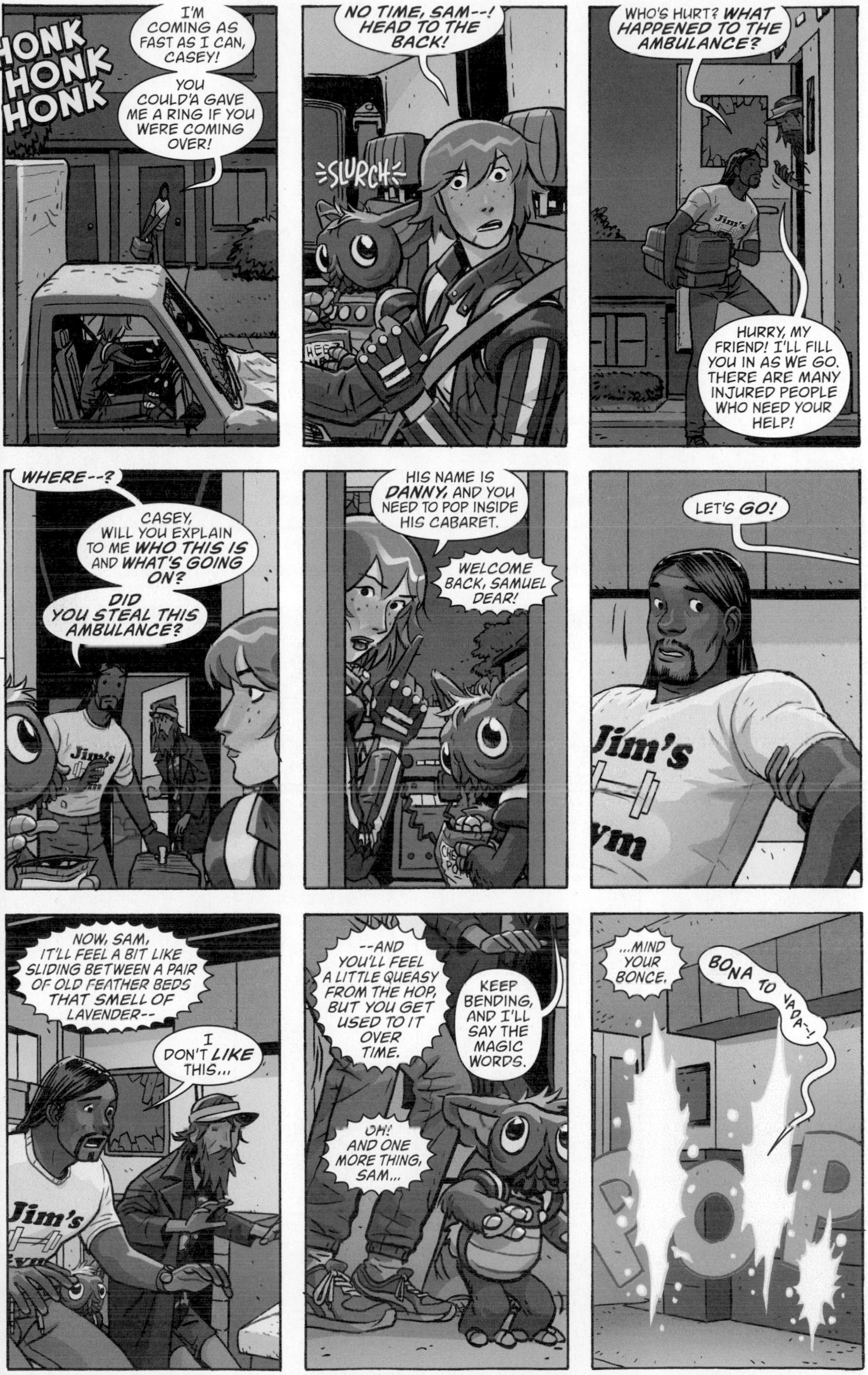
HONK HONK HONK
I'M COMING AS FAST AS I CAN, CASEY!
YOU COULD'A GAVE ME A RING IF YOU WERE COMING OVER!
NO TIME, SAM--! HEAD TO THE BACK!
SLURCH
WHO'S HURT? WHAT HAPPENED TO THE AMBULANCE?
HURRY, MY FRIEND! I'LL FILL YOU IN AS WE GO. THERE ARE MANY INJURED PEOPLE WHO NEED YOUR HELP!
WHERE--?
CASEY, WILL YOU EXPLAIN TO ME WHO THIS IS AND WHAT'S GOING ON?
DID YOU STEAL THIS AMBULANCE?
HIS NAME IS DANNY, AND YOU NEED TO POP INSIDE HIS CABARET.
WELCOME BACK, SAMUEL DEAR!
LET'S GO!
Jim's
NOW, SAM, IT'LL FEEL A BIT LIKE SLIDING BETWEEN A PAIR OF OLD FEATHER BEDS THAT SMELL OF LAVENDER--
I DON'T LIKE THIS...
--AND YOU'LL FEEL A LITTLE QUEASY FROM THE HOP, BUT YOU GET USED TO IT OVER TIME.
KEEP BENDING, AND I'LL SAY THE MAGIC WORDS.
OH! AND ONE MORE THING, SAM...
...MIND YOUR BONCE.
BONA TO VADA--!
POP

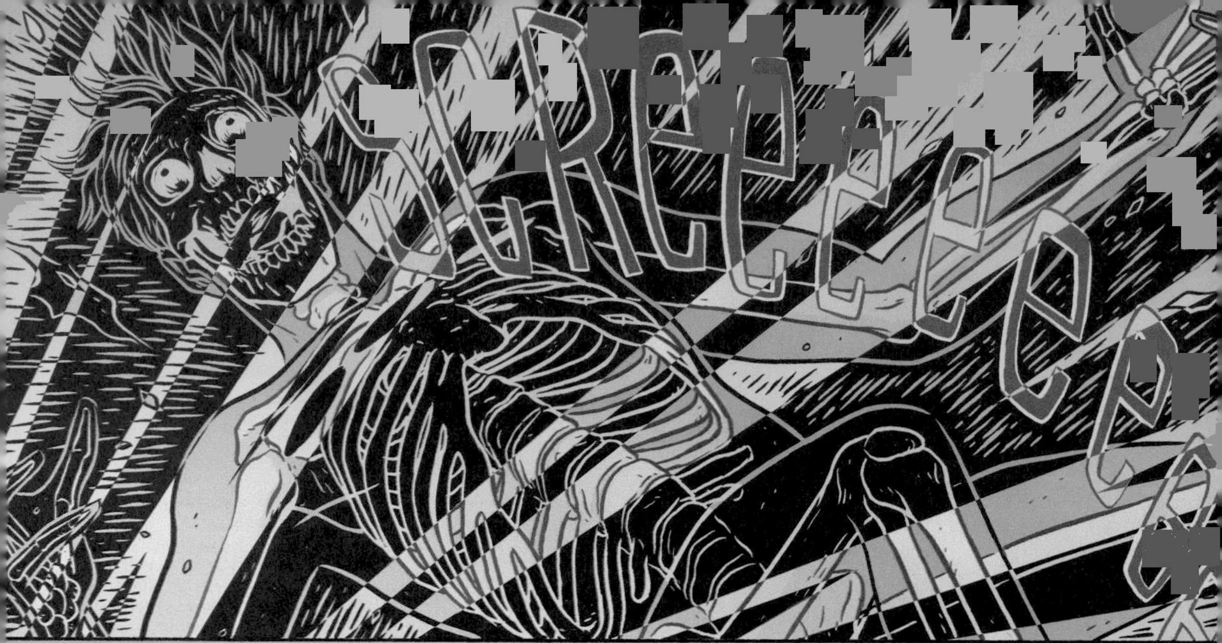

LET'S GO FAST

BRICK by BRICK Part .

GERARD WAY writer | NICK DERINGTON artist & cover | TAMRA BONVILLAIN colorist | LEE LOUGHRIDGE special thanks | TODD KLEIN letterer | MOLLY MAHAN assoc. ed. | JAMIE S. RICH editor | Doom Pa created Arnold Dr

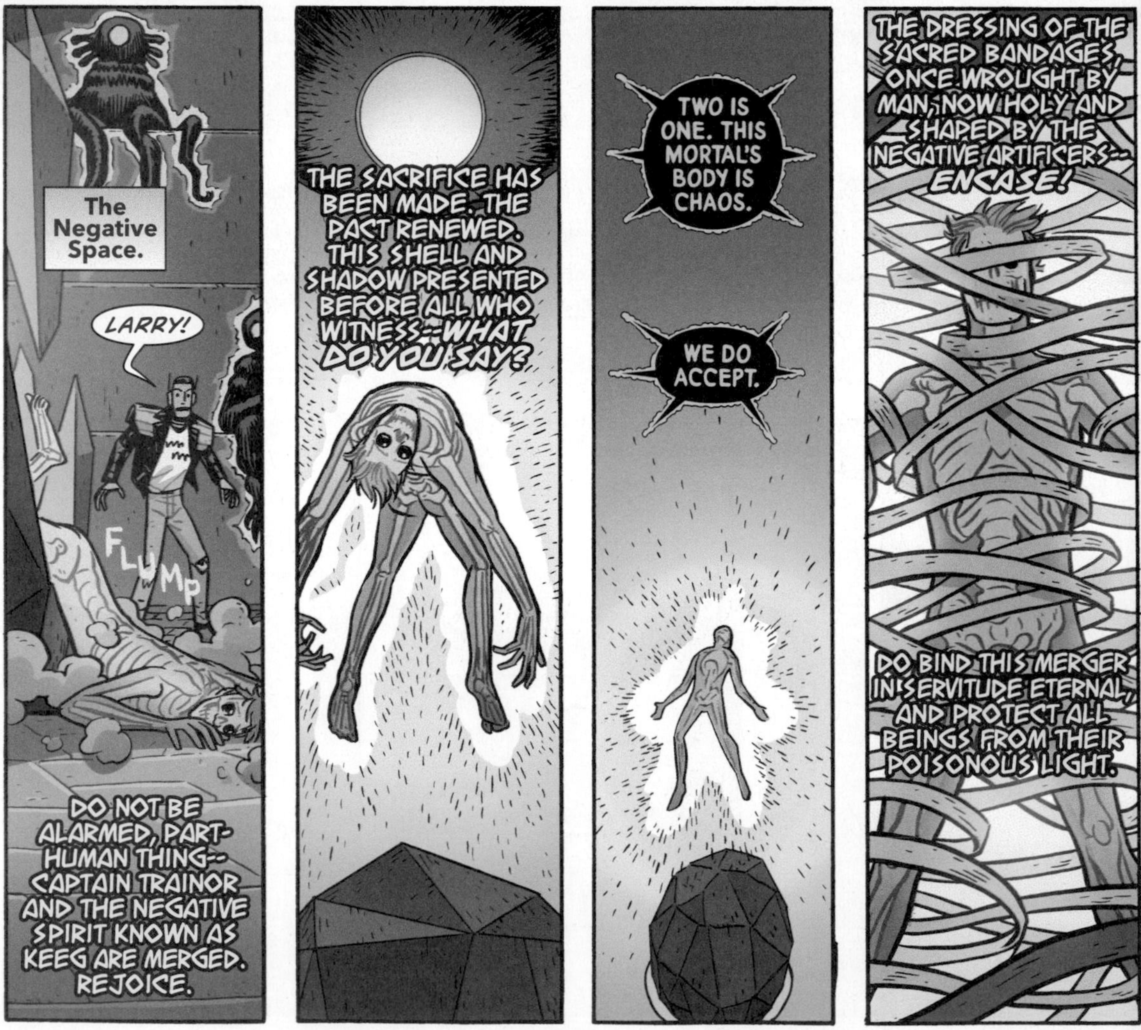
The Negative Space.
LARRY!
FLUMP
DO NOT BE ALARMED, PART-HUMAN THING--CAPTAIN TRAINOR AND THE NEGATIVE SPIRIT KNOWN AS KEEG ARE MERGED. REJOICE.
THE SACRIFICE HAS BEEN MADE. THE PACT RENEWED. THIS SHELL AND SHADOW PRESENTED BEFORE ALL WHO WITNESS--WHAT DO YOU SAY?
TWO IS ONE. THIS MORTAL'S BODY IS CHAOS.
WE DO ACCEPT.
THE DRESSING OF THE SACRED BANDAGES, ONCE WROUGHT BY MAN, NOW HOLY AND SHAPED BY THE NEGATIVE ARTIFICERS--ENCASE!
DO BIND THIS MERGER IN SERVITUDE ETERNAL, AND PROTECT ALL BEINGS FROM THEIR POISONOUS LIGHT.

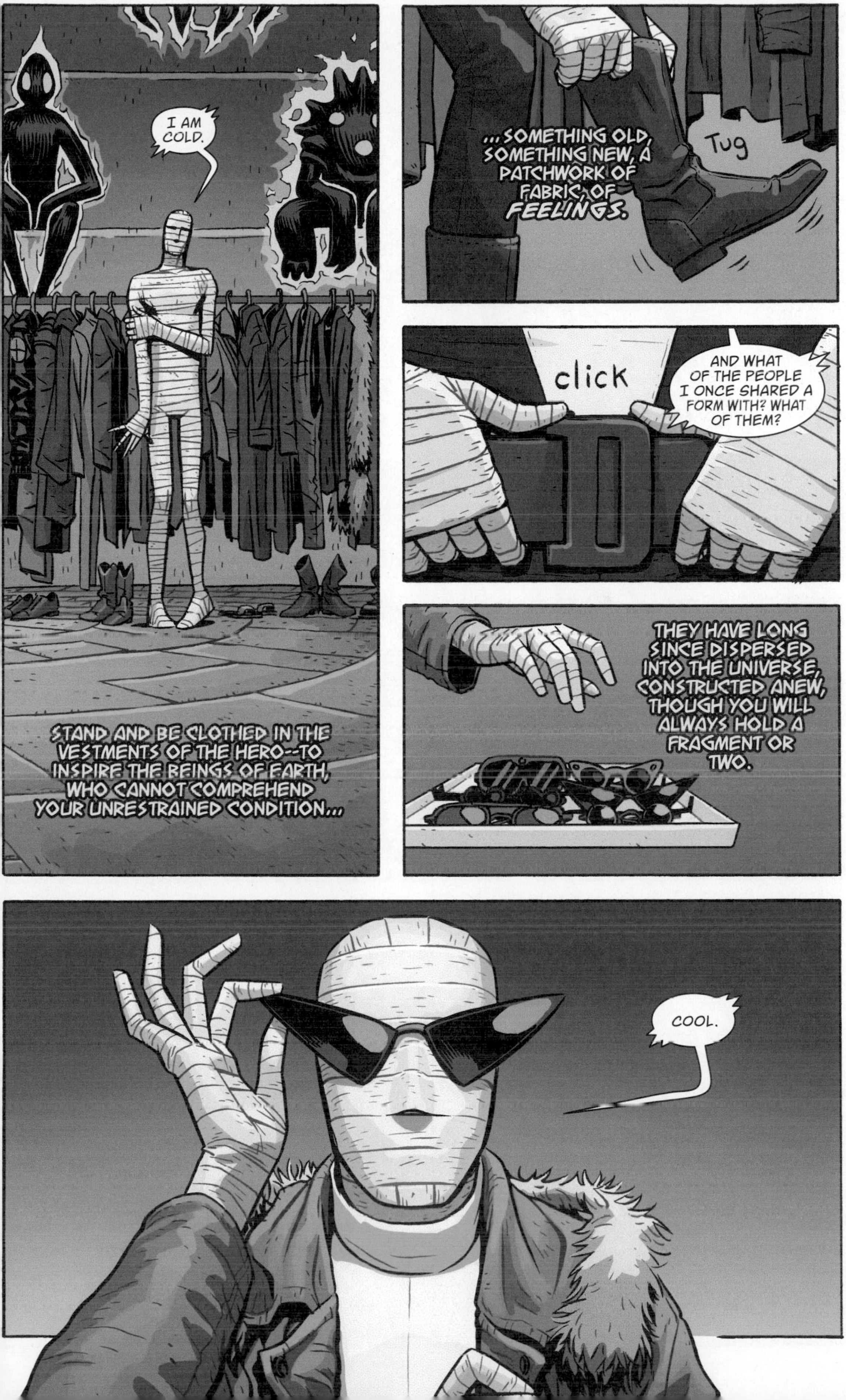
I AM COLD.
STAND AND BE CLOTHED IN THE VESTMENTS OF THE HERO--TO INSPIRE THE BEINGS OF EARTH, WHO CANNOT COMPREHEND YOUR UNRESTRAINED CONDITION...
...SOMETHING OLD, SOMETHING NEW, A PATCHWORK OF FABRIC, OF FEELINGS.
Tug
click
AND WHAT OF THE PEOPLE I ONCE SHARED A FORM WITH? WHAT OF THEM?
THEY HAVE LONG SINCE DISPERSED INTO THE UNIVERSE, CONSTRUCTED ANEW, THOUGH YOU WILL ALWAYS HOLD A FRAGMENT OR TWO.
COOL.

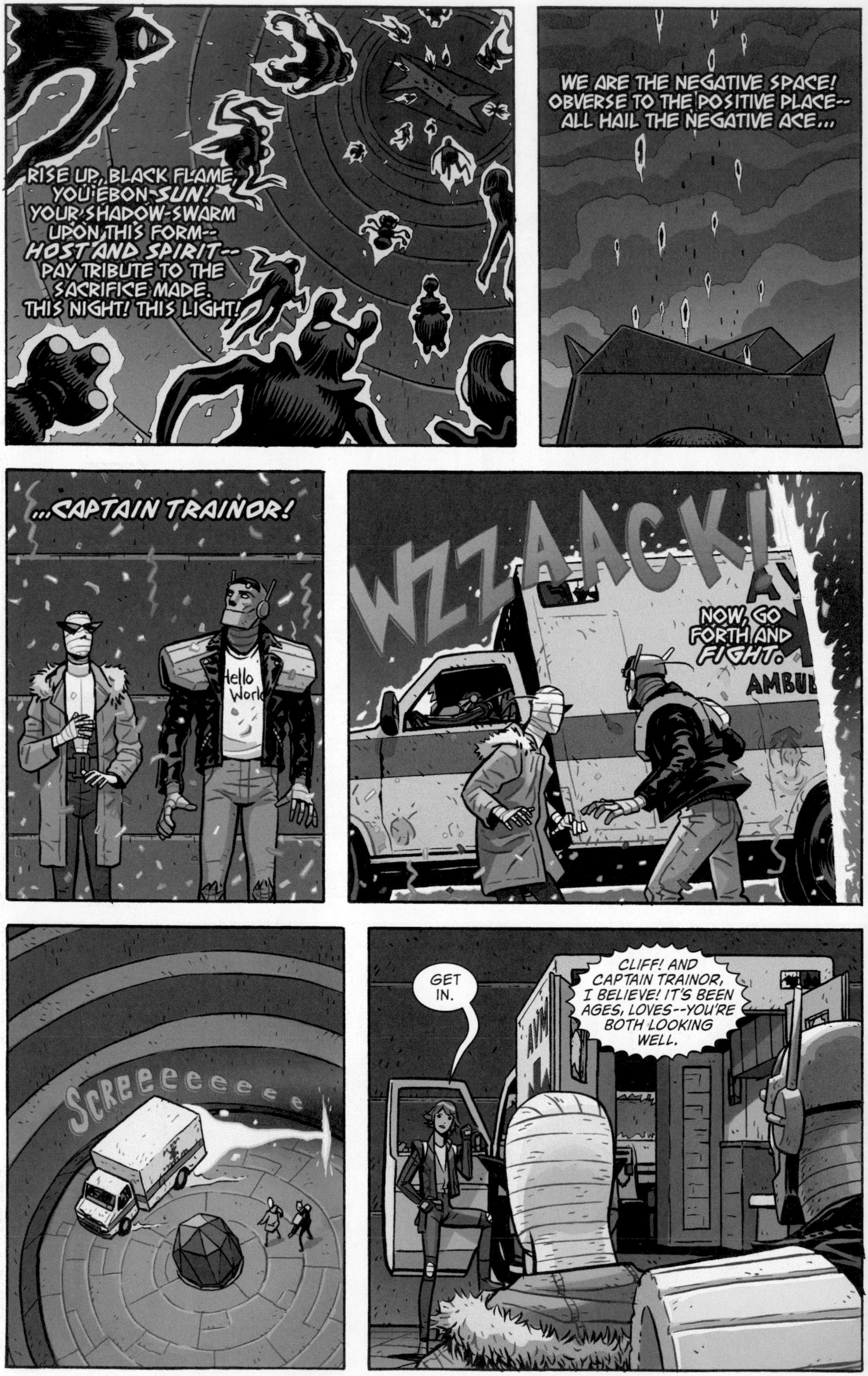
RISE UP, BLACK FLAME, YOU EBON SUN! YOUR SHADOW-SWARM UPON THIS FORM-- HOST AND SPIRIT-- PAY TRIBUTE TO THE SACRIFICE MADE. THIS NIGHT! THIS LIGHT!
WE ARE THE NEGATIVE SPACE! OBVERSE TO THE POSITIVE PLACE-- ALL HAIL THE NEGATIVE ACE...
...CAPTAIN TRAINOR!
WZZAACK!
NOW, GO FORTH AND FIGHT.
Screeeeeeeee
GET IN.
CLIFF! AND CAPTAIN TRAINOR, I BELIEVE! IT'S BEEN AGES, LOVES--YOU'RE BOTH LOOKING WELL.

DANNY?

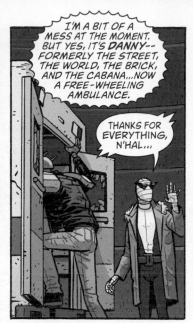

I'M A BIT OF A MESS AT THE MOMENT. BUT YES, IT'S *DANNY*-- FORMERLY THE STREET, THE WORLD, THE BRICK, AND THE CABANA...NOW A FREE-WHEELING AMBULANCE.

THANKS FOR EVERYTHING, N'HAL....

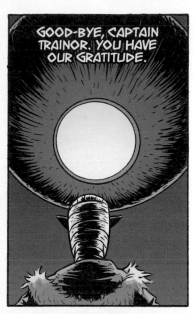

GOOD-BYE, CAPTAIN TRAINOR. YOU HAVE OUR GRATITUDE.

CASEY! IT'S RICARDO-- *ARE YOU THERE?*

GO FOR CASEY.

FLEX MENTALLO IS *DEAD!* PARALYZED TO OBLIVION! DANNYLAND IS IN RUINS....

...WE ARE ADMINISTERING FIRST-AID BUT THERE ARE NOT MANY SURVIVORS....AND NO SIGN OF THE *VECTRA.*

FLEX MENTALLO-- *DEAD?!* WHAT THE HELL IS GOING ON?

NOW, CLIFF....

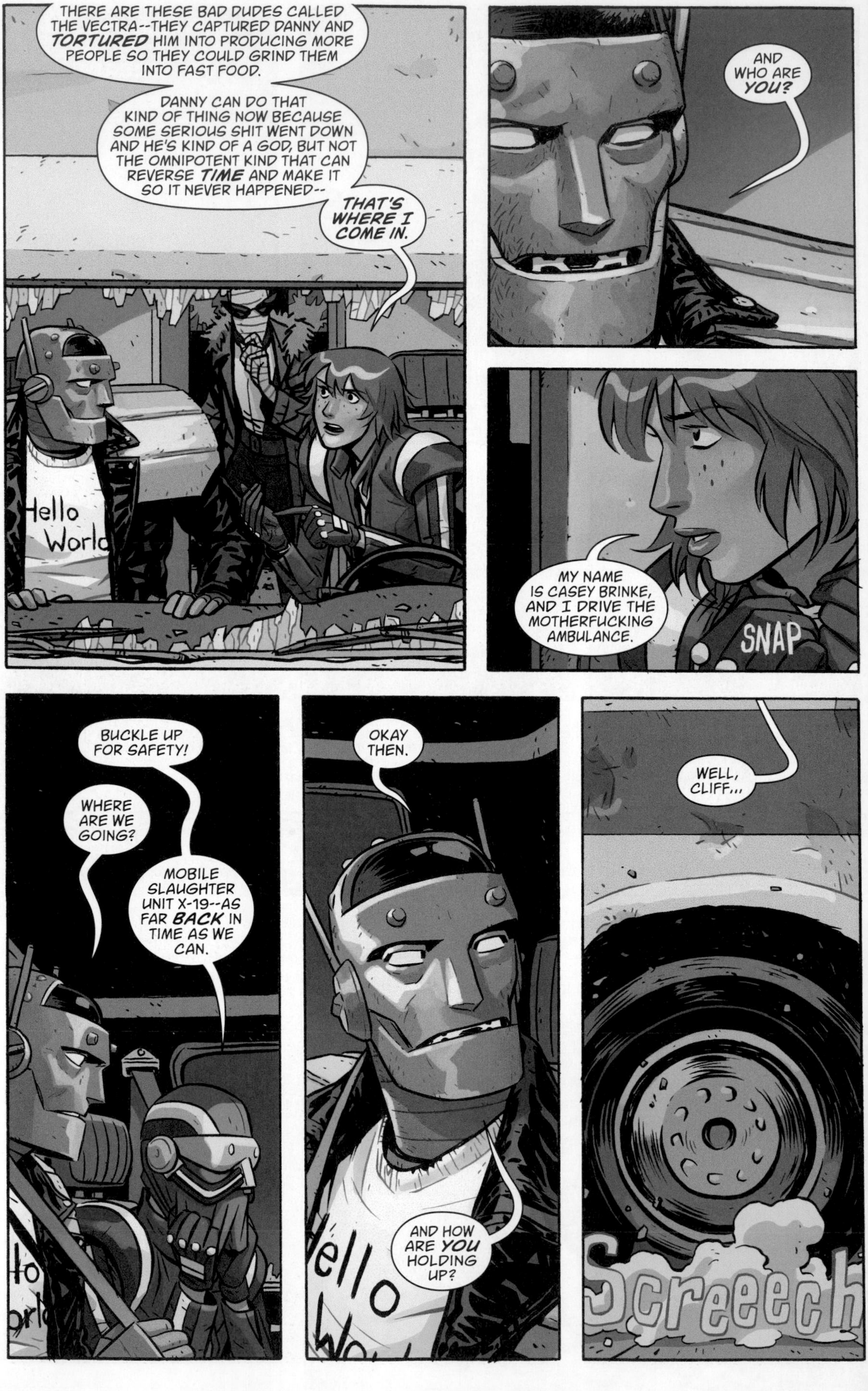
THERE ARE THESE BAD DUDES CALLED THE VECTRA--THEY CAPTURED DANNY AND TORTURED HIM INTO PRODUCING MORE PEOPLE SO THEY COULD GRIND THEM INTO FAST FOOD.
DANNY CAN DO THAT KIND OF THING NOW BECAUSE SOME SERIOUS SHIT WENT DOWN AND HE'S KIND OF A GOD, BUT NOT THE OMNIPOTENT KIND THAT CAN REVERSE TIME AND MAKE IT SO IT NEVER HAPPENED--
THAT'S WHERE I COME IN.
Hello World
AND WHO ARE YOU?
MY NAME IS CASEY BRINKE, AND I DRIVE THE MOTHERFUCKING AMBULANCE.
SNAP
BUCKLE UP FOR SAFETY!
WHERE ARE WE GOING?
MOBILE SLAUGHTER UNIT X-19--AS FAR BACK IN TIME AS WE CAN.
OKAY THEN.
AND HOW ARE YOU HOLDING UP?
WELL, CLIFF...
Screeech

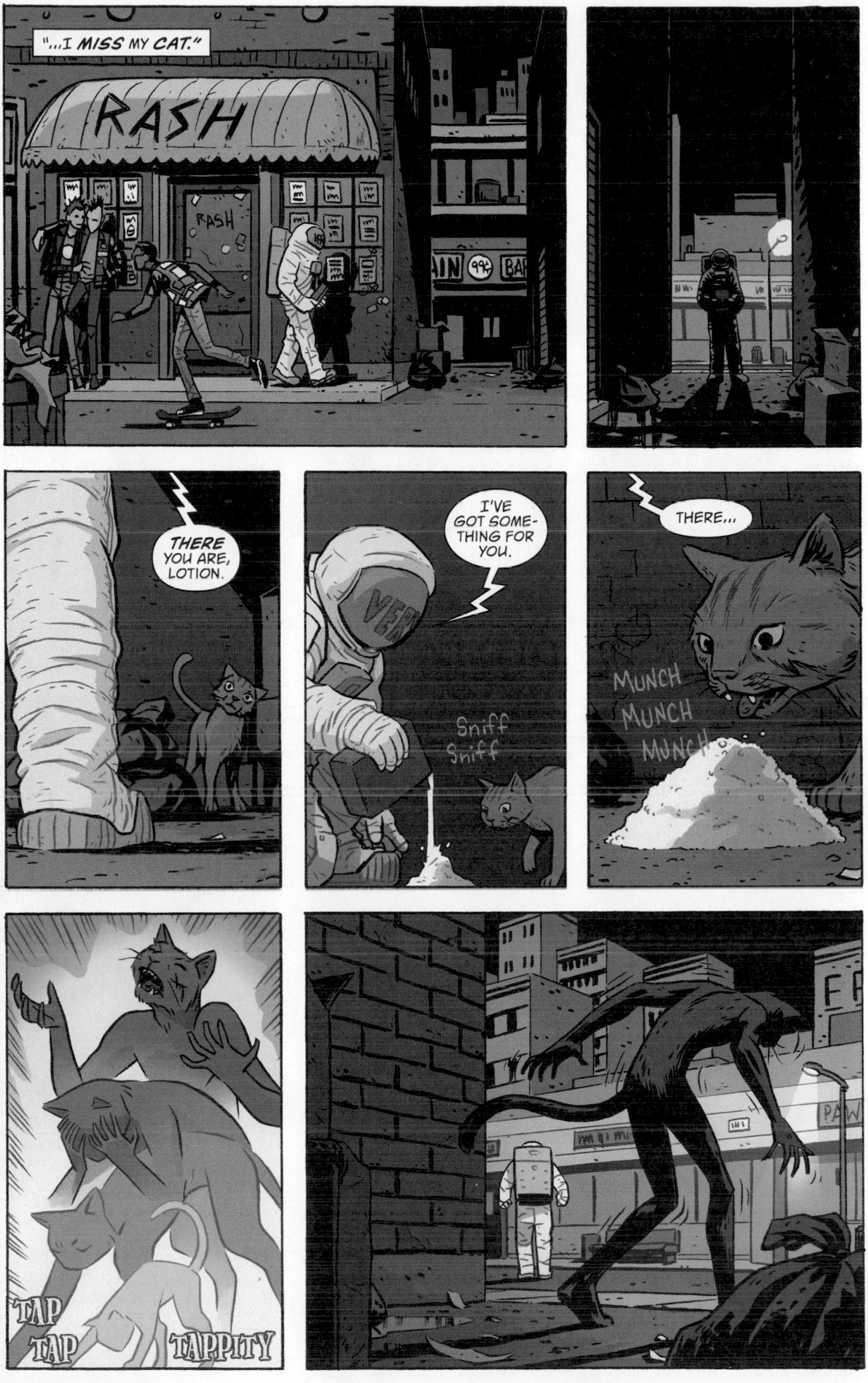
"...I MISS MY CAT."
RASH
RASH
AIN 99¢ BAR
THERE YOU ARE, LOTION.
I'VE GOT SOME-THING FOR YOU.
Sniff Sniff
THERE...
MUNCH MUNCH MUNCH
TAP TAP TAPPITY
FR
PAW

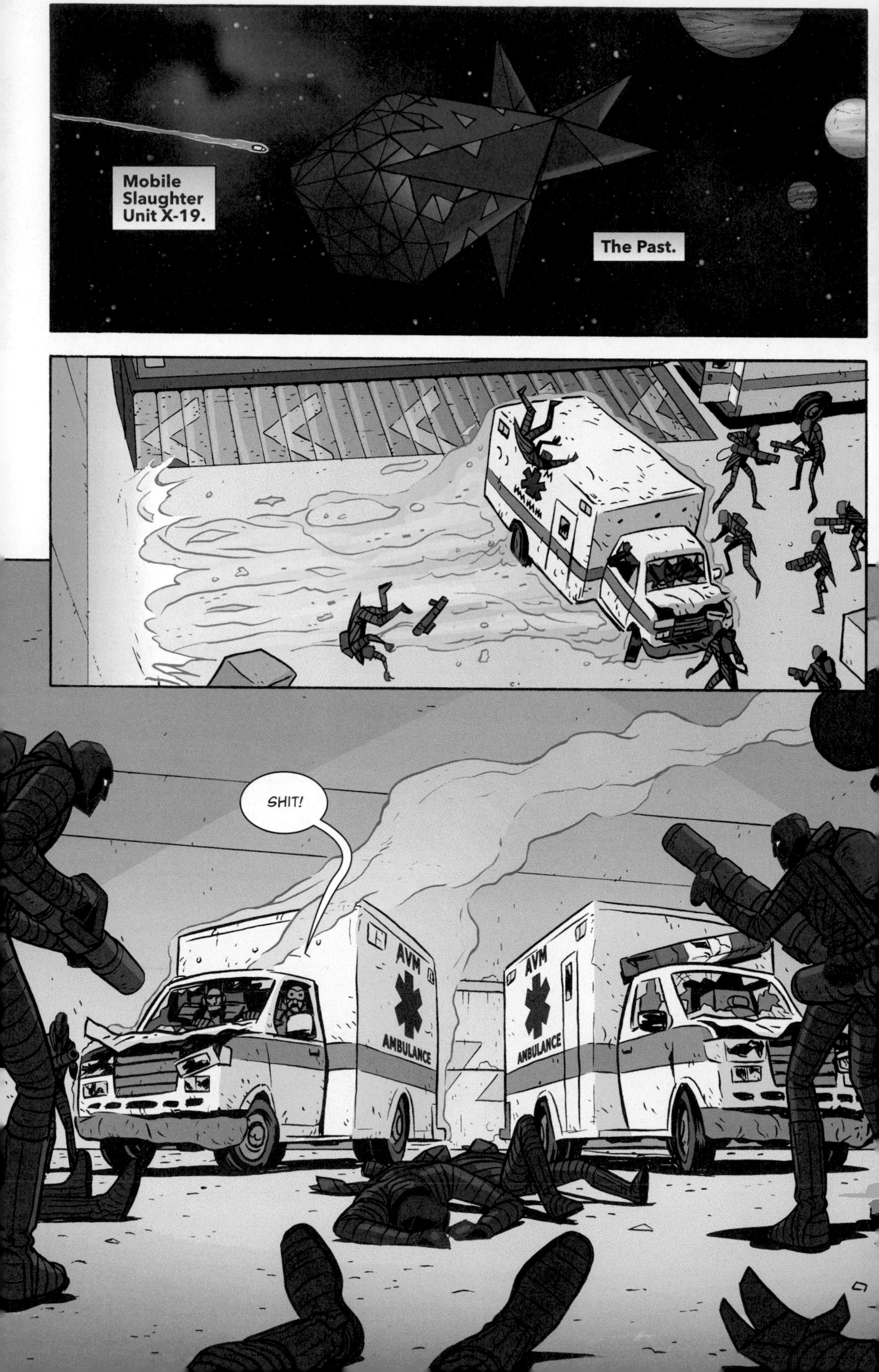
Mobile Slaughter Unit X-19.
The Past.
AVM
SHIT!
AVM
AMBULANCE
AVM
AMBULANCE

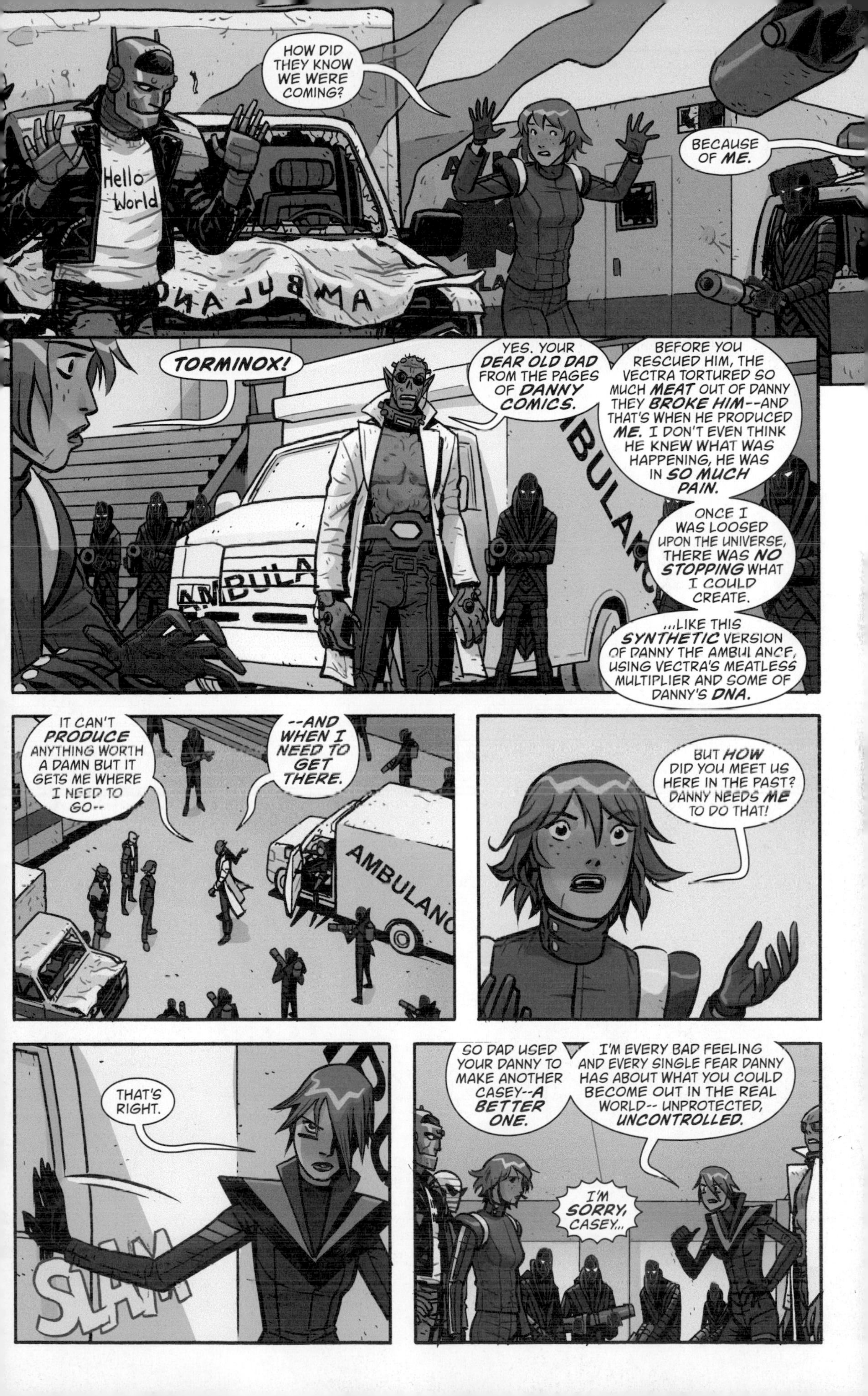

Hello World
HOW DID THEY KNOW WE WERE COMING?
BECAUSE OF ME.
AMBULANCE
TORMINOX!
YES. YOUR DEAR OLD DAD FROM THE PAGES OF DANNY COMICS.
BEFORE YOU RESCUED HIM, THE VECTRA TORTURED SO MUCH MEAT OUT OF DANNY THEY BROKE HIM--AND THAT'S WHEN HE PRODUCED ME. I DON'T EVEN THINK HE KNEW WHAT WAS HAPPENING, HE WAS IN SO MUCH PAIN.
ONCE I WAS LOOSED UPON THE UNIVERSE, THERE WAS NO STOPPING WHAT I COULD CREATE.
...LIKE THIS SYNTHETIC VERSION OF DANNY THE AMBULANCE, USING VECTRA'S MEATLESS MULTIPLIER AND SOME OF DANNY'S DNA.
IT CAN'T PRODUCE ANYTHING WORTH A DAMN BUT IT GETS ME WHERE I NEED TO GO--
--AND WHEN I NEED TO GET THERE.
BUT HOW DID YOU MEET US HERE IN THE PAST? DANNY NEEDS ME TO DO THAT!
THAT'S RIGHT.
SLAM
SO DAD USED YOUR DANNY TO MAKE ANOTHER CASEY--A BETTER ONE.
I'M EVERY BAD FEELING AND EVERY SINGLE FEAR DANNY HAS ABOUT WHAT YOU COULD BECOME OUT IN THE REAL WORLD-- UNPROTECTED, UNCONTROLLED.
I'M SORRY, CASEY...

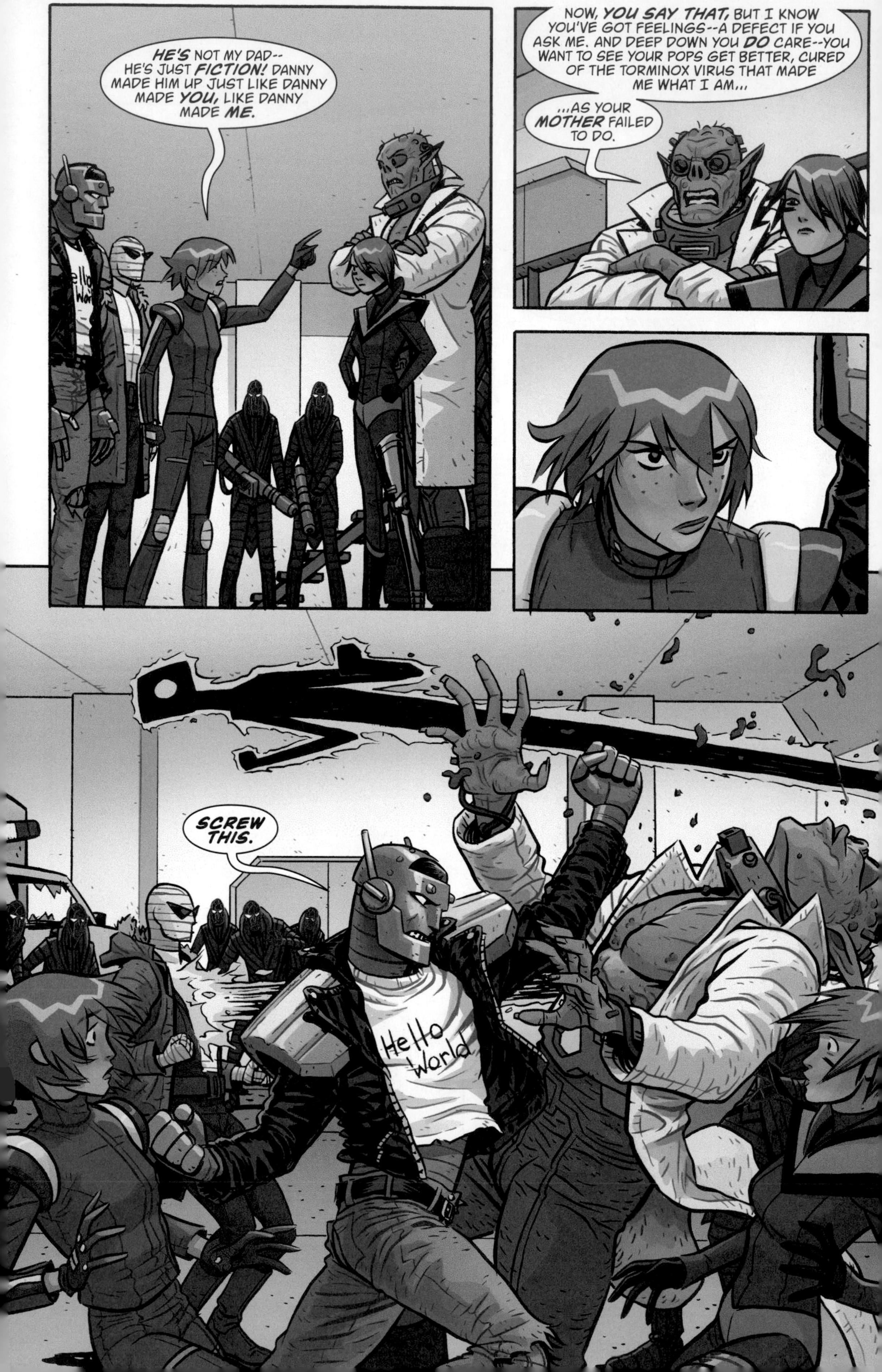
HE'S NOT MY DAD-- HE'S JUST FICTION! DANNY MADE HIM UP JUST LIKE DANNY MADE YOU, LIKE DANNY MADE ME.
NOW, YOU SAY THAT, BUT I KNOW YOU'VE GOT FEELINGS--A DEFECT IF YOU ASK ME. AND DEEP DOWN YOU DO CARE--YOU WANT TO SEE YOUR POPS GET BETTER, CURED OF THE TORMINOX VIRUS THAT MADE ME WHAT I AM...
...AS YOUR MOTHER FAILED TO DO.
SCREW THIS.
Hello World
Hello World

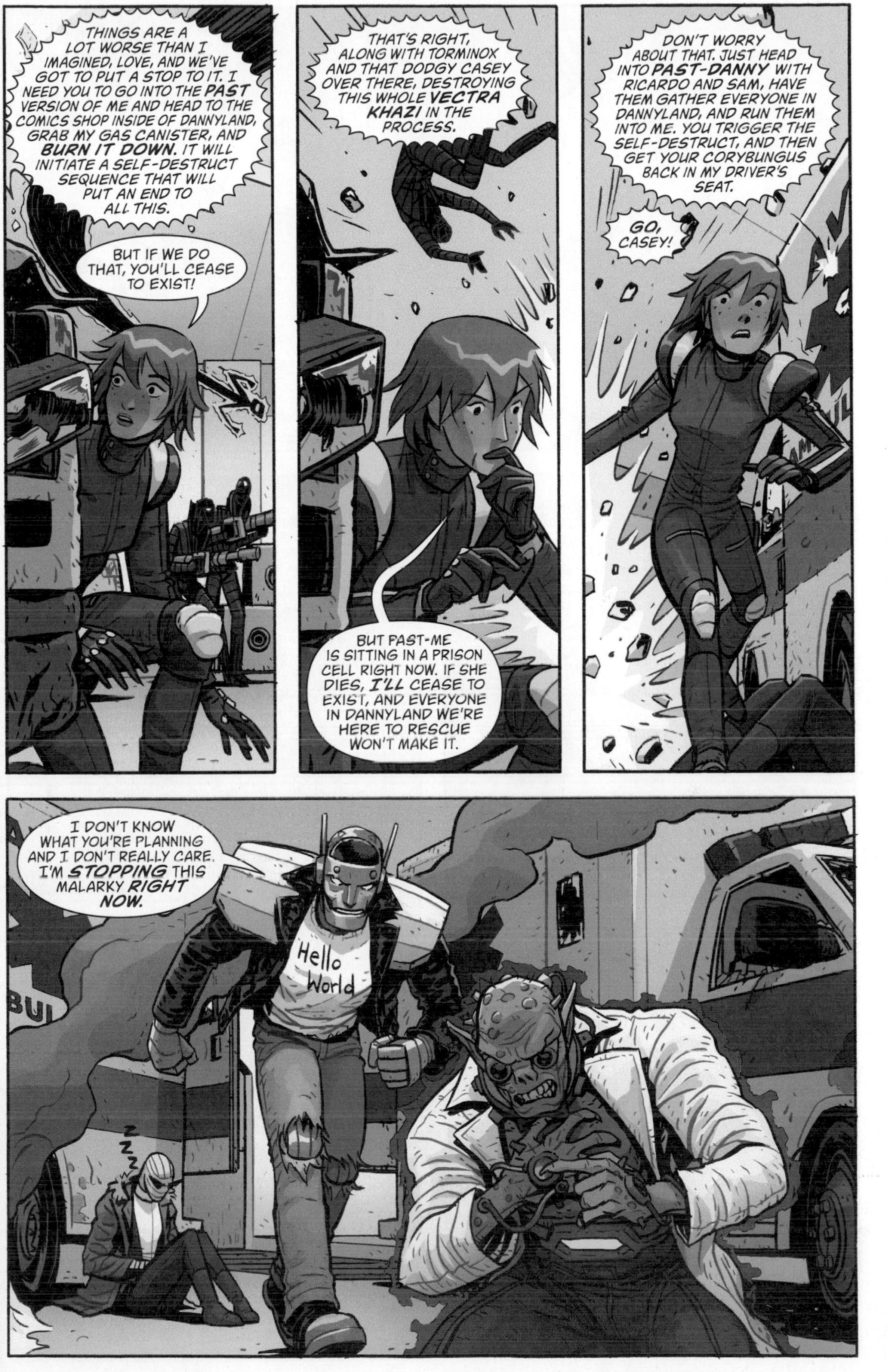
THINGS ARE A LOT WORSE THAN I IMAGINED, LOVE, AND WE'VE GOT TO PUT A STOP TO IT. I NEED YOU TO GO INTO THE PAST VERSION OF ME AND HEAD TO THE COMICS SHOP INSIDE OF DANNYLAND, GRAB MY GAS CANISTER, AND BURN IT DOWN. IT WILL INITIATE A SELF-DESTRUCT SEQUENCE THAT WILL PUT AN END TO ALL THIS.
BUT IF WE DO THAT, YOU'LL CEASE TO EXIST!
THAT'S RIGHT, ALONG WITH TORMINOX AND THAT DODGY CASEY OVER THERE, DESTROYING THIS WHOLE VECTRA KHAZI IN THE PROCESS.
BUT PAST-ME IS SITTING IN A PRISON CELL RIGHT NOW. IF SHE DIES, I'LL CEASE TO EXIST, AND EVERYONE IN DANNYLAND WE'RE HERE TO RESCUE WON'T MAKE IT.
DON'T WORRY ABOUT THAT. JUST HEAD INTO PAST-DANNY WITH RICARDO AND SAM, HAVE THEM GATHER EVERYONE IN DANNYLAND, AND RUN THEM INTO ME. YOU TRIGGER THE SELF-DESTRUCT, AND THEN GET YOUR CORYBUNGUS BACK IN MY DRIVER'S SEAT.
GO, CASEY!
I DON'T KNOW WHAT YOU'RE PLANNING AND I DON'T REALLY CARE. I'M STOPPING THIS MALARKY RIGHT NOW.
Hello World
ZZZ

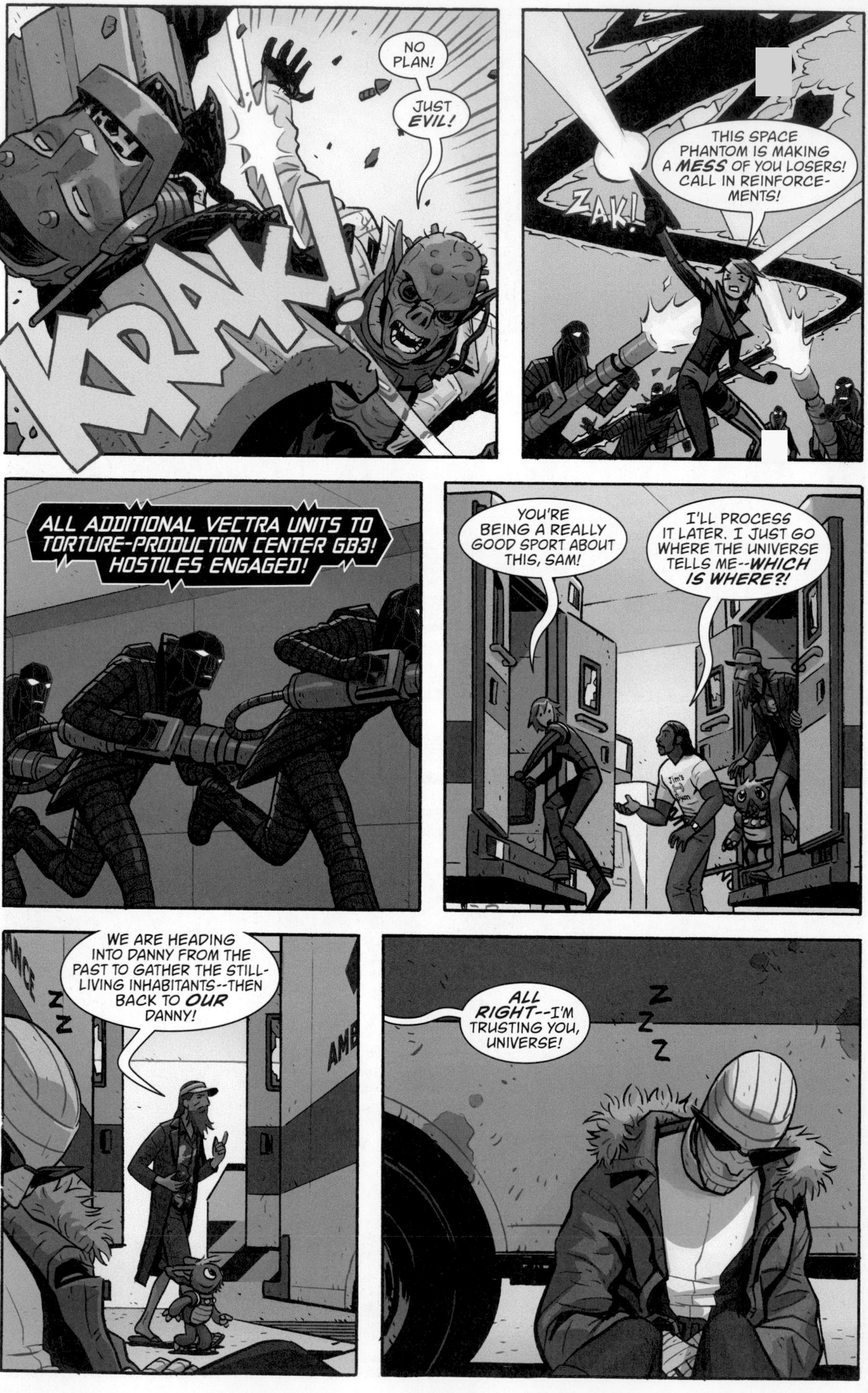
NO PLAN!
JUST EVIL!
KRAK!
ZAK!
THIS SPACE PHANTOM IS MAKING A MESS OF YOU LOSERS! CALL IN REINFORCE-MENTS!
ALL ADDITIONAL VECTRA UNITS TO TORTURE-PRODUCTION CENTER GB3! HOSTILES ENGAGED!
YOU'RE BEING A REALLY GOOD SPORT ABOUT THIS, SAM!
I'LL PROCESS IT LATER. I JUST GO WHERE THE UNIVERSE TELLS ME--WHICH IS WHERE?!
WE ARE HEADING INTO DANNY FROM THE PAST TO GATHER THE STILL-LIVING INHABITANTS--THEN BACK TO OUR DANNY!
Z Z
ALL RIGHT--I'M TRUSTING YOU, UNIVERSE!
Z Z Z

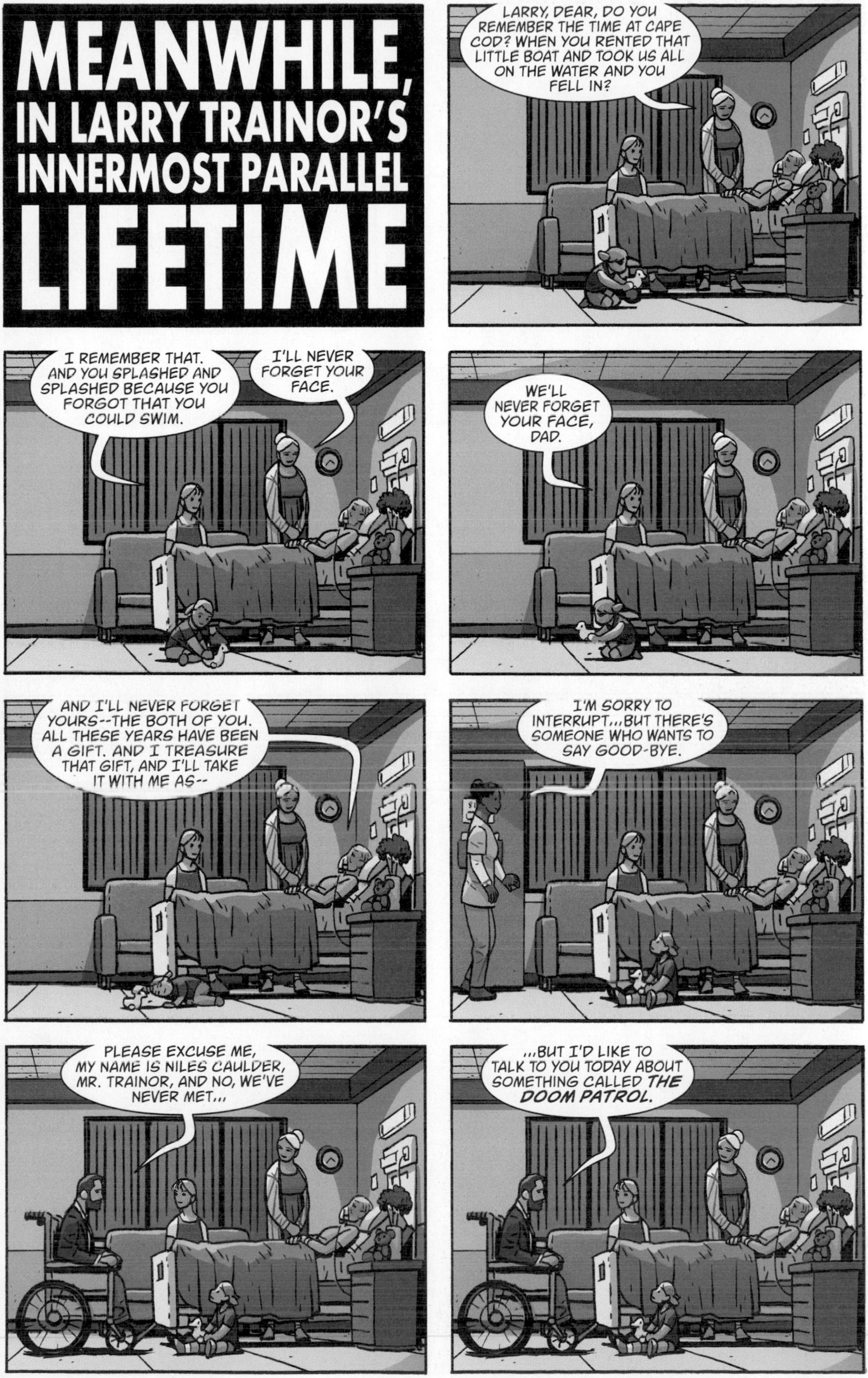
MEANWHILE, IN LARRY TRAINOR'S INNERMOST PARALLEL LIFETIME
LARRY, DEAR, DO YOU REMEMBER THE TIME AT CAPE COD? WHEN YOU RENTED THAT LITTLE BOAT AND TOOK US ALL ON THE WATER AND YOU FELL IN?
I REMEMBER THAT. AND YOU SPLASHED AND SPLASHED BECAUSE YOU FORGOT THAT YOU COULD SWIM.
I'LL NEVER FORGET YOUR FACE.
WE'LL NEVER FORGET YOUR FACE, DAD.
AND I'LL NEVER FORGET YOURS--THE BOTH OF YOU. ALL THESE YEARS HAVE BEEN A GIFT. AND I TREASURE THAT GIFT, AND I'LL TAKE IT WITH ME AS--
I'M SORRY TO INTERRUPT...BUT THERE'S SOMEONE WHO WANTS TO SAY GOOD-BYE.
PLEASE EXCUSE ME, MY NAME IS NILES CAULDER, MR. TRAINOR, AND NO, WE'VE NEVER MET...
...BUT I'D LIKE TO TALK TO YOU TODAY ABOUT SOMETHING CALLED THE DOOM PATROL.

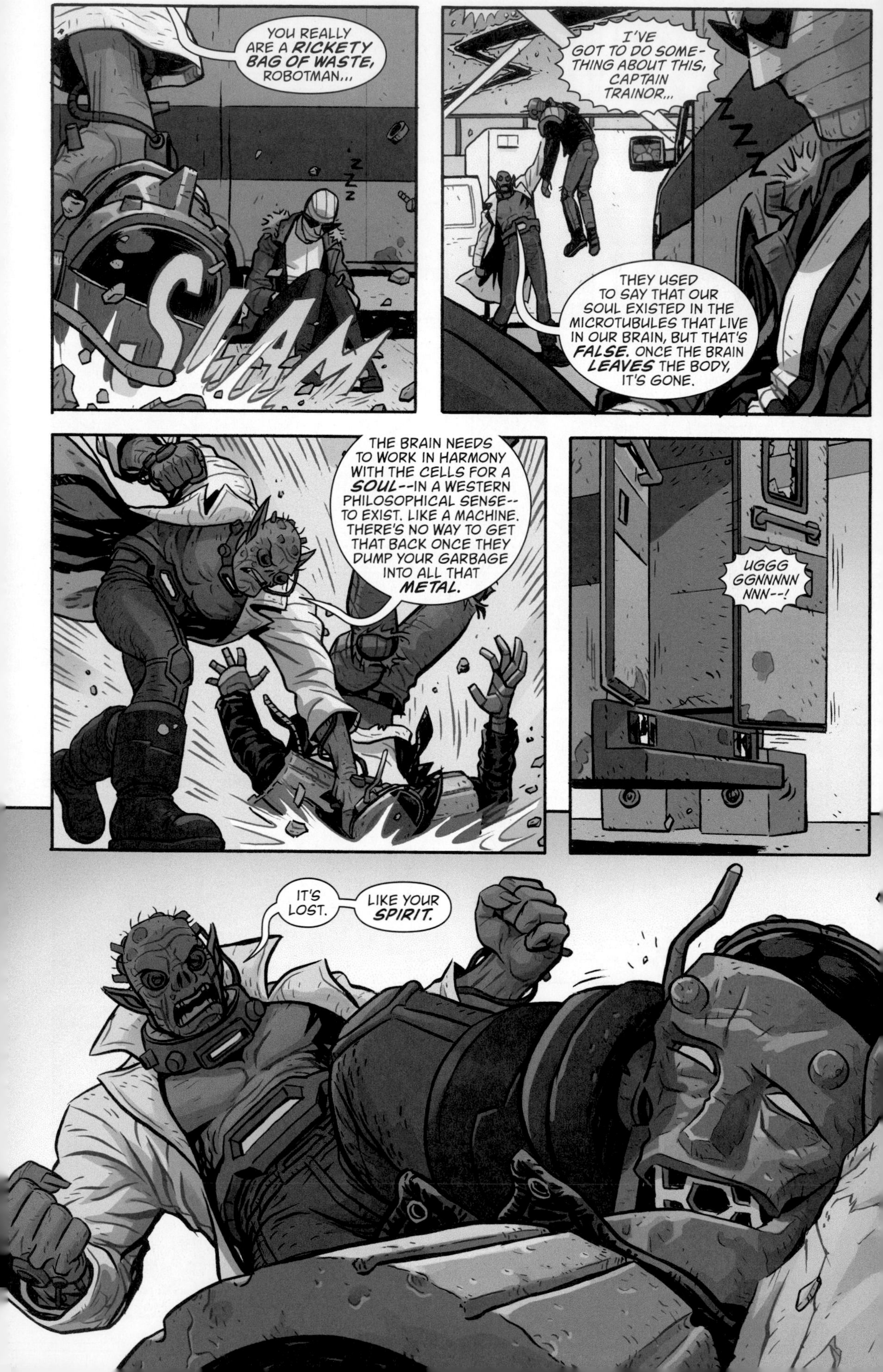
YOU REALLY ARE A RICKETY BAG OF WASTE, ROBOTMAN...
Z Z Z
SLAM
I'VE GOT TO DO SOME-THING ABOUT THIS, CAPTAIN TRAINOR...
Z Z Z
THEY USED TO SAY THAT OUR SOUL EXISTED IN THE MICROTUBULES THAT LIVE IN OUR BRAIN, BUT THAT'S FALSE. ONCE THE BRAIN LEAVES THE BODY, IT'S GONE.
THE BRAIN NEEDS TO WORK IN HARMONY WITH THE CELLS FOR A SOUL--IN A WESTERN PHILOSOPHICAL SENSE--TO EXIST. LIKE A MACHINE. THERE'S NO WAY TO GET THAT BACK ONCE THEY DUMP YOUR GARBAGE INTO ALL THAT METAL.
UGGG GGNNNNN NNN--!
IT'S LOST.
LIKE YOUR SPIRIT.

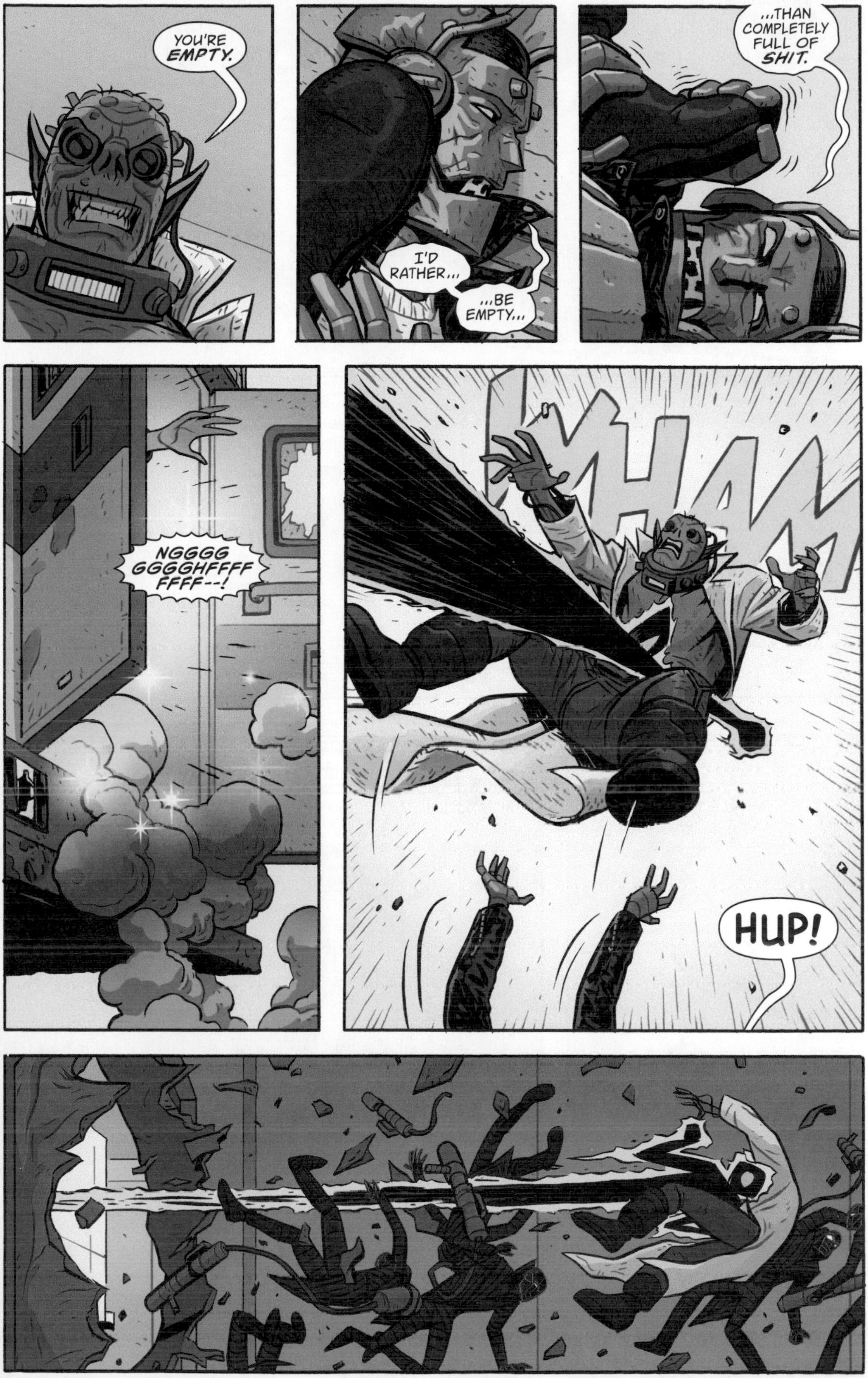
YOU'RE EMPTY.
I'D RATHER...
...BE EMPTY...
...THAN COMPLETELY FULL OF SHIT.
NGGGGGGGGHFFFFFFFF--!
HUP!

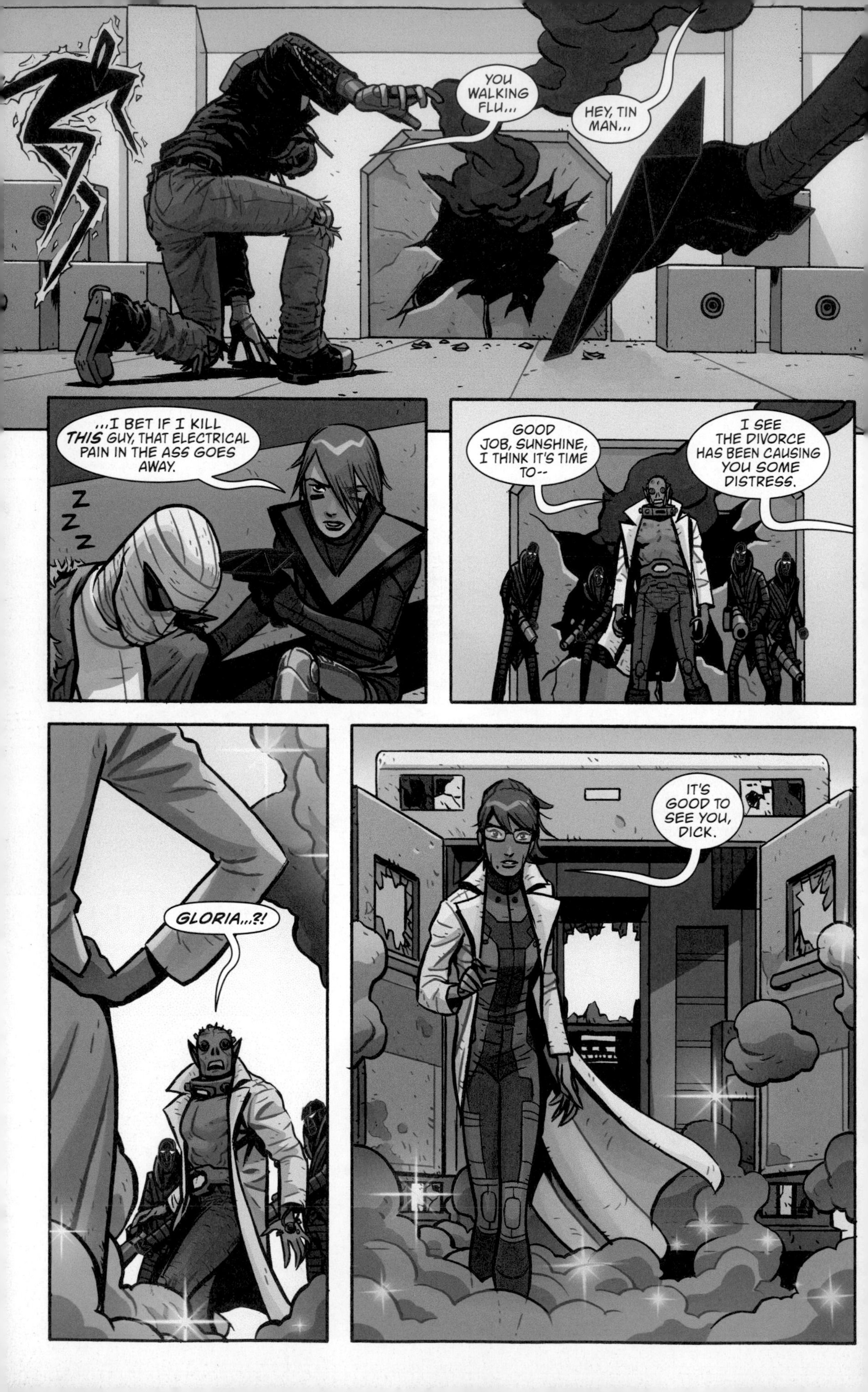
YOU WALKING FLU...
HEY, TIN MAN...
...I BET IF I KILL THIS GUY, THAT ELECTRICAL PAIN IN THE ASS GOES AWAY.
Z Z Z
GOOD JOB, SUNSHINE, I THINK IT'S TIME TO--
I SEE THE DIVORCE HAS BEEN CAUSING YOU SOME DISTRESS.
GLORIA...?!
IT'S GOOD TO SEE YOU, DICK.

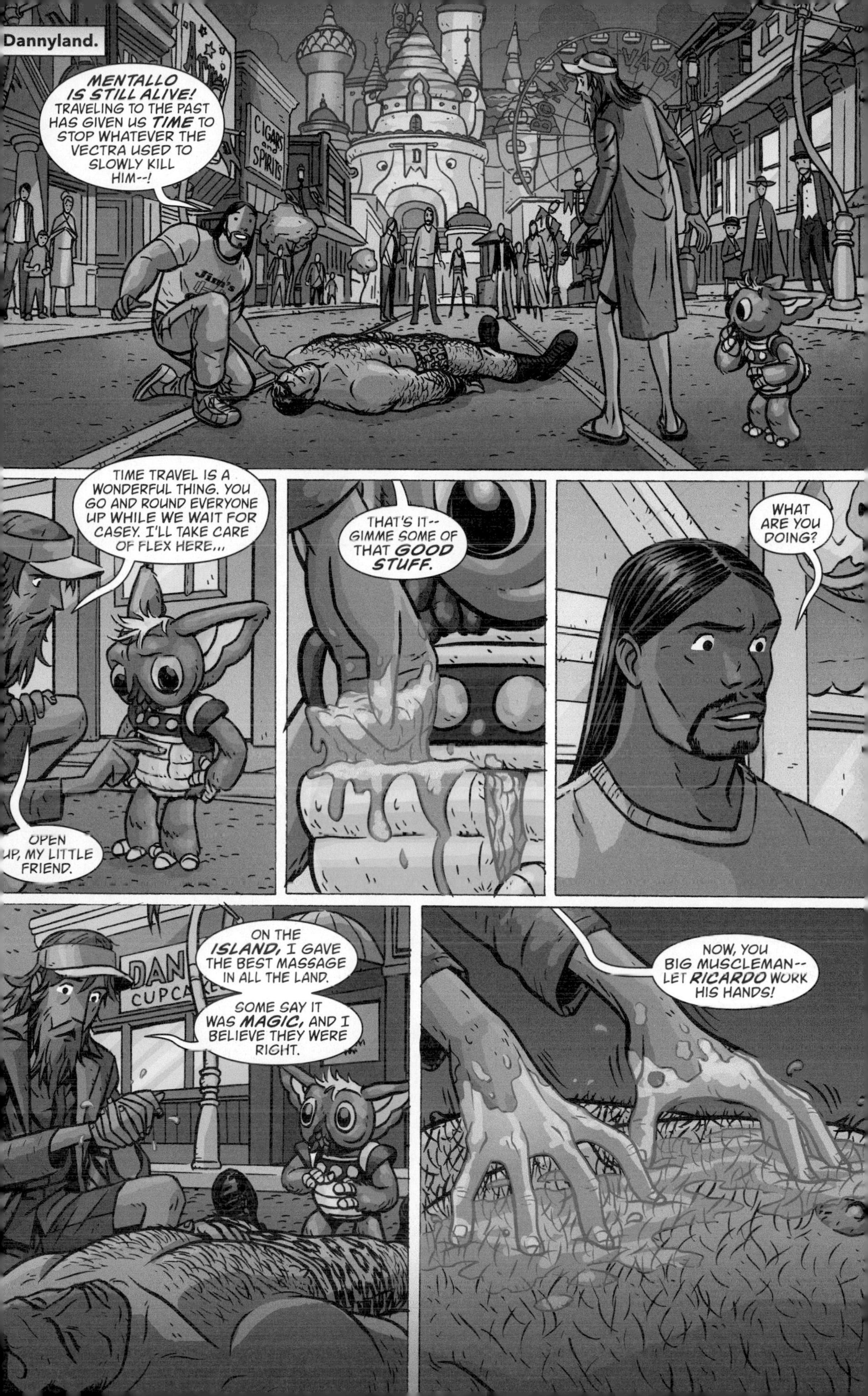
Dannyland.
MENTALLO IS STILL ALIVE! TRAVELING TO THE PAST HAS GIVEN US TIME TO STOP WHATEVER THE VECTRA USED TO SLOWLY KILL HIM--!
TIME TRAVEL IS A WONDERFUL THING. YOU GO AND ROUND EVERYONE UP WHILE WE WAIT FOR CASEY. I'LL TAKE CARE OF FLEX HERE...
OPEN UP, MY LITTLE FRIEND.
THAT'S IT-- GIMME SOME OF THAT GOOD STUFF.
WHAT ARE YOU DOING?
ON THE ISLAND, I GAVE THE BEST MASSAGE IN ALL THE LAND.
SOME SAY IT WAS MAGIC, AND I BELIEVE THEY WERE RIGHT.
NOW, YOU BIG MUSCLEMAN-- LET RICARDO WORK HIS HANDS!

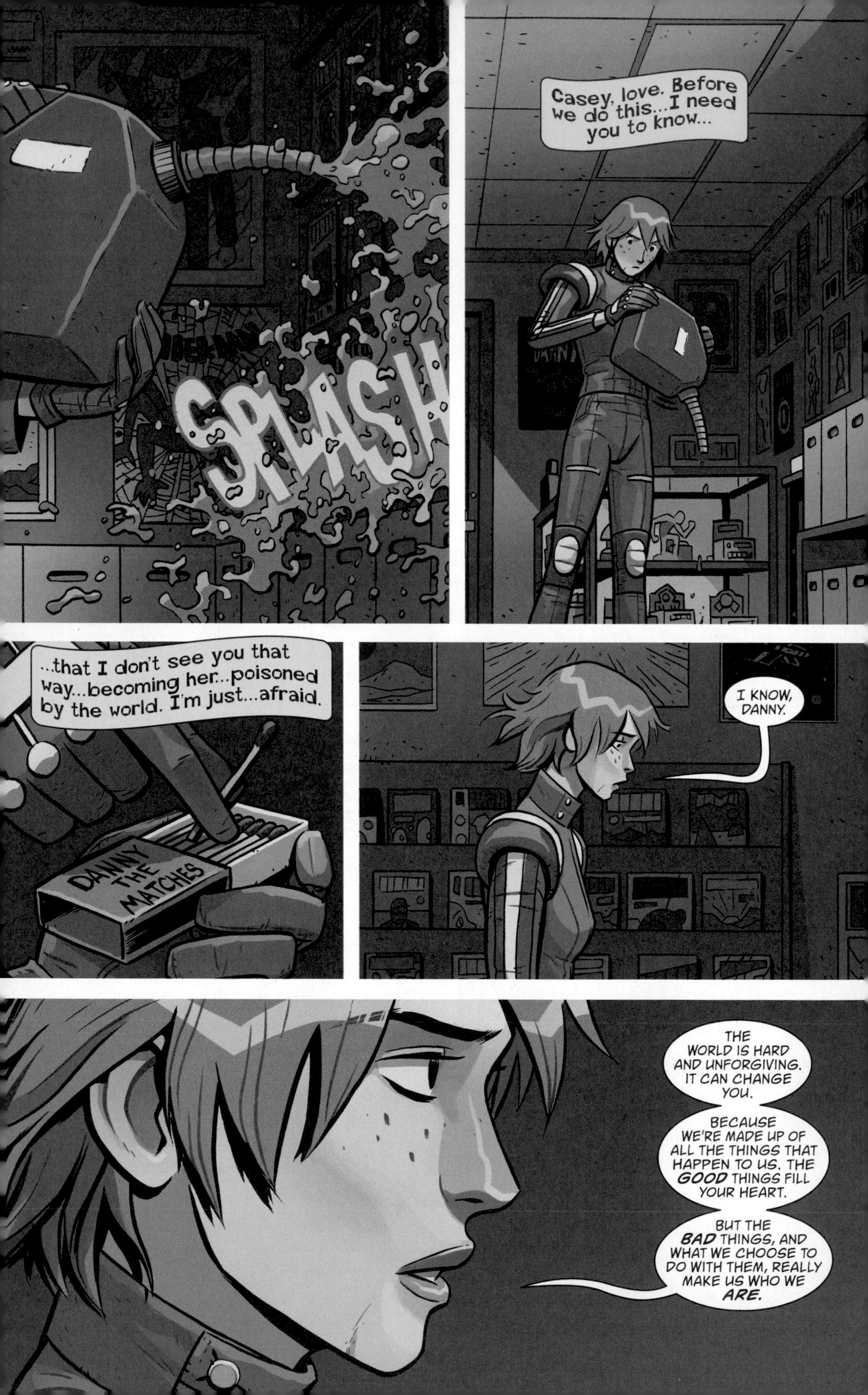
SPLASH
Casey, love. Before we do this...I need you to know...
...that I don't see you that way...becoming her...poisoned by the world. I'm just...afraid.
DANNY THE MATCHES
I KNOW, DANNY.
THE WORLD IS HARD AND UNFORGIVING. IT CAN CHANGE YOU.
BECAUSE WE'RE MADE UP OF ALL THE THINGS THAT HAPPEN TO US. THE GOOD THINGS FILL YOUR HEART.
BUT THE BAD THINGS, AND WHAT WE CHOOSE TO DO WITH THEM, REALLY MAKE US WHO WE ARE.

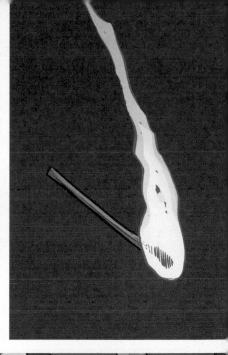

I'LL KEEP CHOOSING LOVE.

I'M SO PROUD OF YOU, CASEY.

I KNOW. IT'S WHY I KEEP BURNING BRIGHT.

SCREEEEEEEEEEE

RUN, CASEY!

GATHER ALL THE PEOPLE AND GET BACK TO YOUR DANNY!

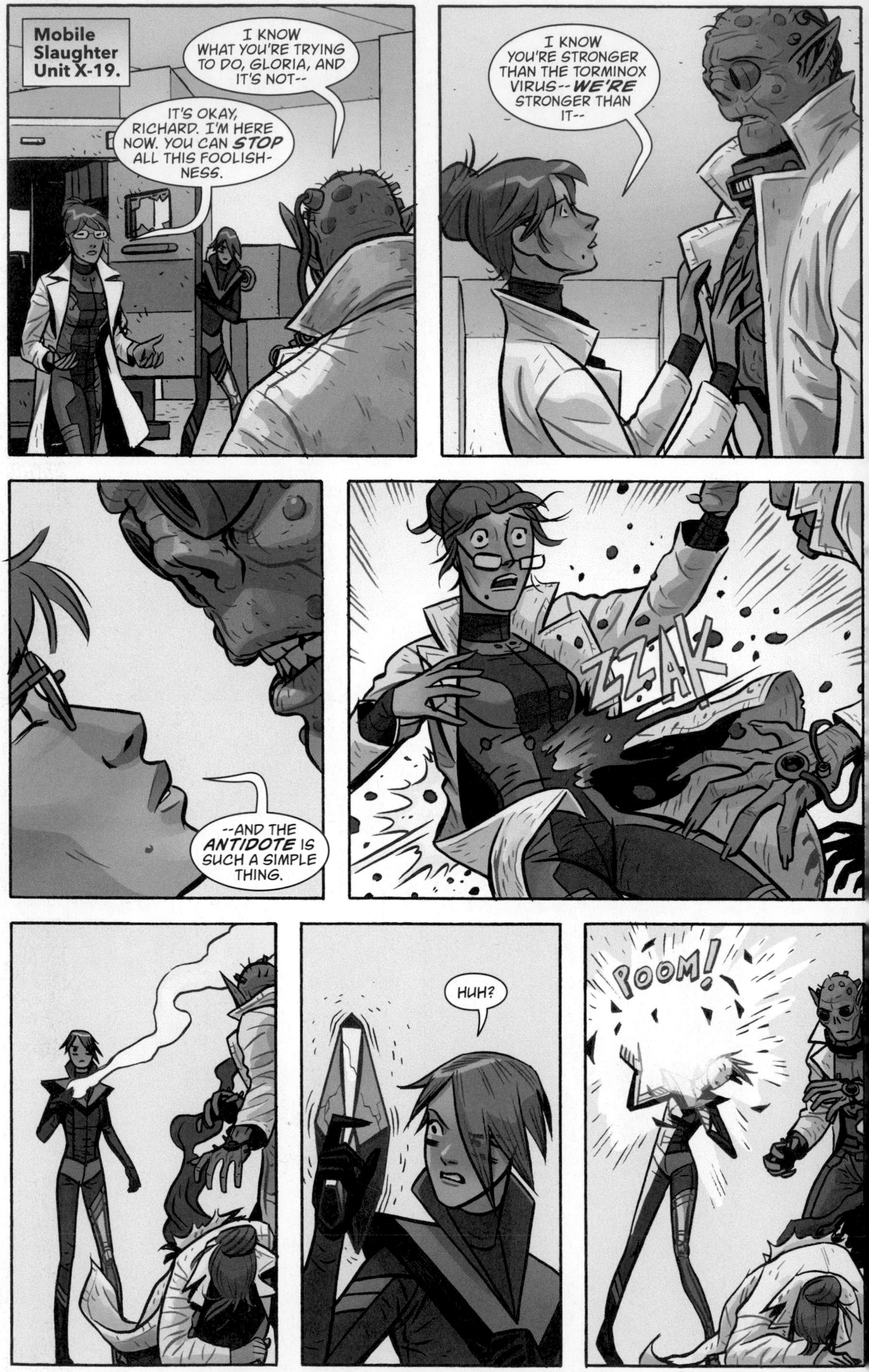
Mobile Slaughter Unit X-19.
I KNOW WHAT YOU'RE TRYING TO DO, GLORIA, AND IT'S NOT--
IT'S OKAY, RICHARD. I'M HERE NOW. YOU CAN STOP ALL THIS FOOLISHNESS.
I KNOW YOU'RE STRONGER THAN THE TORMINOX VIRUS--WE'RE STRONGER THAN IT--
--AND THE ANTIDOTE IS SUCH A SIMPLE THING.
ZZAK
HUH?
POOM!

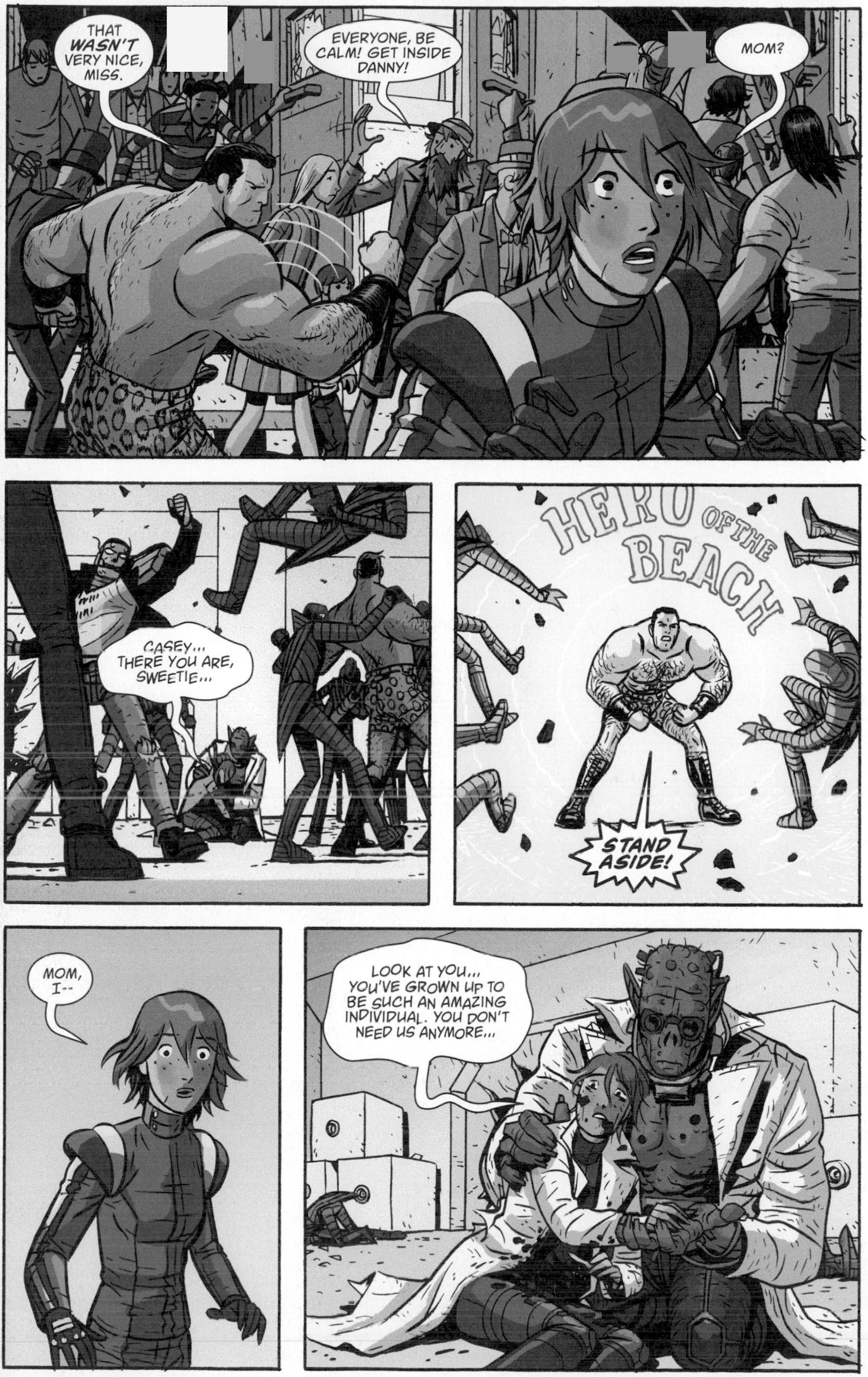

THAT WASN'T VERY NICE, MISS.
EVERYONE, BE CALM! GET INSIDE DANNY!
MOM?
CASEY... THERE YOU ARE, SWEETIE...
HERO OF THE BEACH
STAND ASIDE!
MOM, I--
LOOK AT YOU... YOU'VE GROWN UP TO BE SUCH AN AMAZING INDIVIDUAL. YOU DON'T NEED US ANYMORE...

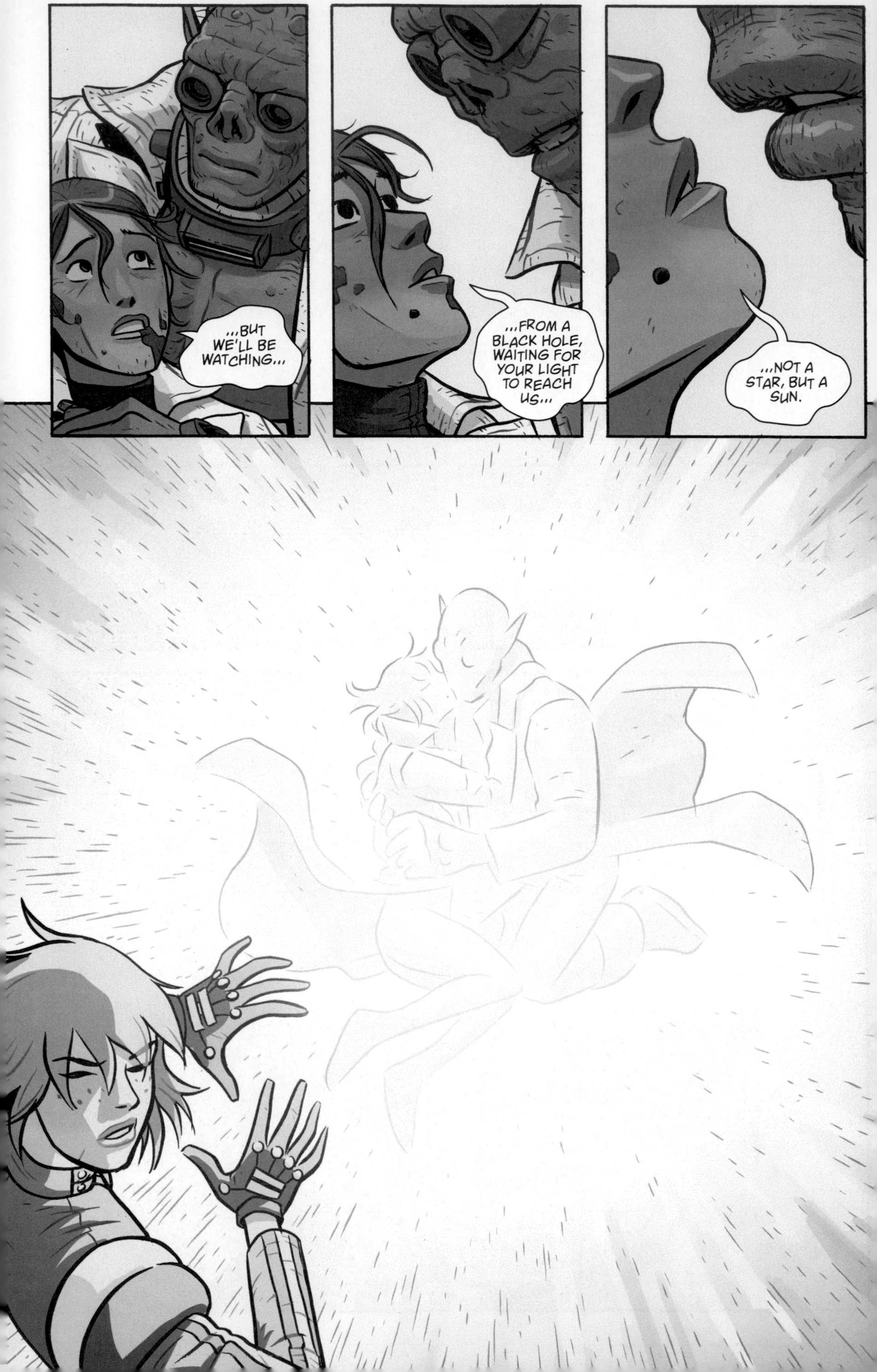
...BUT WE'LL BE WATCHING...
...FROM A BLACK HOLE, WAITING FOR YOUR LIGHT TO REACH US...
...NOT A STAR, BUT A SUN.

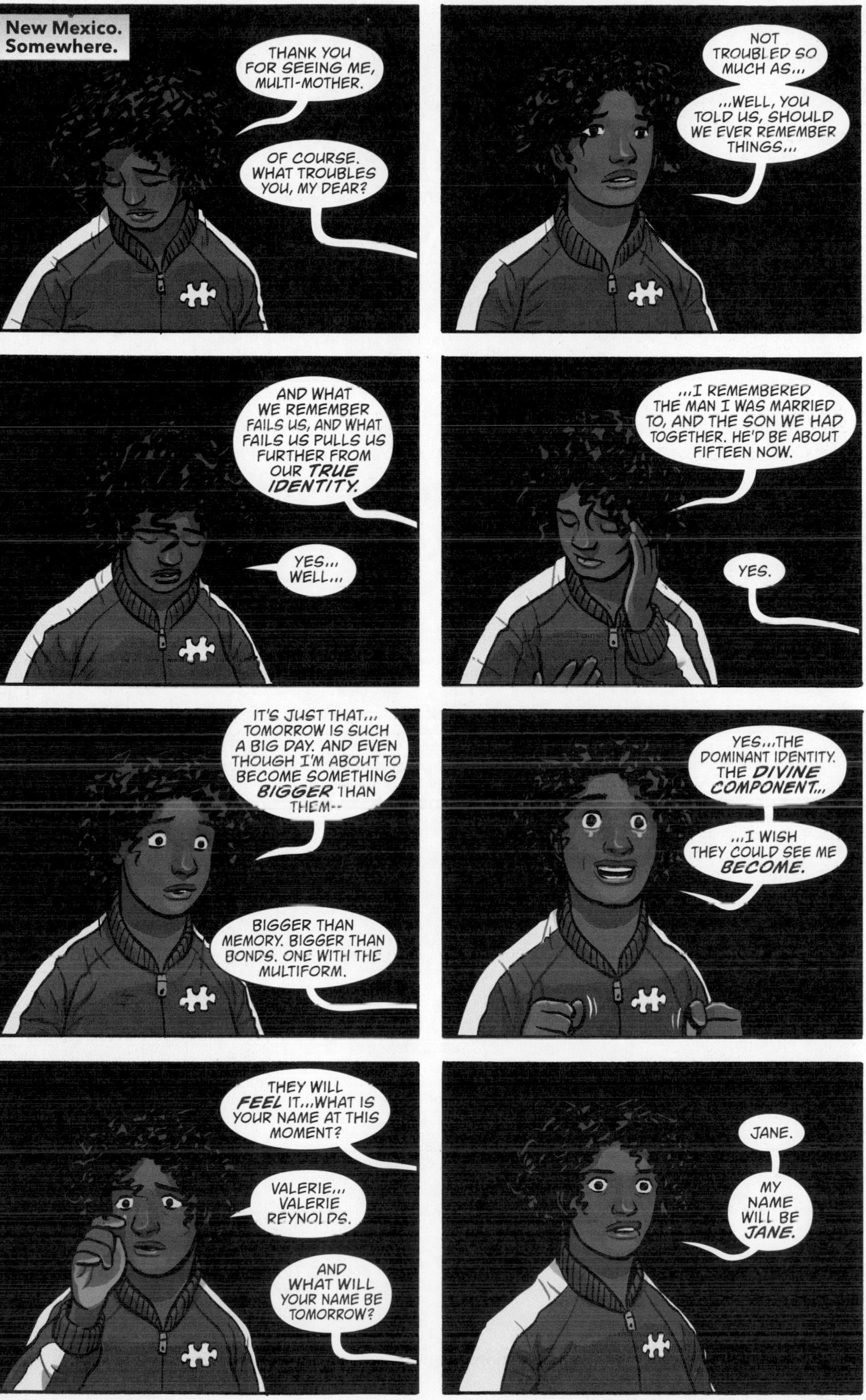
New Mexico. Somewhere.
THANK YOU FOR SEEING ME, MULTI-MOTHER.
OF COURSE. WHAT TROUBLES YOU, MY DEAR?
NOT TROUBLED SO MUCH AS...
...WELL, YOU TOLD US, SHOULD WE EVER REMEMBER THINGS...
AND WHAT WE REMEMBER FAILS US, AND WHAT FAILS US PULLS US FURTHER FROM OUR TRUE IDENTITY.
YES... WELL...
...I REMEMBERED THE MAN I WAS MARRIED TO, AND THE SON WE HAD TOGETHER. HE'D BE ABOUT FIFTEEN NOW.
YES.
IT'S JUST THAT... TOMORROW IS SUCH A BIG DAY. AND EVEN THOUGH I'M ABOUT TO BECOME SOMETHING BIGGER THAN THEM--
BIGGER THAN MEMORY. BIGGER THAN BONDS. ONE WITH THE MULTIFORM.
YES...THE DOMINANT IDENTITY. THE DIVINE COMPONENT...
...I WISH THEY COULD SEE ME BECOME.
THEY WILL FEEL IT...WHAT IS YOUR NAME AT THIS MOMENT?
VALERIE... VALERIE REYNOLDS.
AND WHAT WILL YOUR NAME BE TOMORROW?
JANE.
MY NAME WILL BE JANE.

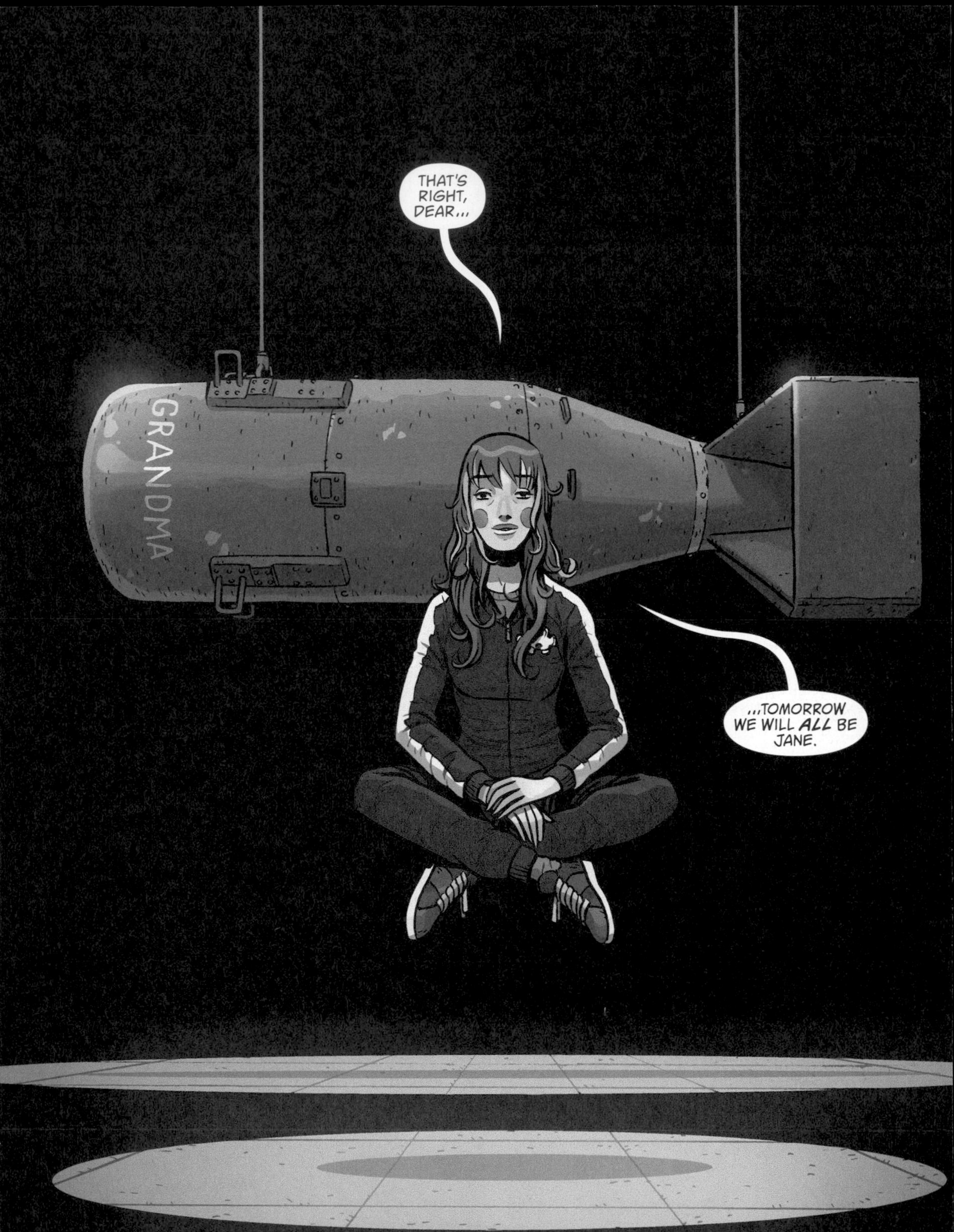
THAT'S RIGHT, DEAR...
GRANDMA
...TOMORROW WE WILL ALL BE JANE.

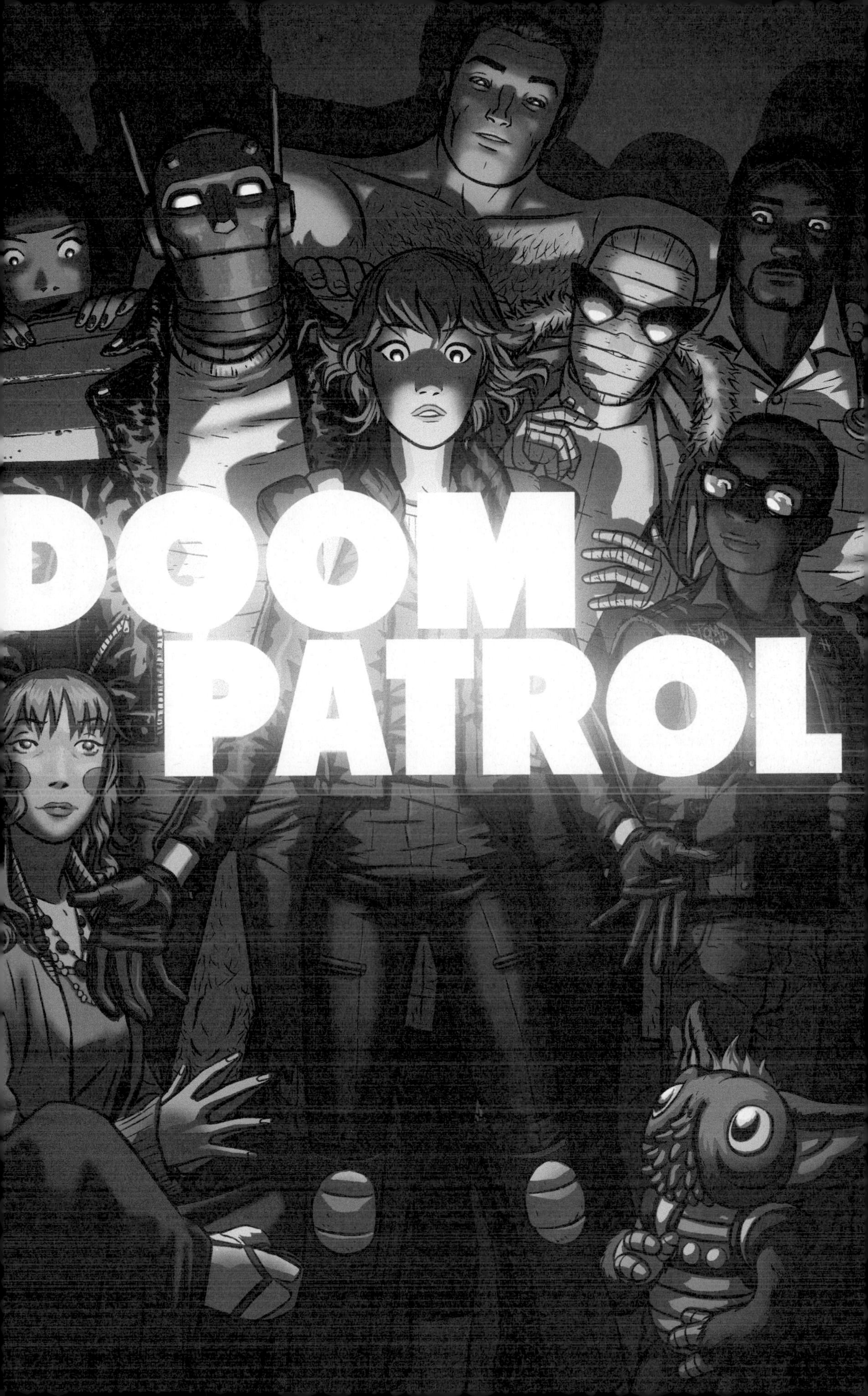
DOOM
PATROL

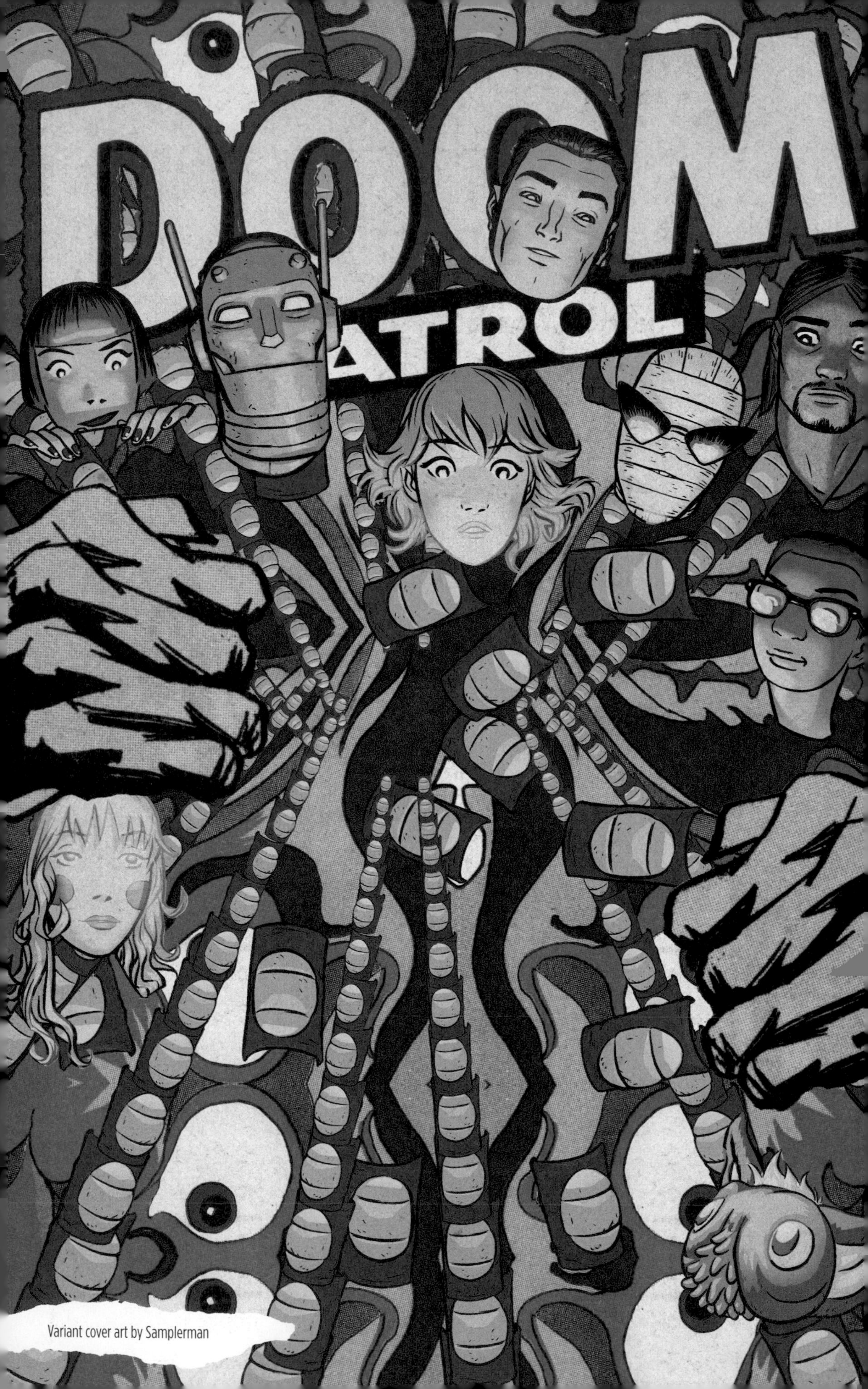
DOOM
ATROL

Variant cover art by Samplerman

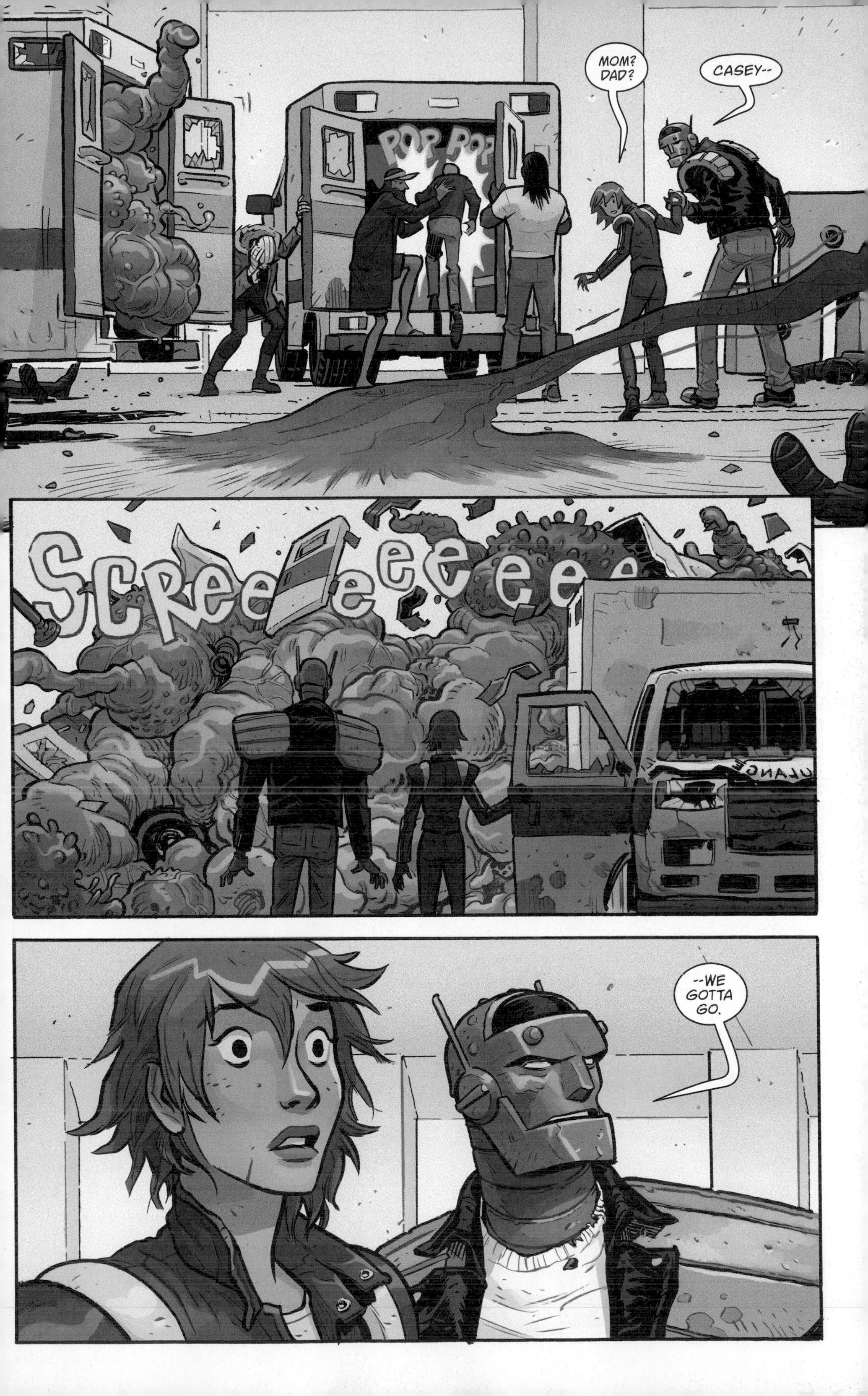
POP POP
MOM? DAD?
CASEY--
SCREEEEEEEE
--WE GOTTA GO.

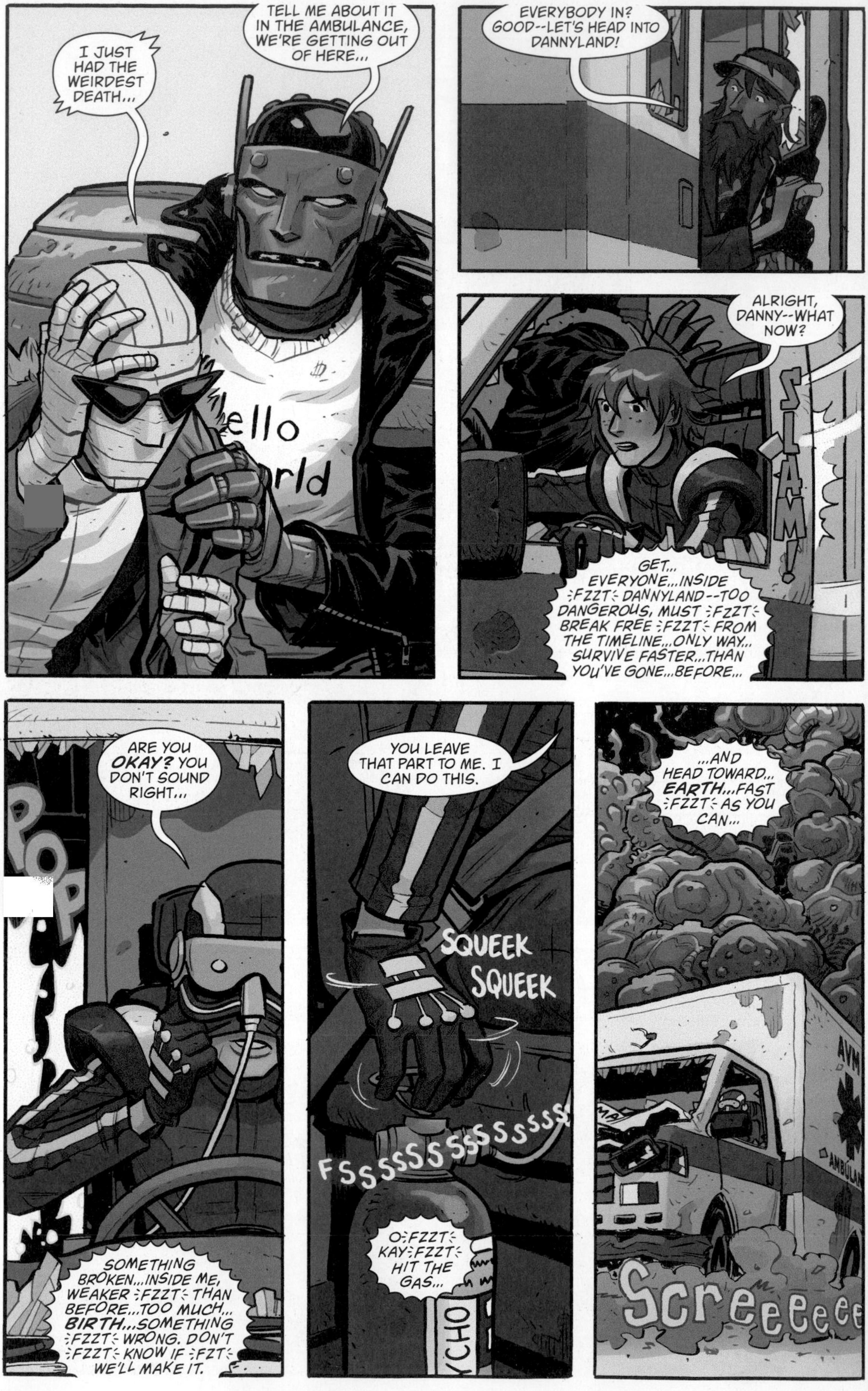
I JUST HAD THE WEIRDEST DEATH...
TELL ME ABOUT IT IN THE AMBULANCE, WE'RE GETTING OUT OF HERE...
Hello World
EVERYBODY IN? GOOD--LET'S HEAD INTO DANNYLAND!
ALRIGHT, DANNY--WHAT NOW?
SLAM!
GET... EVERYONE...INSIDE ⋮FZZT⋮ DANNYLAND--TOO DANGEROUS, MUST ⋮FZZT⋮ BREAK FREE ⋮FZZT⋮ FROM THE TIMELINE...ONLY WAY... SURVIVE FASTER...THAN YOU'VE GONE...BEFORE...
POP
ARE YOU **OKAY?** YOU DON'T SOUND RIGHT...
SOMETHING BROKEN...INSIDE ME, WEAKER ⋮FZZT⋮ THAN BEFORE...TOO MUCH... **BIRTH...**SOMETHING ⋮FZZT⋮ WRONG. DON'T ⋮FZZT⋮ KNOW IF ⋮FZT⋮ WE'LL MAKE IT.
YOU LEAVE THAT PART TO ME. I CAN DO THIS.
SQUEEK
SQUEEK
FSSSSSSSSSSSSSSS
O⋮FZZT⋮ KAY⋮FZZT⋮ HIT THE GAS...
...AND HEAD TOWARD... **EARTH...**FAST ⋮FZZT⋮ AS YOU CAN...
Screeeeeee

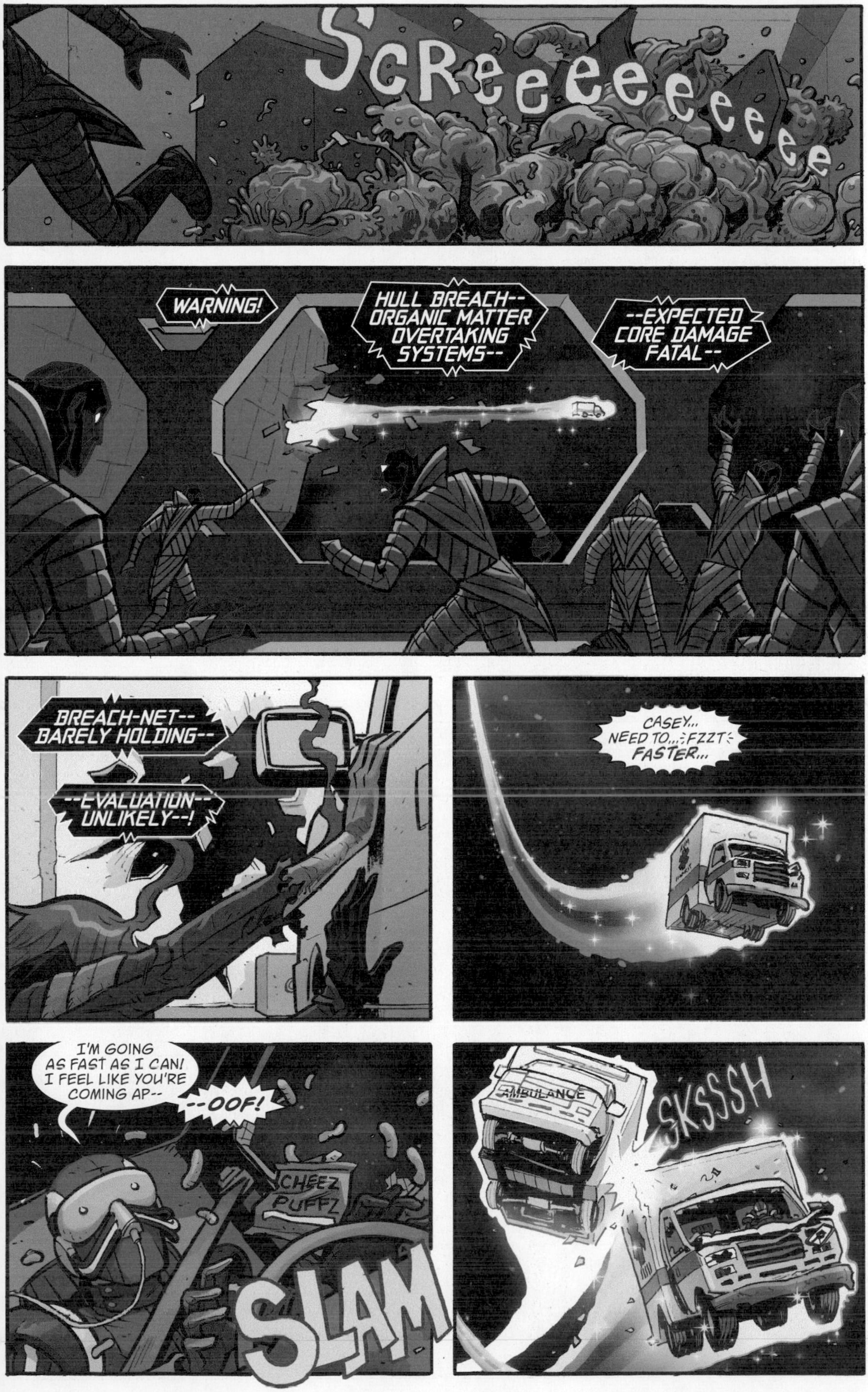
SCREEEEEEEEEE
WARNING!
HULL BREACH-- ORGANIC MATTER OVERTAKING SYSTEMS--
--EXPECTED CORE DAMAGE FATAL--
BREACH-NET-- BARELY HOLDING--
--EVALUATION-- UNLIKELY--!
CASEY... NEED TO... FZZT FASTER...
I'M GOING AS FAST AS I CAN! I FEEL LIKE YOU'RE COMING AP--
--OOF!
CHEEZ PUFFZ
SLAM
AMBULANCE
SKSSSH

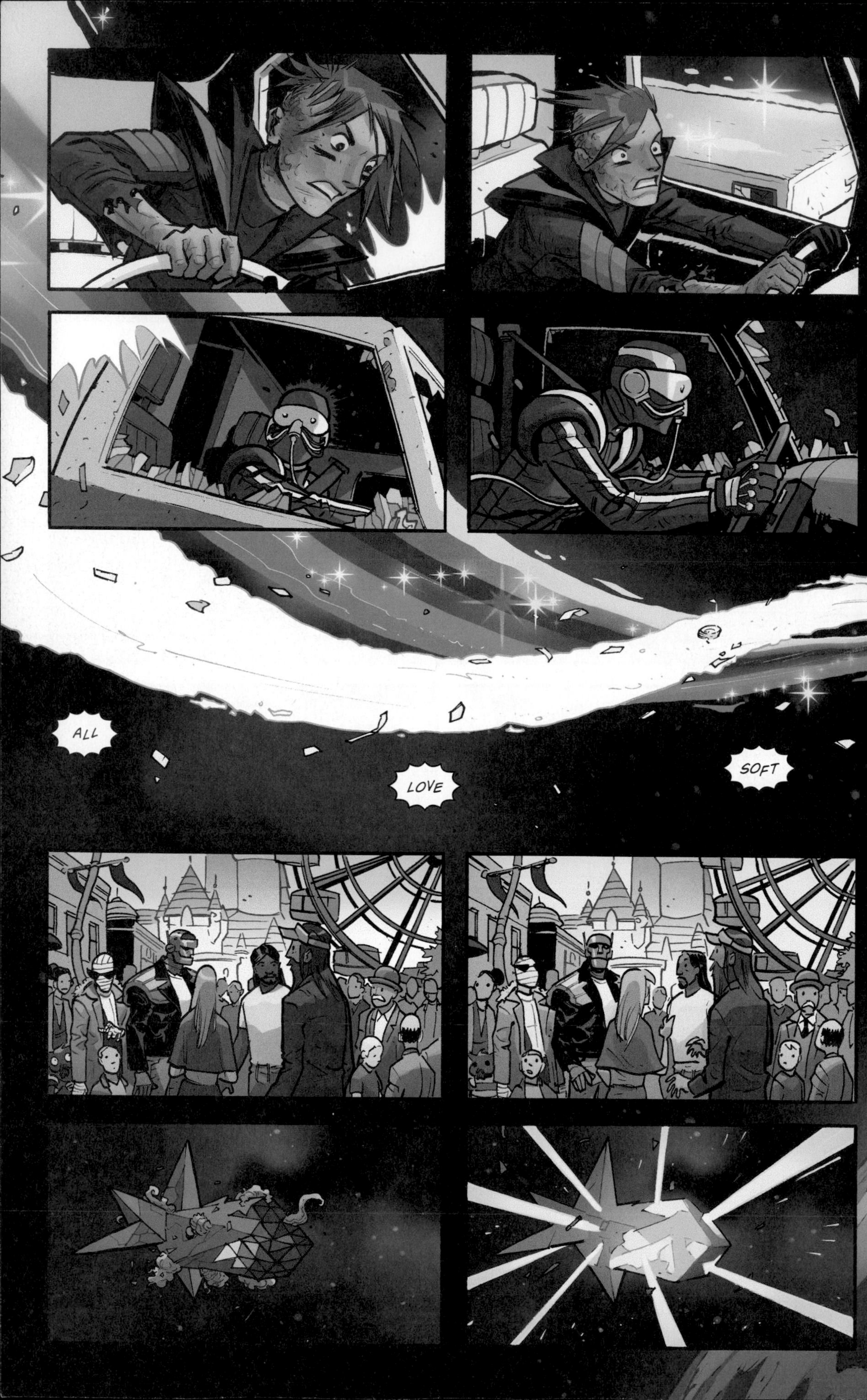
ALL
LOVE
SOFT

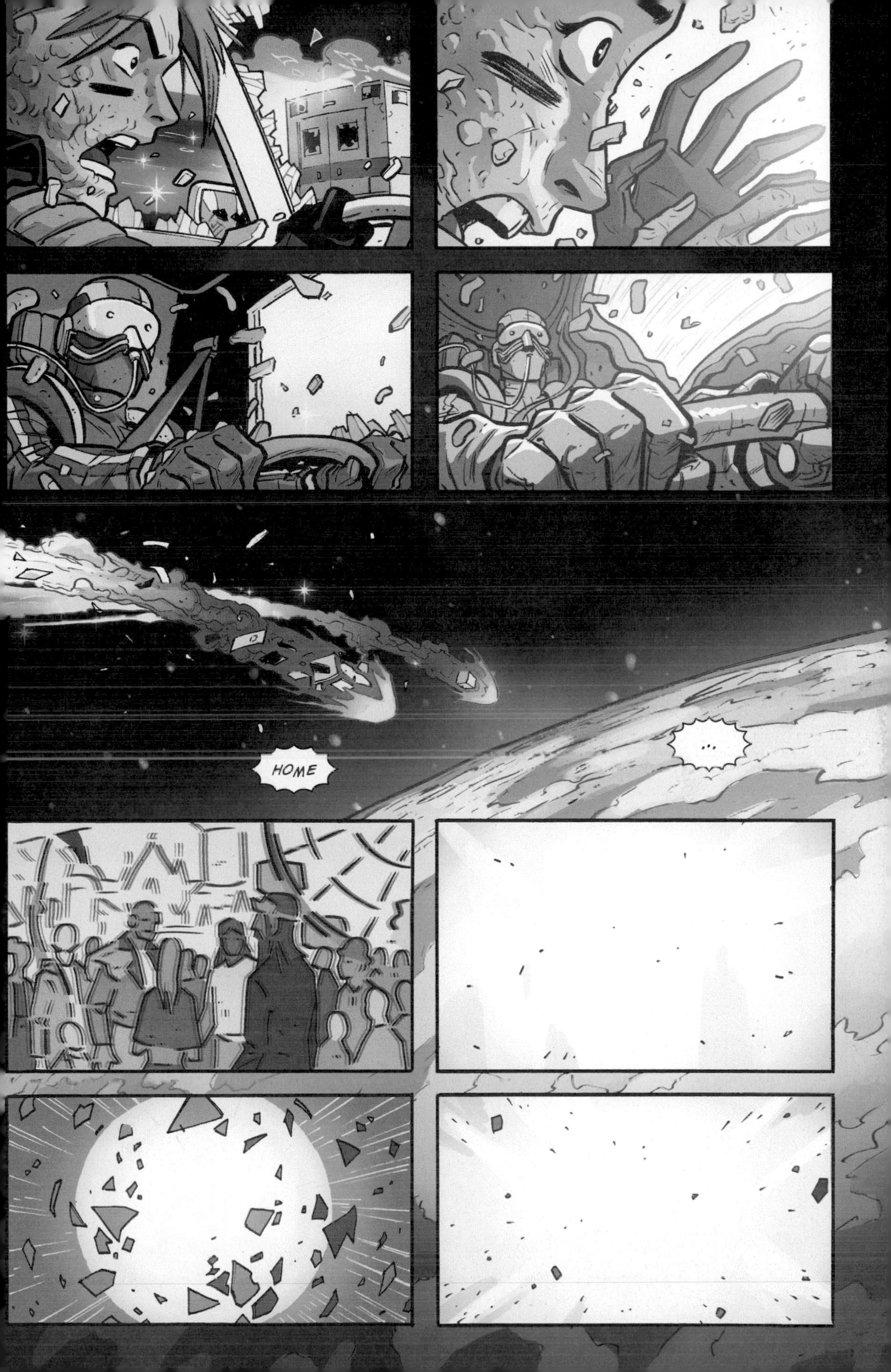
HOME
...

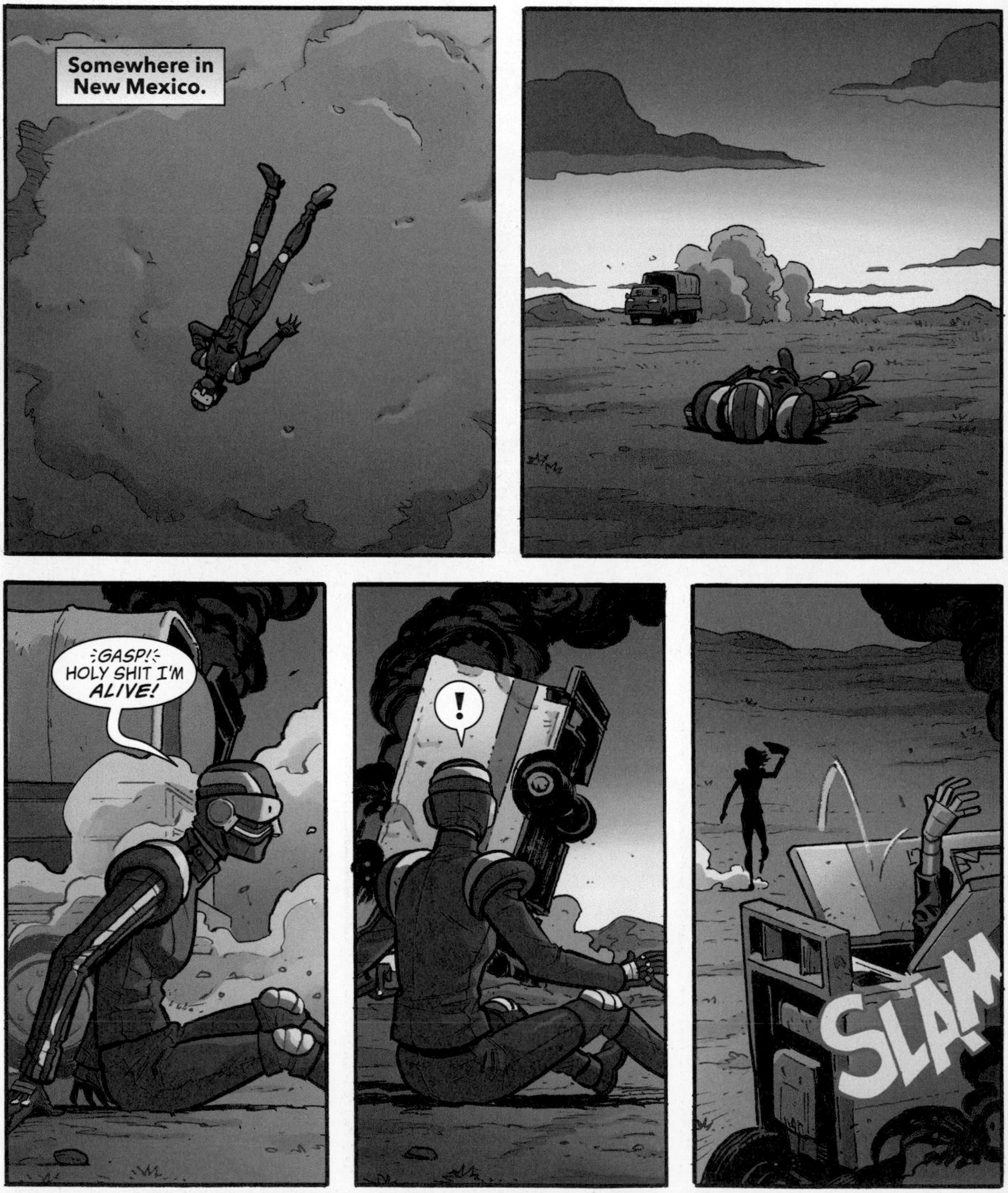
Somewhere in New Mexico.
GASP! HOLY SHIT I'M ALIVE!
!
SLAM

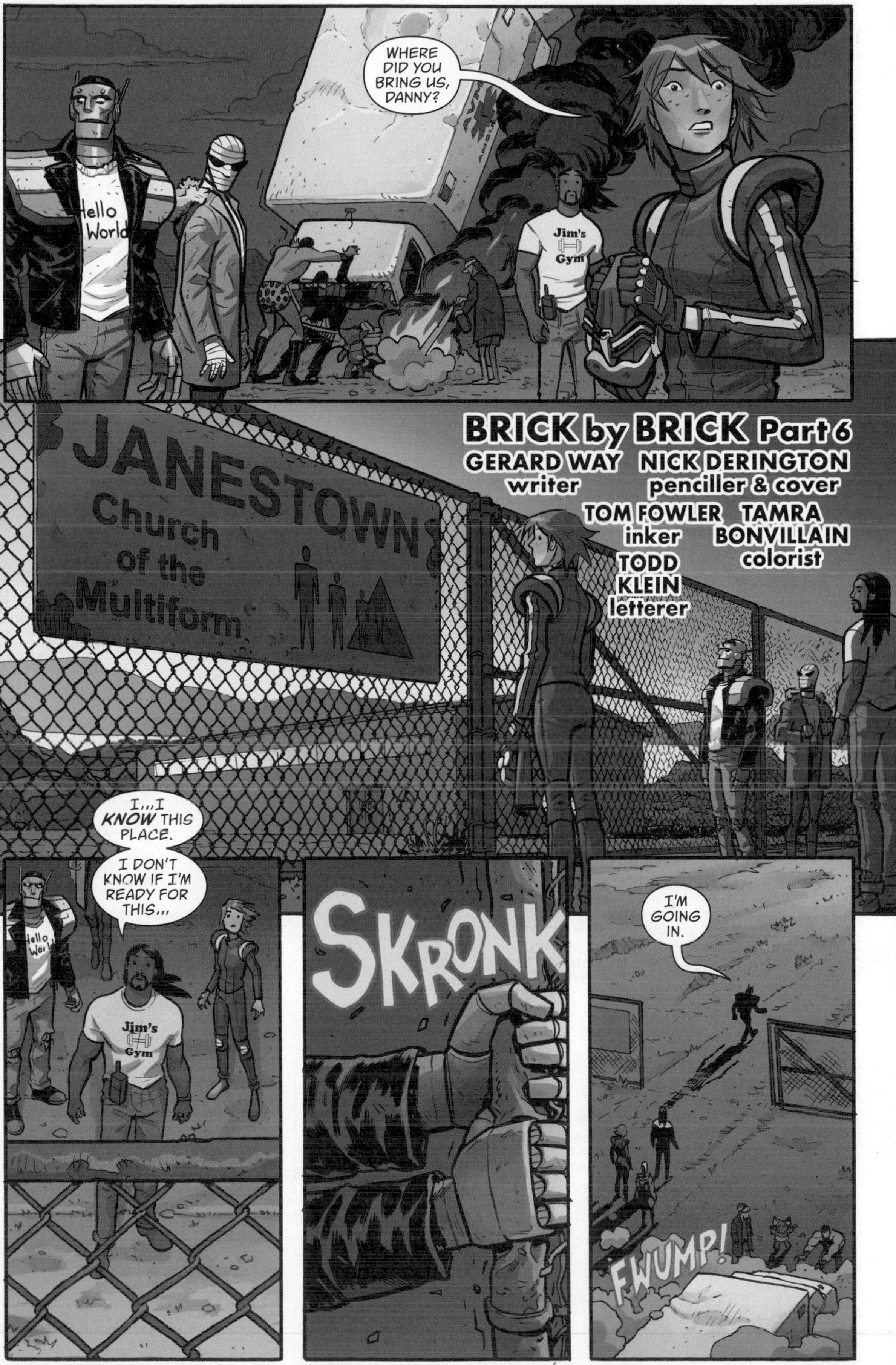
WHERE DID YOU BRING US, DANNY?
Hello World
Jim's Gym
JANESTOWN
Church of the Multiform
BRICK by BRICK Part 6
GERARD WAY writer
NICK DERINGTON penciller & cover
TOM FOWLER inker
TAMRA BONVILLAIN colorist
TODD KLEIN letterer
I...I KNOW THIS PLACE.
I DON'T KNOW IF I'M READY FOR THIS...
SKRONK
I'M GOING IN.
FWUMP!

MOLLY MAHAN assoc. ed. JAMIE S. RICH editor Doom Patrol created by Arnold Drake

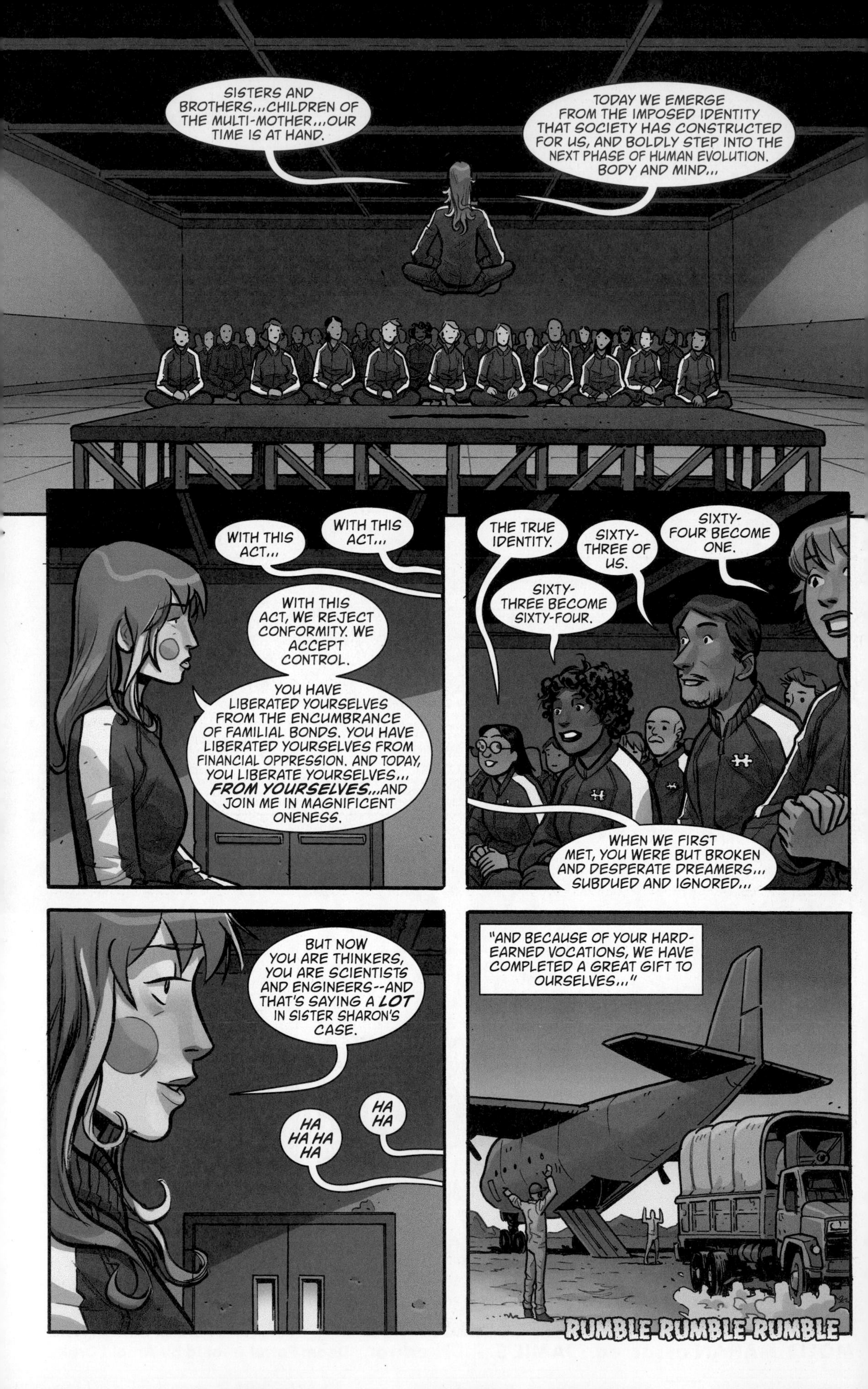
SISTERS AND BROTHERS...CHILDREN OF THE MULTI-MOTHER...OUR TIME IS AT HAND.
TODAY WE EMERGE FROM THE IMPOSED IDENTITY THAT SOCIETY HAS CONSTRUCTED FOR US, AND BOLDLY STEP INTO THE NEXT PHASE OF HUMAN EVOLUTION. BODY AND MIND...
WITH THIS ACT...
WITH THIS ACT...
WITH THIS ACT, WE REJECT CONFORMITY. WE ACCEPT CONTROL.
YOU HAVE LIBERATED YOURSELVES FROM THE ENCUMBRANCE OF FAMILIAL BONDS. YOU HAVE LIBERATED YOURSELVES FROM FINANCIAL OPPRESSION. AND TODAY, YOU LIBERATE YOURSELVES... ***FROM YOURSELVES...*** AND JOIN ME IN MAGNIFICENT ONENESS.
THE TRUE IDENTITY.
SIXTY-THREE BECOME SIXTY-FOUR.
SIXTY-THREE OF US.
SIXTY-FOUR BECOME ONE.
WHEN WE FIRST MET, YOU WERE BUT BROKEN AND DESPERATE DREAMERS... SUBDUED AND IGNORED...
BUT NOW YOU ARE THINKERS, YOU ARE SCIENTISTS AND ENGINEERS--AND THAT'S SAYING A ***LOT*** IN SISTER SHARON'S CASE.
HA HA HA HA
HA HA
"AND BECAUSE OF YOUR HARD-EARNED VOCATIONS, WE HAVE COMPLETED A GREAT GIFT TO OURSELVES..."
RUMBLE RUMBLE RUMBLE

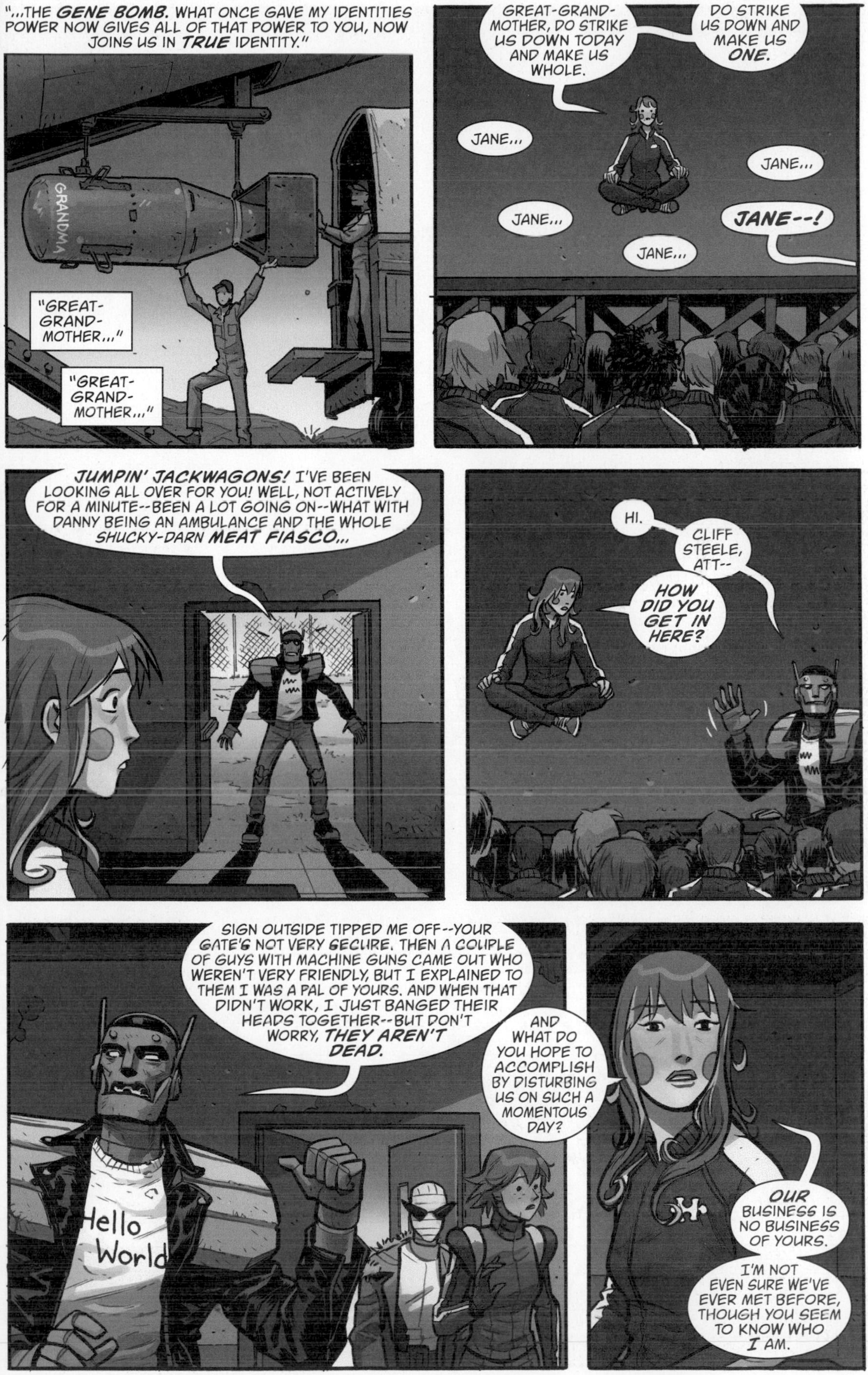
"...THE GENE BOMB. WHAT ONCE GAVE MY IDENTITIES POWER NOW GIVES ALL OF THAT POWER TO YOU, NOW JOINS US IN TRUE IDENTITY."
GRANDMA
"GREAT-GRAND-MOTHER..."
"GREAT-GRAND-MOTHER..."
GREAT-GRAND-MOTHER, DO STRIKE US DOWN TODAY AND MAKE US WHOLE.
DO STRIKE US DOWN AND MAKE US ONE.
JANE...
JANE...
JANE...
JANE...
JANE--!
JUMPIN' JACKWAGONS! I'VE BEEN LOOKING ALL OVER FOR YOU! WELL, NOT ACTIVELY FOR A MINUTE--BEEN A LOT GOING ON--WHAT WITH DANNY BEING AN AMBULANCE AND THE WHOLE SHUCKY-DARN MEAT FIASCO...
HI.
CLIFF STEELE, ATT--
HOW DID YOU GET IN HERE?
SIGN OUTSIDE TIPPED ME OFF--YOUR GATE'S NOT VERY SECURE. THEN A COUPLE OF GUYS WITH MACHINE GUNS CAME OUT WHO WEREN'T VERY FRIENDLY, BUT I EXPLAINED TO THEM I WAS A PAL OF YOURS. AND WHEN THAT DIDN'T WORK, I JUST BANGED THEIR HEADS TOGETHER--BUT DON'T WORRY, THEY AREN'T DEAD.
Hello World
AND WHAT DO YOU HOPE TO ACCOMPLISH BY DISTURBING US ON SUCH A MOMENTOUS DAY?
OUR BUSINESS IS NO BUSINESS OF YOURS.
I'M NOT EVEN SURE WE'VE EVER MET BEFORE, THOUGH YOU SEEM TO KNOW WHO I AM.

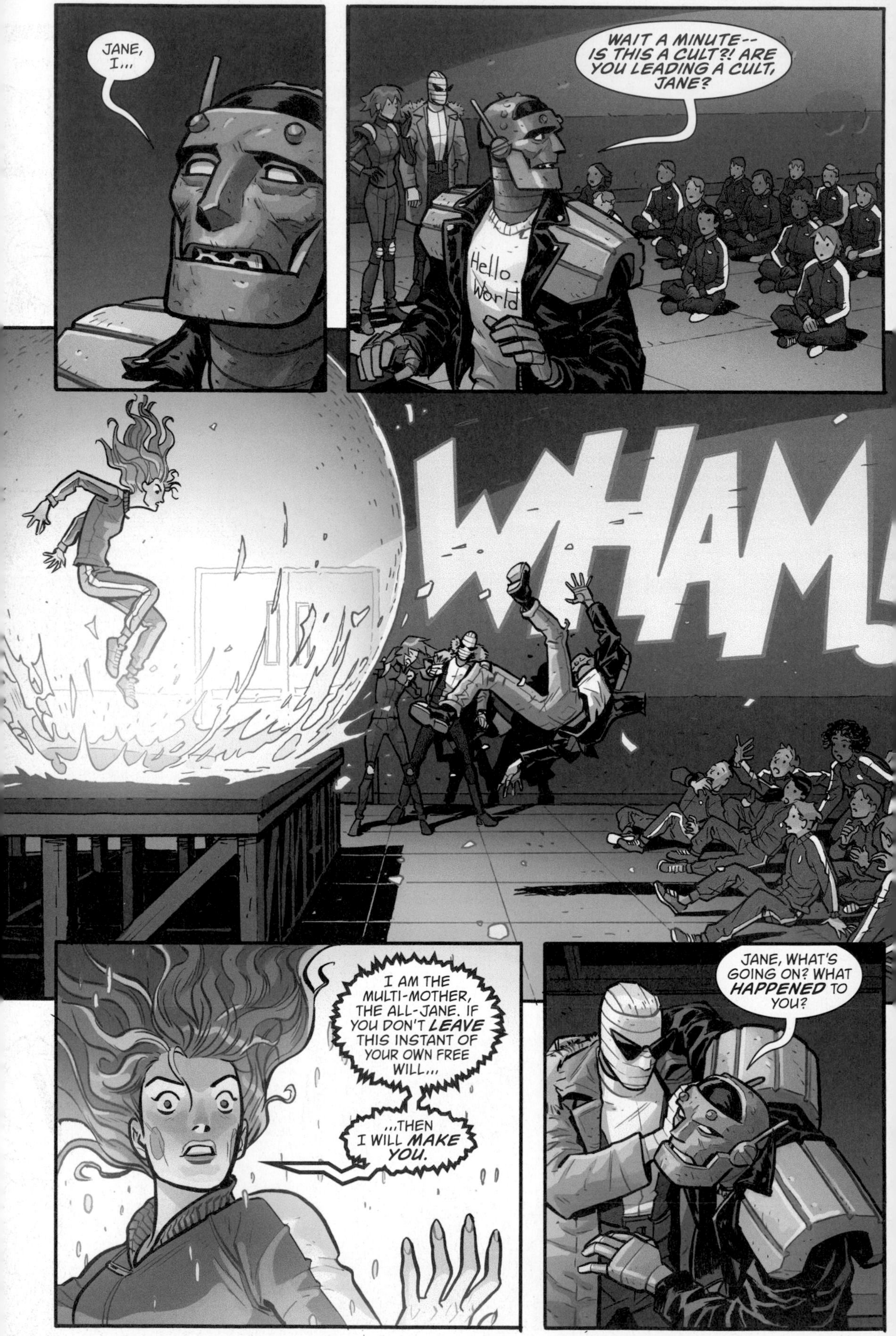
JANE, I...
WAIT A MINUTE-- IS THIS A CULT?! ARE YOU LEADING A CULT, JANE?
Hello World
WHAM!
I AM THE MULTI-MOTHER, THE ALL-JANE. IF YOU DON'T LEAVE THIS INSTANT OF YOUR OWN FREE WILL...
...THEN I WILL MAKE YOU.
JANE, WHAT'S GOING ON? WHAT HAPPENED TO YOU?

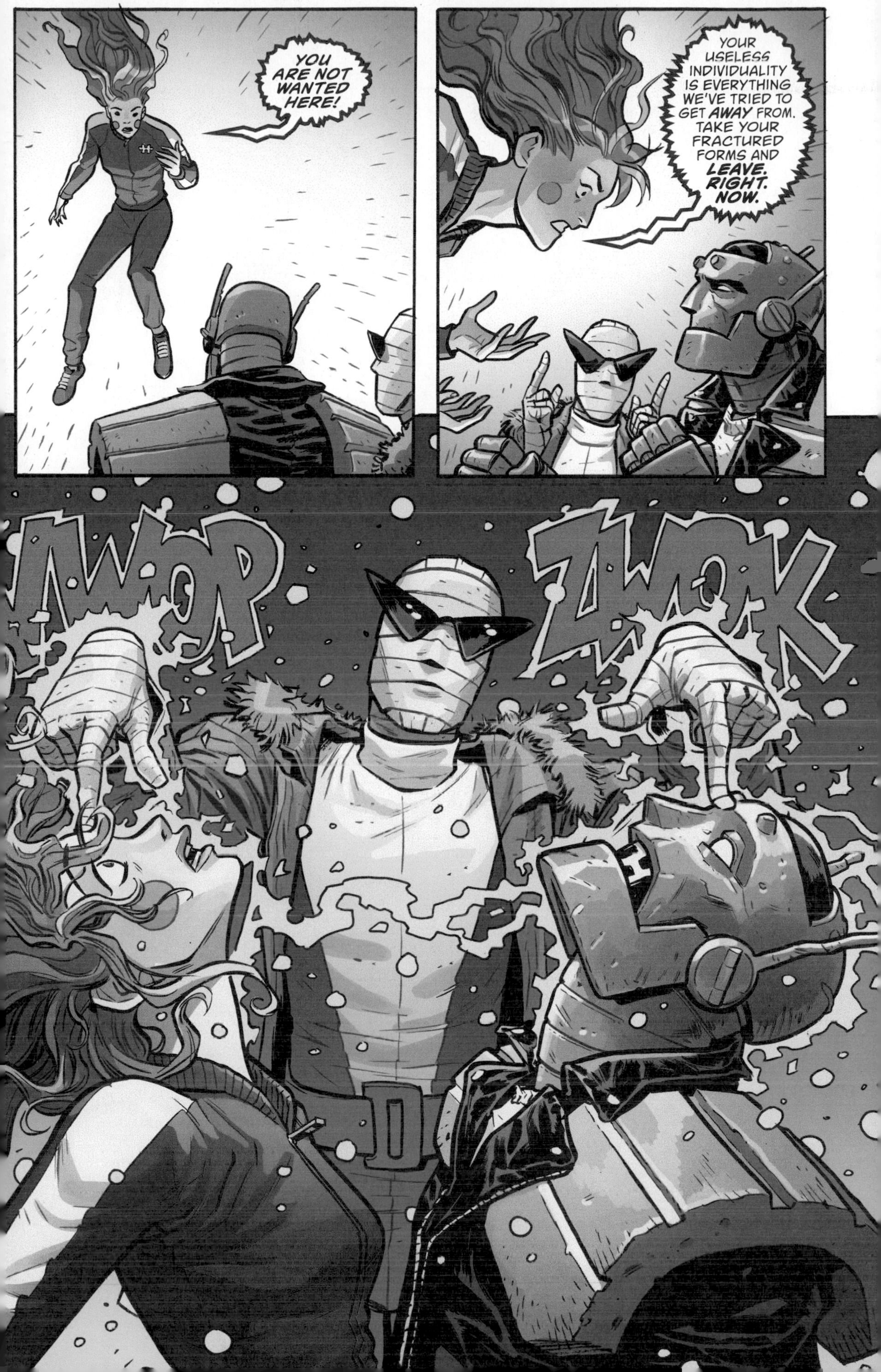
YOU ARE NOT WANTED HERE!
YOUR USELESS INDIVIDUALITY IS EVERYTHING WE'VE TRIED TO GET AWAY FROM. TAKE YOUR FRACTURED FORMS AND LEAVE. RIGHT. NOW.
WOP
ZWOK

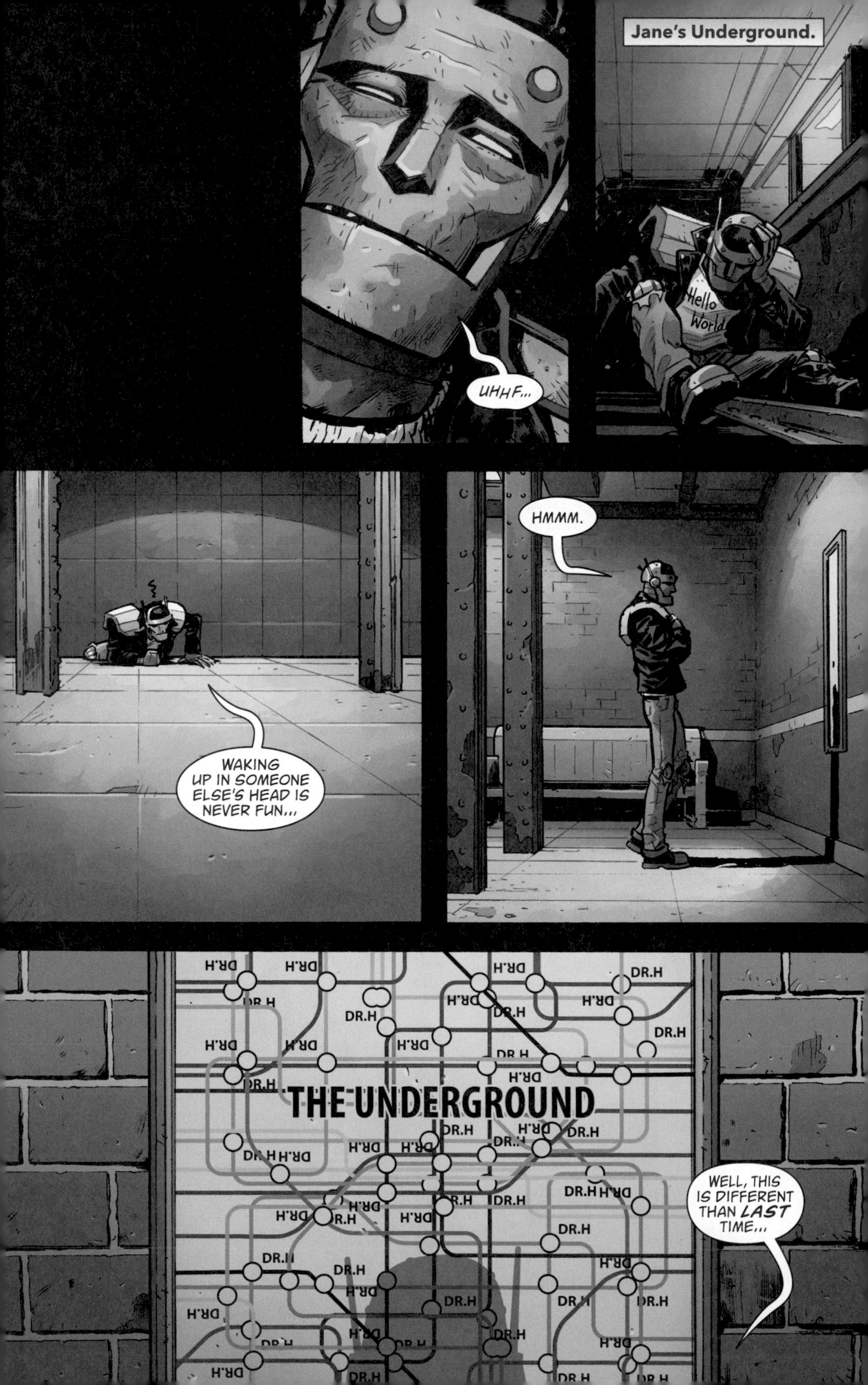
Jane's Underground.
UHHF...
WAKING UP IN SOMEONE ELSE'S HEAD IS NEVER FUN...
HMMM.
THE UNDERGROUND
WELL, THIS IS DIFFERENT THAN LAST TIME...

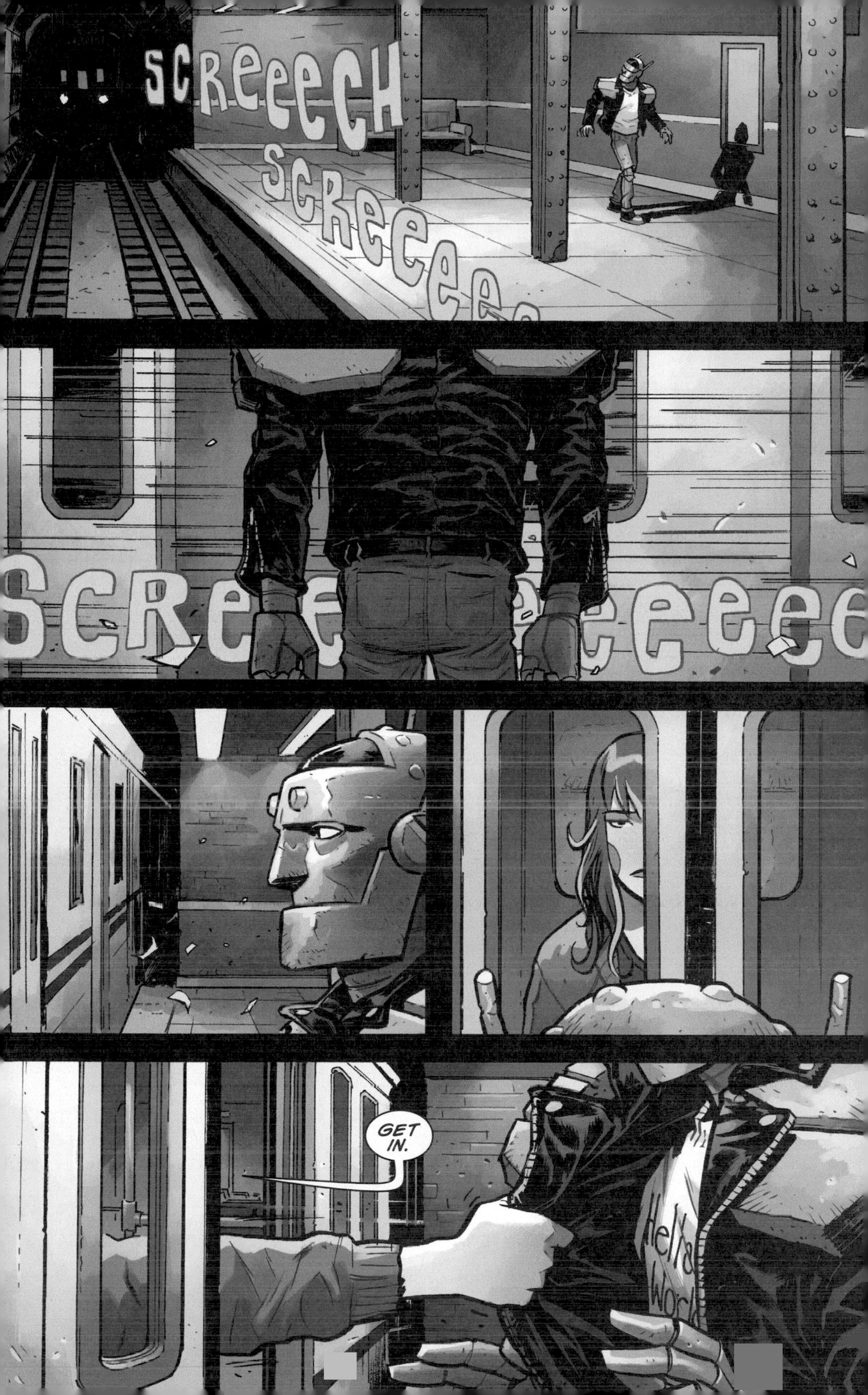
SCREEECH
GET IN.

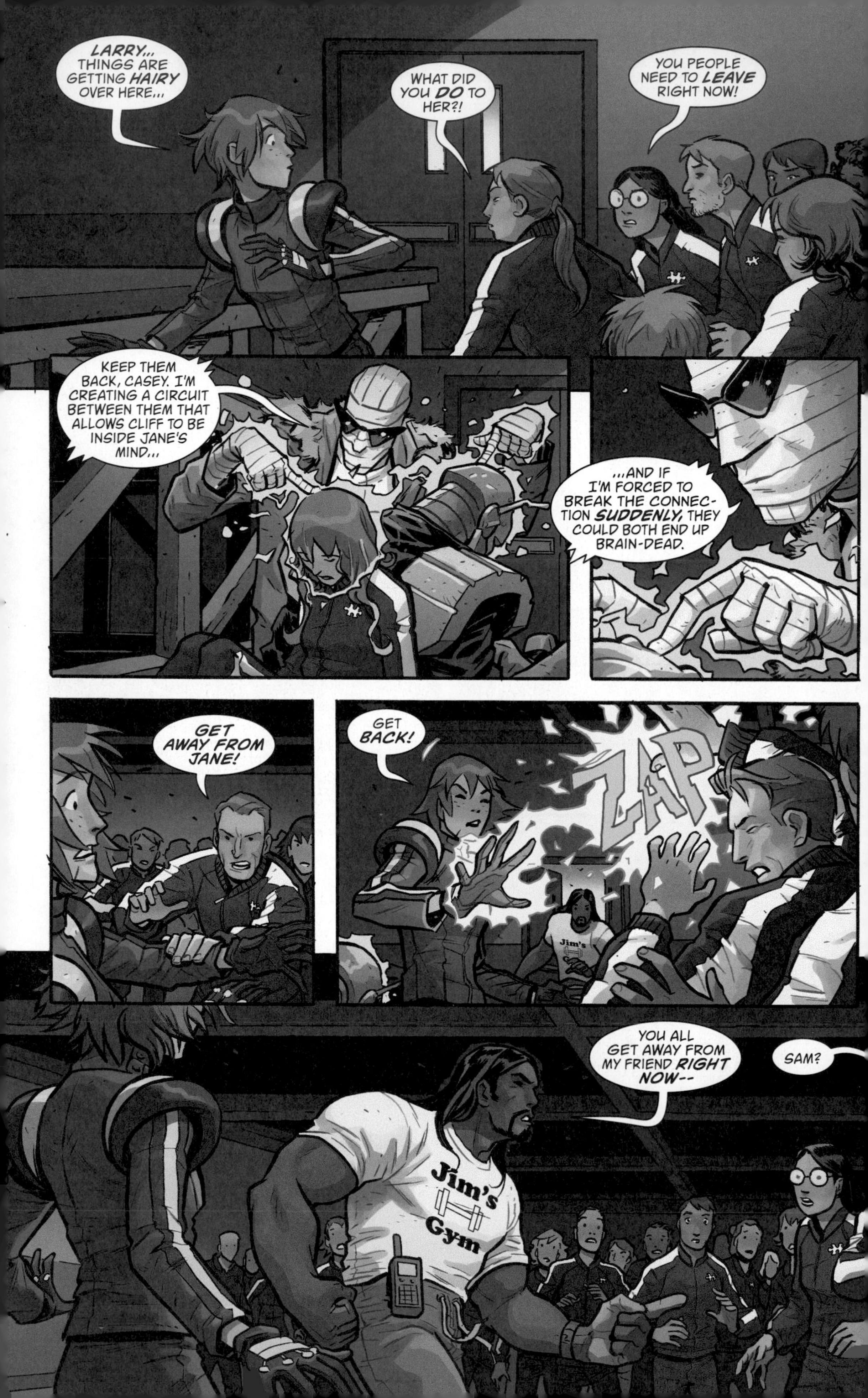
LARRY... THINGS ARE GETTING HAIRY OVER HERE...
WHAT DID YOU DO TO HER?!
YOU PEOPLE NEED TO LEAVE RIGHT NOW!
KEEP THEM BACK, CASEY. I'M CREATING A CIRCUIT BETWEEN THEM THAT ALLOWS CLIFF TO BE INSIDE JANE'S MIND...
...AND IF I'M FORCED TO BREAK THE CONNECTION SUDDENLY, THEY COULD BOTH END UP BRAIN-DEAD.
GET AWAY FROM JANE!
GET BACK!
ZAP
Jim's Gym
YOU ALL GET AWAY FROM MY FRIEND RIGHT NOW--
SAM?
Jim's Gym

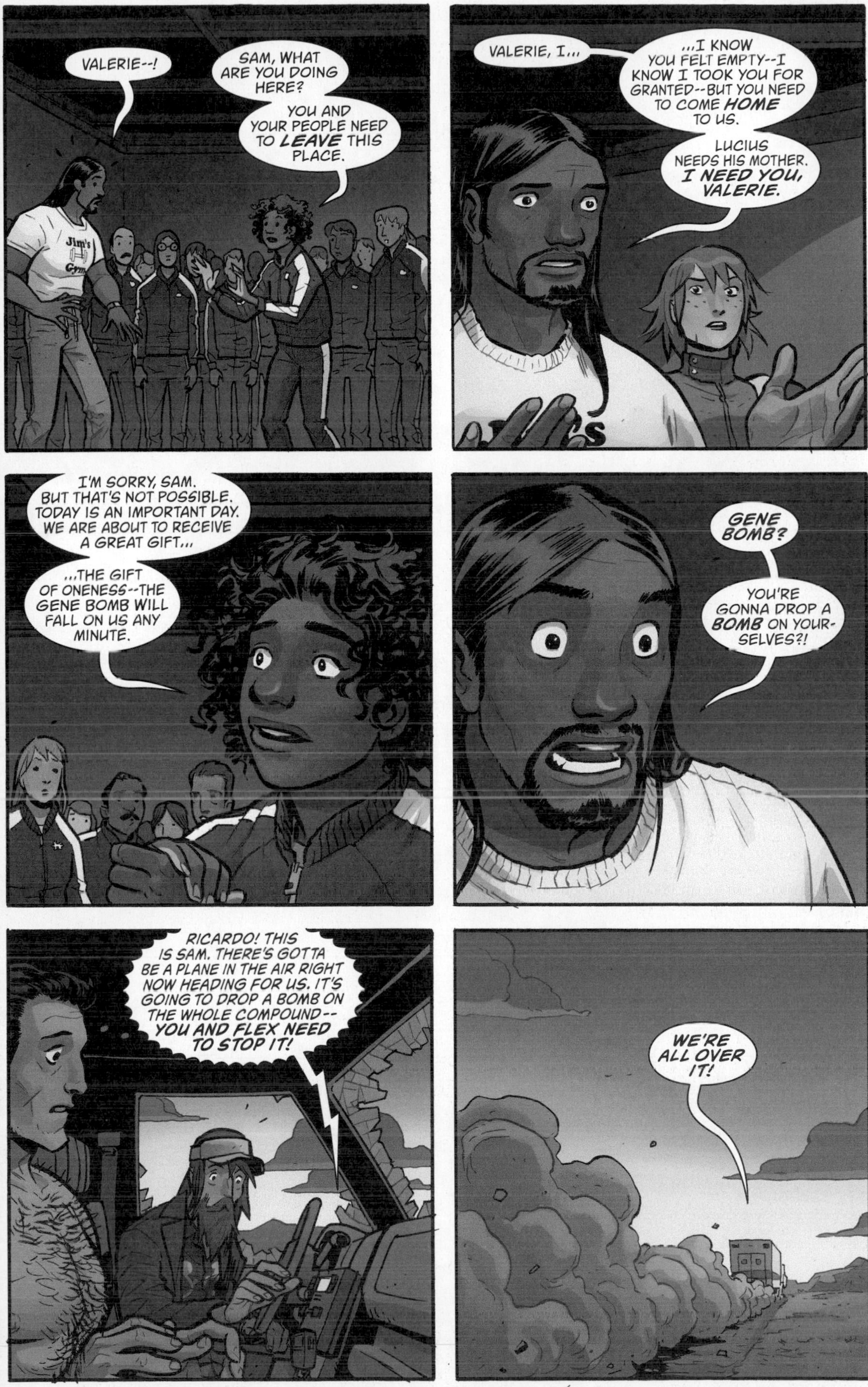
VALERIE--!
SAM, WHAT ARE YOU DOING HERE?
YOU AND YOUR PEOPLE NEED TO LEAVE THIS PLACE.
Jim's Gym
VALERIE, I...
...I KNOW YOU FELT EMPTY--I KNOW I TOOK YOU FOR GRANTED--BUT YOU NEED TO COME HOME TO US.
LUCIUS NEEDS HIS MOTHER. I NEED YOU, VALERIE.
I'M SORRY, SAM. BUT THAT'S NOT POSSIBLE. TODAY IS AN IMPORTANT DAY. WE ARE ABOUT TO RECEIVE A GREAT GIFT...
...THE GIFT OF ONENESS--THE GENE BOMB WILL FALL ON US ANY MINUTE.
GENE BOMB?
YOU'RE GONNA DROP A BOMB ON YOUR-SELVES?!
RICARDO! THIS IS SAM. THERE'S GOTTA BE A PLANE IN THE AIR RIGHT NOW HEADING FOR US. IT'S GOING TO DROP A BOMB ON THE WHOLE COMPOUND--YOU AND FLEX NEED TO STOP IT!
WE'RE ALL OVER IT!

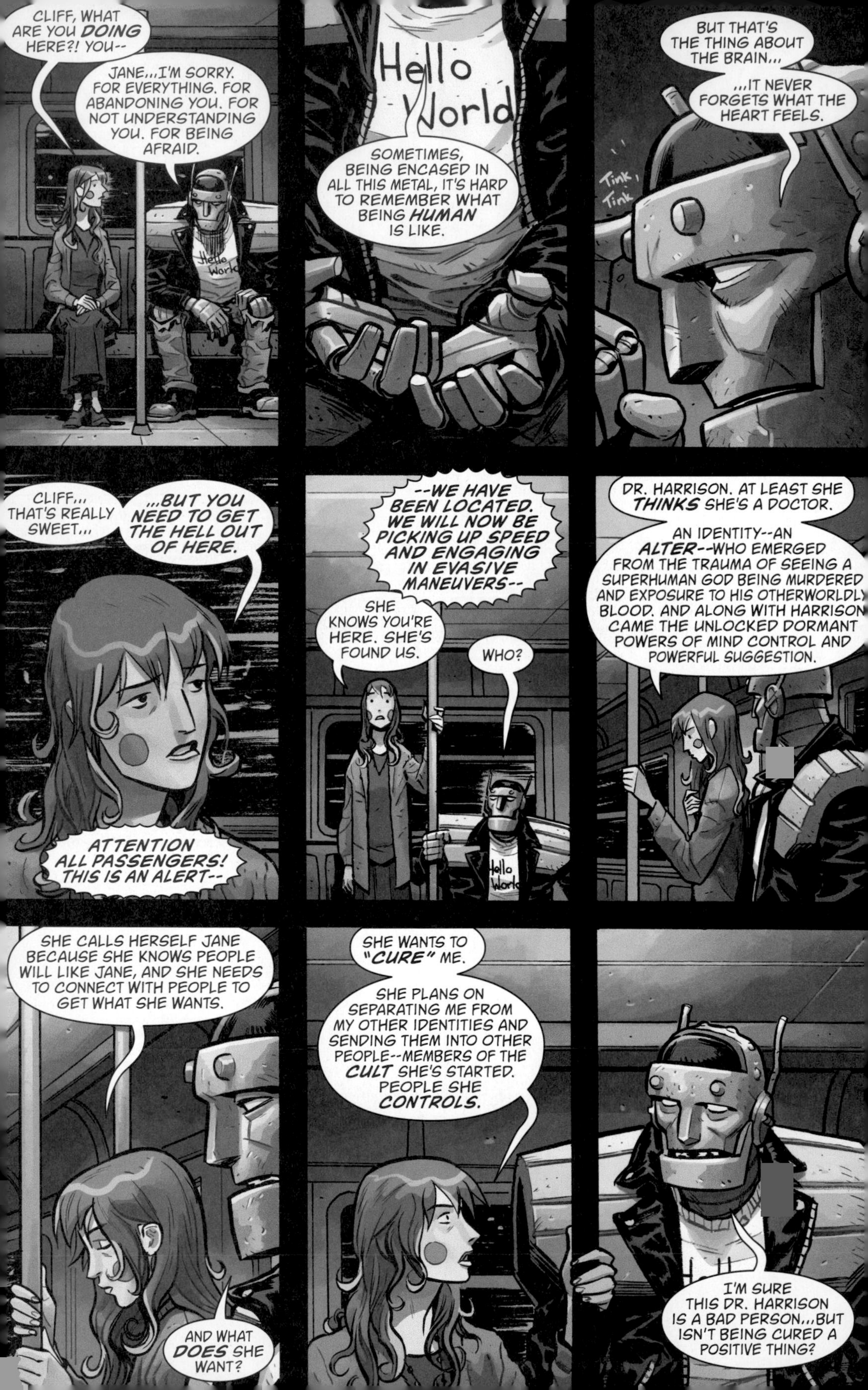
CLIFF, WHAT ARE YOU DOING HERE?! YOU--
JANE... I'M SORRY. FOR EVERYTHING. FOR ABANDONING YOU. FOR NOT UNDERSTANDING YOU. FOR BEING AFRAID.
Hello World
Hello World
SOMETIMES, BEING ENCASED IN ALL THIS METAL, IT'S HARD TO REMEMBER WHAT BEING HUMAN IS LIKE.
BUT THAT'S THE THING ABOUT THE BRAIN...
...IT NEVER FORGETS WHAT THE HEART FEELS.
TINK, TINK
CLIFF... THAT'S REALLY SWEET...
...BUT YOU NEED TO GET THE HELL OUT OF HERE.
ATTENTION ALL PASSENGERS! THIS IS AN ALERT--
--WE HAVE BEEN LOCATED. WE WILL NOW BE PICKING UP SPEED AND ENGAGING IN EVASIVE MANEUVERS--
SHE KNOWS YOU'RE HERE. SHE'S FOUND US.
WHO?
Hello World
DR. HARRISON. AT LEAST SHE THINKS SHE'S A DOCTOR.
AN IDENTITY--AN ALTER--WHO EMERGED FROM THE TRAUMA OF SEEING A SUPERHUMAN GOD BEING MURDERED AND EXPOSURE TO HIS OTHERWORLDLY BLOOD. AND ALONG WITH HARRISON CAME THE UNLOCKED DORMANT POWERS OF MIND CONTROL AND POWERFUL SUGGESTION.
SHE CALLS HERSELF JANE BECAUSE SHE KNOWS PEOPLE WILL LIKE JANE, AND SHE NEEDS TO CONNECT WITH PEOPLE TO GET WHAT SHE WANTS.
AND WHAT DOES SHE WANT?
SHE WANTS TO "CURE" ME.
SHE PLANS ON SEPARATING ME FROM MY OTHER IDENTITIES AND SENDING THEM INTO OTHER PEOPLE--MEMBERS OF THE CULT SHE'S STARTED. PEOPLE SHE CONTROLS.
I'M SURE THIS DR. HARRISON IS A BAD PERSON... BUT ISN'T BEING CURED A POSITIVE THING?

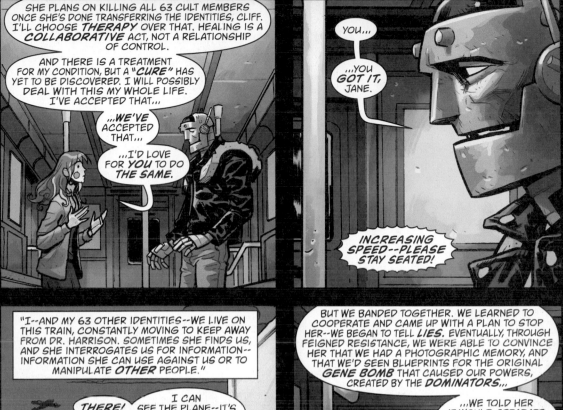

SHE PLANS ON KILLING ALL 63 CULT MEMBERS ONCE SHE'S DONE TRANSFERRING THE IDENTITIES, CLIFF. I'LL CHOOSE *THERAPY* OVER THAT. HEALING IS A *COLLABORATIVE* ACT, NOT A RELATIONSHIP OF CONTROL.

AND THERE IS A TREATMENT FOR MY CONDITION, BUT A "*CURE*" HAS YET TO BE DISCOVERED. I WILL POSSIBLY DEAL WITH THIS MY WHOLE LIFE. I'VE ACCEPTED THAT...

...*WE'VE* ACCEPTED THAT...

...I'D LOVE FOR *YOU* TO DO *THE SAME*.

YOU...

...YOU *GOT IT*, JANE.

INCREASING SPEED--PLEASE STAY SEATED!

"I--AND MY 63 OTHER IDENTITIES--WE LIVE ON THIS TRAIN, CONSTANTLY MOVING TO KEEP AWAY FROM DR. HARRISON. SOMETIMES SHE FINDS US, AND SHE INTERROGATES US FOR INFORMATION-- INFORMATION SHE CAN USE AGAINST US OR TO MANIPULATE *OTHER* PEOPLE."

THERE!

I CAN SEE THE PLANE--IT'S HEADING TOWARD THE COMPOUND!

BUT WE BANDED TOGETHER. WE LEARNED TO COOPERATE AND CAME UP WITH A PLAN TO STOP HER--WE BEGAN TO TELL *LIES*. EVENTUALLY, THROUGH FEIGNED RESISTANCE, WE WERE ABLE TO CONVINCE HER THAT WE HAD A PHOTOGRAPHIC MEMORY, AND THAT WE'D SEEN BLUEPRINTS FOR THE ORIGINAL *GENE BOMB* THAT CAUSED OUR POWERS, CREATED BY THE *DOMINATORS*...

...WE TOLD HER IT WOULD SEPARATE JANE FROM THE OTHER IDENTITIES, AND SHE TRAINED HER FOLLOW- ERS TO BUILD IT.

"ONLY IT'S NOT A GENE BOMB BUT A *PSYCHIC WEAPON* WE LEARNED HOW TO BUILD WHILE TRAINING FOR THE MIONIC MIND-WAR LONG BEFORE HARRISON EMERGED.

"IT'S BIOLOGICALLY CODED TO *KILL MY DOMINANT IDENTITY*."

IF WE CAN GET *UP THERE*, I SHOULD BE ABLE TO JUMP ONTO THE BOMB AND USE MY POWERS TO DEFUSE IT.

COME ON, DANNY, YOU CAN DO IT! COME *BACK* TO US, DANNY!

CLIFF, YOU *CANNOT* STOP THAT BOMB!

PASSENGERS-- BRACE FOR IMPACT--!

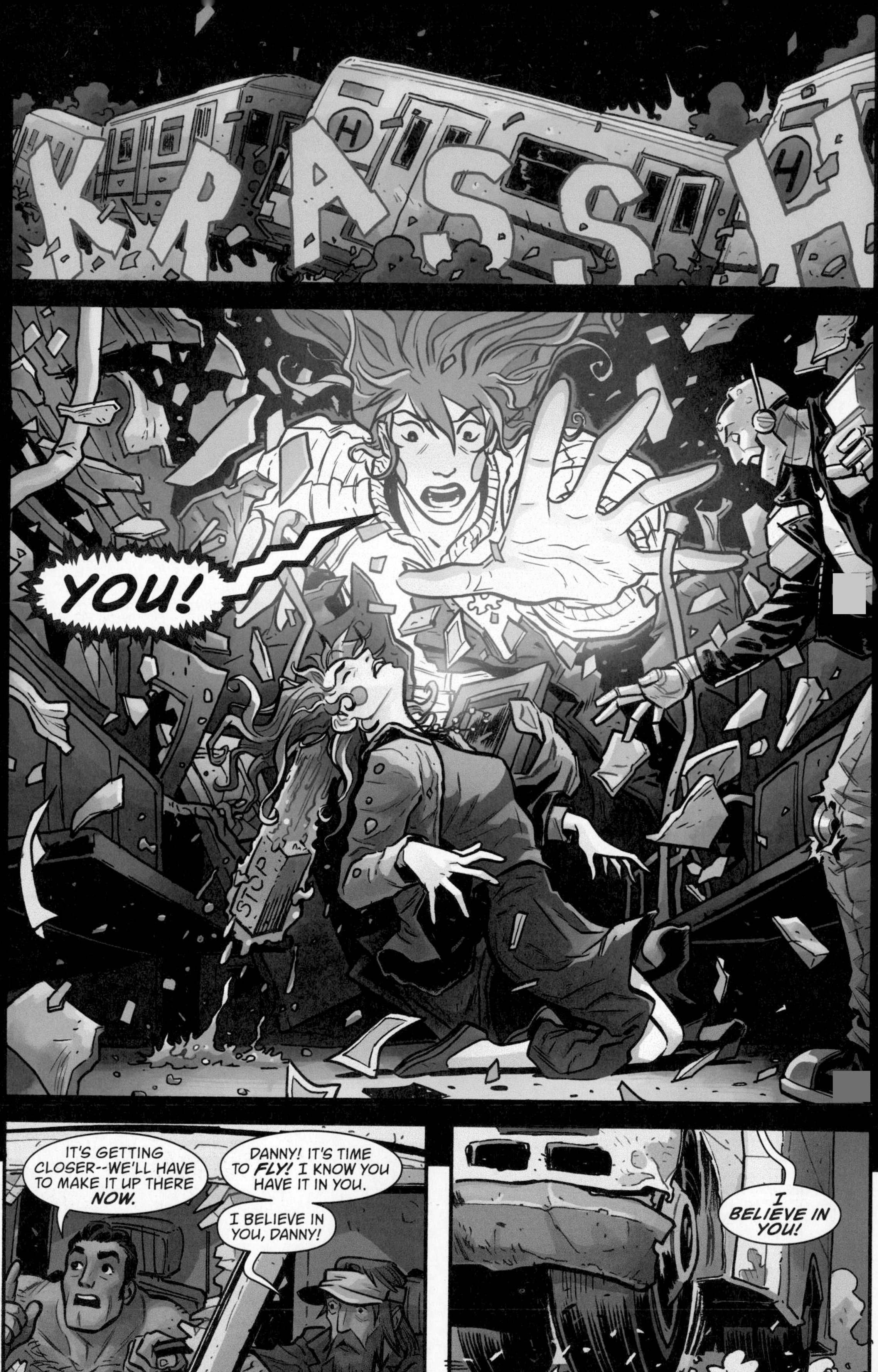
KRASSH
YOU!
IT'S GETTING CLOSER--WE'LL HAVE TO MAKE IT UP THERE NOW.
DANNY! IT'S TIME TO FLY! I KNOW YOU HAVE IT IN YOU.
I BELIEVE IN YOU, DANNY!
STOP
I BELIEVE IN YOU!

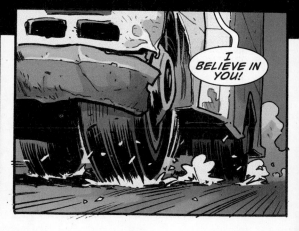

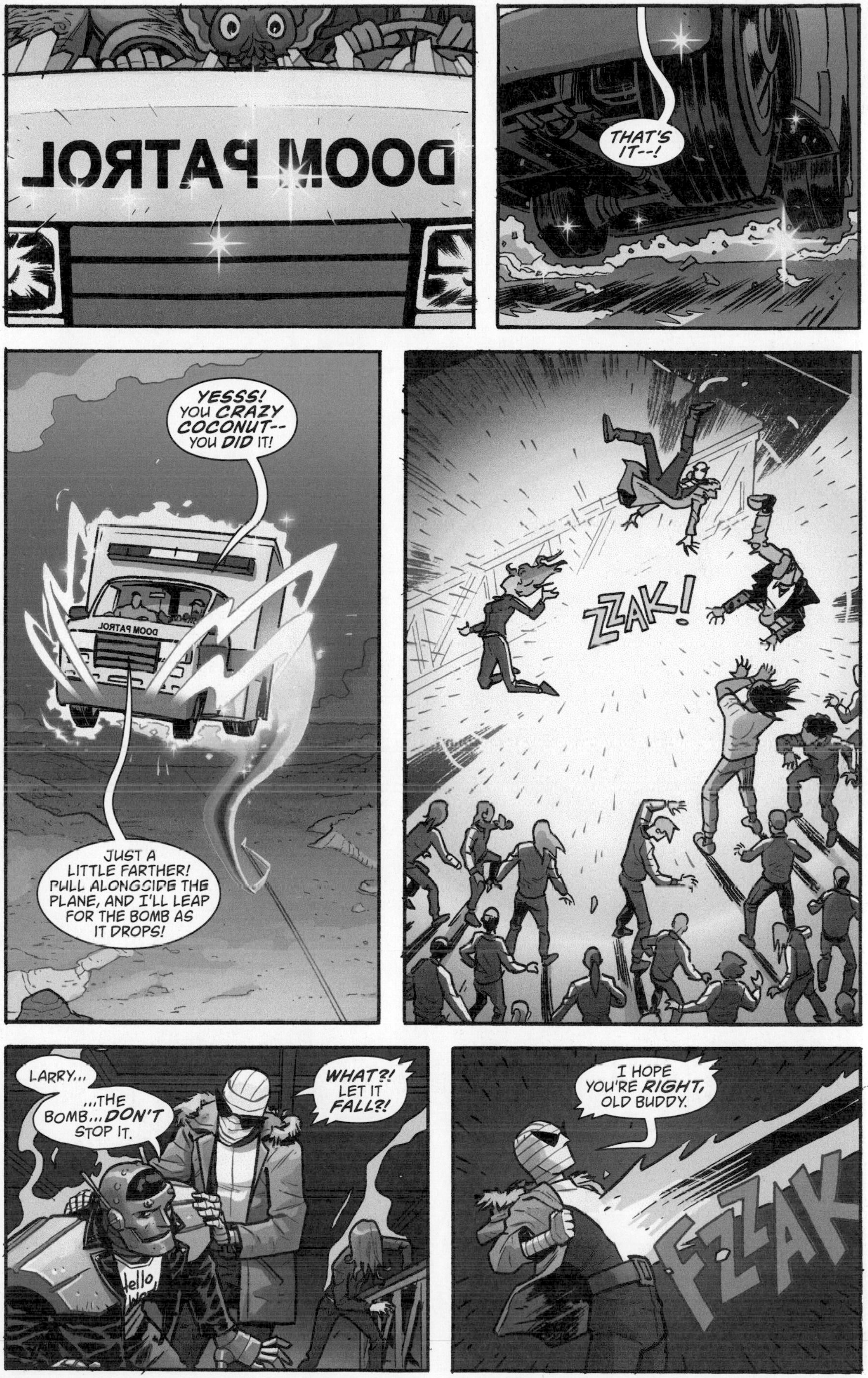
DOOM PATROL
THAT'S IT--!
YESSS! YOU CRAZY COCONUT-- YOU DID IT!
JUST A LITTLE FARTHER! PULL ALONGSIDE THE PLANE, AND I'LL LEAP FOR THE BOMB AS IT DROPS!
ZZZAK!
LARRY...
...THE BOMB... DON'T STOP IT.
WHAT?! LET IT FALL?!
I HOPE YOU'RE RIGHT, OLD BUDDY.
FZZAK

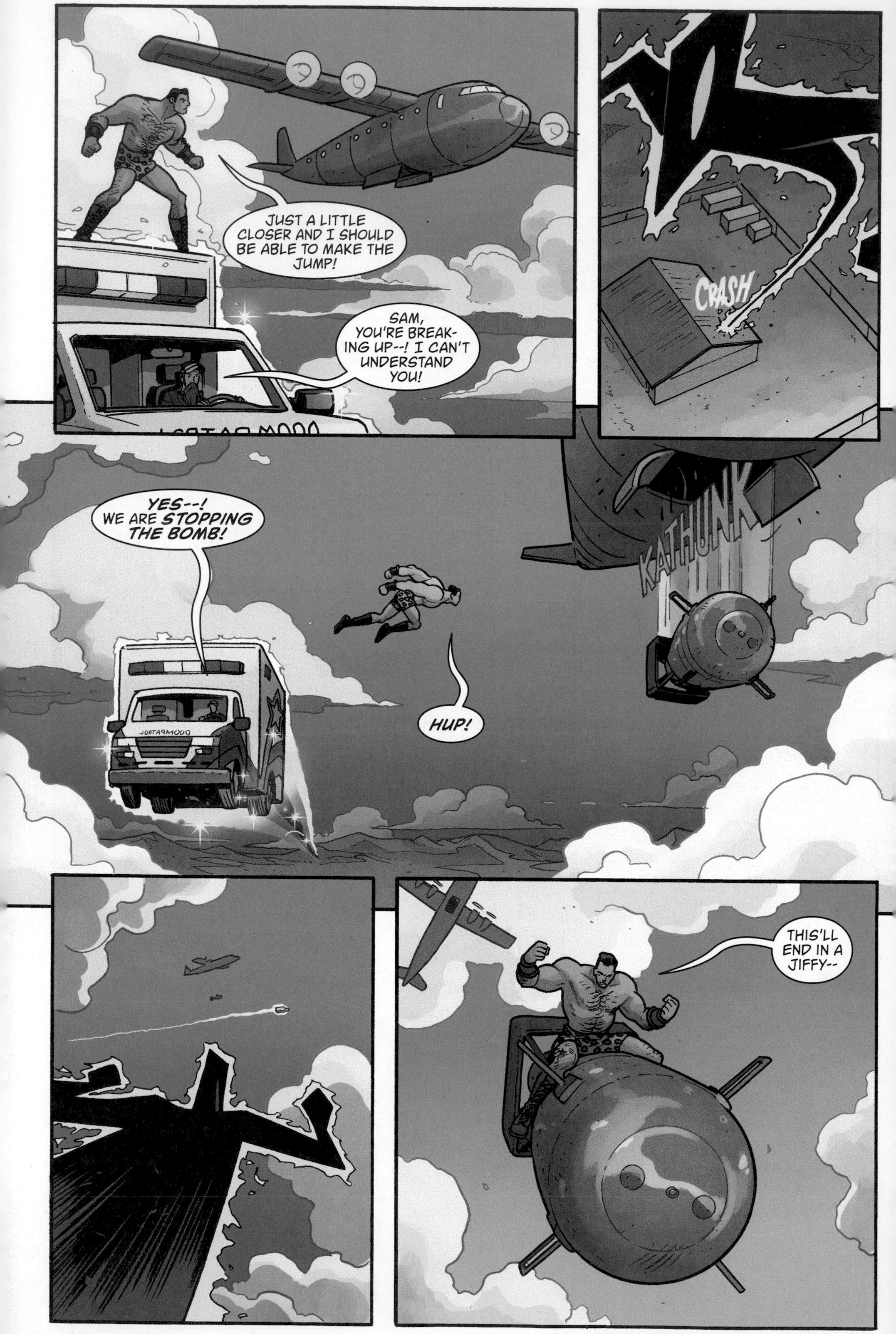
JUST A LITTLE CLOSER AND I SHOULD BE ABLE TO MAKE THE JUMP!
SAM, YOU'RE BREAK-ING UP--! I CAN'T UNDERSTAND YOU!
CRASH
YES--! WE ARE STOPPING THE BOMB!
HUP!
KATHUNK
THIS'LL END IN A JIFFY--

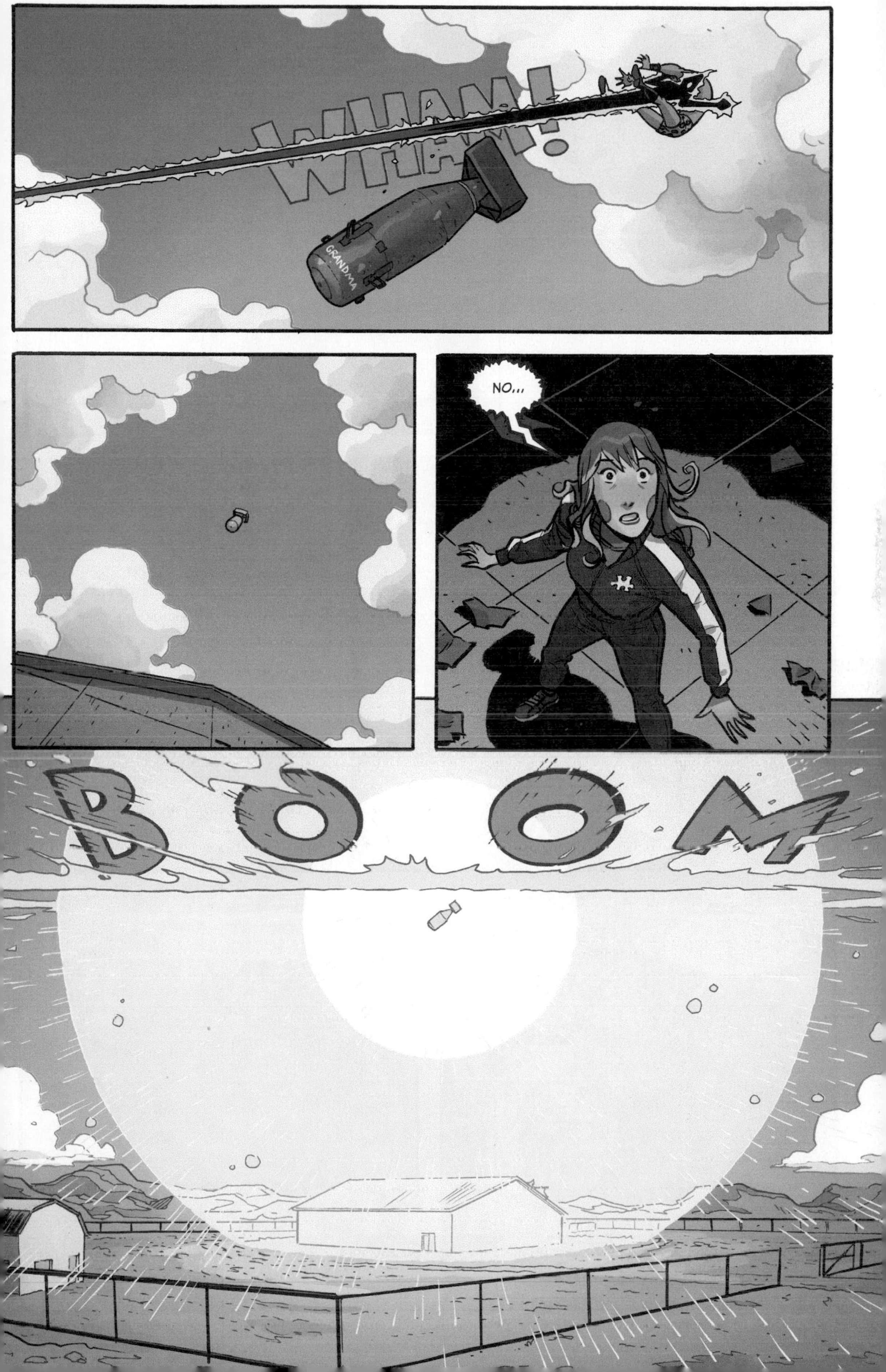
WHAM!
GRANDMA
NO...
BOOM

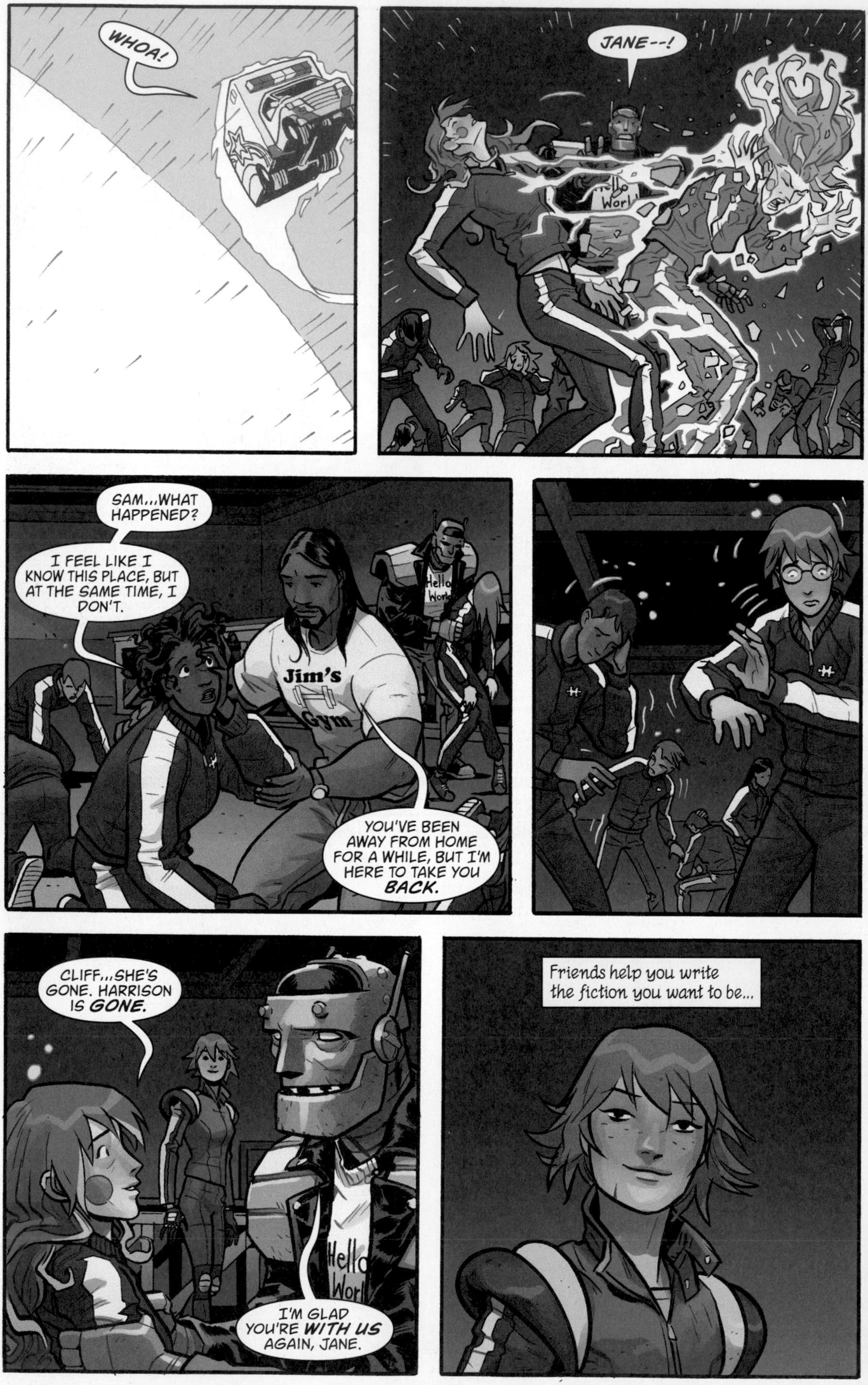
WHOA!
JANE--!
Hello World
SAM...WHAT HAPPENED?
I FEEL LIKE I KNOW THIS PLACE, BUT AT THE SAME TIME, I DON'T.
Jim's Gym
YOU'VE BEEN AWAY FROM HOME FOR A WHILE, BUT I'M HERE TO TAKE YOU BACK.
CLIFF...SHE'S GONE. HARRISON IS GONE.
I'M GLAD YOU'RE WITH US AGAIN, JANE.
Friends help you write the fiction you want to be...

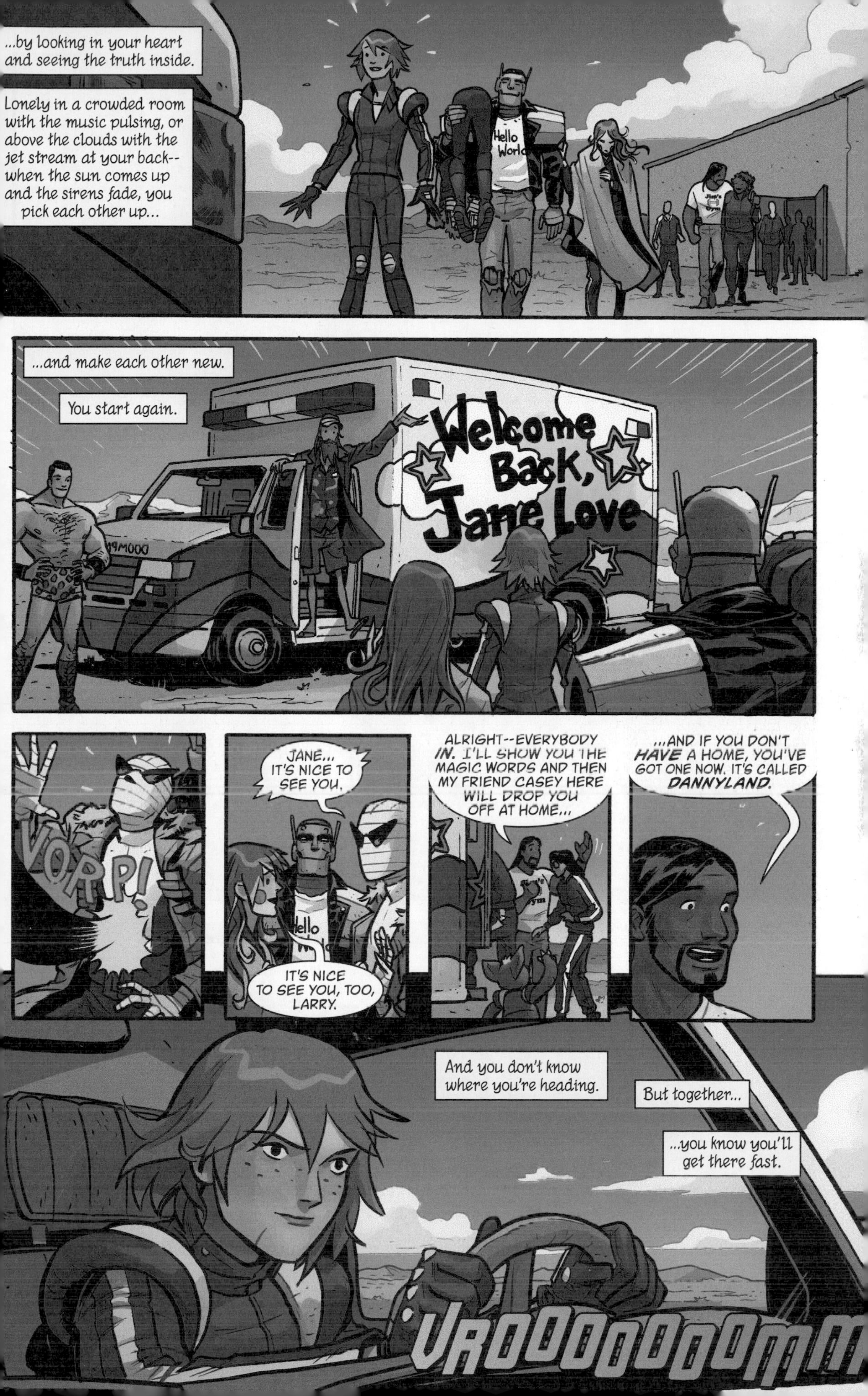
...by looking in your heart and seeing the truth inside.
Lonely in a crowded room with the music pulsing, or above the clouds with the jet stream at your back--when the sun comes up and the sirens fade, you pick each other up...
Hello World
...and make each other new.
You start again.
Welcome Back, Jane Love
VORP!
JANE... IT'S NICE TO SEE YOU.
IT'S NICE TO SEE YOU, TOO, LARRY.
ALRIGHT--EVERYBODY *IN.* I'LL SHOW YOU THE MAGIC WORDS AND THEN MY FRIEND CASEY HERE WILL DROP YOU OFF AT HOME...
...AND IF YOU DON'T *HAVE* A HOME, YOU'VE GOT ONE NOW. IT'S CALLED *DANNYLAND.*
And you don't know where you're heading.
But together...
...you know you'll get there fast.
VROOOOOOOOMM

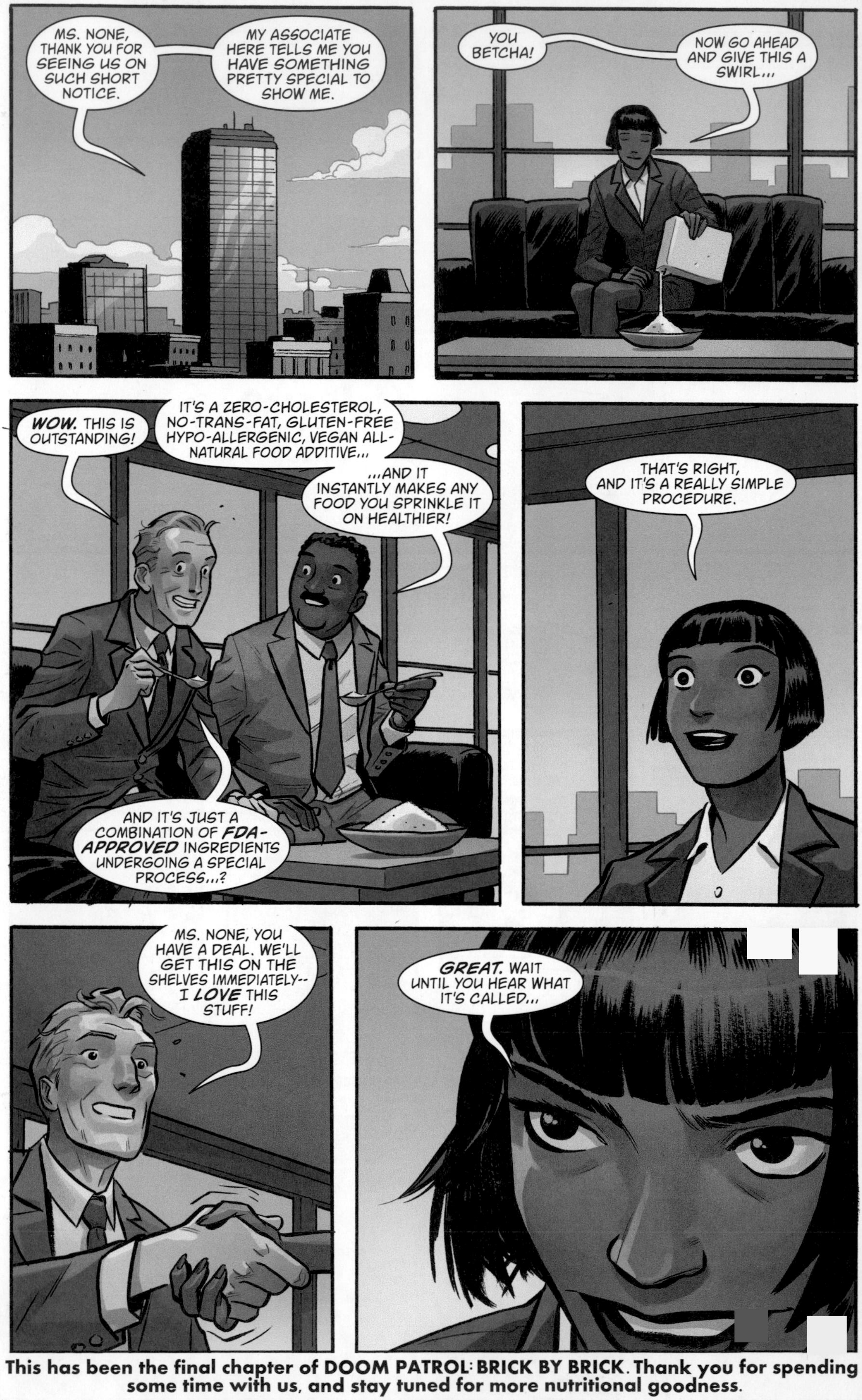
MS. NONE, THANK YOU FOR SEEING US ON SUCH SHORT NOTICE.
MY ASSOCIATE HERE TELLS ME YOU HAVE SOMETHING PRETTY SPECIAL TO SHOW ME.
YOU BETCHA!
NOW GO AHEAD AND GIVE THIS A SWIRL...
WOW. THIS IS OUTSTANDING!
IT'S A ZERO-CHOLESTEROL, NO-TRANS-FAT, GLUTEN-FREE HYPO-ALLERGENIC, VEGAN ALL-NATURAL FOOD ADDITIVE...
...AND IT INSTANTLY MAKES ANY FOOD YOU SPRINKLE IT ON HEALTHIER!
AND IT'S JUST A COMBINATION OF FDA-APPROVED INGREDIENTS UNDERGOING A SPECIAL PROCESS...?
THAT'S RIGHT, AND IT'S A REALLY SIMPLE PROCEDURE.
MS. NONE, YOU HAVE A DEAL. WE'LL GET THIS ON THE SHELVES IMMEDIATELY-- I LOVE THIS STUFF!
GREAT. WAIT UNTIL YOU HEAR WHAT IT'S CALLED...

This has been the final chapter of DOOM PATROL: BRICK BY BRICK. Thank you for spending some time with us, and stay tuned for more nutritional goodness.

BACKWARD By Gerard Way

First.
Wait.
READ THIS LAST.
Heyyy///
WOW.

I get to write DOOM PATROL! What a gift this is! Never in my wildest of wild possible realities and potential outcomes could I ever have imagined I would get to do this. I'm going to keep this casual, because DOOM PATROL is a celebration. One big weird punk rock party at the end of the world, and all of your coolest/strangest friends are invited—stoners, losers, creeps, oddballs, broken dolls, cats, dogs, bugs, musclemen, metalheads, and people who make themselves up into any old wonderful thing they can imagine. Fantabuloso. They're inside. Actualizing. Activating. Shredded latex balloons and broken glass on the floor. A little bit of glitter. Generation arsonists rejoice: this is and isn't your mom and dad's DOOM PATROL.

A long road led to me writing this book—a road that started when I first picked up a random copy of DOOM PATROL in the comic shop that I grew up in (a small, humble shop, which you can see in chapter three of this book). The people in that shop were, in some ways, a gang, and I would continue to be a member of various gangs for most of my life. Because gangs are important. Friends are important. The other lost souls you find in this world—they are important, and it's important to share their stories when you get to hold the megaphone for a moment.

The Doom Patrol was the first superhero team I ever saw participate in a group therapy session. In fact, the scene, in issue #35 of Grant Morrison and Richard Case's run, was the first time I had seen *anyone* in group therapy— something I probably would have benefited from later in life, considering all the time that my fox-hole friends and I spent spitting mad in a van, clawing off our own skin. But the seed was planted: DOOM PATROL was different. There just wasn't anything else like it. It spoke to my young, frustrated, emotional soul on a deep level. It opened my eyes to mental health (something I would learn the hard way to take care of) and softened my heart enough to begin receiving love. It started me on a path to becoming more accepting of things and embracing the differences we have as human beings. In short, DOOM PATROL made me a better person. It sounds pretty dramatic for a comic book, but that's what it did to me. That's what it means to me. I believe in the power of supposedly juvenile things.

The book now in your hands is the result of years of dreaming/hoping/craving. False starts, false alarms, fake fires—it never seemed to be the right time to do it, but it *always* seemed to be the right time to do it, and

Shelly Bond helped me to finally dive into that water. As a visionary team builder and the first editor of the Young Animal imprint, she believed in us. She believed in DOOM PATROL. In writing the first issue—a truly transformative experience—I felt a completion that broke through the rubble and fear of not being good enough (or not being *something* enough) to pull off writing (mostly) monthly comics. It brought me full circle from when I was 15 years old and back in the shop, with ink all over my hands as I banged away at my grandmother's old typewriter.

But enough about me (for a change!). That's only one small part of it, and there are many different parts to this equation, and many different people sweating and screaming and leaping through plate glass windows with their middle fingers out trying to make this book great.

After working with Gabriel Bá on *The Umbrella Academy*, never in my life did I imagine that I would find that kind of special chemistry again. You just don't expect lightning to strike multiple times. Life doesn't work that way. But then I met Nick Derington and all of that changed. I found myself with a new brother and that same kind of wonderful collaboration that I had shared with Bá, but altogether different and unique. Nick not only collaborates, he adds his own ideas. It felt like I was back in the van making up stories with Shaun Simon and my brother, Mikey Way. Nick and I finished each other's sentences, came to the same eventual conclusions (and other times wonderfully different ones), and, most important, we wanted to make the same book that I did. Nick and I talk almost every day about how much fun we're having, because we are indeed having the time of our lives. We're seeing comics through the same oddball lens and making the most of this moment we are trying to manifest. Finding Tamra Bonvillain and having Todd Klein jump on board glued it all together, in a kind of duct-tape-and-blowtorch-it-'til-it's-great kind of way. Todd is a legend, and Tamra is simply one of the most amazing colorists I have ever seen—true gifts as human beings and artists. It's great to be part of another gang, much like the gang you'll find in the pages of this book.

Speaking of which, how special this little (though it's getting larger by the issue) group is to us! Casey Brinke represents exactly what I felt the world needs, because I think she is exactly what Danny felt the world needs: bright lights in black holes, super-positive-to-the-max genuine sunshine, speed, and goodness. Sure, an astute observer and consumer of entertainment could easily say she's a "way in" to the story, but I feel like she's a way *out* of the darkness of modern storytelling—a pedal against the pessimistic world-thought we find ourselves trapped in. And Sam is another great part of the good vibes the world needs: a metaphysical touch, a healthy dose of fitness, and a great partner. I don't know why, but for some reason I always saw the Doom Patrol as EMTs. I felt like the job of an EMT is an actual *doom patrol*—it seemed almost obvious. The original DOOM PATROL script that I wrote in South America (which numbers only six pages) involved another pair of EMTs, but these EMTs were jaded ghouls, and I couldn't find my voice in that scenario when it came time to write the book for real. So everything changed, and Casey and Sam were born. As for bringing back some of the classic characters, well, that was another dream come true. There isn't an issue that goes by where I'm not moved by the fractured humanity of Larry and Jane, or surprised by the logic of Niles Caulder, or astounded by the words that Cliff tells me he wants coming out of his mouth, roller-skating-mother-of-pearl.

Part of writing DOOM PATROL required me to strike a deal with myself: I would (almost) completely shut myself off from outside influence and social media to make the purest art possible. But, at the same time, as a writer, I would try to educate myself as much as possible to do the right thing by the characters, who came with built-in baggage, to reflect how we've progressed as a society and how we've evolved. As it turned out, disconnecting from social media helped with that, because when you're not getting caught up in other people's momentum, you start asking yourself, deep down, what the right thing is, and you do your best. At the end of the day, not making (or reading) tweets was how the scripts got finished. Both my mental health and my editor, Jamie Rich, are very thankful for that.

I'm just going on and on and...

One last thing I'll leave you with: I try not to pay attention to reviews. Not because I feel criticism is useless, but because I feel like positive affirmation and seeking validation can be just as dangerous as falling down the negative spiral of reading bad things about your work. It can all color what you're trying to do, and you have to stay the course—until it's time to change. I hear through dribs and drabs that people like our book, or I meet people who tell me so, and that makes me happy. It doesn't fully drive me, but it's nice to know that someone cares. It is meaningful, yet at the same time it is not something that you should allow to dominate your existence.

However, even in tuning out, there are ways for both positive and negative things to find you, and my favorite assessment of the comic was an insightful combination of both. A reviewer named Patrick started off his review of the book by saying that he felt he wasn't smart enough to get it, which, based on his later statements, I was forced to disagree with. He also had no idea what was going on in the story (which was fair), but he was able to really pinpoint what we were trying to do when he said, "I can't review this book in a meaningful way, because it's not something to be reviewed. It's really a comic to be experienced." And that is exactly the kind of book we were trying to make without fully knowing it at the time. It's supposed to be something you go through. We want to conjure feelings and questions, moods and moments. We want you to feel like it's 3:00 a.m. and you have no idea what's going on—but somehow you do? I can't say I've ever seen an assessment that so accurately describes the instinctive yet unknown original intent. So thank you, Patrick. There are plenty of comics that you can "read," and there are plenty that can be "reviewed," but in very few of them could you simply take the trip. And that's one of the things that makes this book so special to us. Landing in the middle of nowhere with no idea where we are headed next is why we keep going—to experience things. We get to share that experience with you. And trust us, it does make sense in the end. Vroom vroom. Beep beep. Boffo laughs.

Lots of love—thanks for everything and all the cool art and socks,

G

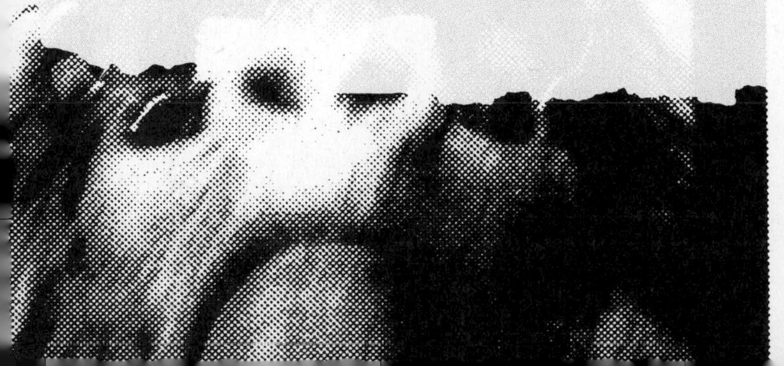

DANNY THE GALLERY

VARIANTS, TEASERS, PROFILES, AND PINUPS

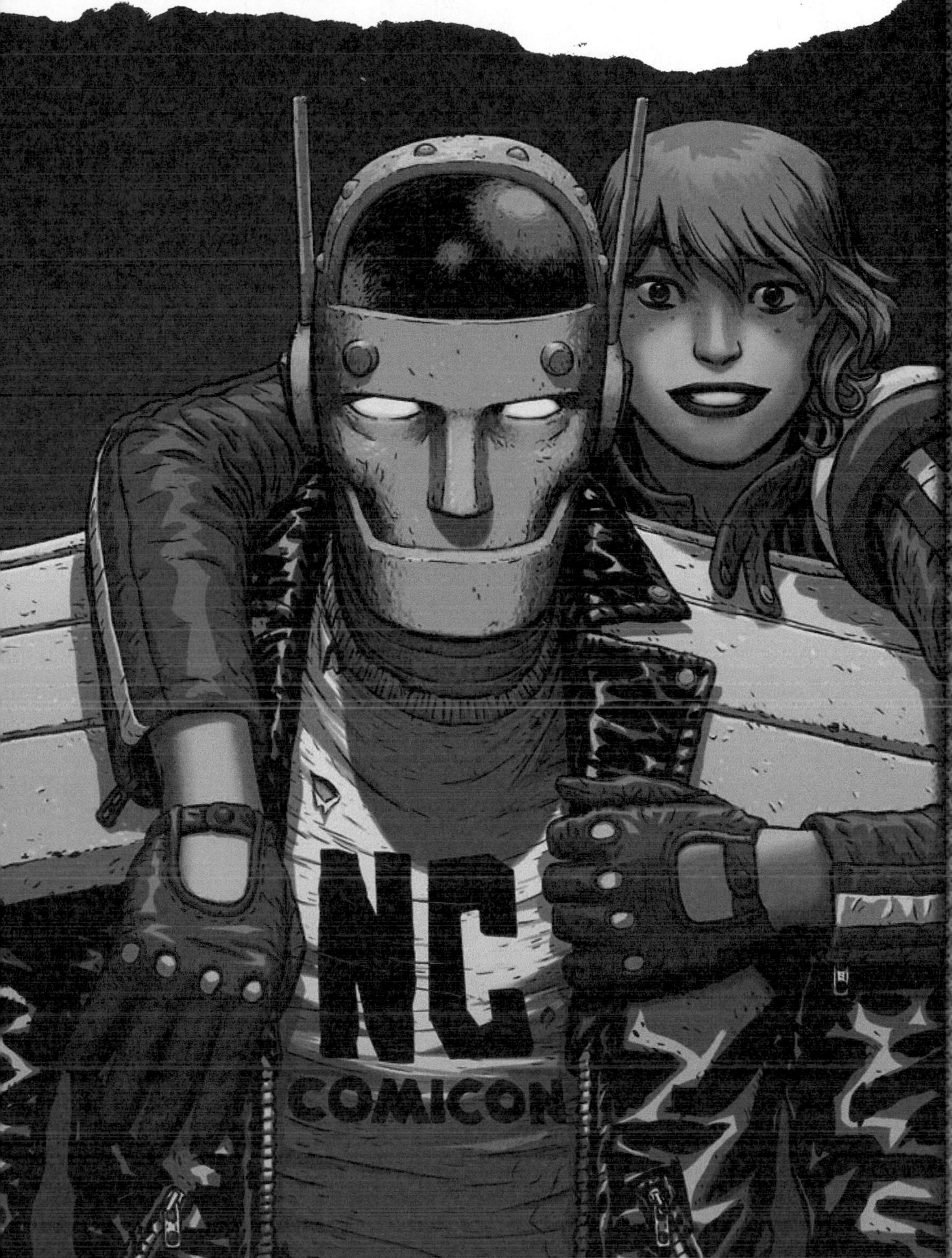
NC
COMICON

Promotional art by Nick Derington for the 2016 North Carolina Comicon program book

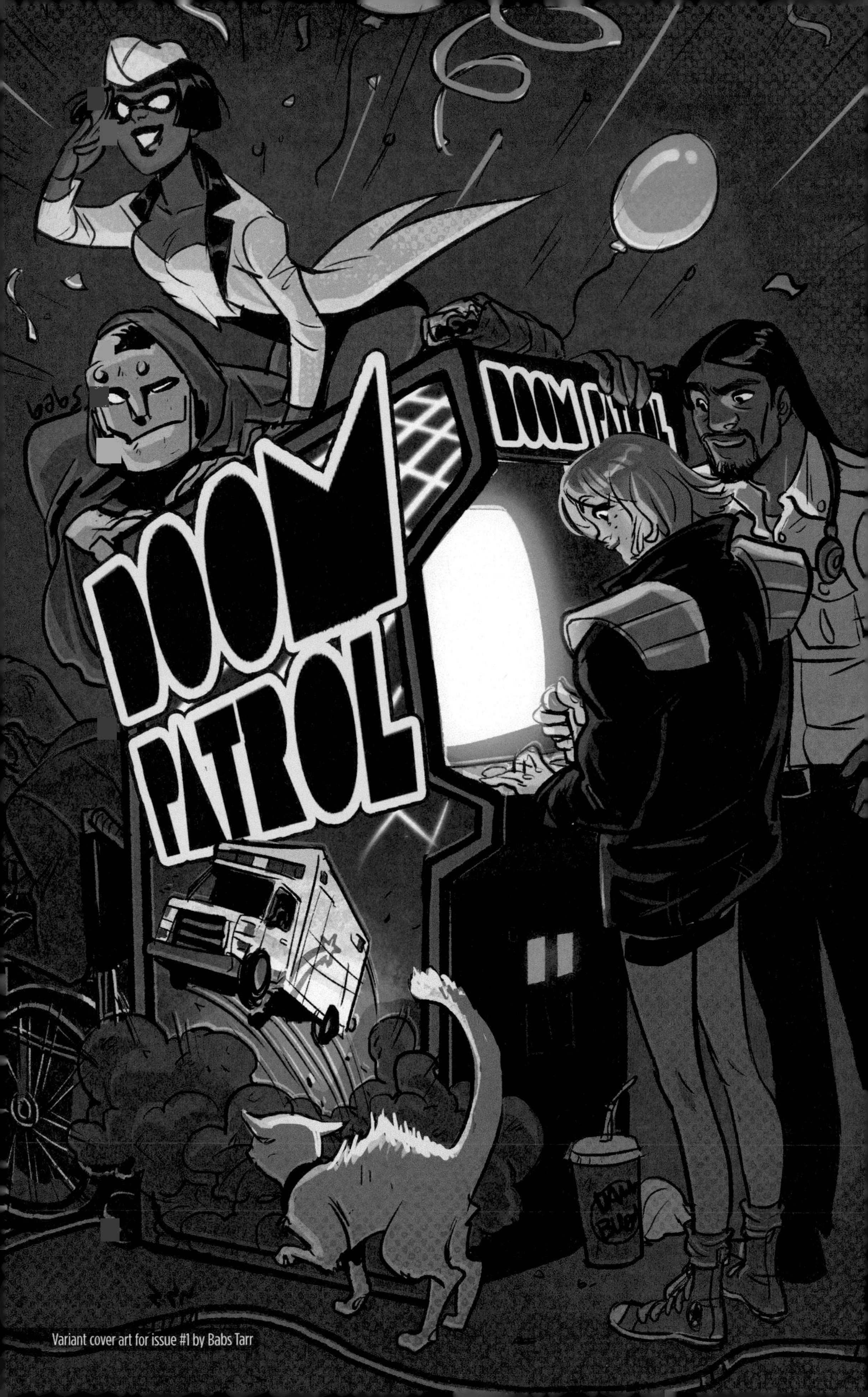
DOOM PATROL
babs

Variant cover art for issue #1 by Babs Tarr

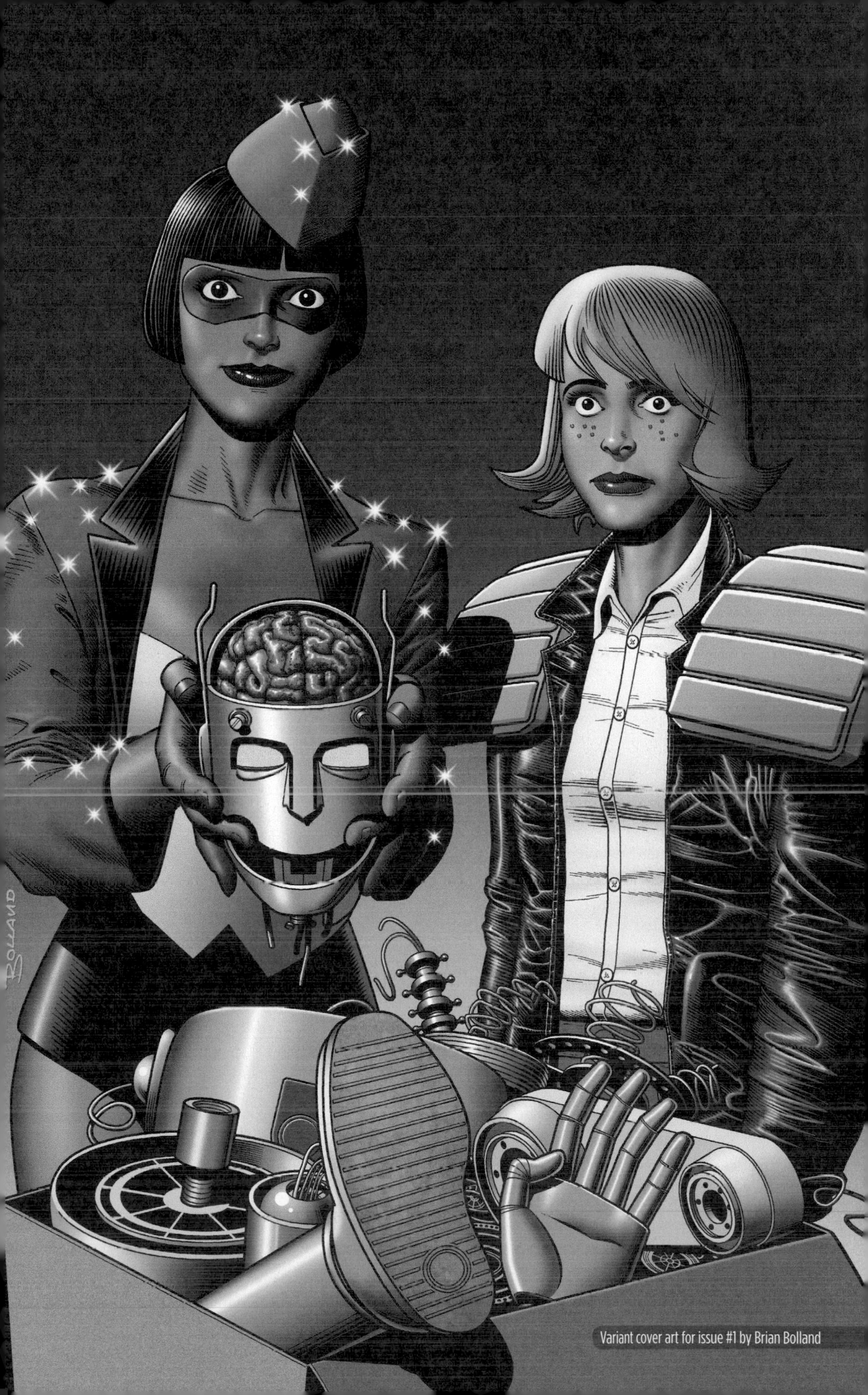
BOLLAND
Variant cover art for issue #1 by Brian Bolland

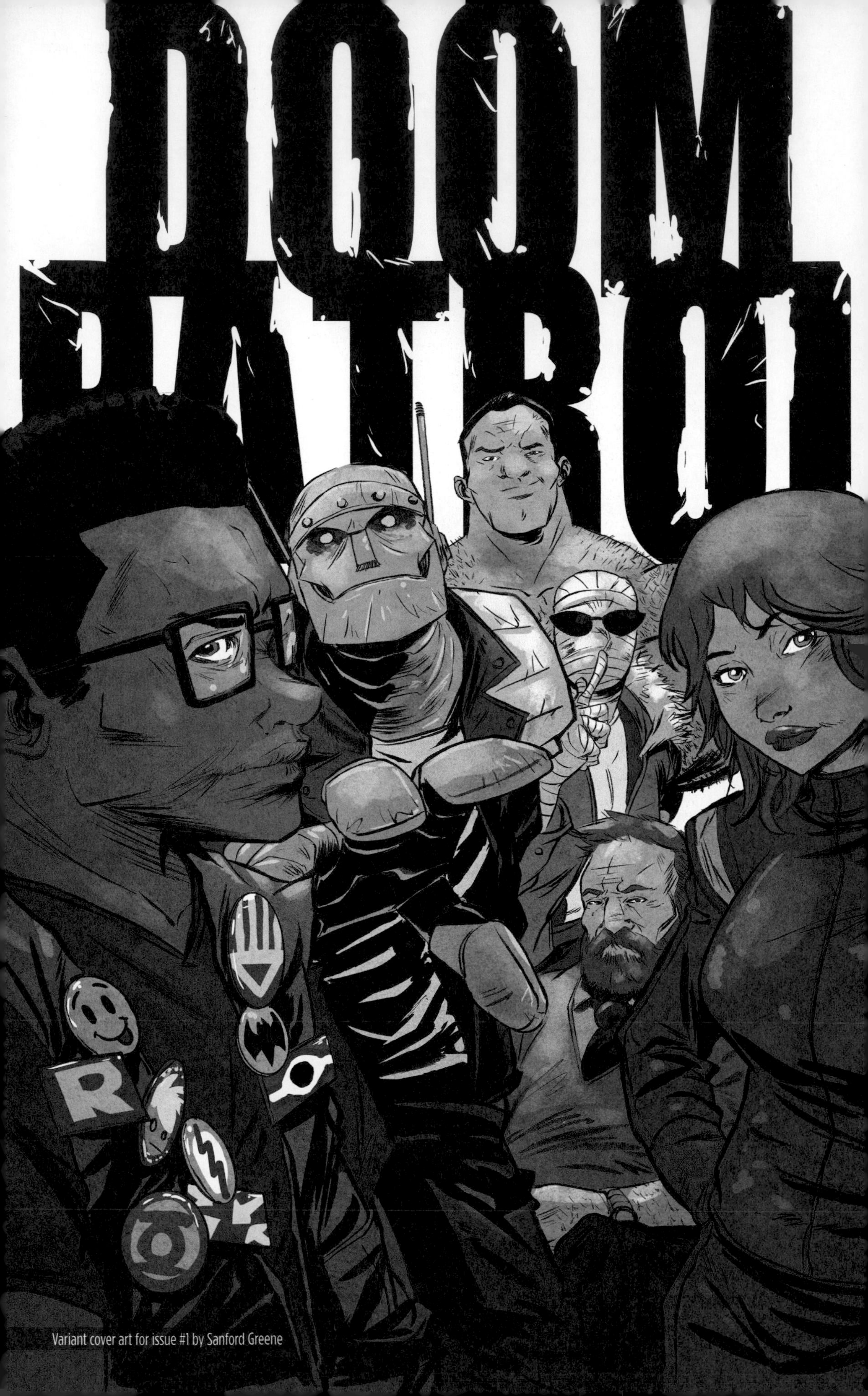
DOOM

Variant cover art for issue #1 by Sanford Greene

Variant cover art for issue #1 by Jaime Hernandez and Laura Allred

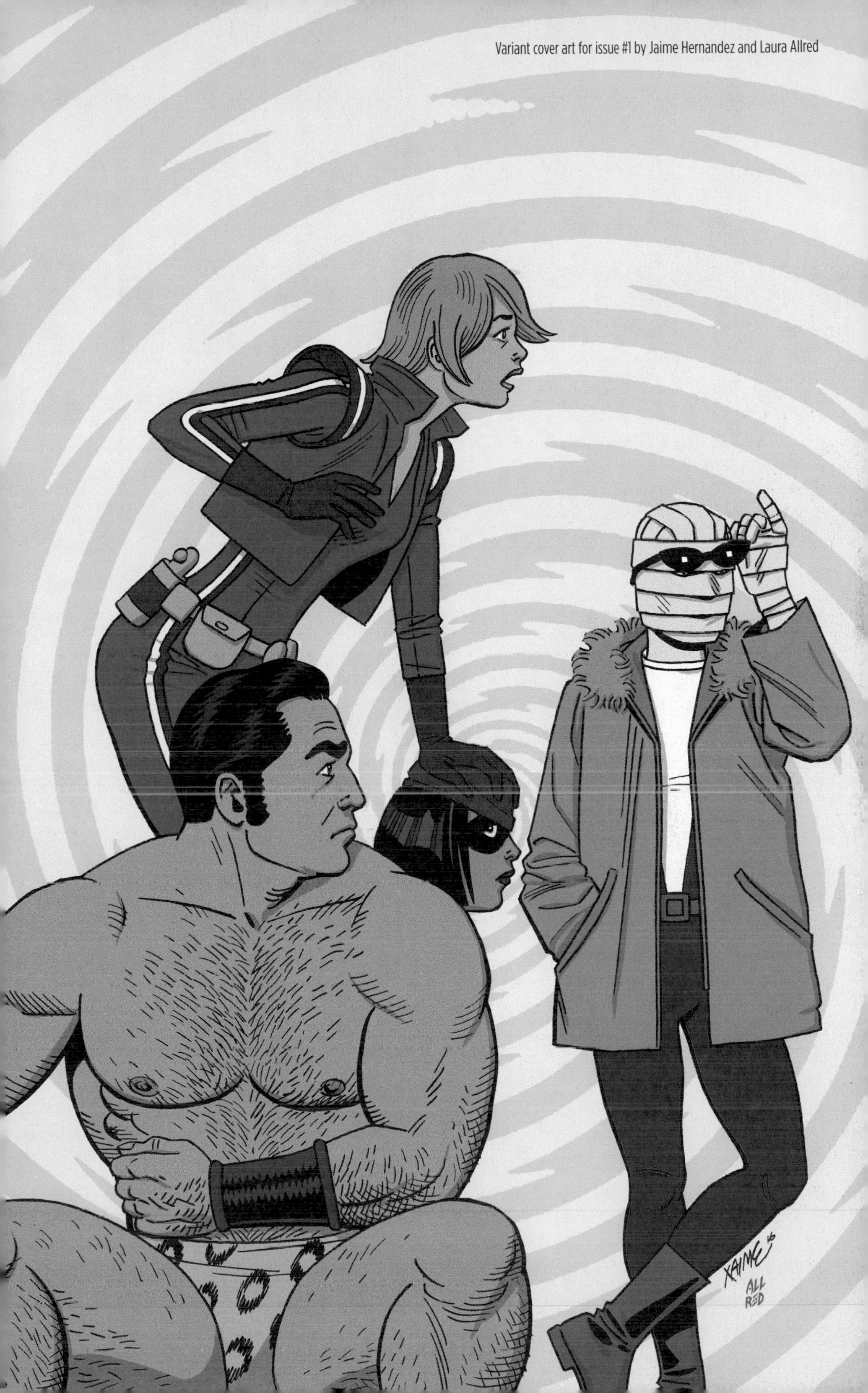
XAIME 16
ALL RED

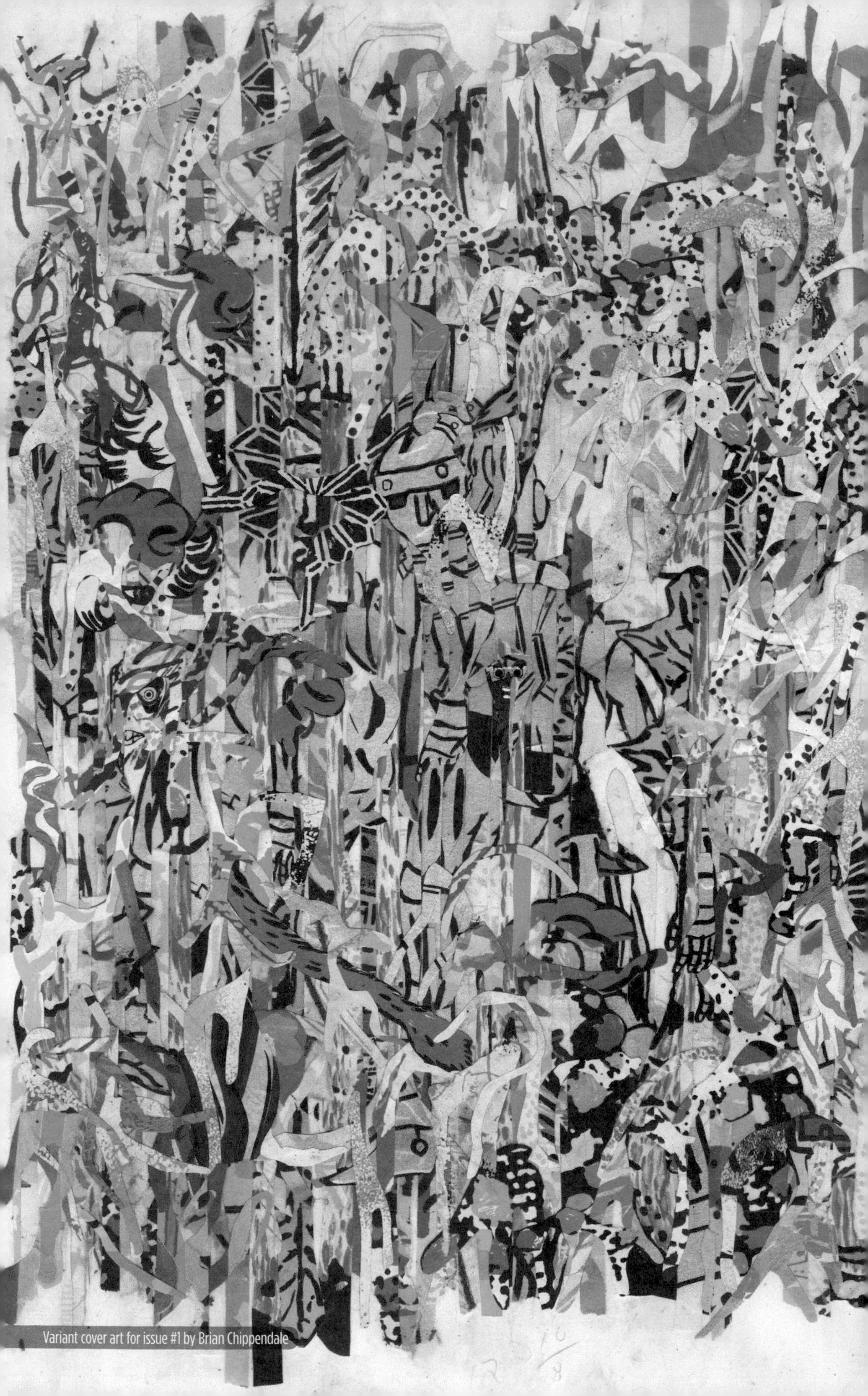

Variant cover art for issue #1 by Brian Chippendale

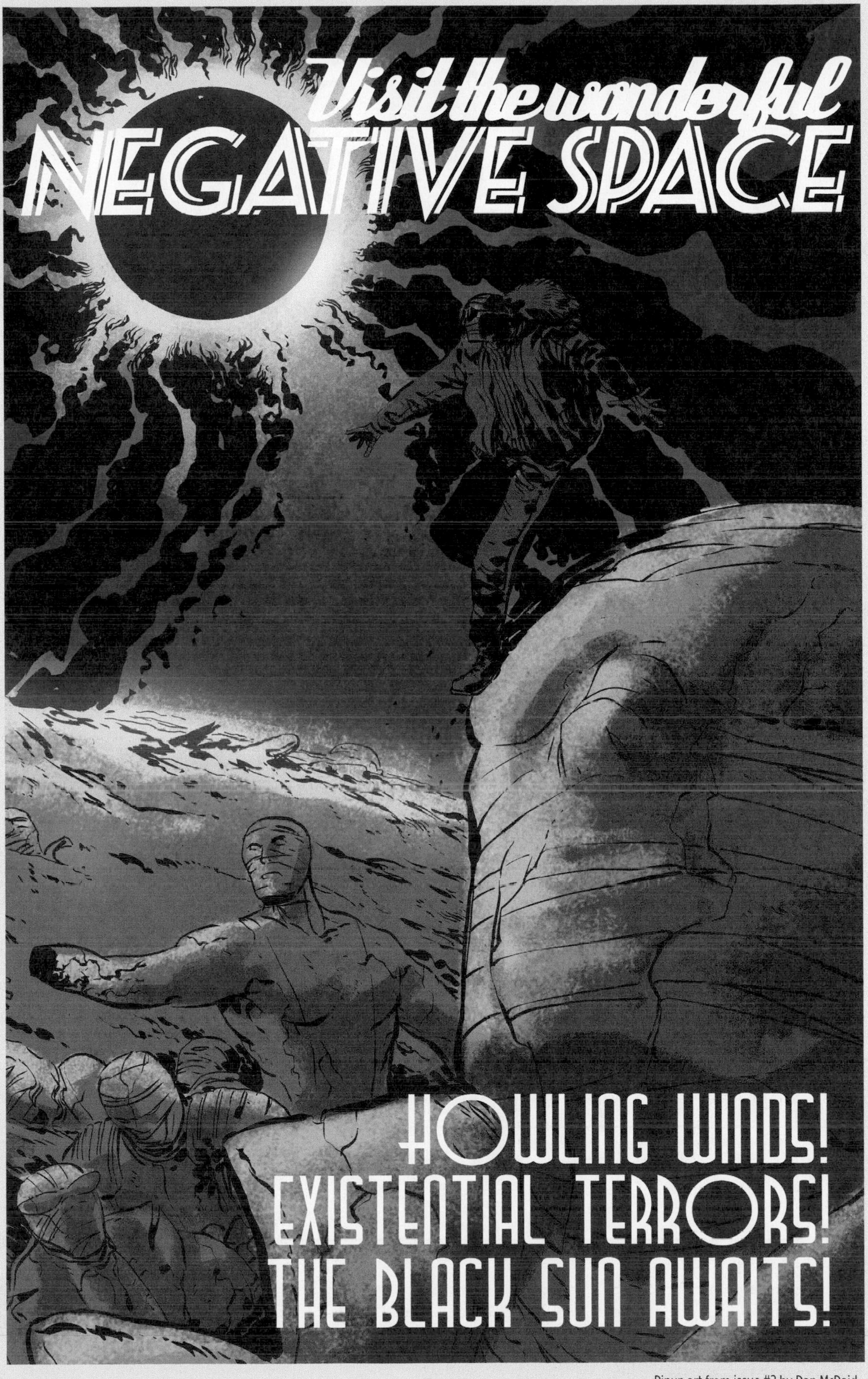
Visit the wonderful
NEGATIVE SPACE
HOWLING WINDS!
EXISTENTIAL TERRORS!
THE BLACK SUN AWAITS!
Pinup art from issue #2 by Dan McDaid

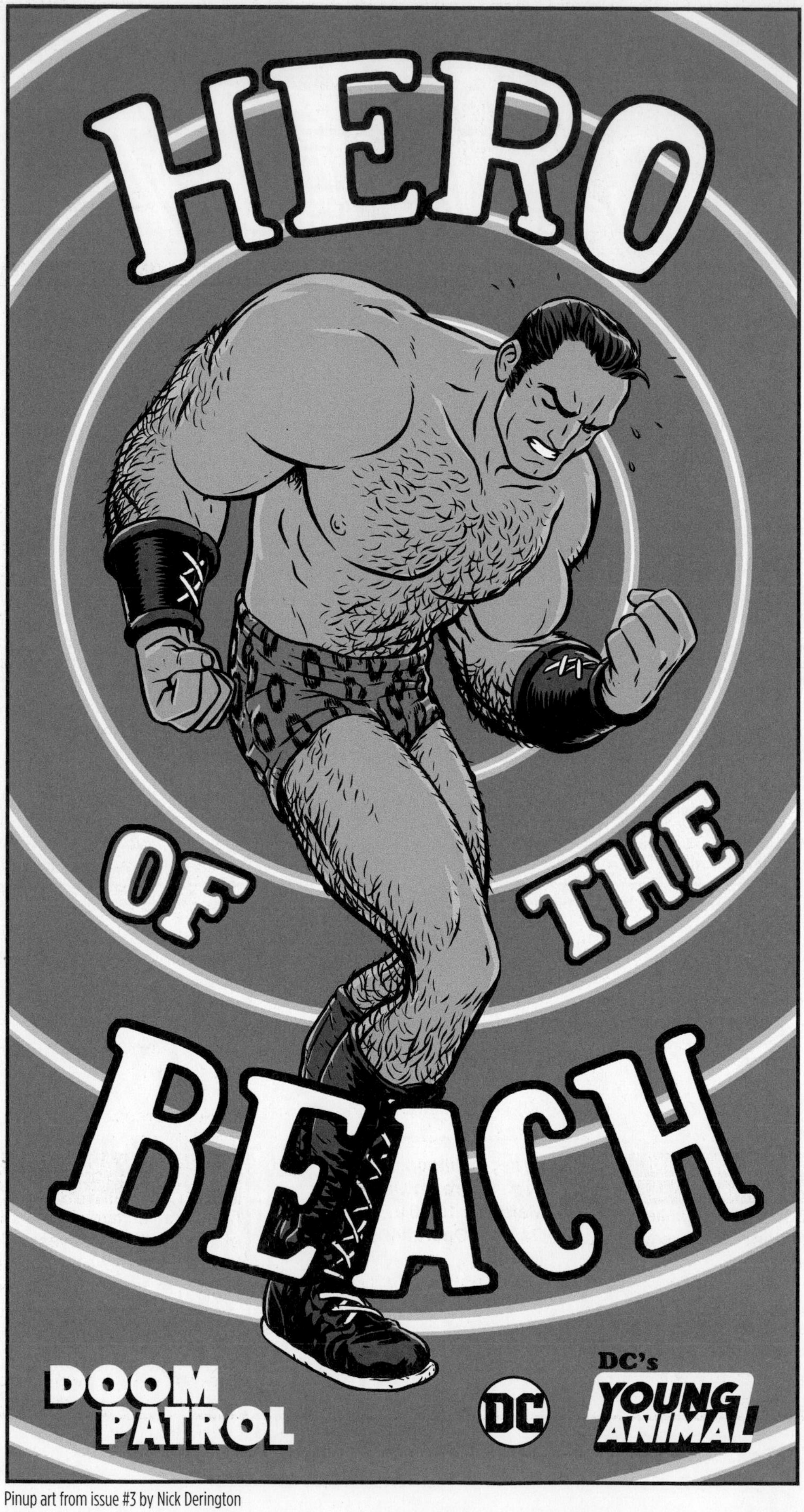
HERO
OF THE
BEACH
DOOM PATROL
DC
DC's YOUNG ANIMAL
Pinup art from issue #3 by Nick Derington

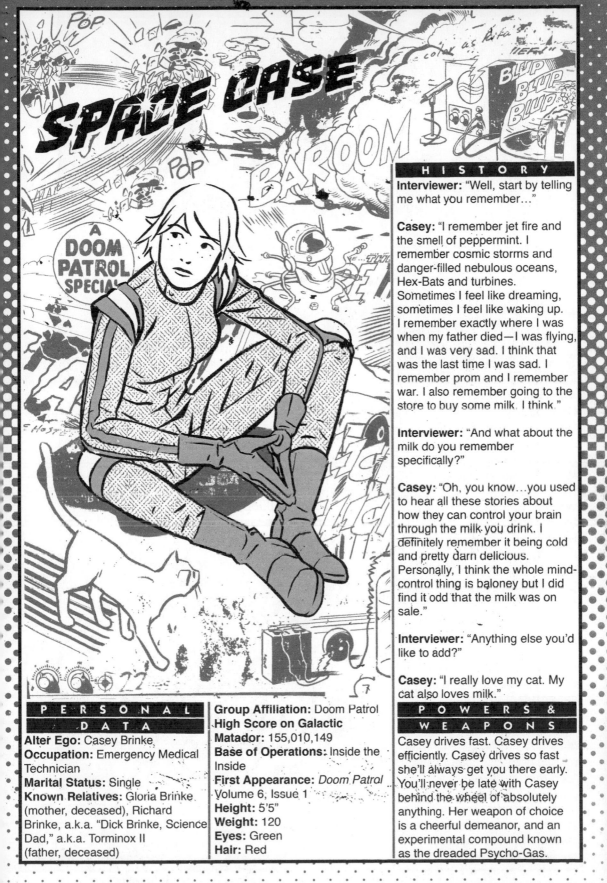

SPACE CASE

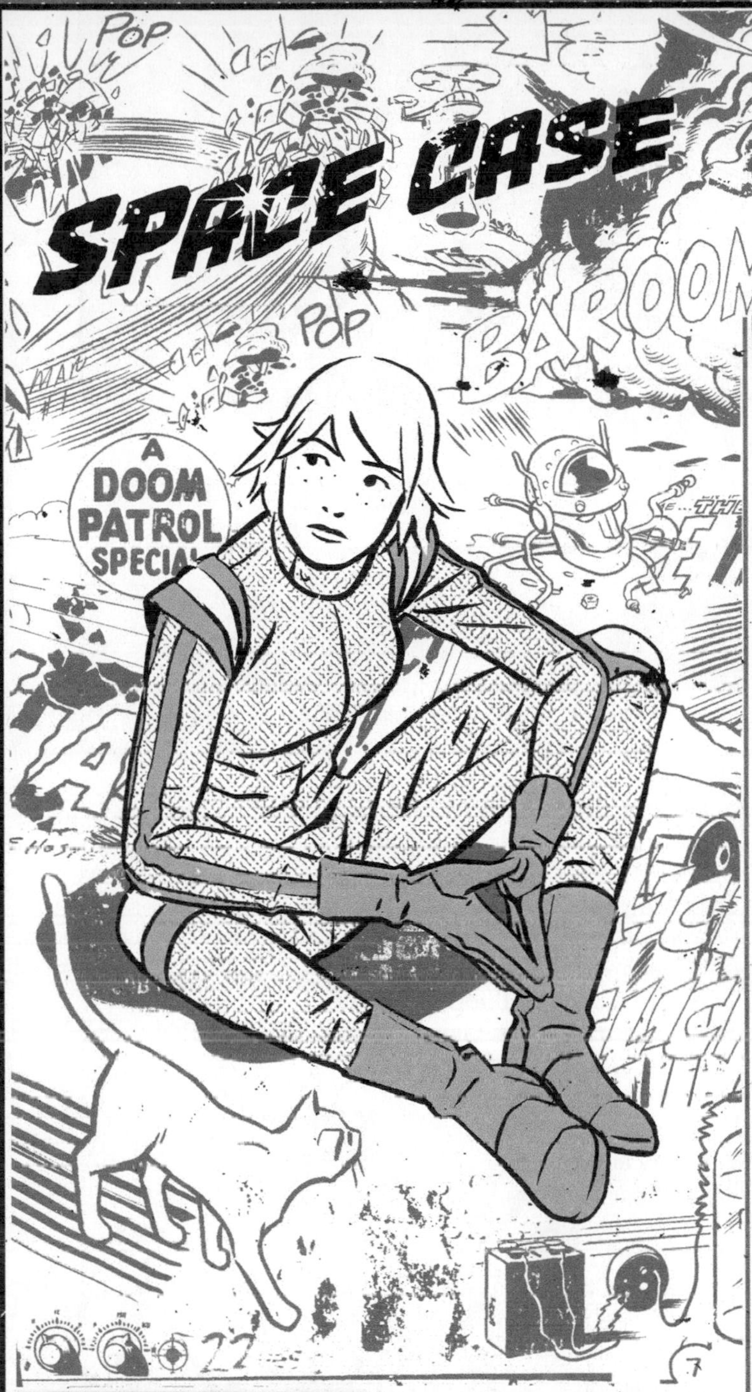
POP
POP
BAROOM
A DOOM PATROL SPECIAL

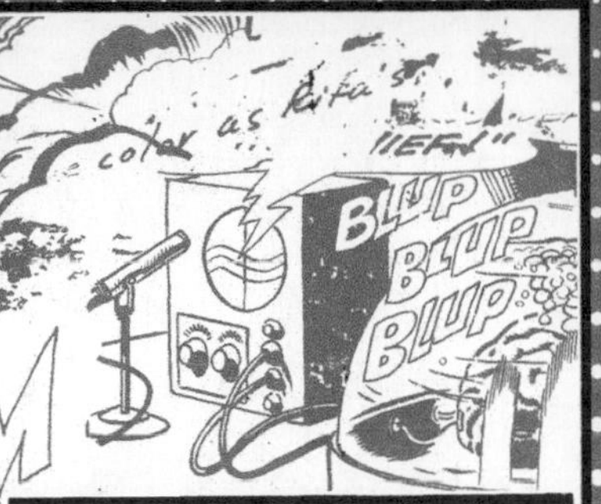
BLUP
BLUP
BLUP

HISTORY

Interviewer: "Well, start by telling me what you remember…"

Casey: "I remember jet fire and the smell of peppermint. I remember cosmic storms and danger-filled nebulous oceans, Hex-Bats and turbines. Sometimes I feel like dreaming, sometimes I feel like waking up. I remember exactly where I was when my father died—I was flying, and I was very sad. I think that was the last time I was sad. I remember prom and I remember war. I also remember going to the store to buy some milk, I think."

Interviewer: "And what about the milk do you remember specifically?"

Casey: "Oh, you know…you used to hear all these stories about how they can control your brain through the milk you drink. I definitely remember it being cold and pretty darn delicious. Personally, I think the whole mind-control thing is baloney but I did find it odd that the milk was on sale."

Interviewer: "Anything else you'd like to add?"

Casey: "I really love my cat. My cat also loves milk."

PERSONAL DATA

Alter Ego: Casey Brinke
Occupation: Emergency Medical Technician
Marital Status: Single
Known Relatives: Gloria Brinke (mother, deceased), Richard Brinke, a.k.a. "Dick Brinke, Science Dad," a.k.a. Torminox II (father, deceased)
Group Affiliation: Doom Patrol
High Score on Galactic Matador: 155,010,149
Base of Operations: Inside the Inside
First Appearance: *Doom Patrol* Volume 6, Issue 1
Height: 5'5"
Weight: 120
Eyes: Green
Hair: Red

POWERS & WEAPONS

Casey drives fast. Casey drives efficiently. Casey drives so fast she'll always get you there early. You'll never be late with Casey behind the wheel of absolutely anything. Her weapon of choice is a cheerful demeanor, and an experimental compound known as the dreaded Psycho-Gas.

ROBOTMAN

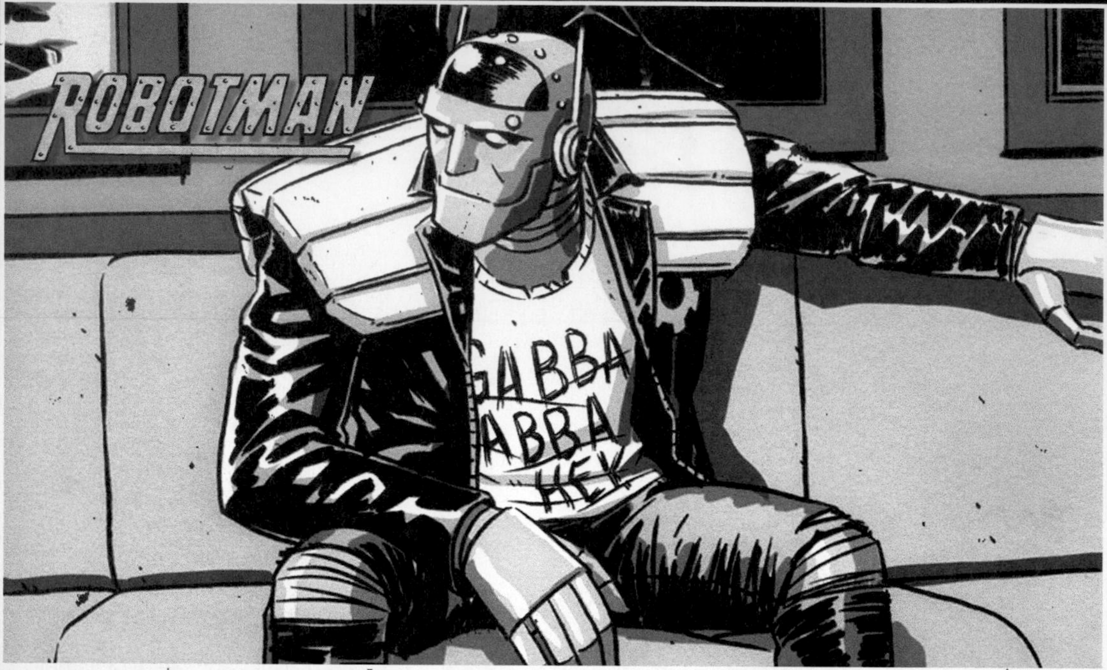
GABBA
GABBA
HEY

PERSONAL DATA

Alter Ego: Clifford Steele, Esq.
Occupation: Former Race Car Driver, Former Adventurer, Former Attorney-at-Law, Adventurer Once More
Marital Status: Single
Height: 6'2"
Weight: 295 lbs.
Eyes: Red
Hair: None
First Appearance:
MY GREATEST ADVENTURE #80

HISTORY

In a previous life Clifford Steele was an international sportsman with a need for speed. In that reckless life his body was destroyed by a fire in a racing car accident. His brain, however, was recovered by Dr. Niles Caulder, who ingeniously decided to transplant it into a robotic body, composed of a "ceramic metal" of his own creation. Originally, Steele was not particularly happy with this arrangement and sought revenge on Caulder for encasing his mind in the metal shell. Luckily, Caulder was able to convince him that a tin man existence was better than none at all, and Steele joined Caulder's superhero team, the Doom Patrol, as Robotman. Over the years, the Doom Patrol has disbanded and reformed many times over. During one such disbandment, Steele returned to his law practice, defending the rights of other robotic entities who have self-actualizing thoughts and awareness, including the Metal Men (LEGENDS OF TOMORROW #4).

POWERS & WEAPONS

Robotman's robotic body has changed many times over the years. The current model—originally constructed by Dr. Will Magnus, but refurbished by Dr. Niles Caulder—accounts for his superhuman strength and speed. His feet are also magnetized, granting him an ability to walk-up walls.

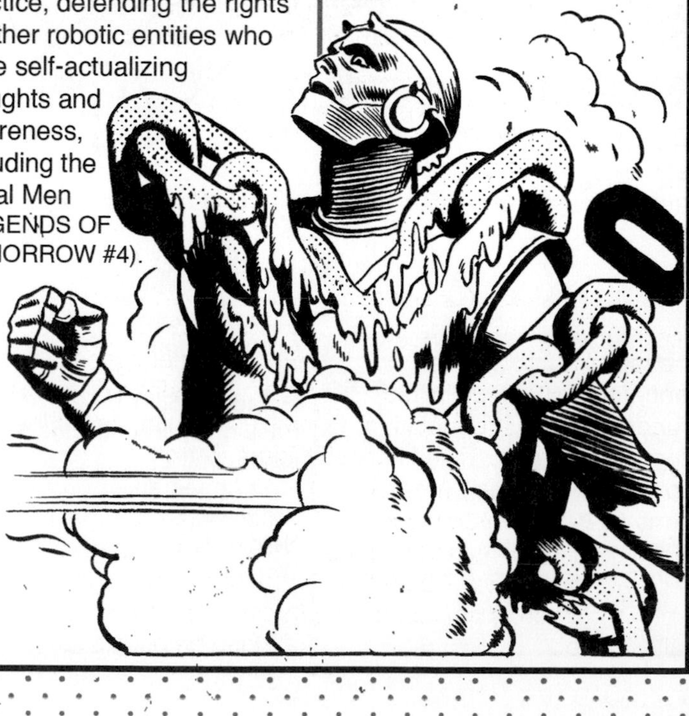

THE CHIEF

PERSONAL DATA

Alter Ego: Dr. Niles Caulder
Occupation: Ex-Research Scientist, Professional Crime-fighter
Marital Status: Married
Height: 5'10"
Weight: 215 lbs.
Eyes: Blue
Hair: Red
First Appearance: MY GREATEST ADVENTURE #80

HISTORY

Dr. Niles Caulder knows the secret to immortality, and it cost him the use of his legs. When he was a young and impoverished scientist, Caulder became a researcher seeking the formula for immortality on behalf of a mysterious benefecator with unlimited funds. Upon the formulation, the benefactor revealed himself to be the infamous General Immortus, who intended to extend his own life and rule the world. Unwilling to give up the secret, Immortus attempted to kill Caulder.

(Apparently, he had forgotten the whole reason he was after Caulder in the first place, which was that Caulder had figured out a way to avoid death. Silver Age villains, amiright?)

Nevertheless, Caulder was mortally wounded. With the assistance of a robot aid, the affliction was mended and Caulder was able to use the formula he had concocted to save his life. Unfortunately, the time duration between the wound and formula consumption was longer than anticipated and Caulder lost the use of his legs permanently. Unable to take on General Immortus on his own, Caulder assembled a team of misfits to fight his battles for him, called the Doom Patrol.

A madman and a genius, Caulder's focus on saving the world from terrible outside forces often comes at the cost of those he enlists as members. In fact, Caulder, unbeknownst to these individuals, at times perpetrates the unfortunate events that befall them, leading to their joining the team. Many members of the Doom Patrol have sacrificed their lives in the name of his cause.

POWERS & WEAPONS

Niles Caulder is one of the most brilliant scientific minds of the 21st century and a natural leader. His wheelchair is occasionally equipped with various weapons, including a flamethrower.

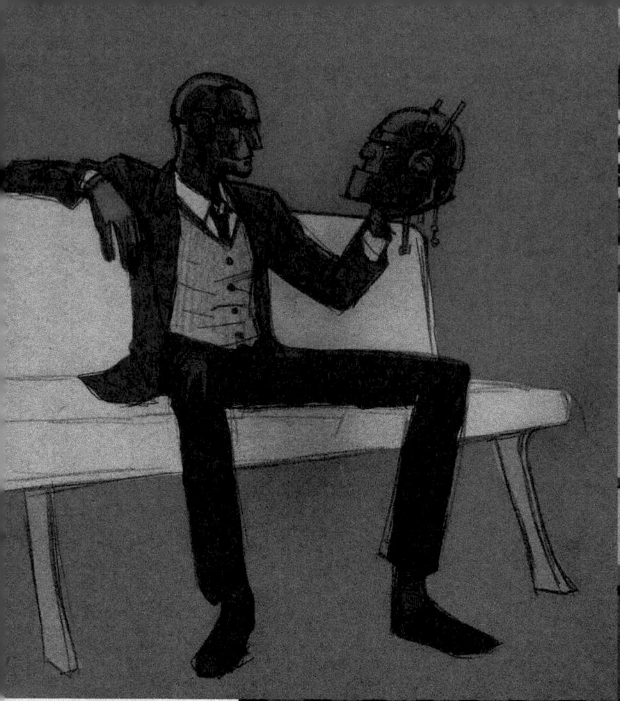

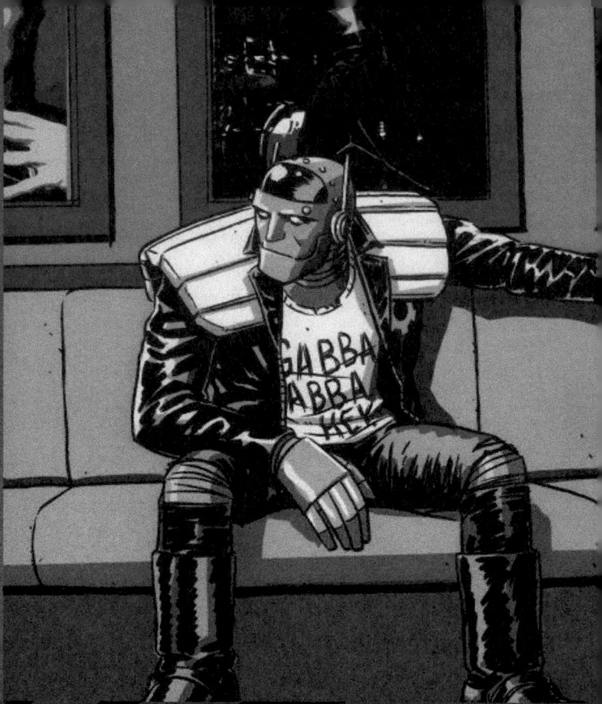
GABBA
ABBA
HEY

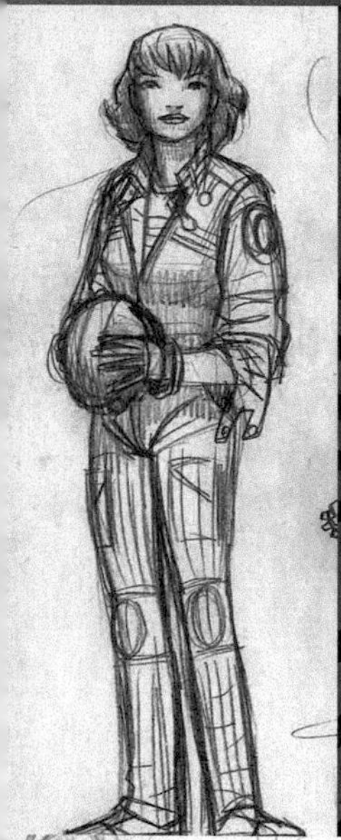

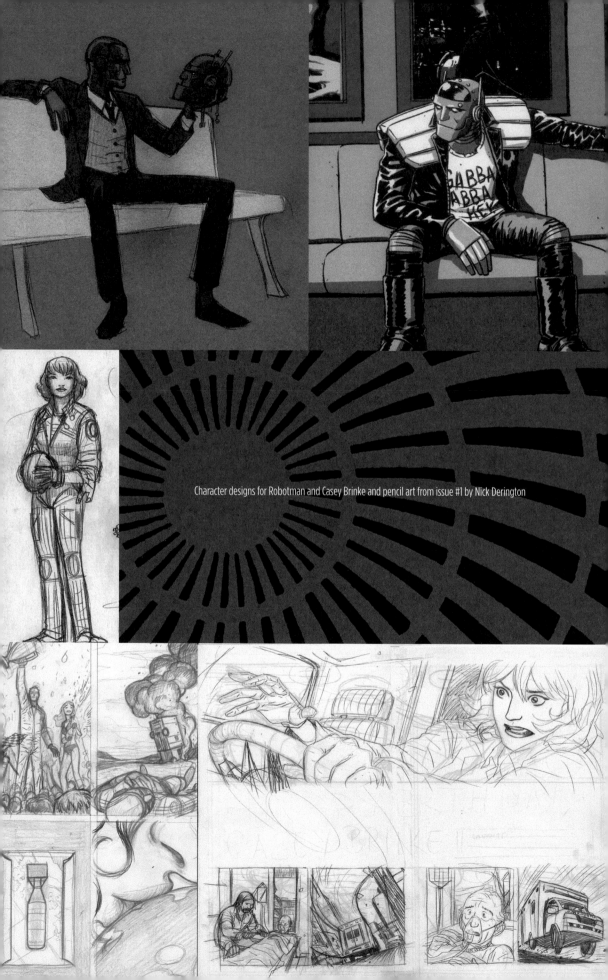

Character designs for Robotman and Casey Brinke and pencil art from issue #1 by Nick Derington

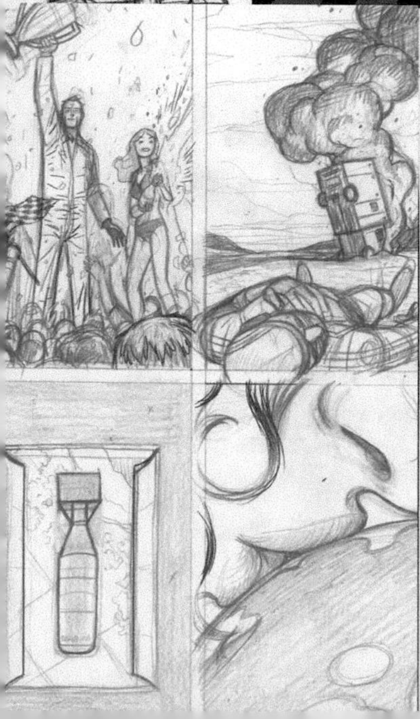

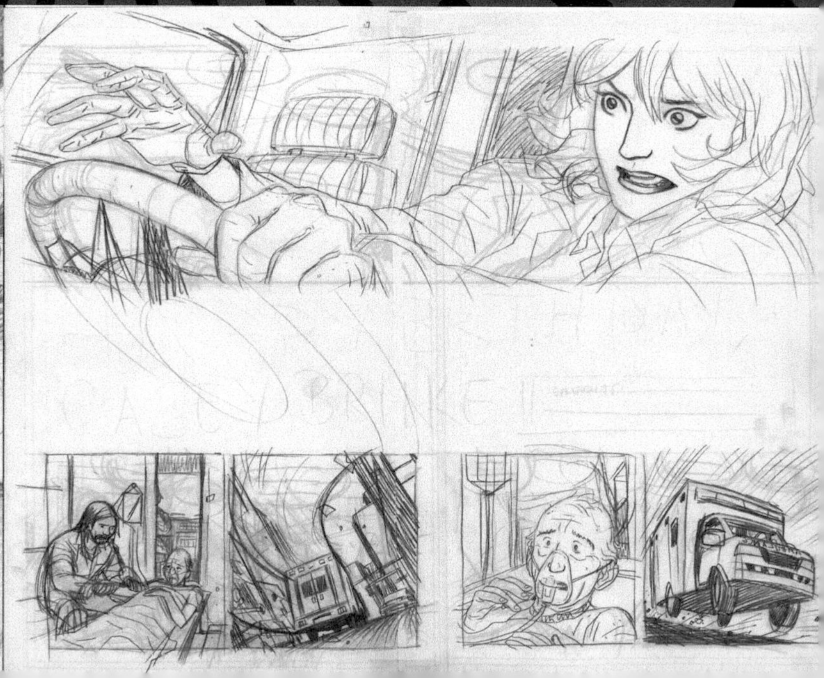

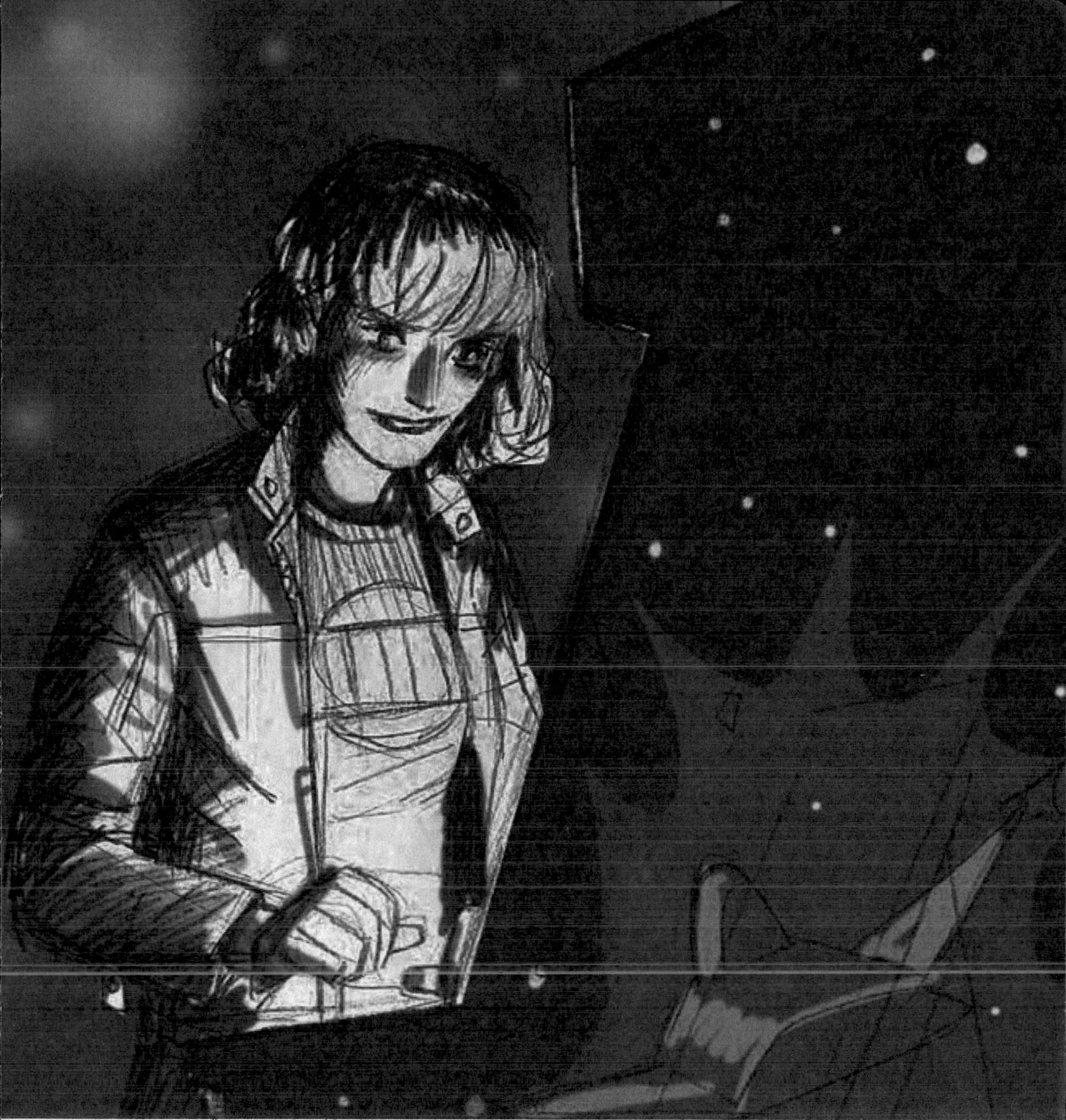

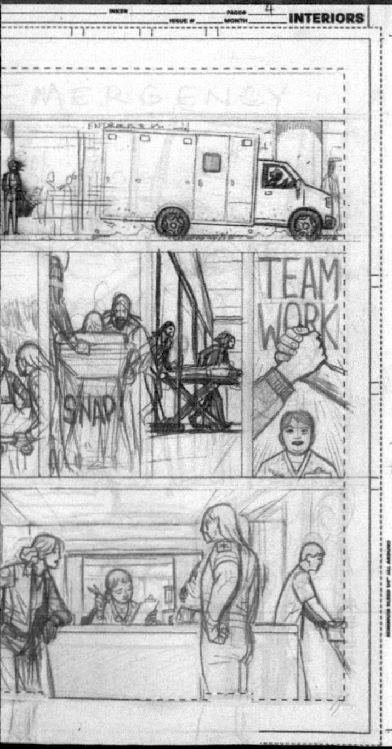
INTERIORS
TEAM
WORK
SNAP!

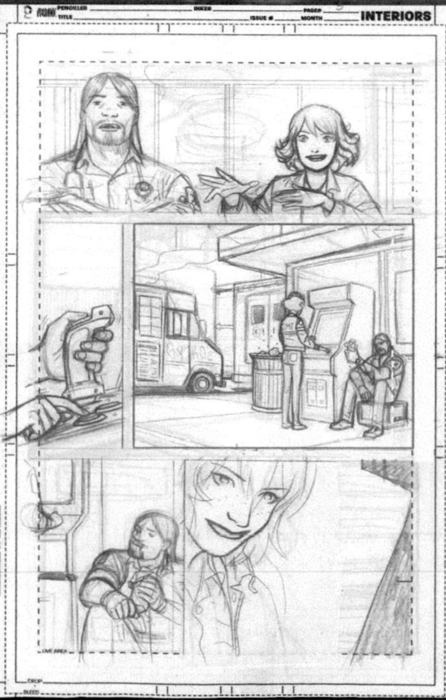
INTERIORS

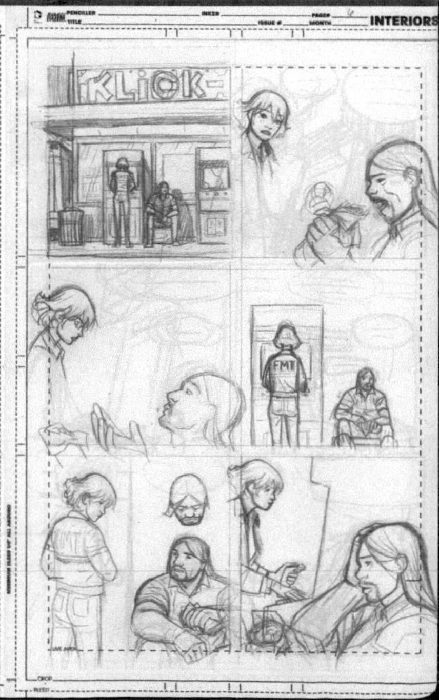
INTERIORS
KLICK-

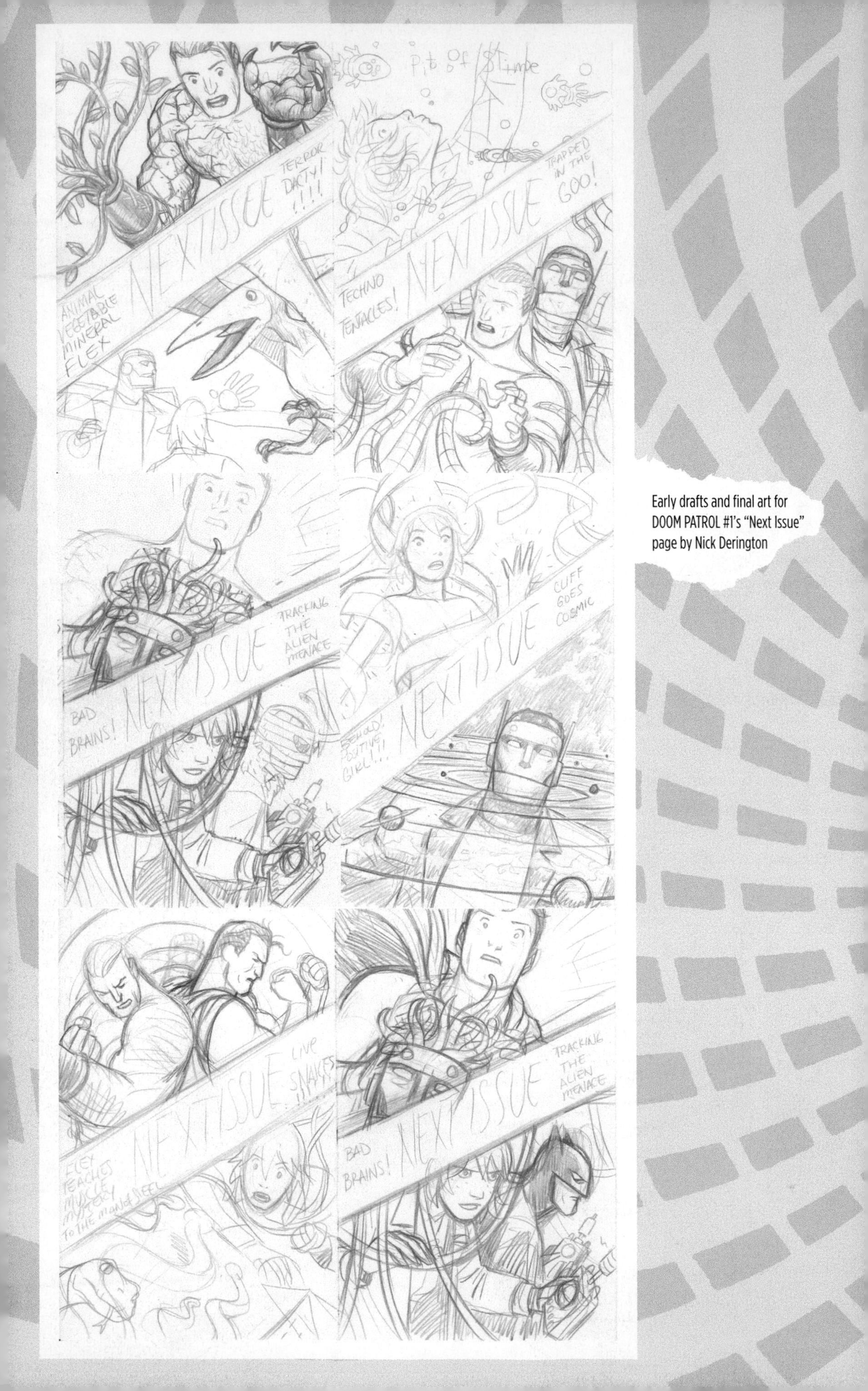
TERROR DACTYL!!!!!
NEXT ISSUE
ANIMAL VEGETABLE MINERAL FLEX
Pit of Slime
TRAPPED IN THE GOO!
NEXT ISSUE
TECHNO TENTACLES!
TRACKING THE ALIEN MENACE
NEXT ISSUE
BAD BRAINS!
CLIFF GOES COSMIC
NEXT ISSUE
BEHOLD! POSITIVE GIRL!!!
LIVE SNAKES !!!
NEXT ISSUE
FLEX TEACHES MUSCLE MYSTERY TO THE man of STEEL
TRACKING THE ALIEN MENACE
NEXT ISSUE
BAD BRAINS!

Early drafts and final art for DOOM PATROL #1's "Next Issue" page by Nick Derington

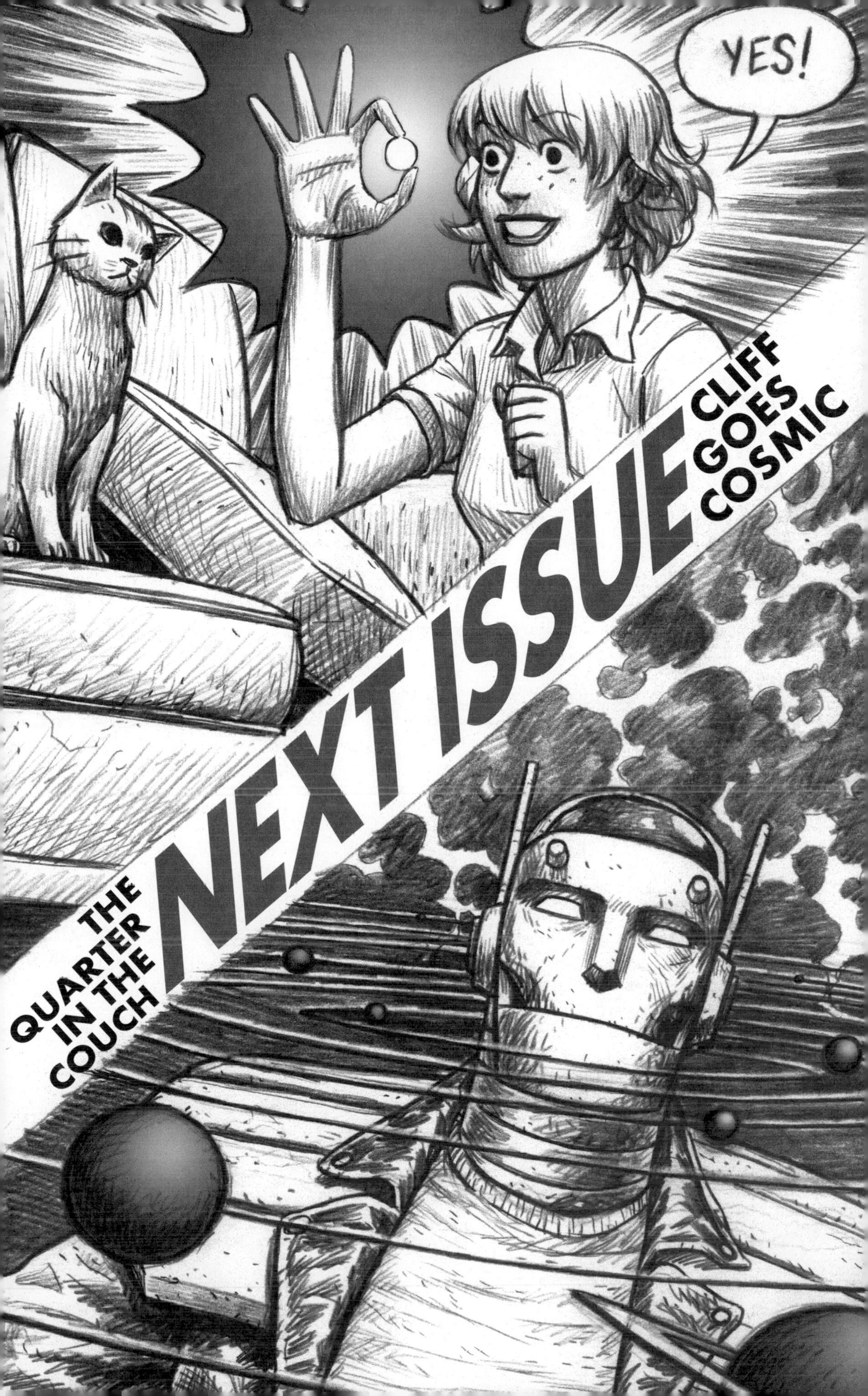
YES!
NEXT ISSUE
THE QUARTER IN THE COUCH
CLIFF GOES COSMIC

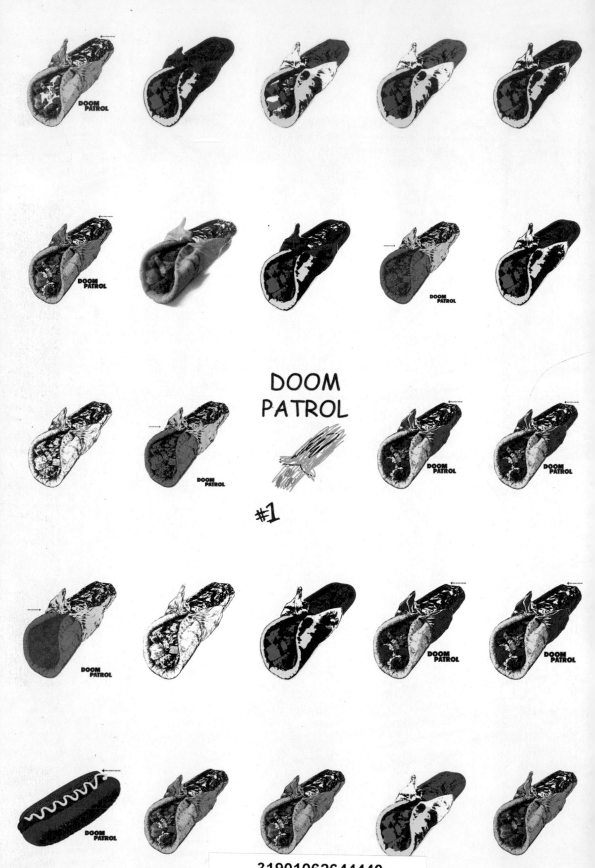

DOOM
PATROL

#1

Cover design development for issue #1 by Gerard Way, Nick Derington and James Harvey